EARLY CHILDHOOD EDUCATION 98/99

Nineteenth Edition

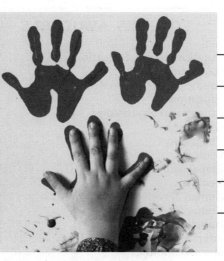

Editors

Karen Menke Paciorek

Eastern Michigan University

Karen Menke Paciorek is a professor of early childhood education at Eastern Michigan University in Ypsilanti. She has degrees in early childhood education from the University of Pittsburgh, George Washington University, and Peabody College of Vanderbilt University. She and Joyce Huth Munro coedit *Sources: Notable Selections in Early Childhood Education,* also published by Dushkin/McGraw-Hill Publishers. Dr. Paciorek presents at local and national conferences on a variety of topics, including curriculum planning, establishing a quality learning environment, guiding young children's behavior, and working with families.

Joyce Huth Munro

Joyce Huth Munro is Interim Director of Extended Programs and Distance Learning at Francis Marion University in Florence, South Carolina. She is an editor for a teaching cases series and coeditor (with Karen Menke Paciorek) of *Sources: Notable Selections in Early Childhood Education.* At regional and national conferences, she presents seminars on innovative methods of teacher education and curriculum design. Dr. Munro holds an M.Ed. from the University of South Carolina and a Ph.D. from Peabody College at Vanderbilt University.

Annual Editions

A Library of Information from the Public Press

Dushkin/McGraw·Hill

Sluice Dock, Guilford, Connecticut 06437

*Visit us on the Internet—*http://www.dushkin.com/

The Annual Editions Series

ANNUAL EDITIONS, including GLOBAL STUDIES, consist of over 70 volumes designed to provide the reader with convenient, low-cost access to a wide range of current, carefully selected articles from some of the most important magazines, newspapers, and journals published today. ANNUAL EDITIONS are updated on an annual basis through a continuous monitoring of over 300 periodical sources. All ANNUAL EDITIONS have a number of features that are designed to make them particularly useful, including topic guides, annotated tables of contents, unit overviews, and indexes. For the teacher using ANNUAL EDITIONS in the classroom, an Instructor's Resource Guide with test questions is available for each volume. GLOBAL STUDIES titles provide comprehensive background information and selected world press articles on the regions and countries of the world.

VOLUMES AVAILABLE

ANNUAL EDITIONS

Abnormal Psychology
Accounting
Adolescent Psychology
Aging
American Foreign Policy
American Government
American History, Pre-Civil War
American History, Post-Civil War
American Public Policy
Anthropology
Archaeology
Astronomy
Biopsychology
Business Ethics
Canadian Politics
Child Growth and Development
Comparative Politics
Computers in Education
Computers in Society
Criminal Justice
Criminology
Developing World
Deviant Behavior
Drugs, Society, and Behavior
Dying, Death, and Bereavement

Early Childhood Education
Economics
Educating Exceptional Children
Education
Educational Psychology
Environment
Geography
Geology
Global Issues
Health
Human Development
Human Resources
Human Sexuality
International Business
Macroeconomics
Management
Marketing
Marriage and Family
Mass Media
Microeconomics
Multicultural Education
Nutrition
Personal Growth and Behavior
Physical Anthropology
Psychology
Public Administration
Race and Ethnic Relations

Social Problems
Social Psychology
Sociology
State and Local Government
Teaching English as a Second
 Language
Urban Society
Violence and Terrorism
Western Civilization, Pre-Reformation
Western Civilization, Post-Reformation
Women's Health
World History, Pre-Modern
World History, Modern
World Politics

GLOBAL STUDIES

Africa
China
India and South Asia
Japan and the Pacific Rim
Latin America
Middle East
Russia, the Eurasian Republics, and
 Central/Eastern Europe
Western Europe

Cataloging in Publication Data
Main entry under title: Annual editions: Early Childhood Education. 1998/99.
   1. Education, Preschool—Periodicals. 2. Child development—Periodicals. 3. Child rearing—United States—Periodicals. I. Paciorek, Karen Menke, *comp.*; Munro, Joyce Huth, *comp.* II. Title: Early Childhood Education.
ISBN 0–697–39129–9   372.21'05   77–640114   ISSN: 0272–4456

© 1998 by Dushkin/McGraw-Hill, Guilford, CT 06437, A Division of The McGraw-Hill Companies.

Copyright law prohibits the reproduction, storage, or transmission in any form by any means of any portion of this publication without the express written permission of Dushkin/McGraw-Hill, and of the copyright holder (if different) of the part of the publication to be reproduced. The Guidelines for Classroom Copying endorsed by Congress explicitly state that unauthorized copying may not be used to create, to replace, or to substitute for anthologies, compilations, or collective works.

Annual Editions® is a Registered Trademark of Dushkin/McGraw-Hill, A Division of The McGraw-Hill Companies.

Nineteenth Edition

Cover image © 1998 PhotoDisc, Inc.

Printed in the United States of America   34567890BAHBAH901234098   Printed on Recycled Paper

Editors/Advisory Board

Members of the Advisory Board are instrumental in the final selection of articles for each edition of ANNUAL EDITIONS. Their review of articles for content, level, currentness, and appropriateness provides critical direction to the editor and staff. We think that you will find their careful consideration well reflected in this volume.

EDITORS

Karen Menke Paciorek
Eastern Michigan University

Joyce Huth Munro

ADVISORY BOARD

Anna Lou Blevins
University of Pittsburgh

Glen T. Dixon
University of British Columbia

Linda C. Edwards
College of Charleston

Richard Fabes
Arizona State University

Kathy Fite
Southwest Texas State University

Samuel T. Harris
Wright State University

John R. Hranitz
Bloomsburg University

Joan Isenberg
George Mason University

Mary Renck Jalongo
Indiana University of Pennsylvania

Richard T. Johnson
University of Hawaii

Katharine C. Kersey
Old Dominion University

Dene G. Klinzing
University of Delaware

Charles R. May
University of Northern Iowa

Judy Spitler McKee
Eastern Michigan University

Joan S. McMath
Ohio University

George S. Morrison
University of North Texas

Linda S. Nelson
Indiana University of Pennsylvania

R. Robert Orr
University of Windsor

Karen L. Peterson
Washington State University

Jack V. Powell
University of Georgia

William H. Strader
Fitchburg State College

Lewis H. Walker
Shorter College

John Worobey
Rutgers University

Staff

Ian A. Nielsen, Publisher

EDITORIAL STAFF

Roberta Monaco, Developmental Editor
Dorothy Fink, Associate Developmental Editor
Addie Raucci, Senior Administrative Editor
Cheryl Greenleaf, Permissions Editor
Deanna Herrschaft, Permissions Assistant
Diane Barker, Proofreader
Lisa Holmes-Doebrick, Program Coordinator

PRODUCTION STAFF

Brenda S. Filley, Production Manager
Charles Vitelli, Designer
Lara M. Johnson, Design/Advertising Coordinator
Shawn Callahan, Graphics
Laura Levine, Graphics
Mike Campbell, Graphics
Joseph Offredi, Graphics
Juliana Arbo, Typesetting Supervisor
Jane Jaegersen, Typesetter
Marie Lazauskas, Word Processor
Kathleen D'Amico, Word Processor
Larry Killian, Copier Coordinator

To the Reader

In publishing ANNUAL EDITIONS we recognize the enormous role played by the magazines, newspapers, and journals of the *public press* in providing current, first-rate educational information in a broad spectrum of interest areas. Many of these articles are appropriate for students, researchers, and professionals seeking accurate, current material to help bridge the gap between principles and theories and the real world. These articles, however, become more useful for study when those of lasting value are carefully *collected, organized, indexed,* and *reproduced* in a *low-cost format,* which provides easy and permanent access when the material is needed. That is the role played by ANNUAL EDITIONS. Under the direction of each volume's *academic editor,* who is an expert in the subject area, and with the guidance of an *Advisory Board,* each year we seek to provide in each ANNUAL EDITION a current, well-balanced, carefully selected collection of the best of the public press for your study and enjoyment. We think that you will find this volume useful, and we hope that you take a moment to let us know what you think.

Early childhood education is an interdisciplinary field that includes child development, family issues, educational practices, behavior guidance, and curriculum. *Annual Editions: Early Childhood Education 98/99* brings you the latest information in the field from a wide variety of recent journals, newspapers, and magazines. In selecting articles, we were careful to provide you with a well-balanced look at the issues and concerns facing teachers, families, society, and children. This edition begins with a look at the ramifications that new brain research holds for early childhood education.

The three themes found in readings chosen for this nineteenth edition of *Annual Editions: Early Childhood Education* are (1) the recent release of key findings on how the brain develops, (2) strategies for adapting regular classroom activities for children with special needs, and (3) child-centered learning that begins with more thoughtful themes.

The lead articles in unit 1, *Perspectives,* discuss the latest information on the development of young children's brains and the importance of early experiences. As we find out more about children's early capacity for learning, it is vital to include all children in activities. For a direct application of how this new research on the brain influences early childhood education, read unit 1's first two articles as well as the essay "New Ways of Learning = New Ways of Teaching" in unit 6.

In *Care and Educational Practices,* unit 3, we have chosen several articles dealing with specific ways to plan for inclusion. Whether children have limited motor, sight, or perceptual abilities, their needs must be met by adapting learning centers, activities, or environments. Four articles in this unit deal directly with planning and adapting for special needs children. Several of the articles in *Curricular Issues,* unit 5, are also helpful to consider for ideas on adapting learning activities.

A new and exciting feature that has been added to this edition of *Annual Editions: Early Childhood Education* is selected *World Wide Web* sites that can be used to further explore topics addressed in the articles. These sites will be cross-referenced by number in the *topic guide.*

Given the wide range of topics it includes, *Annual Editions: Early Childhood Education 98/99* may be used with

several groups: undergraduate or graduate students studying early childhood education, professionals pursuing further development, or parents seeking to improve their skills.

The selection of readings for this edition has been a cooperative effort between the two editors. We meet each year with members of our advisory board, who share with us in the selection process. The production and editorial staff of Dushkin/McGraw-Hill ably support and coordinate our efforts.

To the instructor or reader interested in the history of early childhood care and education programs throughout the years, we invite you to review our latest book, also published by Dushkin/McGraw-Hill. *Sources: Notable Selections in Early Childhood Education* (1998) is a collection of numerous writings of enduring historical value by influential people in the field. All of the selections are primary sources that allow you to experience first-hand the thoughts and views of these important educators. The instructor interested in using both *Sources* and *Annual Editions* may contact the editors for a list of compatible articles from the two books.

We are grateful to readers who have corresponded with us about the selection and organization of previous editions. Your comments and articles for consideration are welcomed and will serve to modify future volumes. Please take the time to fill out and return the postage-paid *article rating form* on the last page. You may also contact either one of us on-line at: *ted_paciorek@online.emich.edu* or *jhmunro@aol.com*

We look forward to hearing from you.

Karen Menke Paciorek

Joyce Huth Munro
Editors

Contents

UNIT 1

Perspectives

Five selections consider both the national and international development of early childhood education.

The concepts in bold italics are developed in the article. For further expansion please refer to the Topic Guide and the Index.

UNIT 2

Child Development and Families

Five selections consider the effects of family life on the growing child and the importance of parent education.

UNIT 3

Care and Educational Practices

Eleven selections examine various educational programs, assess the effectiveness of some teaching methods, and consider some of the problems faced by students with special needs.

The concepts in bold italics are developed in the article. For further expansion please refer to the Topic Guide and the Index.

vi

The concepts in bold italics are developed in the article. For further expansion please refer to the Topic Guide and the Index.

UNIT 5

Curricular Issues

Ten selections consider various curricular choices. The areas covered include creating, inventing, emergent literacy, motor development, and conceptualizing curriculum.

The concepts in bold italics are developed in the article. For further expansion please refer to the Topic Guide and the Index.

The concepts in bold italics are developed in the article. For further expansion please refer to the Topic Guide and the Index.

x

UNIT 6

Reflections

Four selections consider the present and future of early childhood education.

The concepts in bold italics are developed in the article. For further expansion please refer to the Topic Guide and the Index.

Topic Guide

This topic guide suggests how the selections in this book relate to topics of traditional concern to students and professionals involved with the study of early childhood education. It is useful for locating interrelated articles for reading and research. The guide is arranged alphabetically according to topic. Articles may, of course, treat topics that do not appear in the topic guide. In turn, entries in the topic guide do not necessarily constitute a comprehensive listing of all the contents of each selection. **In addition, relevant Web sites, which are annotated on pages 4 and 5, are noted in bold italics under the topic articles.**

TOPIC AREA	TREATED IN	TOPIC AREA	TREATED IN
Abuse	26. Creating a Community of Learning for Homeless Children *(18, 21, 23, 24)*	**Curriculum**	15. New Preschool 16. Understanding through Play 19. "SMART" Planning for Inclusion 27. Off with a Theme 28. 10 Ways to Improve Theme Teaching 30. Fostering Creativity in the Early Childhood Classroom 33. Sharing Books with Infants and Toddlers *(15, 16, 17, 19, 20, 25, 26, 27, 28, 29, 30)*
Advocacy	8. Families and Schools 39. Child Advocacy Directory *(3, 7, 18, 21, 22, 23, 24, 34, 35)*		
Assessment	11. It May Cause Anxiety 14. Nurturing Kids 17. Your Learning Environment 19. "SMART" Planning for Inclusion 29. Documenting Children's Learning 40. New Ways of Learning = New Ways of Teaching *(11, 13, 16, 17, 28, 31, 32, 35)*	**Developmentally Appropriate Practice**	14. Nurturing Kids 20. "Can I Play Too?" 21. Together Is Better *(14, 17, 18, 22, 34)*
		Discipline	23. Beyond Discipline to Guidance 24. Getting Along 25. Caring Classroom's Academic Edge *(5, 8, 14, 15, 16, 17, 18, 19)*
Brain Development	1. How to Build a Baby's Brain 2. New Brain Development Research *(5)*	**Diversity**	18. Labeled for Life? 22. Challenges to Family Involvement
Child Care: Full Day/Half Day	5. Child Care 11. It May Cause Anxiety 12. Meeting Basic Needs 13. Who Cares for the Children? 19. "SMART" Planning for Inclusion 22. Challenges to Family Involvement *(3)*	**Emergent Literacy**	32. "Hey! Where's the Toys?" 33. Sharing Books with Infants and Toddlers 34. Back to the Basics of Whole Language 35. Interactive Writing in a Primary Classroom *(25)*
Child Development	1. How to Build a Baby's Brain 7. Prenatal Drug Exposure 16. Understanding through Play 18. Labeled for Life 26. Creating a Community for Learning for Homeless Children *(5, 18, 21, 23, 24)*	**Emotional Development**	6. Bundle of Emotions *(5)*
		Families	5. Child Care 8. Families and Schools 11. It May Cause Anxiety 13. Who Cares for the Children? 15. New Preschool 22. Challenges to Family Involvement 26. Creating a Community of Learning for Homeless Children 38. Where Are the Good Old Days? *(3, 7, 8, 9, 12, 13, 23)*
Collaboration	8. Families and Schools 26. Creating a Community of Learning for Homeless Children 39. Child Advocacy Directory *(3, 7, 18, 21, 23, 24)*		
Constructivist Practice	40. New Ways of Learning = New Ways of Teaching *(19, 25, 27, 33, 34, 35)*	**Guiding Behavior**	23. Beyond Discipline to Guidance 24. Getting Along 25. Caring Classroom's Academic Edge *(15, 16, 17, 18, 19)*
Creativity	30. Fostering Creativity in the Early Childhood Classroom *(19, 25, 26, 27, 28, 29, 30)*	**Health and Safety**	12. Meeting Basic Needs *(5, 14)*
		History	38. Where Are the Good Old Days?

TOPIC AREA	TREATED IN	TOPIC AREA	TREATED IN
Homeless	5. Child Care 26. Creating a Community of Learning for Homeless Children 38. Where Are the Good Old Days? *(7, 18, 21, 23, 24)*	Prenatal Drug Exposure	7. Prenatal Drug Exposure
Inclusion	19. "SMART" Planning for Inclusion 20. "Can I Play Too?" 21. Together Is Better	Preschool	15. New Preschool 19. "SMART" Planning for Inclusion *(18)*
Infants and Infant Care	1. How to Build a Baby's Brain 2. New Brain Development Research 6. Bundle of Emotions 7. Prenatal Drug Exposure 12. Meeting Basic Needs 31. Active Living 33. Sharing Books with Infants and Toddlers *(5, 11, 14)*	Primary Grades	32. "Hey, Where's the Toys?" 35. Interactive Writing in a Primary Classroom *(25, 26, 27, 28, 29, 30)*
		Quality	3. Highlights of Quality 2000 Initiative 11. It May Cause Anxiety 15. New Preschool *(6)*
Learning	10. Integrating Learning Styles and Multiple Intelligences 29. Documenting Children's Learning 40. New Ways of Learning = New Ways of Teaching *(9, 10, 11, 12, 13, 35)*	Self-Esteem	23. Beyond Discipline to Guidance *(29, 30)*
		Social Development	23. Beyond Discipline to Guidance 24. Getting Along 25. Caring Classroom's Academic Edge *(25, 26, 27, 28, 29, 30)*
Mathematics	16. Understanding through Play 17. Your Learning Environment 40. New Ways of Learning = New Ways of Teaching *(26, 27, 29, 33, 35)*	Special Needs	17. Your Learning Environment 18. Labeled for Life? 19. "SMART" Planning for Inclusion 20. "Can I Play Too?" 21. Together Is Better *(4, 5, 7, 10, 11, 12, 13, 17, 18, 19, 21, 22, 23, 24)*
Motor Development	20. "Can I Play Too?" 31. Active Living *(22)*	Teachers/Teaching	8. Families and Schools 15. New Preschool 17. Your Learning Environment 19. "SMART" Planning for Inclusion 20. "Can I Play Too?" 21. Together Is Better 23. Beyond Discipline to Guidance 24. Getting Along 25. Caring Classroom's Academic Edge 26. Creating a Community of Learning for Homeless Children 27. Off with a Theme 28. 10 Ways to Improve Theme Teaching 29. Documenting Children's Learning 37. Let's Be Real *(2, 9, 13, 15, 16, 17, 19, 20, 22, 25, 26, 27, 28, 29, 30, 31, 33, 35)*
Multicultural	8. Families and Schools 9. Education of Hispanics in Early Childhood *(3, 10, 12, 13, 34, 35)*		
Multiple Intelligences	10. Integrating Learning Styles and Multiple Intelligences 14. Nurturing Kids *(9, 10, 11, 12, 13)*		
Observation	16. Understanding through Play *(15, 16, 19)*		
Play	16. Understanding through Play 17. Your Learning Environment 20. "Can I Play Too?" 32. "Hey! Where's the Toys?" *(15, 16, 19)*	Technology	19. "SMART" Planning for Inclusion 36. Outstanding Developmental Software *(6, 9, 16, 29, 33)*
		Theme Teaching	27. Off with a Theme 28. 10 Ways to Improve Theme Teaching
Policy	5. Child Care 13. Who Cares for the Children? *(2, 6, 35)*	Violence	4. National Television Violence Study 26. Creating a Community of Learning for Homeless Children *(21, 23)*
Portfolio	29. Documenting Children's Learning		
Poverty	5. Child Care 38. Where Are the Good Old Days? *(7, 21, 24)*	Whole Language	34. Back to the Basics of Whole Language

Selected World Wide Web Sites for
AE: Early Childhood Education

All of these Web sites are hot-linked through the *Annual Editions* home page:
http://www.dushkin.com/annualeditions (just click on this book's title). In addition, these sites are referenced by number and appear where relevant in the Topic Guide on the previous two pages.

Some Web sites are continually changing their structure and content, so the information listed may not always be available.

General Sources

1. Educational Resources Information Center (ERIC)—*http://www.aspensys.com/eric/index.html*—This invaluable site provides links to all ERIC sites: clearinghouses, support components, and publishers of ERIC materials. You can search the massive ERIC database, find out what is new in early childhood education, and ask questions about ERIC.

2. National Education Association—*http://www.nea.org/*—Something—and often quite a lot—about virtually every education-related topic can be accessed at or through this site of the 2.3-million-strong National Education Association.

3. National Parent Information Network/ERIC—*http://npin.org/*—This is a clearinghouse of information on elementary and early childhood education as well as urban education. Browse through its links for information for parents and for people who work with parents.

4. U.S. Department of Education—*http://www.ed.gov/pubs/TeachersGuide/*—Government goals, projects, grants, and other educational programs are listed here as well as many links to teacher services and resources.

Perspectives

5. American Psychological Association (APA)—*http://www.apa.org/psychnet/*—By exploring the APA's PsychNET, you will be able to find links to an abundance of articles and other resources that are useful in understanding the factors that are involved in brain development.

6. Goals 2000: A Progress Report—*http://www.ed.gov/pubs/goals/progrpt/index.html*—Open this site to survey a progress report by the U.S. Department of Education on the Goals 2000 reform initiative. It provides a sense of what goals that educators are reaching for as they look toward the future.

7. Poverty in America Research Index—*http://www.mindspring.com/~nexweb21/povindex.htm*—Open this page to find definitions and tables related to poverty and poverty areas. The site provides answers to FAQs, facts about poverty, and discussion of poverty myths vs. realities. Welfare reform is also addressed.

Child Development and Families

8. Association for Moral Education (AME)—*http://www.wittenberg.edu/ame/*—AME is dedicated to fostering communication, cooperation, training, curriculum development, and research that links moral theory with educational practices. From here it is possible to connect to several sites on ethics, character building, and moral development.

9. Global SchoolNet Foundation—*http://www.gsn.org/*—Access this site for multicultural education information. The site includes news for teachers, students, and parents; as well as chat rooms, links to educational resources, programs, and contests and competitions.

10. Multicultural Publishing and Education Council—*http://www.mpec.org/*—This is the home page of the MPEC, a networking and support organization for independent publishers, authors, educators, and librarians fostering authentic multicultural books and materials. It has excellent links to a vast array of resources related to multicultural education.

11. The National Academy for Child Development (NACD)—*http://www.nacd.org/*—NACD, an international organization, is dedicated to helping children and adults reach their full potential. Its home page presents links to various programs, research, and resources into such topics as learning disabilities, ADD/ADHD, brain injuries, autism, accelerated and gifted, and other similar topic areas.

12. National Immigration Forum—*http://www.immigrationforum.org/national.htm*—The National Immigration Forum offers this page to examine the effects of immigration on the U.S. economy and society. Click on the links for discussion of underground economies, immigrant economies, and other topics.

13. World Education Exchange/Hamline University—*http://www.hamline.edu/~kjmaier/*—This site, which aims for "educational collaboration," takes you around the world to examine virtual classrooms, trends, policy, and infrastructure development. It leads to information about school reform, multiculturalism, technology in education, and much more.

Care and Educational Practices

14. American Academy of Pediatrics (AAP)—*http://www.aap.org/*—AAP provides information for optimal physical, mental, and social health for infants, children, adolescents, and young adults.

15. Canada's Schoolnet Staff Room—*http://www.schoolnet.ca/adm/staff/*—Here is a resource and link site for anyone involved in education, including special-needs educators, teachers, parents, volunteers, and administrators.

16. Classroom Connect—*http://www.classroom.net/*—A major Web site for K–12 teachers and students, this site provides links to schools, teachers, and resources online. It includes discussion of the use of technology in the classroom.

17. ERIC Clearinghouse on Disabilities and Gifted Education—*http://www.cec.sped.org/gifted/gt-faqs.htm*—Information on identifying and teaching gifted children, attention deficit disorders, and other topics in gifted education may be accessed at this site.

18. National Resource Center for Health and Safety in Child Care—*http://nrc.uchsc.edu/*—Search through this site's extensive links to find information on health and safety in child care. Health and safety tips are provided, as are other child-care information resources. In addition, national U.S. health and safety performance standards are reproduced here.

19. Online Innovation Institute—*http://oii.org/*—A collaborative project among Internet-using educators, proponents of systemic reform,

content-area experts, and teachers who desire professional growth, this site provides a learning environment for integrating the Internet into educators' individual teaching styles.

20. Scholastic/Instructor Magazine—*http://place.scholastic.com/ instructor/curriculum/index.htm*— Open this *Instuctor* magazine home page for data on curriculum activies and srategies for teachers. The goal of this site is to provide professional development tools to help teachers successfully meet the challenges of today's classrooms.

Supporting Young Children and Their Families

21. Child Welfare League of America (CWLA)—*http://www.cwla.org/*—The CWLA is the United States' oldest and largest organization devoted entirely to the well-being of vulnerable children and their families. Its Web site provides links to information about issues related to morality and values in education.

22. Early Intervention Solutions (EIS)—*http://www.earlyintervention. com/library4.htm*—EIS presents this site to address concerns about child stress and reinforcement. It suggests ways to deal with negative behaviors that may result from stress and anxiety among children.

23. National Network for Family Resiliency—*http://www.nnfr.org/nnfr/*—This organization's home page will lead you to a number of resource areas of interest in learning about resiliency, including General Family Resiliency, Violence Prevention, and Family Economics.

24. World Hunger Year (WHY)—*http://www.iglou.com/why/ria.htm*—WHY offers this site as part of its program called *Reinvesting in America,* and its effort to help people fight hunger and poverty in their communities is examined. Various resources and models for grassroots action are included here.

Curricular Issues

25. California Reading Initiative—*http://www.sdcoe.k12.ca.us/score/ prreadin.html*—The California Reading Initiative site provides valuable insight into topics related to emergent literacy. Many resources for teachers and staff developers are provided here.

26. Education Week on the Web—*http://www.edweek.org/*—At this *Education Week* home page, you will be able to open archives, read special reports, keep up on current events, look at job opportunities, and access a variety of articles of relevance in educational psychology. A great deal of material is helpful in learning and instruction.

27. Kathy Schrock's Guide for Educators—*http://www.capecod.net/ schrockguide/*—This is a classified list of sites on the Internet found to be useful for enhancing curriculum and teacher professional growth. It is updated daily.

28. Phi Delta Kappa—*http://www.pdkintl.org/home.htm*—This important organization publishes articles about all facets of education. By clicking on the links in this site, for example, you can check out the journal's online archive, which has resources such as articles having to do with assessment.

29. Teachers Helping Teachers—*http://www.pacificnet.net/~mandel/*—Basic teaching tips, new teaching-methodology ideas, and forums for teachers to share their experiences are provided on this Web site. Download software and participate in chat sessions. It features educational resources on the Web, with new ones added each week.

30. Verio Pittsburgh—*http://pittsburgh.verio.net/*—Formerly known as PREPnet, this site contains Web sites for educators. It covers a wide range of topics dealing with K-12 resources and curricula. Its links will prove useful for examining issues ranging from curricular concerns to teaching values.

Reflections

31. Awesome Library for Teachers—*http://www.neat-schoolhouse.org/ teacher.html*—Open this page for links and access to teacher information on everything from educational assessment to general child development topics.

32. Carfax—*http://www.carfax.co.uk/subjeduc.htm*—Look through this superb index for links to education publications such as *Journal of Beliefs and Values, Educational Philosophy and Theory,* and *Assessment in Education.* The site also provides links to articles and research that will prove helpful in assessment.

33. EdWeb/Andy Carvin—*http://edweb.cnidr.org/*—The purpose of Ed-Web is to explore the worlds of educational reform and information technology. Access educational resources around the world, learn about trends in education policy and information infrastructure development, examine success stories of computers in the classroom, and much more.

34. National Institute on the Education of At-Risk Students—*http:// www.ed.gov/offices/OERI/At-Risk*—The At-Risk Institute supports a range of research and development activities designed to improve the education of students at risk of educational failure due to limited English proficiency, race, geographic location, or economic disadvantage. Access numerous links and summaries of the Institute's work at this site.

35. Prospects: The Congressionally Mandated Study of Educational Growth and Opportunity—*http://www.ed.gov/pubs/Prospects/index.html*—This report analyzes cross-sectional data on language-minority and LEP students in the United States and outlines what actions are needed to improve their educational performance. Family and economic situations are addressed. Information on related reports and sites is provided.

We highly recommend that you review our Web site for expanded information and our other product lines. We are continually updating and adding links to our Web site in order to offer you the most usable and useful information that will support and expand the value of your Annual Editions. You can reach us at: *http://www. dushkin.com/annualeditions/.*

Perspectives

The field of early childhood education received a major shot in the arm during the past year with the wide dissemination of research on how a baby's brain develops. The information scientists are gathering that supports brain development activity during the early years of a child's life has brought significant attention to the field of early childhood care and education. As recently as 15 years ago it was believed that brain structure and capacity were set at birth. We now know that the types of early experiences a child has, the frequency in which they occur, and with whom they happen can determine a child's future learning capacity.

We begin this issue of *Annual Editions: Early Childhood Education* with two articles on brain development research. For professionals in the field, now is the time to capitalize on the interest and resources available. It is our responsibility to provide stimulating environments in which young children best learn. We must be responsive to each child and provide many opportunities for language, music, and literature to be heard on a daily basis. We can educate parents as to their responsibility in providing an appropriate environment that allows the brain to develop to its full capacity.

With many political leaders talking of welfare reform, the key message to remember is this: Welfare reform will work only if child care works. Most people on welfare are children, and most of the adults on welfare are the mothers of those children. The recent welfare reform and the push to have mothers in the workforce will only be successful if the mothers have affordable, quality, and regulated or licensed child care for their children. Families who receive reimbursements so small that they can pay only for low-quality, unstimulating care will not be contributing members of the workforce. In California, parents were twice as likely to drop out of a welfare-to-work program during the first year if their children were in unlicensed and poor-quality care. Many welfare reform proponents want to skimp on the funding available for quality child care to make their reforms work. This is unwise. Quality early care and education should be the cornerstone of successful welfare reform. The essay on the Child Care and Early Education section from the *Children's Defense Fund 1998 Yearbook on the State of America's Children* addresses the necessity for quality programs for our most vulnerable children. We have too many children in poor quality care who are not receiving the types of early experiences that will provide a strong foundation for later learning.

Effective parenting and teaching require the adult to monitor a wide variety of the experiences children encounter. This has become increasingly true today as television, video, and computer games occupy a great deal of children's time.

The amount of violence a young child witnesses on a screen does affect his or her behavior. The presentations made in "The National Television Violence Study: Key Findings and Recommendations" lead one to conclude that television violence has increased at an alarming rate. Children do not see perpetrators of violence punished in 73 percent of violent scenes. In real life, our behavior has consequences. Children do not see those consequences on television and are, thus, not learning the true effects of violent behavior from this medium. As violence increases in our communities, teachers, parents, and public leaders must work together to develop ways to use the media and technology we have established to entertain and educate in appropriate ways. Indeed, many teachers are beginning to see themselves not only as educators but also as strong advocates for children.

Looking Ahead: Challenge Questions

How can quality preschool programs benefit children?

What types of early experiences are beneficial to the development of a healthy brain?

What should be done to capitalize on the window of opportunity in early care and education?

What are the key goals of the Quality 2000 Initiative? How can they best be attained?

UNIT 1

THE BRAIN

A baby is born with a head on her shoulders and a mind primed for learning. But it takes years of experience—looking, listening, playing, interacting with parents—to wire the billions of complex neural circuits that govern language, math, music, logic and emotions.

How to Build a Baby's Brain

By Sharon Begley

YOU CANNOT SEE WHAT IS GOING ON INSIDE YOUR newborn's brain. You cannot see the electrical activity as her eyes lock onto yours and, almost instantaneously, a neuron in her retina makes a connection to one in her brain's visual cortex that will last all her life. The image of your face has become an enduring memory in her mind. And you cannot see the explosive release of a neurotransmitter—brain chemical—as a neuron from your baby's ear, carrying the electrically encoded sound of "ma," connects to a neuron in her auditory cortex. "Ma" has now commandeered a cluster of cells in the infant's brain that will, as long

53% of all parents say that they read to their child every day; 55% of parents say they sing to or play music for their child every day

as the child lives, respond to no other sound.

You cannot see any of this. But Dr. Harry Chugani can come close. With positron-emission tomography (PET), Chugani, a pediatric neurobiologist at Wayne State University in Detroit, watches the regions of a baby's brain turn on, one after another, like city neighborhoods having their electricity restored after a blackout. He can measure activity in the primitive brain stem and sensory cortex from the moment the baby is born. He can observe the visual cortex burn with activity in the second and third months of life. He can see the frontal cortex light up at 6 to 8 months. He can see,

From *Newsweek*, Spring/Summer 1997, pp. 28-32. © 1997 by Newsweek, Inc. All rights reserved. Reprinted by permission.

in other words, that the brain of a baby is still forming long after the child has left the womb—not merely growing bigger, as toes and livers and arms do, but forming the microscopic connections responsible for feeling, learning and remembering. For doing, in short, everything that a brain is born to do but that it is born without knowing how to do.

Scientists are just now realizing how experiences after birth, rather than something innate, determine the actual wiring of the human brain. "Only 15 years ago," reports the Families and Work Institute in the just-released study "Rethinking the Brain," "neuroscientists assumed that by the time babies are born, the structure of their brains [had been] genetically determined." But by last year re-searchers knew that was wrong. Instead, early-childhood experiences exert a dramatic and precise impact, physically determining how the intricate neural circuits of the brain are wired (NEWSWEEK, Feb. 19, 1996). Since then they have been learning how those experiences shape the brain's circuits.

At birth, the brain's 100 billion or so neurons form more than 50 trillion connections (synapses). The genes the baby carries—from the egg and sperm that made him—have already determined his brain's basic wiring. They have formed the connections in the brain stem that will make the heart beat and the lungs respire. But that's all. Of a human's 80,000 different genes, fully half are believed to be involved in forming and running the central nervous system. Yet even that doesn't come close to what the brain needs. In the first months of life, the number of synapses will increase 20-fold—to more than 1,000 trillion. There simply are not enough genes in the human species to specify so many connections.

That leaves experience—all the signals that a baby receives from the world. Experience seems to exert its effects by strengthening synapses. Just as a memory will fade if it is not accessed from time to time, so synapses that are not used will also wither away in a process called pruning. The way to reinforce these wispy connections has come to be known as stimulation. Contrary to the claims of entrepreneurs preying on the anxieties of new parents, stimulation does not mean subjecting a toddler to flashcards.

Rooting for Intelligence

Breast-feeding is good for health and bonding. And mother's milk may have another payoff: boosting a child's IQ scores.

BY DANIEL GLICK

BREAST MILK MAY be Mother Nature's ultimate food. It's potent enough to keep babies alive for the first 16 weeks of life. It contains antibodies to ward off illness; breast-fed babies suffer fewer ear infections, respiratory infections, rashes and allergies than bottle-fed babies. For mothers, nursing lowers the chance of getting breast cancer later in life, accelerates weight loss after pregnancy and may act as a natural (though imperfect) contraceptive.

But can breast-feeding also make a baby smarter?

The answer is still uncertain. But a series of studies shows everything from "small but still detectable" increases in cognitive development to an eight-point IQ difference between breast- and bottle-fed babies. Various measurements, including standard infant testing and even report cards from grade-school children, all give a statistically significant nod to babies who nursed. In one widely publicized 1992 study by Alan Lucas of the Dunn Nutrition Unit in Cambridge, Mass., preterm infants who were tube-fed breast milk scored much higher on developmental tests than babies who were tube-fed formula. "It's hard to come out and say, 'Your baby is going to be stupider or sicker if you don't breast-feed'," says Dr. Lawrence Gartner, chair of the American Academy of Pediatrics' working group on breast-feeding. "But that's what the literature says." (The academy recommends that infants be fed breast milk for the first 6 to 12 months of life, with appropriate solid foods added between the ages of 4 and 6 months.)

No one can explain exactly why breast milk may be such good brain food. The precise mix of en-zymes, long-chain fatty acids and proteins that make up breast milk is so complex that no human engineer could ever duplicate it. And each ingredient has a purpose. Specific fatty acids found in breast milk have been shown to be critical for neurological development. Certain amino acids are a central component for the development of the retina, which could account for breast-fed babies' increased visual acuity—another way of measuring advanced brain development.

Critics say that trying to quantify the developmental advantages of breast-feeding is an epidemiologist's nightmare. Confounding factors include race, age, socioeconomic status and parental intelligence. But even formula makers acknowledge that their product will always be a pale imitation. Cow's-milk-based formula, even fortified with iron or fatty acids, simply can't match the complexity of nature's own. "Breast milk gives you things we don't even know about," says Dr. William Goldman, medical director of Wyeth Nutritionals International. The U.S. Food and Drug Administration is currently assessing a fierce debate over adding to formula a polyunsaturated fat that has been shown in some studies to stimulate eye and brain development—and in others to stunt growth.

Food for thought: The controversy will likely get louder, as breast-feeding advocates seize on the latest studies to bolster their case. Some researchers, on the other hand, suggest that different factors, like a loving home environment, may ultimately prove to be more important than what a child is fed. In a 1996 commentary in the British journal Lancet, William and Mark Feldman of the Hospital for Sick Children in Toronto wrote: "The best evidence is that intelligent, loving and caring mothers are more likely to have intelligent children, irrespective of how they feed their babies." But wouldn't it be something if mother's milk turns out to be, ahem, the mother's milk of intelligence?

The native languages a baby hears will cre

Rather, it is something much simpler—sorting socks by color or listening to the soothing cadences of a fairy tale. In the most extensive study yet of what makes a difference, Craig Ramey of the University of Alabama found that it was blocks, beads, peekaboo and other old-fashioned measures that enhance cognitive, motor and language development—and, absent traumas, enhance them permanently.

The formation of synapses (synaptogenesis) and their pruning occurs at different times in different parts of the brain. The sequence seems to coincide with the emergence of various skills. Synaptogenesis begins in the motor cortex at about 2 months. Around then, infants lose their "startle" and "rooting" reflexes and begin to master purposeful movements. At 3 months, synapse formation in the visual cortex peaks; the brain is fine-tuning connections allowing the eyes to focus on an object. At 8 or 9 months the hippocampus, which indexes and files memories, becomes fully functional; only now can babies form explicit memories of, say, how to move a mobile. In the second half of the first year, finds Chugani, the prefrontal cortex, the seat of forethought and logic, forms synapses at such a rate that it consumes twice as much energy as an adult brain. That furious pace continues for the child's first decade of life.

Research on language has shown how "neuroplastic" an infant's brain is, and how that plasticity lessens with age. Patricia Kuhl of the University of Washington studies the "auditory maps" that infants' brains construct out of phonemes (the smallest units of sound in a language, such as "ee" or "l"). At first, neurons in the auditory cortex are like laborers to whom jobs have not yet been assigned. But as a newborn hears, say, the patter of English, a different cluster of neurons in the auditory cortex is recruited to respond to each phoneme. Each cluster then fires only when a nerve from the ear carries that particular sound, such as "pa" or "ma." If one sound is clearly distinct from another, as "ra" and "la" are in English, then the neurons whose job it is to hear one will lie far from those whose job it is to hear the other. (Kuhl makes noninvasive electrical measurements, through the babies' scalps, to identify which neurons fire in response to a particular sound.) But if the sounds are nearly identical, as "ra" and "la" are in Japanese, then the two sets of neurons are so close that the baby will have trouble distinguishing the two phonemes. By 12 months, an infant's auditory map is formed. He will be unable to pick out

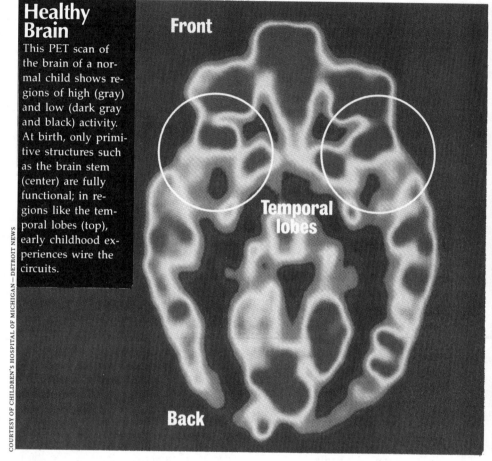

Healthy Brain
This PET scan of the brain of a normal child shows regions of high (gray) and low (dark gray and black) activity. At birth, only primitive structures such as the brain stem (center) are fully functional; in regions like the temporal lobes (top), early childhood experiences wire the circuits.

Front

Temporal lobes

Back

COURTESY OF CHILDREN'S HOSPITAL OF MICHIGAN – DETROIT NEWS

phonemes he has not heard thousands of times for the simple reason that no cluster of neurons has been assigned the job of responding to that sound. And the older he gets, the more he will struggle to learn a new language: fewer unassigned neurons are available for the job of hearing new phonemes.

Experience counts in building vocabulary, too, and at a very young age. The size of a toddler's vocabulary is strongly correlated with how much a mother talks to the child, reports Janellen Huttenlocher of the University of Chicago. At 20 months, children of chatty mothers averaged 131 more words than children of less talkative mothers; at 2 years, the gap had more than doubled, to 295 words. "The critical factor is the number of times the child hears different words," says Huttenlocher. The effect holds for the complexity of sentence structure, too, she finds. Mothers who used complex sentences (those with dependent clauses, such as "when ..." or "because ...") 40 percent of the time had toddlers who did so 35 percent of the time; mothers who

used such sentences in only 10 percent of their utterances had children who did so only 5 percent of the time.

NLY "LIVE" LANGUAGE, not television, produced these vocabulary- and syntax-boosting effects. Why doesn't all the gabbing on TV stimulate language development? Huttenlocher suspects that "language has to be used in relation to ongoing events, or it's just noise." That may hold for other sorts of cognition, too. Information embedded in an emotional context seems to stimulate neural circuitry more powerfully than information alone. A child will more readily learn the concept of "more" if it refers to the happy prospect of more cookies, and "later" if it is attached to a frustrating wait for a trip to the playground, than if the word is presented in isolation from things the baby cares about. There is nothing mysterious about this: adults form a

ate a permanent auditory map in his brain

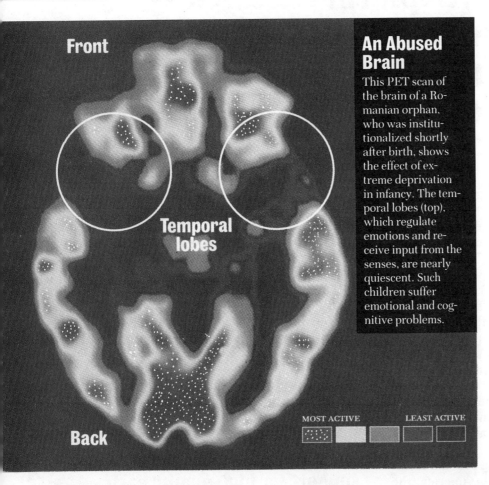

Front

Temporal lobes

Back

MOST ACTIVE   LEAST ACTIVE

An Abused Brain

This PET scan of the brain of a Romanian orphan, who was institutionalized shortly after birth, shows the effect of extreme deprivation in infancy. The temporal lobes (top), which regulate emotions and receive input from the senses, are nearly quiescent. Such children suffer emotional and cognitive problems.

memory much more readily if it has emotional content (how did you hear that the space shuttle had exploded?) than if it doesn't (what's the difference between a sine and a cosine?). Causality, a key component of logic, is also best learned through emotion: if I smile, Mommy smiles back. A sense that one thing causes another forms synapses that will eventually support more abstruse concepts of causality. Feelings, concepts and language begin to be linked in this way in the months from 7 through 12.

Another route to brain wiring seems to be tapping into its natural harmonies. In the last year, new studies have nailed down how music affects spatial-temporal reasoning—the ability to see a disassembled picture of, say, a rabbit and mentally piece it back together. Such reasoning underlies math, engineering and chess. In a study published in February in the journal Neurological Research, scientists report how spatial-temporal reasoning in 3- and 4-year-olds was affected by weekly piano lessons. After six months, the budding Horowitzes—all of whom scored at the national average on tests of spatial recogni-

tion—scored 34 percent *above* average on this reasoning skill. None of the other children (who had received computer keyboard and mouse lessons, singing lessons or nothing at all) had improved. What explains the effect? Physicist Gordon Shaw of the University of California, Irvine, suspects that in playing the piano, "you are seeing how patterns work in space and time." When sequential finger and key patterns make melodies, neural circuits that connect positions (keys) to sounds in space and time (the melody) are strengthened. "Music training produces long-term modifications in neural circuitry," says Shaw. What scientists do not know is whether the effects of early music training endure—whether the preschoolers will be math wizards in high school.

The downside of the brain's great plasticity is that it is acutely vulnerable to trauma. "Experience may alter the behavior of an adult," says Dr. Bruce Perry of Baylor College of Medicine, but it "literally provides the organizing framework" for the brain of a child. If the brain's organization reflects its experience, and the experience of the

traumatized child is fear and stress, then the neurochemical responses to fear and stress become the most powerful architects of the brain. "If you have experiences that are overwhelming, and have them again and again, it changes the structure of the brain," says Dr. Linda Mayes of the Yale Child Study Center. Here's how:

■ Trauma elevates stress hormones, such as cortisol, that wash over the tender brain like acid. As a result, regions in the cortex and in the limbic system (responsible for emotions, including attachment) are 20 to 30 percent smaller in abused children than in normal kids, finds Perry; these regions also have fewer synapses.

■ In adults who were abused as children, the memory-making hippocampus is smaller than in nonabused adults. This effect, too, is believed to be the result of the toxic effects of cortisol.

■ High cortisol levels during the vulnerable years of zero to 3 increase activity in the brain structure involved in vigilance and arousal. (It's called the locus ceruleus.) As a result the brain is wired to be on hair-trigger alert, explains Perry: regions that were activated by the original trauma are immediately reactivated whenever the child dreams of, thinks about or is reminded of the trauma (as by the mere presence of the abusive person). The slightest stress, the most inchoate fear, unleashes a new surge of stress hormones. This causes hyperactivity, anxiety and impulsive behavior. "The kids with the higher cortisol levels score lowest on inhibitory control," says neuroscientist Megan Gunnar of the University of Minnesota. "Kids from high-stress environments [have] problems in attention regulation and self-control."

Trauma also scrambles neurotransmitter signals, ratcheting up some and depressing others. Since neurotransmitters play key roles in telling growing neurons where to go and what to connect to, children exposed to chronic and unpredictable stress—a mother's boyfriend who lashes out in fury, an alcoholic uncle who is kind one day and abusive the next—will suffer deficits in their ability to learn. "Some percentage of capacity is lost," says Perry. "A piece of the child is lost forever."

That is tragedy enough, of course, but it is made even greater by the loss of what could have been. Babies are born into this world with their brain primed to learn. But they cannot do it alone.

With ANDREW MURR *in Los Angeles*

New Brain Development Research—
A Wonderful Window of Opportunity
to Build Public Support for
Early Childhood Education!

Julee J. Newberger

More than 20 years of brain development research is finally making news. Articles have appeared recently in *Time* (see Nash 1997), *Working Mother* (see Jabs 1996), *The Chicago Tribune, Newsweek* (see Begley 1996), and *The Washington Post*. A special edition of *Newsweek* focusing on learning in the early years is on the newsstands this spring in conjunction with the April 28, ABC-TV special "I Am Your Child." Receiving unprecedented attention, they kick off a massive three-year campaign to engage the public. What is the significance of this new research on the brain, and what does it mean for early childhood professionals?

New brain-imaging technologies have enabled scientists to investigate how the brain develops and works. Stimulated in part by growing concern about the overall well-being of children in America, the findings affirm what many parents and caregivers have known for years: (1) good prenatal care, (2) warm and loving attachments between young children and adults, and (3) positive, age-appropriate stimulation from the time of birth really do make a difference in children's development for a lifetime.

In addition to giving us a glimpse of the complex activity that occurs in the brain during infancy, the new research tools have stimulated dialogue between scientists and educators. In June 1996 Families and Work Institute sponsored a conference, "Brain Development in Young Children: New Frontiers for Research, Policy, and Practice," at the University of Chicago (see Families and Work Institute 1996). Convening professionals from the media, human services, business, and public policy, the conference explored how knowledge about the brain can inform our efforts to make better beginnings for

> **Just as experts agree that we have only begun to understand the complexities of the growing brain, so we have only begun to bridge the gap between neuroscience and education. The question for early childhood professionals is, How can we take advantage of the public interest that these stories and events have sparked to build support for high-quality early childhood education?**

children and families. One month later, a workshop sponsored by the Education Commission of the States and the Charles A. Dana Foundation brought together 74 neuroscientists, cognitive psychologists, and education researchers and practitioners to foster communication and bridge a "historical communications gap" (ECS 1996). Similar events have followed, such as President Clinton's White House Conference on Early Childhood Development and Learning on April 17, 1997.

Just as experts agree that we have only begun to understand the complexities of the growing brain, so we have only begun to bridge the gap between neuroscience and education. The question for early childhood professionals is, How can we take advantage of the public interest that these stories and events have sparked to build support for high-quality early childhood education?

Julee J. Newberger, M.F.A., is a communications specialist in the NAEYC public affairs division. She is the primary author of "Early Years Are Learning Years" news releases.

From *Young Children*, May 1997, pp. 4-9. © 1997 by the National Association for the Education of Young Children. Reprinted by permission.

What we know about how children learn

Although the scientists of all varieties who have been researching biology-versus-environment issues for much of this century have long agreed that both are enormously important influences on growth and development, only about 20 years ago neuroscientists believed that the genes we are born with determine the structure of our brains. They held that this fixed structure determines the way we develop and interact with the world. But recent brain research, enabled by new technologies, disproves this notion. Heredity may determine the basic number of neurons (brain cells) children are born with, and their initial arrangement, but this is merely a framework. A child's environment has enormous impact on how the circuits of the brain will be laid. Nature and nurture together—not nature or nurture alone—determine the outcome of our lives.

Beginning even before birth, the kind of nourishment and care a child receives affects not only the "wiring" of her brain but also the qualities of her experiences beyond the first few years of life. Many parents and caregivers have understood intuitively that warm, everyday interaction—cuddling infants closely or singing to toddlers—actually helps prepare children for learning throughout life. More and more we begin to understand the biological reasons behind this.

When a child is born, the brain produces trillions more neurons and synapses (connections between the brain cells) than she will ultimately need. Positive interactions with caring adults stimulate a child's brain profoundly, causing synapses to grow and existing connections to be strengthened. Those synapses in a child's brain that are used tend to be-

© The Growth Program

Many parents and caregivers have understood intuitively that warm, everyday interaction—cuddling infants closely or singing to toddlers—actually helps prepare children for the learning they will do throughout life. More and more we begin to understand the biological reasons behind this.

come permanent fixtures; those that are not used tend to be eliminated. If a child receives little stimulation early on, synapses will not sprout or develop, and the brain will make fewer connections. Therefore, a child's experiences during the first few days, months, and years may be more decisive than scientists once believed.

We now know that during the early years the brain has the greatest capacity for change. Neural plasticity, the brain's ability to adapt with experience, confirms that early stimulation sets the stage for how children will continue to learn and interact with others throughout life.

Neural plasticity: The brain's ability to adapt

Particularly during the first three years of life, brain connections develop quickly in response to outside stimulation. A child's experiences—good or bad—influence the wiring of his brain and the connections in his nervous system. Thus, when we snuggle a baby or talk to him in a singsong, undulating rhythm, we are contributing to the growth of his brain. How do we know this?

Recent research examining one of the body's "stress-sensitive" systems demonstrates how outside experiences shape a child's developing brain (Gunnar et al. 1996). One stress-sensitive system in particular is activated when children are faced with physical or emotional trauma. Activation of this system produces a steroid hormone called *cortisol*. High levels of cortisol cause the death of brain cells and a reduction in connections between the cells in certain areas of the brain. Research in adults who have experienced chronic or intense activation of the system that produces cortisol shows shrinkage

Particularly during the first three years of life, brain connections develop quickly in response to outside stimulation. Thus, when we snuggle a baby or talk to him in a singsong, undulating rhythm, we are contributing to the growth of his brain.

of a certain brain region that is important in learning and memory. Clearly, a link exists between physical or emotional trauma and long-term impairments to learning and development.

But nature has provided a way of buffering the negative effects of these stress systems in the brain: strong attachments between children and their parents or caregivers. Studies measuring the levels of cortisol in children's saliva showed that those who received warm and responsive care were able to turn off this stress-sensitive response more quickly and efficiently. Babies with strong emotional bonds to their caregivers showed consistently lower levels of cortisol in their brains.

While positive, nurturing experiences can help brighten a child's future, negative experiences can do the opposite. Children who are emotionally neglected or abandoned early in life not only are more likely to have difficulty in learning but also may have more trouble experiencing empathy, attachment, and emotional expression in general. An excess of cortisol in the brain is linked to impaired cognitive ability and difficulty in responding appropriately or productively in stressful situations. Healthy relationships during the early years help children create a framework for interactions with others throughout life.

Windows of opportunity

Studies have increased our understanding of "windows of opportunity" or critical periods in children's lives when specific types of learning take place. For instance, scientists have determined that the neurons for vision begin sending messages back and forth rapidly at two to four months of age, peaking in intensity at eight months. It is no coincidence that babies begin to take notice of the world during this period. A well-known experiment conducted in the 1970s prompted research on the window of opportunity in development of vision in children. The original study demonstrated that sewing shut

one eye of a newborn kitten caused the kitten's brain to be "rewired." Because no synapses were created in the brain to allow the kitten to see with the eye that had been closed, the kitten was blind in that eye even after scientists reopened it. The results could not be repeated in adult cats, whose brains were already wired for sight in both eyes. We now know that by the age of two these synapses in the human brain have matured as well. The window of opportunity for vision has already closed.

Scientists believe that language is acquired most easily during the first decade of life. Infants under six months respond with equal interest to the sounds of all languages, but they soon develop "perceptual maps" that direct them toward the sounds of the language they hear most frequently and away from the sounds of other languages. They start by forming connections for specific vowel sounds they hear repeatedly. The circuits in children's brains then become wired for those sounds that are significant in their own language, diminishing their ability to discern sounds that are not. As a result, the brains of babies in Japan, for example, begin to develop differently than those of babies in the United States. These perceptual maps eventually account for regional accents—and the increasing difficulty in acquiring new languages as we grow older.

Studies well-known to early childhood educators make one thing clear: Talking to an infant increases the number of words she will recognize and eventually come to understand. She also will learn better when spoken to in brief phrases, preferably in singsong tones. Researchers report that infants whose parents and caregivers frequently speak to them recognize far more words later on than do infants whose parents are less vocal or less engaged. An infant's repeated exposure to words clearly helps her brain build neural circuitry that will enable her to learn more words later on. For infants, individual attention and responsive, sensitive care-giving are critical for later language and intellectual development.

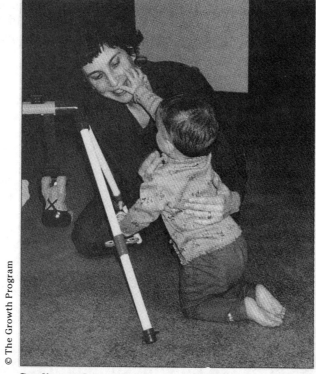

© The Growth Program

Studies make one thing clear: Talking to an infant increases the number of words she will recognize and eventually come to understand. She also will learn better when spoken to in brief phrases, preferably in singsong tones.

Children who are emotionally neglected or abandoned early in life not only are more likely to have difficulty in learning but also may have more trouble experiencing empathy, attachment, and emotional expression in general. An excess of cortisol in the brain is linked to impaired cognitive ability and difficulty in responding appropriately or productively in stressful situations.

Many reports on brain research point to the implications for the introduction of second-language learning during the early years (ECS 1996). We now know that if children are to learn to speak a second language like a native, they should be introduced to the language by age ten. Mastering an additional language is still possible after this point, but the window of opportunity for easy acquisition is gone.

Research does not suggest drilling children in alphabet songs from different languages or using flash cards to promote rote memorization of letters and numbers. Rather, it reinforces the principles of developmentally appropriate practice. Children learn any language best in the context of meaningful, day-to-day interactions with adults or other children who speak the language.

More windows of opportunity in children's learning may exist. Studies show that the most effective time to begin music lessons, for instance, is between the ages of three and ten. Few professional musicians began later in life. Music also seems to be linked to spatial orientation, so providing a child with the opportunity to play an instrument and using basic music education to spark her interest may do more than help her become musically inclined. With such knowledge, scientists and educators can work together to create the best plans for developing the whole child during the early years of life.

Implications for early care and education programs

Now that scientific research has reinforced what many already knew about early childhood education, what impact will this knowledge have on programs and centers across the country? We know that enriched home and school environments can help make the most of children's mental capacities. We also know that when we bring an understanding of child development to our interactions with children, we can meet their developmental needs more than just adequately. Parents and the general pub-

lic, having children's best interests in mind, may raise issues about early education practices. Here are some questions that are likely to arise.

1. Should new parents put off employment and stay at home?

The relationship between secure attachment and healthy brain development makes this a reasonable question, although working parents should not be blamed for any and every developmental obstacle their children encounter. At a time when 55% of women provide about half or more of their families' income, decisions as to whether parents should put off employment remain a personal, family matter (Families and Work Institute 1996). Research shows that the best scenario for children and families if child care is used involves high-quality parenting and access to high-quality, affordable child care and early education that enhances—not disrupts—attachments between parents and children. Flexible workplace policies can help accommodate and support modern family life.

2. Is it too late for children to develop cognitive skills after the early years?

While scientists have found that the early years may be even more important than anticipated, human development continues throughout the life span. It may not be as easy to acquire a second language at the age of fifty, but learning new skills is always possible. A meaningful context and the desire to develop new skills make learning more likely at any age.

The significance of this new research, according to Harry Chugani (1997) of Wayne State University, is for all of us to "be aware and take advantage of these critical periods nature has provided us with." Chugani says, "We must create innovations to make learning fun." Parents and educators should focus on ways to take advantage of windows of opportunity that remain open.

Research does not suggest drilling children in alphabet songs from different languages or using flash cards to promote rote memorization of letters and numbers. Rather, it reinforces the principles of developmentally appropriate practice. Children learn any language best in the context of meaningful, day-to-day interactions with adults or other children who speak the language.

3. To take advantage of the early years of learning, should I invest more in toys and new products for my child?

New developments in research may prompt manufacturers to market products that claim to make the most of children's learning potential. Remember that scientific evidence does not change the fundamental principles of developmentally appropriate practice. In fact, research supports the theory that learning must take place in a meaningful context and in an environment of love and support. A developing brain doesn't know the difference between an inexpensive set of measuring cups and a pricey set of stackables purchased at a toy store.

The key to fostering early childhood learning is understanding that there will be a range in the amount of stimulation children are comfortable with and can tolerate. Before children can move on to new skills, they must have time to practice and master those they have already learned. Parents or caregivers who push children too fast or too hard can do as much damage as those who do not challenge children at all. Chugani recommends, "Be rigorous, but be aware of early signs of overload" (1997). Continue to respect the child as a human being and use common sense in determining when he enjoys what he is learning and when he is resistant.

Bridging the gaps

The ECS workshop on neuroscience and education outlined the following conflicts between research and current education practice (ECS 1996):
- While we know that development of children's capacity to learn is crucial in the first few years of life, children during these years receive the least attention from the educational world.
- Interactive environments enhance development, but many children are in child care programs today with staff who are underpaid, lack training in early childhood and brain development, and may be responsible for too many children.

- Although some adverse effects can be reversed or prevented for much less than it costs to provide special services later on, our educational system waits for children to fall behind, then places them in special education programs at high costs to states.

In light of this research, shouldn't parents have more options to stay home with children during the years in which this critical learning takes place? Parental leave policies must be put on the table for discussion. And what about new welfare reform policies that push single mothers into the workforce without guaranteeing high-quality child care to promote children's optimum development and learning? The concerns raised and the dialogue generated at this workshop and other conferences may be timely in preventing more children from growing up without the benefit of the kind of education that early childhood professionals, utilizing years of research and practice, can provide.

Where we go from here

The Families and Work Institute conference on brain development offered the following recommendations for parents, caregivers, policymakers, and the public to institute policies and practices that improve the day-to-day experiences of all young children and families.

First, do no harm.

- Allow parents to fulfill their all-important role in providing and arranging sensitive, predictable care for their children.

Parents or caregivers who push children too fast or too hard can do as much damage as those who do not challenge children at all.

• Work to reform policies that prevent parents from forming strong, secure attachments with their infants in the first months of life.

• Mount intensive efforts to improve the quality of child care and early education so that families can be sure their young children's learning and emotional development are being fostered while parents are at work.

Prevention is best, but when a child needs help, intervene quickly and intensively.

• Ensure consistent and responsive care to help cushion children against the stresses of everyday life.

• Provide timely, intensive, sustained assistance to help children recover from serious trauma or overcome developmental problems.

Promote healthy development and learning for every child.

• Be aware that missed opportunities to promote healthy development may result later on in more expensive and less effective attempts at remediation.

• Support ongoing efforts to enhance the cognitive, emotional, and social development of children and adults in every phase of the life cycle.

Improve health and protection by providing health care coverage for expectant and new parents and their young children.

• Medical care, including preventive health screening, well-baby care, timely immunization, and attention to children's emotional and physical development, is cost-effective and provides a foundation for lifetime development.

Promote responsible parenthood by expanding proven approaches.

• Identify parent education and family support programs that promote the healthy development of children, improve the well-being of parents, and are cost-effective.

Safeguard children in early care and education from harm and promote their learning and development.

• Ensure that children will learn and thrive by improving the quality of early childhood programs and centers.

> **While we know that development of children's capacity to learn is crucial in the first few years of life, children during these years receive the least attention from the educational world.**

Enable communities to have the flexibility and resources they need to mobilize on behalf of young children and their families.

• Bring together leaders from business, media, community organizations, and religious institutions to develop goals and strategies for achieving the kind of community that supports all children and families.

*　　*　　*

Increased public awareness prompted by news-breaking reports on brain research may represent a window of opportunity in the early childhood field. With plans to make further links between science and education, early childhood professionals and advocates may find increased support for our cause— public understanding and support for child care that guarantees proper nutrition, well-planned physical environments, and developmentally appropriate practices to ensure the most promising future for all young children and families. The window of opportunity is open and the time for action is now.

References

Begley, S. 1996. I am your child. *Newsweek*, 19 February, 55–61.

Chugari, H. 1997. Personal communication, 21 March.

ECS (Education Commission of the States). 1996. *Bridging the gap between neuroscience and education: Summary of the workshop co-sponsored by Education Commission of the States and the Charles A. Dana Foundation.* Denver: Author.

Families and Work Institute. 1996. Rethinking the brain: New insights into early development. Executive summary of the Conference on Brain Development in Young Children: New frontiers for Research, Policy, and Practice. University of Chicago, June.

Gunnar, M. R., L. Brodersen, K. Krueger, & R. Rigatuso. 1996. Dampening of behavioral and adrenocortical reactivity during early infancy: Normative changes and individual differences. *Child Development* 67 (3): 877–89.

Jabs, C. 1996. Your baby's brain power. *Working Mother*, November, 24–28.

Nash, M. 1997. Fertile Minds. *Time*, 3 February, 48–56.

Highlights of the Quality 2000 Initiative:
Not by Chance

Sharon L. Kagan and Michelle J. Neuman

The quality crisis in early care and education

Each day 13 million children spend time in early care and education centers or family child care homes. This should be heartening given that quality early care and education contributes to the healthy cognitive, social, and emotional development of all young children (CQ&O Study Team 1995) and in particular children from low-income families (Schweinhart, Barnes, & Weikart 1993; Barnett 1995; Gomby et al. 1995; Phillips 1995; Yoshikawa 1995). Yet we know that the quality of a majority of these settings does not optimize children's healthy development; in fact, many settings seriously jeopardize it (Galinsky et al. 1994; CQ&O Study Team 1995).

We well understand many of the reasons for low quality: underfinanced services, poorly compensated teachers, precarious turnover rates, inadequate and inconsistent regulation and enforcement, fragmented training and delivery mechanisms—the litany goes on. We understand less well how to alter the situation and what it would *really* take to reverse the

Sharon L. Kagan, *Ed.D., senior associate at Yale University's Bush Center in Child Development and Social Policy in New Haven, Connecticut, is recognized nationally and internationally for her work related to the care and education of young children and their families and investigation of issues, including policy development, family support, early childhood pedagogy, strategies for collaboration and service integration, and evaluation of social programs.*

Michelle J. Neuman *was recently a research assistant at the Yale Bush Center in Child Development and Social Policy. Her research has focused on issues related to children and families, including early care and edcuation policy, family support, children's transitions to school, school readiness, and French family policy.*

pattern of neglect and provide quality early care and education to all young children.

The Quality 2000 initiative

For the past four years, hundreds of experts in early childhood education and allied fields have been examining these very questions under the auspices of an inventive initiative, Quality 2000: Advancing Early Care and Education. The primary goal of this initiative is that by the year 2010, high-quality early care and education programs will be available and accessible to all children from birth to age five whose parents choose to enroll them. Funded by the Carnegie Corporation of New York, with supportive funding from the David and Lucile Packard, W.K. Kellogg, A.L. Mailman Family, and Ewing Marion Kauffman foundations, the initiative carried out its work through a series of commissioned papers, cross-national literature reviews, task forces, and working groups. Informed by national and international research, the fruit of that work, *Not by Chance: Creating an Early Care and Education System for America's Children*, offers a comprehensive, long-range vision for the field.

The vision is not about adding more services or disparate programs to what exists, although additional funds and services are essential to the vision. Rather, consisting of eight recommendations, the vision sets forth new patterns of thinking and pathways for action. Some of the recommendations seem familiar; others may sound bold, if not audacious. However they are interpreted, the recommendations are not modest or quick fixes; they will take time and energy to accomplish. That is why we set them in the

From *Young Children*, September 1997, pp. 54-62. © 1997 by the National Association for the Education of Young Children. Reprinted by permission.

context of the year 2010, not the year 2000 as the project's name suggests.

Recommendations for eight essential functions

The Quality 2000 recommendations are broad and represent eight essential functions or areas where action to improve quality is needed; each recommendation is accompanied by suggested strategies to be tailored to fit individual community needs. Finally, the recommendations, although individualized to reflect each of the eight essential functions, need to be read in the aggregate—as a set of linked ideas.

1. Program quality

Imagine a time when we expect and support quality in all family child care and center-based programs (Head Start, for-profit and nonprofit child care centers, prekindergartens, nursery schools), allowing staff flexibility in using state-of-the-art strategies, technologies, and resources creatively and cost effectively.

To address the quality crisis, early care and education programs need the flexibility to explore and implement fresh ideas and strategies—strategies that consider changing demographic and technological realities as well as strategies that focus on the total program and individual classrooms or settings.

STRATEGIES

Promote cultural sensitivity and cultural pluralism. Children, staff, and families need opportunities to better understand and express their own cultural values and beliefs and to learn about other cultures (Derman-Sparks & the A.B.C. Task Force 1989; Phillips 1994; Phillips & Crowell 1994; Chang, Pulido-Tobiassen, & Muckelroy 1996). Staff should be trained to promote cultural sensitivity and cultural pluralism, and where possible, staff should come from the communities they serve. Children should be encouraged to cherish diversity.

Encourage pedagogical inventiveness in family child care and centers. Quality may result from a variety of strategies, including working with children in mixed-age groups (Katz, Evangelou, & Hartman 1990) and working inventively with families, grouping children in new ways, and considering ways of adapting child-staff ratios to capitalize on staff abilities to meet preschoolers' needs.

Focus on improving the overall organizational climate. The organizational climate of the total early care and education program —not only classrooms— must be considered as we create positive environments for all staff, parents, and families. Such environments should focus on the program as a learning organization ready to experiment, adapt, and grow.

Increase the number of accredited programs. Research indicates that accreditation—a voluntary process of self-assessment—significantly raises program quality. Because accredited centers provide higher quality services than nonaccredited programs (Bredekamp & Glowacki 1995; Bloom 1996; Whitebook, Sakai, & Howes 1997) and because the process promotes professionalism in the field, concerted efforts must be made to significantly increase the numbers of accredited programs.

Link programs to networks, supportive services, or other community resources. Linking early care and education programs with other services, especially resource-and-referral agencies, can help address unmet needs, expedite service delivery, minimize duplication of services, ensure smooth transitions for children, and help parents navigate through the social services maze (NACCRRA 1996). In addition, by creating family child care systems or networks, family child care providers can reduce their isolation and be more effectively linked to each other and community services.

2. Results for children

Imagine a time when clear results and expectations are specified and used to guide individual planning for all three- and four-year-old children, based on all domains of development (social/emotional, physical/motor, cognitive, language) and approaches to learning.

Traditionally, researchers have focused on inputs (e.g., child-staff ratios, group size, staff training and education) and on the manner in which services are delivered (e.g., the nature of adult-child interactions) (Hofferth & Chaplin 1994). Recently, however, there has been mounting interest in gauging quality in terms of the results that programs or interventions produce for preschool-age children and their families (Schorr 1994; CCSSO 1995). A focus on results for three- and four-year-olds can assist teachers with pedagogical planning and improvement as well as for purposes of evaluation and accountability. By defining desired goals and results, practitioners who work with young children can plan and tailor their activities to foster individual children's development. In addition, specified goals and results can provide programs with the feedback they need to evaluate their effectiveness and identify areas for improvement. Results also can be used to help assess the overall status of young children in communities, states, and the nation (Schorr 1994). With this information in hand, parents, practitioners, and the public can hold decisionmakers at all levels accountable for investing in early care and education (Kagan, Rosenkoetter, & Cohen 1997).

STRATEGIES

Identify appropriate results. To move toward a results-focused approach and to safeguard children from the misuses of results, parents, practitioners, policymakers, and the public need to come together to define results and expectations for three- and four-year-old children, taking into consideration the child, family, and community conditions that promote healthy development. In particular, results should be considered from the perspective of children—across programs and over time. Results should be specified at the local, state, and national levels, increasing the customization and specificity at each level.

Develop appropriate strategies and instruments. Developmentally appropriate and culturally sensitive instruments should be developed to evaluate progress toward the achievement of specified results in all domains of development. These strategies should include capturing children's development via portfolios and other documentation of children's work.

Share results effectively, ensuring safeguards for children. Demonstration projects, evaluation, and basic research will expand the knowledge base of what helps children achieve positive results. This information needs to be shared in ways that increase public understanding of the connection among child results, effective services, and the expenditure of public funds, not in ways that may label or stigmatize children. Guidelines for the effective use of results should be developed.

3. Parent and family engagement

Imagine a time when parents of young children are actively involved in their children's programs and when programs provide diverse opportunities for such involvement. Imagine a time when parents have the user-friendly information and support they need to be effective consumers in choosing programs for their children. Imagine a time when employers provide policies that enable parents to become involved in their children's early learning and education.

Research shows that parent and family engagement in early care and education programs improves results for children, increasing the likelihood of children's success and achievement and decreasing the likelihood of negative outcomes, both in school and later in life (Bronfenbrenner 1974; Bronson, Pierson, & Tivnan 1984; Powell 1989).

STRATEGIES

Support parents as partners in early care and education programs. By focusing on developing regular communication among practitioners and parents (Weissbourd 1987), parents can be more effectively engaged as equals, with valuable information and resources. To that end, programs can offer multiple activities to involve parents (Henderson, Marburger, & Ooms 1986; Epstein 1995), taking into consideration how parent's interests, needs, and work and family responsibilities may influence their participation. Parents also should be engaged in governance opportunities (Kagan 1994).

Support parents as effective consumers. Parents can benefit from objective information about programs so they can make educated decisions that will promote their children's early development and learning. Well-funded resource-and-referral agencies, along with other parenting education efforts, can assist parents in learning about and evaluating their early care and education options. Such efforts must acknowledge and respect parents' diverse backgrounds, cultures, and needs.

Increase the family-friendliness of workplaces. Parents need support from their employers so they can fulfill their roles as partners in their children's programs, as effective consumers of early care and education services, and as productive employees (Staines & Galinsky 1991; Galinsky, Bond, & Friedman 1993). Employers should consider offering significantly greater employee benefits, at a minimum providing time for parents to find a program and monitor and participate in their children's early care and education. Corporations should offer parents the choice of working part-time, paid sick days to care for sick children, and job-protected paid maternity and parental leave.

4. Staff credentialing

Imagine a time when all individuals working with children in early care and education programs have—or are actively in the process of obtaining—credentials related to the position they hold or seek. Imagine a time when all staff are encouraged to pursue ongoing training and education—a course of lifelong learning.

An Approach to Licensing Individuals: Requirements for Early Care and Education Staff

Administrator license

For center directors and directors of family child care support services,

• at least a bachelor's or master's degree in early childhood education or child development from an accredited institution, including at least 15 credits in early childhood administration

• certification in pediatric first aid

• demonstration of competency in management and in working with children and families

Educator license

For center teachers and public school teachers of children ages three and four,

• at least an associate's or bachelor's degree in early childhood education or child development from an accredited institution

• practicum with the age of children with whom individuals would work

• certification in pediatric first aid

• demonstration of competency in working with children and families

Associate educator license

For lead providers in large family child care homes and assistant teachers in centers,

• at least a Child Development Associate (CDA) credential, the revised National Association for Family Child Care (NAFCC) accreditation or equivalent—meaning at least 120 clock hours of formal education in child development/early childhood education and the demonstration of competency in working with children and families

• practicum with the age group with which individuals would work

• certification in pediatric first aid

Entry-level position requirement

For aides in centers and in large family child care homes and for family child care providers in small family child care homes,

• interest in and aptitude for working with children and families

• commitment to participating in ongoing training leading to licensure

Because individuals who work with children in early care and education programs have a major impact on children's early development and learning experiences, their credentialing/licensing is critical. Licensing individual early childhood educators has many benefits. Licensing

• holds promise for increasing the compensation of staff,

• increases professionalization in the field,

• promotes the creation and coordination of quality training and education as well as career mobility, and

• helps prevent harm to children and ensure the quality of programs (APHA & AAP 1992).

The model for individual licensing can be found in Western European nations and Japan, which require significantly more training and education of practitioners and a more coordinated and sequenced training delivery system (Pritchard 1996). Structures to support licensing individuals are well established in many other occupations in the United States, including help-ing professionals (e.g., social workers, registered and licensed practical nurses, teachers), technical professionals (e.g., architects, engineers), tradespeople (e.g., electricians), and even service workers (e.g., cosmetologists) (Mitchell 1996).

Individual licenses should be distinct from, but complementary to, facility licenses. They should specify the preparatory and ongoing training that staff need to work with children in a variety of roles. While there are many approaches to individual licensing, Quality 2000 offers one that calls for a series of three licenses for early care and education workers (see "An Approach to Licensing Individuals" chart).

STRATEGIES

Create early childhood administrator licenses. All center directors and directors of family child care support services would be required to have early childhood administrator licenses. To obtain this license, an individual would need at least a bachelor's or master's degree in early childhood education or child development from an accredited institution, including at least 15 credits in early childhood administration, certification in first aid, and demonstrated competency in management and in working with children and families.

Create early childhood educator licenses. All teachers in centers would be required to have early childhood educator licenses. Teachers of three- and four-year-old children in public schools would have the option of obtaining public school teacher certification/licenses or the early childhood educator license. To obtain the early childhood educator license, individuals would need to have at least an associate's or bachelor's degree in early childhood education or child development from an accredited institution; have practicum experience with the age group with which they would work; be certified in pediatric first aid; and pass a competency-based assessment in working with children and families.

Create early childhood associate educator licenses. All assistant teachers in centers, as well as lead providers in large family child care homes, would be required to have early childhood associate educator licenses. To obtain the license, an individual working in a center would need to have a Child Development Associate (CDA) credential or the equivalent; an individual working in a family child care home would need to have a CDA, the revised National Association for Family Child Care (NAFCC) accreditation, or equivalent certification. Each of these certifications requires at least 120 clock hours of formal education in early childhood development and education and the demonstration of the competencies needed to work with young children and their families. Assistant teachers and lead providers also would need to have practicum experience with the age group with which they would work and certification in pediatric first aid.

Maintain access to entry-level positions. Individuals who do not have training or education in child development or early childhood education, but who have an interest in and aptitude for working with young children and families and a commitment to seeking training in the field, would have access to entry-level jobs as aides in child care centers and in large-group family child care homes or as providers in small family child care homes. These individuals would be considered an integral part of the profession as long as they are actively pursuing training to achieve licensure as early childhood associate educator or educator.

5. Staff training and preparation

Imagine a time when all training for early childhood positions is child and family focused, reflecting and respecting cultural and linguistic diversity. Imagine a time when all approved training bears credit, leads to increased credentials and compensation, and equips individuals for diverse and advanced roles.

The quality of the credentials just discussed is contingent upon the quality of the training individuals receive. All training and education sequences should, at a minimum, address the CDA competency areas (establishing and maintaining a safe, healthy learning environment; advancing physical and intellectual competence; supporting social and emotional development and providing positive guidance; establishing positive and productive relationships with families; ensuring a well-run, purposeful program that is responsive to participant needs; and maintaining a commitment to professionalism [Council for Early Childhood Professional Recognition 1992]). More preservice and inservice training, particularly at intermediate and advanced levels, needs to be developed and made available to practitioners in the following areas (Morgan et al. 1993): engaging and supporting families; developing cultural competency; observing and assessing children; working with mixed-age groups and larger groups, and team teaching; working with infants and toddlers; working with children with special needs; promoting ethics; working across human service disciplines; and developing management and leadership skills.

STRATEGIES

Revise and develop staff training/preparation curricula and sequences. Revamping the content of and opportunities for practitioner training/preparation will necessitate the participation of many stakeholders. State licensing boards for early care and education should require staff to have appropriate ranges of skills to earn and maintain licenses, including appropriate preparatory and ongoing course work. Colleges and community organizations that educate and train early care and education staff should revise and develop curricula and sequences to address the broad-based knowledge (early childhood pedagogy and content from allied disciplines) and skills that practitioners need to be competent in today's early care and education programs.

Promote the development of leaders and managers. To promote the development of leaders and managers at the local, state, and national levels, program administrators with strong leadership potential should be supported through fellowships and training and mentoring opportunities. Such mentoring programs are an effective strategy to support staff as they acquire knowledge and skills and to enhance the professional development of more skilled and experienced mentor-teachers (Whitebook, Hnatiuk, & Bellm 1994; Breunig & Bellm 1996).

6. Program licensing

Imagine a time when all early care and education programs are licensed, without any legal exemptions. Imagine a time when facility licensing procedures are streamlined and enforced to ensure that all programs promote children's safety, health, and development. Imagine a time when incentives exist for programs to continually enhance their facilities.

Research demonstrates that about 40% of center-based programs—including many part-day, school-based, and church-based programs (Adams 1990)—and as many as 80 to 90% of family child care providers (Willer et al. 1991) are legally exempt from regulation despite the fact that states with more stringent regulation yield higher quality programs (CQ&O Study Team 1995).

STRATEGIES

Eliminate exemptions. All programs available to the general public should be required to meet basic safeguards that protect children's well-being and foster equity in the early care and education field; there should be no legal exemptions. For example, programs should not be legally exempt from facility regulations because of their size, hours of operation, location, or auspices.

Streamline facility licensing. State facility licensing should be streamlined to focus on essential safeguards of safety, health, and development and to complement the system of individual licensing described earlier (U.S. ACIR 1994; Gormley 1995; Gwen Morgan, personal communication, 22 March 1996). Standards for staffing levels should allow programs the flexibility to group children and organize staff in ways that maximize quality.

Enforce requirements. To fully promote children's safety, health, and development, states must not only eliminate exemptions and streamline regulations but also enforce requirements. Licensing agencies must have the appropriate resources to carry out enforcement functions. State monitoring and enforcement systems should employ positive, incentive-based strategies to enable programs to

meet licensing requirements. State licensing systems also should provide incentives for programs to invest in facility enhancement to increase capacity for meeting the increasing demand for early care and education services.

Develop national licensing guidelines. Although the main responsibility for the development and issue of facility licensing requirements should remain at the state level, national licensing guidelines should be developed to promote regulatory consistency across the country.

7. Funding and financing

Imagine a time when young children's early care and education is funded by the public and private sectors at per-child levels commensurate with funding for elementary-age children and when 10% of the funds are set aside for professional and staff development, enhanced compensation, parent information and engagement, program accreditation, resource-and-referral services, evaluation, research, planning, and licensing and facility enhancement.

Adequate funding is essential to ensuring that all children have access to quality early care and education services and that their parents have choice in selecting services. The costs must be shared by the public at large, parents (according to income), employers, government, and community organizations. While parents need access to and choice of quality early care and education services, they also need the option of caring for their own very young children; therefore, paid parental leave for parents of very young children should be provided. These efforts to increase investment necessitate additional research and planning.

STRATEGIES

Estimate the actual cost of a quality early care and education system. The field needs to estimate the actual cost of mounting and sustaining a comprehensive quality early care and education system. In making such estimates, early care and education professionals need to work closely with funding and financing experts, using cost-calculation approaches that other fields have found useful. Such an analysis also should estimate the revenues that the early care and education system would generate in both the short and long term. Longer-term cost-benefit accounting should be used to determine the extended benefits of a quality early care and education system, benefits that include savings in special education, corrections, public assistance, and other social services.

Identify several revenue-generation mechanisms. Several revenue-generation options for funding for a comprehensive early care and education system—including increased staff compensation—need to be considered and implemented. Some possible mechanisms include establishing individual and corporate income taxes, federal payroll taxes, and new sales or excise taxes; expanding the populations eligible to receive the school aid formula; cutting other government expenditures to raise some of the needed funds; and procuring funds as part of a larger revenue-generation package designed to support a range of social services that families need. None of these approaches are easy to sell to the public or policymakers, but each would help improve the amount of funding available to support early care and education.

Develop model approaches for distributing funds to parents. State-level agencies may be best suited for administering funds to parents. Mechanisms to distribute funds to parents should promote parent choice, such as vouchers, direct payments to programs of parents' choice, and/or tax credits. Parents should receive assistance in paying for early care and education programs based on a sliding scale linked to parents' income. (As family income increases over time, public assistance for early care and education would decrease proportionately but not be completely cut off [Stangler 1995]).

Create a targeted, coordinated funding initiative. Scholarship and knowledge of how to generate increased revenues for the development of a comprehensive early care and education system is emerging but remains piecemeal and embryonic. Focused research is needed to carry out the analyses mentioned above. Therefore, it will be necessary to create a targeted, coordinated initiative focused on funding a quality early care and education system.

8. Governance structures

Imagine a time when early care and education is governed rationally. Imagine a time when mechanisms (councils, boards) are established or built upon in every community and state to carry out planning, governance, and accountability roles in early care and education.

To increase coordination, efficiency, and continuity of services for young children and their families, it is critical to establish a rational governance system.

Quality 2000 recommends establishing governance entities in every state and locality—to be called State Early Care and Education Board and Local Early Care and Education Board, respectively. Where these governing boards or coordinating councils already exist, the State or Local Early Care and Education Board could be built from the existing body or created in collaboration with it.

STRATEGIES

Establish state boards. State boards should be responsible for ensuring quality and achieving agreed-upon results for children. They should engage in planning, collecting, and analyzing data; defining eligibility and subsidy levels and parental-leave conditions; and determining how to allocate funds to parents. They would also develop state standards for results to align with national goals. As with other governance entities, state boards would facilitate collaboration, service integration, and comprehensive services delivery. State boards would be composed of appointed or elected board members, including equal numbers of parents/consumers; practitioners; community and state leaders, including clergy; and municipal or government agency representatives.

Establish local boards. Local boards would have responsibility for both the governance and the coordination of early care and education for children birth to age five. They could be geographically aligned with school districts, but would be distinct entities. Like their state counterparts, they should be composed of a broad-based group of appointed or elected board members who would be responsible for developing performance benchmarks for child results, taking into consideration local strengths, needs, priorities, and resources. Local boards would involve consumers and citizens in comprehensive needs assessment and planning.

Support effective federal governance. To support these efforts, the federal government will need to provide mandates and incentives to these boards. In addition, the federal government will guide states as they develop standards and communities as they develop benchmarks to meet state standards and national goals. The federal government also will collect national data, provide funding for evaluating demonstration efforts, and offer technical assistance to states and localities. Their well-being, and the nation's, simply cannot be left to chance.

* * *

The quality of daily life for millions of American children and families depends on how the United States solves—or fails to solve—the quality crisis in early care and education. Quality 2000 and the *Not by Chance* report address this crisis by recommending that the nation make a planned, significant, and immediate advance to improve quality and to create a system of services. It is the hope of those involved in the Quality 2000 initiative that the ideas put forth in these recommendations will provoke discussion, advance our collective thinking, and spark bold, new action on behalf of our nation's children. Their well-being, and the nation's, simply cannot be left to chance.

References

Adams, G. 1990. *Who knows how safe? The status of state efforts to ensure quality child care.* Washington, DC: Children's Defense Fund.

APHA (American Public Health Association), & AAP (American Academy of Pediatrics). 1992. *Caring for our children: National health and safety performance standards—Guidelines for out-of-home child care programs.* Washington, DC: APHA.

Barnett, W.S. 1995. Long-term effects of early childhood programs on cognitive and school outcomes. *The Future of Children* 5 (3): 25–50.

Bloom, P.J. 1996. The quality of work life in early childhood programs: Does accreditation make a difference? In *NAEYC accreditation: A decade of learning and the years ahead*, eds. S. Bredekamp & B.A. Willer, 13–24. Washington, DC: NAEYC.

Bredekamp, S., & S. Glowacki. 1995. The first decade of NAEYC accreditation: Growth and impact on the field. Paper prepared for an invitational conference sponsored by the Robert McCormick Tribune Foundation and NAEYC, 18–20 September, Wheaton, Illinois.

Breunig, G.S., & D. Bellm. 1996. *Early childhood mentoring programs: A survey of community initiatives.* Washington, DC: National Center for the Early Childhood Work Force.

Brofenbrenner, U. 1974. *A report on longitudinal evaluations of preschool programs, Vol. 2: Is early intervention effective?* Washington, DC: Office of Child Development, U.S. Department of Health, Education, and Welfare.

Bronson, M.B., D.E. Pierson, & T. Tivnan. 1984. The effects of early education on children's competence in elementary school. *Evaluation Review* 8: 615–29.

Chang, H.N., D. Pulido-Tobiassen, & A. Muckelroy. 1996. *Looking in, looking out: Redefining care and early education in a diverse society.* San Francisco: California Tomorrow.

CCSSO (Council of Chief State School Officers). 1995. *Moving toward accountability for results: A look at ten states' efforts.* Washington, DC: Author.

Council for Early Childhood Professional Recognition. 1992. *Child Development Associate assessment system and competency standards.* Washington, DC: Author.

CQ&O (Cost, Quality, & Outcomes) Study Team. 1995. *Cost, quality, and child outcomes in child care centers.* Denver: Department of Economics, University of Colorado at Denver.

Derman-Sparks, L., & the A.B.C. Task Force. 1989. *Anti-bias curriculum: Tools for empowering young children.* Washington, DC: NAEYC.

Epstein, J.L. 1995. School/family/community partnerships: Caring for the children we share. *Phi Delta Kappan* (May): 701–12.

Galinsky, E., J.T. Bond, & D.E. Friedman. 1993. *The changing workforce: Highlights of the National Study.* New York: Families and Work Institute.

Galinsky, E., C. Howes, S. Kontos, & M. Shinn. 1994. *The study of children in family child care and relative care.* New York: Families and Work Institute.

Gomby, D.S., M.B. Larner, C.S. Stevenson, E.M. Lewit, & R.E. Behrman. 1995. Long-term outcomes of early childhood programs: Analysis and recommendations. *The Future of Children* 5 (3): 6–24.

Gormley, W.T. 1995. *Everybody's children: Child care as a public problem.* Washington, DC: Brookings Institution.

Henderson, A.T., C.L. Marburger, & T. Ooms. 1986. *Beyond the bake sale: An educator's guide to working with parents.* Columbia, MD: National Committee for Citizens in Education.

Hofferth, S.L., & D. Chaplin. 1994. *Child care quality versus availability: Do we have to trade one for the other?* Washington, DC: Urban Institute Press.

Kagan, S.L. 1994. *Defining America's commitments to parents and families: An historical-conceptual perspective.* Kansas City, MO: Ewing Marion Kauffman Foundation.

Kagan, S.L., S. Rosenkoetter, & N.E. Cohen, eds. 1997. *Considering child-based outcomes for young children: Definitions, desirability, feasibility, and next steps.* New Haven, CT: Bush Center in Child Development and Social Policy, Yale University.

Katz, L.G., D. Evangelou, & J.A. Hartman. 1990. *The case for mixed-age grouping in early education.* Washington, DC: NAEYC.

Mitchell, A. 1996. Licensing: Lessons from other occupations. In *Reinventing early care and education: A vision for a quality system*, eds. S.L. Kagan & N.E. Cohen, 101–123. San Francisco: Jossey-Bass.

Morgan, G., S.L. Azer, J.B. Costley, A. Genser, I.F. Goodman, J. Lombardi, & B. McGimsey. 1993. *Making a career of it: The state of the states report on career development in early care and education.* Boston: Center for Career Development in Early Care and Education, Wheelock College.

NACCRRA (National Association of Child Care Resource and Referral Agencies). 1996. *Creating and facilitating health linkages: The role of child care resource and referral.* Washington, DC: Author.

Phillips, C.B. 1994. The movement of African-American children through sociocultural contexts: A case of conflict resolution. In *Diversity and developmentally appropriate practices: Challenges for early childhood education*, eds. B.L. Mallory & R.S. New, 137–54. New York: Teachers College Press.

Phillips, D.A., ed. 1995. *Child care for low-income families: Summary of two workshops.* Washington, DC: National Academy Press.

Phillips, D.A., & N.A. Crowell, eds. 1994. *Cultural diversity in early education: Results of a workshop.* Washington, DC: National Academy Press.

Powell, D.R. 1989. *Families and early childhood programs.* Washington, DC: NAEYC.

Pritchard, E. 1996. Training and professional development: International approaches. In *Reinventing early care and education: A vision for a quality system*, eds. S.L. Kagan & N.E. Cohen, 124–41. San Francisco: Jossey-Bass.

Schorr, L.B. 1994. The case for shifting to results-based accountability. In *Making a difference: Moving to outcome-based accountability for comprehensive service reforms*, eds. N. Young, S. Gardner, S. Coley, L. Schorr, & C. Bruner, 13–28. Falls Church, VA: National Center for Service Integration.

Schweinhart, L.J., H.V. Barnes, & D.P. Weikart, with W.S. Barnett, & A.S. Epstein. 1993. *Significant benefits: The High/Scope Perry Preschool Study through age 27.* Ypsilanti, MI: High/Scope Press.

Staines, G.L., & E. Galinsky. 1991. *Parental leave and productivity: The supervisor's view.* New York: Families and Work Institute.

Stangler, G. 1995. Lifeboats vs. safety nets: Who rides. . .who swims? In *Dollars and sense: Diverse perspectives on block grants and the Personal Responsibility Act,* 67–72. Washington, DC: The Finance Project and Institute for Educational Leadership.

U.S. ACIR (Advisory Commission on Intergovernmental Relations). 1994. *Child care: The need for federal-state-local coordination.* Washington, DC: Author.

Weissbourd, B. 1987. A brief history of family support programs. In *America's family support programs*, eds. S.L. Kagan, D.R. Powell, B. Weissbourd, & E.F. Zigler, 38–56. New Haven, CT: Yale University Press.

Whitebook, M., P. Hnatiuk, & D. Bellm. 1994. *Mentoring in early care and education: Refining an emerging career path.* Washington, DC: National Center for the Early Childhood Work Force.

Whitebook, M., L. Sakai, &, C. Howes. 1997. *NAEYC accreditation as a strategy for improving child care quality, executive summary.* Washington, DC: National Center for the Early Childhood Work Force.

Willer, B., ed. 1990. *Reaching the full cost of quality in early childhood programs.* Washington, DC: NAEYC.

Willer, B., S. Hofferth, E. Kisker, P. Divine-Hawkins, E. Farquhar, & F. Glantz. 1991. *The demand and supply of child care in 1990: Joint findings from the National Child Care Survey 1990 and a profile of child care settings.* Washington, DC: NAEYC.

Yoshikawa, H. 1995. Long-term effects of early childhood programs on social outcomes and delinquency. *The Future of Children* 5 (3): 51–75.

The National Television Violence Study: Key Findings and Recommendations

Editor's note: *The National Television Violence Study is a three-year effort to assess violence on television. Underwritten by the National Cable Television Association, the independent analysis is coordinated by an autonomous nonprofit organization, Mediascope. Oversight is provided by a council whose members reflect national leadership in education, medicine, violence prevention, the creative community, law, psychology, and communication, with one-third of the council representing the entertainment industry. Four universities are involved in three study components. The Universities of California at Santa Barbara and Texas at Austin are doing a content analysis to assess the amount and context of television violence. The University of Wisconsin at Madison is researching how children respond to viewer advisories and ratings, and the University of North Carolina at Chapel Hill is examining adolescents' responses to antiviolence messages on television. This report is excerpted from the* National Television Violence Study 1994–95 Executive Summary, *the first in a series of three annual reports. Here we present a summary of key findings related to the content analysis and the study's recommendations.*

Preventing violence involves identifying the combination of factors that contribute to it, from biological and psychological causes to broader social and cultural ones. Among these, television violence has been recognized as a significant factor contributing to violent and aggressive antisocial behavior by an overwhelming majority of the scientific community.

However, it is also recognized that televised violence does not have a uniform effect on viewers. The outcome of media violence depends both on the nature of the depiction and the sociological and psychological makeup of the audience. In some cases, the same portrayal of violence may have different effects on different audiences. For example, graphically portrayed violence may elicit fear in some viewers and aggression in others. Family role models, social and economic status, educational level, peer influences, and the availability of weapons can each significantly alter the likelihood of a particular reaction to viewing televised violence.

The context in which violence is portrayed may modify the contributions to viewer behaviors and attitudes. Violence may be performed by heroic characters or villains. It may be rewarded or it may be punished. Violence may occur without much victim pain and suffering or it may cause tremendous physical anguish. It may be shown close-up on the screen or at a distance.

This study is the most comprehensive scientific assessment yet conducted of the context in which violence is depicted on television, based on some 2,500 hours of programming randomly selected from 23 television channels between 6 A.M. to 11 P.M. over a 20-week period. Television content was analyzed at three distinct levels: (1) how characters interact with one another when violence occurs (violent interaction); (2) how violent interactions are grouped together (violent scene); and (3) how violence is presented in the context of the overall program.

Violence is defined as any overt depiction of the use of physical force—or the credible threat of such force—intended to physically harm an animate being or group of beings. Violence also includes certain depictions of physically harmful consequences against an animate being or group that occur as a result of unseen violent means.

Key findings

• *The context in which most violence is presented on television poses risks for viewers.* The majority of programs analyzed in this study contain some violence. But more important than the prevalence of violence is the contextual pattern in which most of it is shown. The risks of viewing the most common depictions of televised violence include learning to behave violently, becoming more desensitized to the harmful consequences of violence, and becoming more fearful of being attacked. The contextual patterns noted below are found consistently across most channels, program types, and times of day. Thus, there are substantial risks of harmful effects of viewing violence throughout the television environment.

• *Perpetrators go unpunished in 73% of all violent scenes.* This pattern is highly consistent across different types of programs and channels. The portrayal of rewards and punishments is probably the most important of all contextual factors for viewers as they interpret the meaning of what they see on television. When violence is presented without punishment, viewers are more likely to learn the lesson that violence is successful.

• *The negative consequences of violence are not often portrayed in violent programming.* Most violent portrayals do not show the victim experiencing any serious physical harm or pain at the time the violence occurs. For example, 47% of all violent interactions show no harm to victims and 58% show no pain. Even less frequent is the depiction of any long-term consequences of violence. In fact, only 16% of all programs portray the long-term nega-

From *Young Children*, March 1996, pp. 54-55. © 1996 by Mediascope, Inc. Reprinted by permission.

tive repercussions of violence, such as psychological, financial, or emotional harm.

• *One out of four violent interactions on television (25%) involves the use of a handgun.* Depictions of violence with guns and other conventional weapons can instigate or trigger aggressive thoughts and behaviors.

• *Only 4% of violent programs emphasize an antiviolence theme.* Very few violent programs place emphasis on condemning the use of violence or on presenting alternatives to using violence to solve problems. This pattern is consistent across different types of programs and channels.

• *On the positive side, television violence is usually not explicit or graphic.* Most violence is presented without any close-up focus on aggressive behaviors and without showing any blood and gore. In particular, less than 3% of violent scenes feature close-ups on the violence and only 15% of scenes contain blood and gore. Explicit or graphic violence contributes to desensitization and can enhance fear.

• *There are some notable differences in the presentation of violence across television channels.* Public broadcasting presents violent programs least often (18%) and those violent depictions that appear pose the least risk of harmful effects. Premium cable channels present the highest percentage of violent programs (85%) and those depictions often pose a greater risk of harm than do most violent portrayals. Broadcast networks present violent programs less frequently (44%) than the industry norm (57%), but when violence is included its contextual features are just as problematic as those on most other channels.

• *There are also some important differences in the presentation of violence across types of television programs.* Movies are more likely to present violence in realistic settings (85%) and to include blood and gore in violent scenes (28%) than other program types. The contextual pattern of violence in children's programming also poses concern. Children's programs are the least likely of all genres to show the long-term negative consequences of violence (5%), and they frequently portray violence in a humorous context (67%).

Recommendations

These recommendations are based both on the findings of this study and extensive research upon which this study is based.

For the television community

• Produce more programs that avoid violence. When violence does occur, keep the number of incidents low, show more negative consequences, provide nonviolent alternatives to solving problems, and consider emphasizing antiviolence themes.

• Increase portrayals of powerful nonviolent heroes and attractive characters.

Although violence in society has many causes, the effect of thousands of messages conveyed through the most powerful medium of mass communication cannot be ignored.

• Programs with high levels of violence, including reality programs, should be scheduled in late-evening hours when children are less likely to be watching.

• Increase the number of program advisories and content codes. In doing so, however, use caution in language so that such messages do not serve as magnets to children.

• Provide information about advisories and the nature of violent content to viewers in programming guides.

• Limit the time devoted to sponsor, station, or network identification during public service announcements (PSAs) so that it does not compete with the message.

For policy and public interest leaders

• Recognize that context is an essential aspect of television violence and that the basis of any policy proposal should consider the types of violent depictions that pose the greatest concern.

• Consider the feasibility of technology that would allow parents to restrict access to inappropriate content.

• Test antiviolence PSAs, including the credibility of spokespersons, with target audiences prior to production. Provide target audiences with specific and realistic actions for resolving conflicts peacefully.

• When possible, link antiviolence PSAs to school-based or community efforts and target young audiences, 8 to 13 years old, who may be more responsive to such messages.

For parents

• Watch television with your child. In this study, children whose parents were routinely involved with their child's viewing were more likely to avoid inappropriate programming.

• Encourage critical evaluation of television content.

• Consider a child's developmental level when making viewing decisions.

• Be aware of the potential risks associated with viewing television violence: the learning of aggressive attitudes and behaviors, fear, desensitization or loss of sympathy toward victims of violence.

• Recognize that different kinds of violent programs pose different risks.

The *National Television Violence Study Executive Summary 1994–95* is published by Mediascope, Inc., and is available for $10 prepaid. For further information, contact Mediascope at 12711 Ventura Boulevard, Studio City, CA 91604; 818-508-2080; fax 818-508-2088; e-mail: mediascope@mediascope.org

CHILD CARE

Good-quality child care and early education programs are essential for millions of American families. Thirteen million preschool children—including 6 million infants and toddlers—spend all or part of their day being cared for by someone other than their parents. In addition, millions of school-age children need supervision during the hours when their parents are at work, and their schools are closed. Many parents, however, are hard pressed to find affordable, reliable child care that gives them peace of mind about their children while they work.

The number of parents for whom adequate child care is a constant concern has grown dramatically over the past 25 years. In 1973 approximately 30 percent of mothers with children under age 6 were in the work force, as were more than 50 percent of mothers of school-age children. By 1997 these percentages had grown to 65 percent and 77 percent, respectively. As recent changes in the welfare laws compel recipients of government assistance to work, the numbers will keep climbing. In addition, because income is declining for young families, many simply cannot make ends meet unless both parents work. About half of America's families with young children earn less than $35,000 per year, and the Families and Work Institute reports that the majority of

working women provide half or more of their household income. More than ever, American families desperately need child care that is affordable and of high quality.

Child Care: 1973 to 1998

Families in 1973 found little help from either the government or the private sector as they searched for child care that would enable them to work and ensure their children's safety and well-being. President Nixon had just vetoed the 1971 Comprehensive Child Development Act, which would have provided $2 billion to help states and local communities expand and improve families' access to quality child care. Head Start, now a widely acclaimed early childhood development program, was a relatively new initiative serving 379,000 low-income children—many in summer programs only. The federal government provided only limited funds for child care services, primarily for families receiving welfare.

Past problems. In 1972 *Windows on Day Care,* a study by the National Council of Jewish Women (NCJW), exposed the glaring inadequacies of the nation's child care system. The study, based on observations of pro-

grams and interviews with families across the country, revealed problems that are strikingly familiar today: substandard care, insufficient supply (particularly for infants, toddlers, and school-age children), and a lack of funds to help families pay for care.

NCJW members visited 431 child care centers enrolling nearly 24,000 children. They found that only 1 percent of the for-profit centers and 9 percent of the nonprofit centers provided what NCJW members regarded as truly developmental care, including educational, health, nutritional, and, where needed, social services. A significant proportion of programs were of poor quality and should have been closed.

A 1971 *Washington Post* article likewise described poor conditions at a center in Washington, D.C.:

> In one corner of the large, neat, and very bare room, 21 children, ages 3 to 6 years old, and two adults sit, watching "Captain Kangaroo" on a small-screen black-and-white television perched far above their heads on a room divider. About half the children seem attentive, a handful are squinting or glassy-eyed, and five have their heads down on the table either resting or sleeping.... There is no talk, either during commercials or after the program ends.

According to the reporter, there were few books in the center, no educa-

 From *The State of America's Children Yearbook,* 1998, pp. 37-47. © 1998 by the Children's Defense Fund. Reprinted by permission.

tional toys, and little if anything to stimulate creative play.

Windows on Day Care also documented a serious shortage of child care for two large groups—children under age 3 (infants and toddlers) and those of school age. One of the most distressing findings of the report "was the almost total absence of quality care for infants and toddlers outside the home." Similarly, interviewees in almost every community spoke of "a large need for before- and after-school care . . . about which very little, if anything, was being done." Mother after mother reported that there was no care of any kind available for after-school hours.

Low wages for child care providers were another problem in the 1970s. In 1977 almost two out of three caregivers had annual earnings below the poverty line for a family of four.

Current issues. Although more resources are now available to families, many of the problems highlighted in *Windows on Day Care* in 1972 remain just as challenging today. National studies continue to reveal alarming deficiencies in the quality of care in many communities. According to *Cost, Quality, and Child Outcomes in Child Care Centers,* a 1995 study conducted by researchers at the University of Colorado at Denver, the University of California at Los Angeles, the University of North Carolina at Chapel Hill, and Yale University, six out of seven child care centers provide care that is mediocre to poor. One in eight might actually be jeopardizing children's safety and development. Equally disturbing problems in home-based care were documented by Ellen Galinsky and others in a 1994 report for the Families and Work Institute. According to their *Study of Children in Family Child Care and Relative Care: Highlights of Findings,* one in three settings provided care that could conceivably hinder a child's development.

Low wages continue to be the norm for child care providers, just

as they were 25 years ago. Child care teachers and providers today earn less per year than the average bus driver ($20,150) or garbage collector ($18,100). Staff employed in child care centers typically earn about $12,000 per year (only slightly above minimum wage) and receive no benefits or paid leave. As a result, turnover among child care providers is high, shattering the stable relationship that infants and children need to feel safe and secure.

In addition, many states have woefully inadequate health and safety standards for child care. Staff education and training are among the most critical elements in improving children's experiences in child care. Yet 39 states and the District of Columbia do not require prior training for providers who look after children in their homes, and 32 states do not demand prior training for teachers in child care centers. In contrast, becoming a licensed haircutter or manicurist typically requires about 1,500 hours of training at an accredited school.

Even the standards that are in place are often poorly enforced because of a growing number of child care facilities coupled with insufficient inspection staff. A 1994 Inspector General's report on licensed child care centers in five states found unsafe and unsanitary conditions in a significant number. Moreover, relatively few child care centers meet the higher standards required for accreditation. In 1997, for example, only 6 percent of all child care centers were accredited by the National Association for the Education of Young Children.

A 1996 report by the Carnegie Corporation, *Years of Promise: A Comprehensive Strategy for America's Children,* states that child care and early education services "have so long been neglected that they now constitute some of the worst services for children in Western society." The report observes that the care most children receive not only can "threaten their immediate health and safety, but also can compromise their long-term

development." Kindergarten teachers estimate that one in three children enters the classroom unprepared to meet the challenges of school.

Families with children under 3 continue to face especially daunting obstacles to finding safe and supportive child care. Both the supply and the quality have been found wanting. A 1995 Urban Institute study of child care needs found shortages of infant care in the majority of the cities examined. The *Cost, Quality, and Child Outcomes* study revealed that 40 percent of the rooms serving infants and toddlers in child care centers provided such poor care as to jeopardize children's health, safety, and development.

The need for before- and after-school care has barely been addressed. The U.S. Census Bureau estimates that nearly 5 million children are left unsupervised by an adult after school each week. The consequences are grim; according to the U.S. Department of Justice, juvenile crime peaks between 3 and 7 p.m. A study by Kathleen Dwyer and others, published in the September 1989 issue of *Pediatrics,* found that eighth-graders who were left home alone after school reported greater use of cigarettes, alcohol, and marijuana than those in adult-supervised settings. The lack of good after-school options is especially acute in low-income neighborhoods. In 1993 only one-third of schools in such neighborhoods offered before- and after-school programs.

Finally, many low-income working families have little hope of receiving help to pay for child care. In 1997 New Jersey, for example, reported that as many as 15,000 children were on waiting lists for child care subsidies, and Texas had a waiting list of 37,000 families. New York state can provide child care subsidies to only one in 10 eligible children. According to the Census Bureau, poor families earning less than $14,400 in 1993 spent 25 percent of their income on child care. The annual cost of center-based care for one child in an urban area can range from $5,000 to $12,000 for infants and $4,000 to $8,000 for preschoolers. Moreover, the average American family has two children.

About one-quarter of employed mothers with children under 6 care for their children while they work, or rely on their spouses to do so. Another quarter leave their children with other relatives. But these are not always options, and low-income families who need outside child care face extraordinary pressures. Many are forced to make choices between placing their children in potentially harmful care settings or leaving their jobs and turning to welfare. The 1996 welfare law, which imposes work requirements on recipients and limits the amount of time they can get public assistance, intensifies the need to make child care affordable for parents in low-wage jobs. These families must have reliable child care whether they are moving off welfare or struggling to avoid dependence on it.

More resources. Over the past 25 years some additional help for families has been provided. In the late 1980s a major initiative, the Act for Better Child Care, moved through Congress with bipartisan support. That legislation, which established

what is today the Child Care and Development Block Grant (CCDBG), now provides a significant portion of the federal resources for child care. Largely through the CCDBG program, the federal government currently invests $3 billion a year on child care needs, and the states supply additional funds. The money goes to help low-income families pay for child care, to support resource and referral programs that help families find care, to train providers, to monitor child care programs, and to expand the supply of care.

In addition, families recoup some of their outlays for child care through the Dependent Care Tax Credit, which costs the federal treasury $2.8 billion a year. Approximately half the states likewise offer state tax credits or deductions for families with child care expenses. Close to 800,000 children now participate in Head Start—more than twice as many as in 1973. Almost $300 million is invested in the Early Head Start Program, providing comprehensive child care and family support services to families with infants and toddlers. States spend about $1 billion on prekindergarten initiatives for 3- and 4-year-olds. Finally, more than 2.5 million children

in child care centers, Head Start, and neighborhood family child care homes receive nutritious meals and snacks through the Child and Adult Care Food Program.

Although greater resources are devoted to child care today, the number of children needing care is also much greater. As a result, the gap between the supply of adequate, affordable care and the demand for it remains as wide today as it was 25 years ago.

Federal Action in 1997

In 1997 several events brought home the importance of good child care and the serious shortcomings in America's present approach. The "I Am Your Child" campaign, a far-reaching public education initiative, emphasized the need for better care for babies and toddlers by focusing attention on the critical brain development that takes place during the first three years of life. *Kids These Days*, a report on a survey by the Public Agenda Foundation, revealed deep and widespread concern about today's children. A majority of respondents, however, believed that after-school programs

- Every day, 13 million children—including 6 million infants and toddlers—are in child care.

- Two-thirds of mothers of young children work outside the home—many out of economic necessity. Fifty-five percent of working women provide half or more of their family's income.

- Half of American parents with young children earn less than $35,000 per year, and two parents working full-time at minimum wage earn only $21,400 per year. Yet child care can easily cost $4,000 to $10,000 for a single child.

- Forty percent of infant and toddler rooms in centers provide care that could jeopardize children's safety and development.

- Thirty-two states require no prior training for child care teachers. They are among the lowest-paid workers in America, earning only $12,058 per year, on average, and receiving no benefits or paid leave.

- Juvenile crime peaks between 3 and 7 p.m., when nearly 5 million children are left home alone after school.

would be a very effective way to help children. Finally, in October the White House Conference on Child Care cast a national spotlight on the myriad challenges of child care.

Members of Congress responded to the growing concern about child care by introducing an array of bills that would increase federal funds to help families with the costs of child care, strengthen the quality of child care, create better options for families with infants and young children, expand before- and after-school programs, and create incentives for businesses to become involved in child care. Although no action was taken on any of these proposals in 1997, Congress seems likely to devote much more attention to child care this year.

The Administration is also making child care a priority for 1998. In his State of the Union address in January, President Clinton proposed a variety of new federal subsidies and tax breaks to ease the burdens of child care for working families. The President's new proposal amounts to almost a $22 billion investment in child care and Head Start and provides a solid and significant foundation for congressional action.

Uneven Progress by States

Changes in the welfare system that require millions of women on welfare to work are causing an enormous surge in the demand for child care. How are states responding?

In 1997 every state should have been able to improve its policies and increase its investment in child care. State economies were strong, and welfare caseloads were shrinking. Furthermore, states received approximately $600 million in new federal child care money (if they provided matching funds), and they were allowed to use a portion of their new federal welfare grants under the Temporary Assistance for

Needy Families (TANF) program for child care.

Setbacks. Given these favorable conditions, it is disheartening that a number of states took steps backward. For example, half the states no longer guarantee child care assistance to welfare families. Fourteen states reduced eligibility for child care assistance, and one in five states increased or plans to increase copayments for low-income parents. Four states froze or reduced reimbursement rates to providers. Minnesota took a giant step in the wrong direction by passing legislation that undermines efforts to ensure the health and safety of children enrolled in family child care homes. Providers may now care for a total of five children without being licensed, and those wishing to seek a license will actually be prohibited from doing so. Michigan lowered the minimum age at which relatives and at-home providers can receive public funds, allowing adolescents as young as 16 to take on the significant responsibility of child care for up to 10 hours each day.

Financial help for needy parents. Several states, however, recognized the importance of providing child care assistance to low-income families, regardless of whether they are receiving TANF. Although these states have not made such assistance a legal entitlement for all families below a certain income level, state officials believe they have appropriated or otherwise secured enough funds to help every family currently eligible for child care subsidies. For example, Illinois increased state funding by $100 million, making it possible to provide child care assistance to all families earning less than 50 percent of the state median income (roughly $22,000 for a family of three in 1997). The state of Washington transferred $152 million from TANF to the CCDBG to help families earning up to 175 percent of the federal poverty level. Wisconsin is using $80.1 million transferred from

TANF to provide child care assistance to working families with income below 165 percent of the poverty level.

Although these are important steps to address child care needs, some aspects of the initiatives raise serious policy concerns. For example, Wisconsin families are given a financial incentive to opt for less expensive child care with providers who have no training, making it more difficult for financially strapped families to choose higher quality care. The state also has a "light touch" policy directing welfare caseworkers to inform welfare recipients only of services they ask for or need. Washington state has lowered the rates it pays providers who serve children receiving public child care funds. Consequently, many providers may limit the spaces open to poor children, charge parents additional fees, or even leave the child care business, all of which reduce parents' options. Illinois has raised families' fees in order to help finance child care assistance. High fees make it possible for state governments to provide aid to more families, but they can severely strain a low-income family's budget.

Over the next several years, as work requirements for TANF families increase, all states will face greater demand for child care and growing needs for funding. As a result, even larger investments in child care will be necessary to enable parents to find and keep jobs and to protect children's safety and development.

Prekindergarten programs. Responding to heightened interest in ensuring that children enter school ready to learn, states continue to support prekindergarten programs, either by investing in state initiatives or by supplementing the federal Head Start program with state dollars. In 1997 three states—Connecticut, New Jersey, and New York—took strides forward by developing new plans for prekindergarteners. Connecticut will support full-day, full-year programs for children whose parents work outside the home. In New Jersey, by the 2001–02 school year, 125 school districts serving large numbers of low-income children will be required to offer full-day kindergarten for all 5-year-olds and prekindergarten for 4-year-olds. New York approved a universal program that is expected to grow to $500 million by 2001–02. Meanwhile, Ohio estimates that by using state and federal funds, it will be able to provide Head Start to 84 percent of the state's eligible children in 1998.

Recent Research Findings

Reports issued in 1997 highlight the paucity of child care options available to families. The General Accounting Office released *Implications of Increased Work Participation for Child Care*, a study of four sites (Baltimore, Chicago, and two largely rural counties—Benton and Linn—in Oregon). In all four areas, the current supply of child care is inadequate to serve children in certain age groups, particularly children from low-income families. For example, Chicago was expected to meet just 14 percent of the demand for infant care at the end of 1997. By 2002 the demand for infant care could exceed the existing supply by almost 24,000 spaces. The study identified other problems, too, that could affect low-income families' access to care, including its steep cost, the limited availability of both high-quality care and nonstandard-hour care, and limited or unaffordable transportation.

Another study, *"Back to School" Is Not for Everybody* by the National Law Center on Homelessness and Poverty, reported that homeless children in particular are underserved by preschool programs. Staff in almost 50 percent of the family shelters surveyed said that few, if any, eligible homeless children attend preschool. Staff in 70 percent of the shelters indicated that current federal, state, and local funding is inadequate to meet the preschool needs of these children.

Other research suggests that preschool is far less accessible to low-income families than to those with higher income. A 1997 study by the National Education Goals Panel found that about 55 percent of all 3- to 5-year-olds participated in preschool programs in 1996. However, families earning more than $75,000 enrolled their children at nearly twice the rate of families with income of $10,000 a year or less.

Similar findings are presented in *An Unfair Head Start: California Families Face Gaps in Preschool and Child Care Availability*, a 1997 report by the PACE Center at the University of California at Berkeley, the California Child Care Resource and Referral Network, and the University of Chicago. According to the report, children's opportunity to attend preschool or child care programs in California depends largely on family income and where they live. In some counties, notably Los Angeles, parents in affluent areas are twice as likely to find a child care or preschool slot as parents in poor areas. . . .

Moving Forward: A 1998 Agenda for Action

Three ongoing developments provide a powerful impetus for action on child care issues: escalating work requirements for families on welfare, increasing awareness of the importance of the first three years of life, and growing concern about school-age children left home alone. In 1998 we must move forward with new strategies and investments ensuring that parents have reliable child care, that infants and toddlers get the nurturing and stimulation they need for future learning, that older children have after-school activities that keep them

out of trouble and help them succeed in school, and that parents who wish to stay home during their children's early years have the opportunity and support to do so.

We can meet these goals only through partnerships that draw together resources from the public and private sectors. In 1998 a broad-based coalition will be working at all levels—federal, state, and local—to expand the child care options of American families.

At the federal level, advocates should:

- Lobby for a guaranteed $20 billion to the states over five years to strengthen the quality of child care for all families and make child care more affordable. Improving the quality and availability of care for children under 3 and children of school age should be a special priority, given the alarming gaps in the quality and supply of care for these groups.
- Campaign to reauthorize Head Start with more funds targeted to infants and toddlers and additional funds to move Head Start toward serving all eligible children who need it.
- Support an extension of the Family and Medical Leave Act to cover all employers with 25 or more workers. The act guarantees up to 12 weeks of unpaid leave to employees with a new child or a serious illness in the family, but it currently applies only to private employers with 50 or more workers and to all public employers.
- Support paid parental leave through family leave insurance or other means to help parents stay home with their children during the critical early months of life.
- Support changes in the Child and Adult Care Food Program that would make it easier for schools to participate and allow more school-age children (up to age 18) to be served. Provide

funds for meals and snacks at for-profit child care centers serving low-income children, and increase funding for family child care providers.

At the state level, advocates should:

- Encourage states to expand their investments in child care assistance to help more families afford care. In addition, states should guarantee child care assistance to all low-income working families.
- Call for child care policies that ensure a true choice of good providers for families receiving child care assistance. Such policies might stipulate reimbursement rates for providers that are based on current market-rate costs, higher reimbursement rates for accredited programs, and reasonable fees for families.
- Work to strengthen state licensing standards and enforcement so that parents can be confident their children are in safe and supportive child care settings.
- Ensure that resource and referral programs are available in com-

munities to help families find child care that meets their needs.
- Urge lawmakers to provide resources to local communities for initiatives to improve the quality and expand the supply of child care.
- Expand training and career opportunities in child care and link increased education and training to increased compensation. Support or replicate programs . . . that motive and reward caregivers who seek professional development.
- Support initiatives to expand and improve child care for infants and toddlers, such as family child care networks, better training for caregivers, and higher reimbursement rates for infant care.
- Press for the funding of high-quality prekindergarten programs that offer comprehensive services and operate on a full-day, full-year basis.
- Support creative before-school, after-school, and summer programs for both elementary and middle-school students.

At the community level, advocates should:

- Build the local supply of high-quality child care to give families more and better options. Encourage religious institutions, schools, and other community organizations to make child care and after-school programs a top priority, mobilizing funds, volunteers, space, and other resources.
- Encourage local government leaders to play a greater role in improving the quality, affordability, and supply of child care and school-age programs.
- Encourage employers to contribute to community child care funds that help families pay for child care and bolster the quality of care in the community.
- Urge businesses to establish family-friendly policies (such as flex-time and compressed work weeks), help employees find and pay for quality child care, and operate child care centers on-site or nearby. Not only do such efforts benefit families, but with unemployment at its lowest point since the mid-1970s, they make good business sense as a means of attracting and retaining workers.

Child Development
and Families

Startling information about brain development has been released that has brought on a flurry of speculation about the best ways to prepare children for a lifetime of learning. The information pediatric neurobiologists now have indicates that the types of experiences children have prior to the age of 10 can affect their future capacity to learn. Early experiences, once thought to be useless, now have been found to help support the developing neurons in a child's brain. These neurons, which make successful complete connections when a child is young, will be used in the future to work complicated mathematical problems, learn a second language, or play a musical instrument.

Knowledge of the way a child's brain develops led the writers of the Carnegie Corporation Starting Points Report to conclude, "How children function from the preschool years all the way through adolescence, and even adulthood, hinges in large part on their experiences before the age of three." This information is exciting to early childhood professionals. It has been the focus for over a year of planning on a public engagement campaign called "I Am Your Child" that started in the spring of 1997. This campaign educates parents and the general public on the correlation of the experiences of a young child's early years to future learning. The care and education received prior to the age of three can determine the success a child will have in developing new skills. There is a danger that parents and others will try to push learning on a young child.

What the findings on brain development do indicate is that experiences that allow a child to investigate and explore a variety of sounds, objects, and materials can foster the development of neurons. It is also important to note that parents who did not provide for a stimulating early environment for their children should not be seen as failures. Learning experiences that will affect future learning can be offered throughout life. The lead article,

"A Bundle of Emotions," from the *Newsweek* special issue on brain development outlines stages of emotional development.

We cannot separate the child from his or her family or home environment. Therefore, for professionals in early childhood education, much of what is done involves the child's family. Families come in many different arrangements, and the more familiar teachers and caregivers are with the people whom the child sees on a regular basis, the easier communication with those individuals will be. Professionals who are aware of the enormously varied life circumstances that children and parents experience today are mindful not to offer a magic formula, quick remedies, or simplistic solutions to complicated, long-standing problems.

Instead, parents appreciate a sense that they are respected and given up-to-date, objective information about their child. These strategies can be shared with families. Collaborative efforts to build bridges between home and school allow for maximized learning for all children.

Looking Ahead: Challenge Questions

Why is it important for teachers and caregivers to know about major changes affecting young children and their families?

Discuss how parents and caregivers can take advantage of the stages of emotional development of infants.

What are some of the negative effects of prenatal drug exposure on an infant? How can parents and caregivers minimize these conditions?

How can the cultural values emphasized in each family help children to develop a sense of who they are and to assist them in learning?

What strategies have been found to be successful when working with children of different intelligences?

UNIT 2

A Bundle of Emotions

Whether by smiling or screaming, crying or cuddling, babies find ways early on to tell us how they feel. Good behavior comes along later. What to watch and listen for:

A Repertoire of Cries

All babies cry, and usually for good reason. Before they learn to talk, crying is one way to express their needs and send out signals of distress. Examples of three typical cries, and their differences in volume, pitch and rhythm:

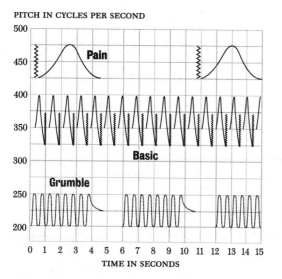

PITCH IN CYCLES PER SECOND

TIME IN SECONDS

Pain A cry of pain or distress usually begins with an inward gasp followed by a long, rising shriek. There is a long pause until the next painful scream. Soothe the baby by rocking or with music.

Basic A basic cry rises and falls rhythmically, broken up with a breath and a pause. The child may cry this way when demanding food or attention.

Grumble A grumble cry is the first attempt at communication. It has a lower pitch and volume, often sounding whimpery and whiny. It is a signal that the child may be getting restless. Move the child to a different environment and provide new stimulation.

0–2 months old

❶ month old
Behavior Alert to stimuli like loud sounds and bright patterns. Quiets to holding or cuddling.
Interaction Child may recognize parent's voice or make eye-to-eye contact.
Tips Spend special time with siblings who may feel abandoned or jealous.

❷ months old
Emotions Cries to show distress or pain, coos when happy or excited.
Tips If leaving child with a sitter, choose someone both you and the baby know, like a grandparent or close friend. Keep a list of emergency numbers handy.

Toys and Games for Curious Tots

Children love playtime, especially when parents or siblings join in the fun. Look for educational toys and games that encourage development:

1–3 months old Mobiles, unbreakable mirrors and activity centers attached to crib, rattles, stuffed toys with black and white patterns, music boxes, large colorful rings.

4–6 months old Beach balls, chunky bracelets, building blocks, squeaky toys, paper streamers, books made of cloth or vinyl, playing peekaboo or come-and-get-me with others.

7–9 months old Stuffed animals, balls, nesting cylinders, pop-up toys, large dolls and puppets, bath toys, performing "so big" or pat-a-cake.

10–12 months old Push-and-pull toys like miniature cars, ordinary household objects like empty egg cartons and large spoons, stacked rings on a spindle, playing simple ball games.

13–15 months old Toy telephones, acrobatics, pushing a carriage or toy horse, playing with cups and clothespins.

16–18 months old Sandbox, simple musical instruments like a drum or tambourine, large colored beads, jack-in-the-boxes, blowing bubbles.

19–21 months old Rocking horse, toys to take apart and fit back together, small rubber balls, digging toys, large crayons, kiddie cars, water games, easy jigsaw puzzles, making mud pies, playing tag or hide-and-seek.

22–24 months old Kiddie lawn mowers and kitchen sets for make-believe play, modeling clay, construction sets, action toys like trains, telephones, dump trucks and fire engines, old magazines, baskets, tubes and containers with lids.

2–3 years Beginner tricycle, mini-trampoline, roller skates or Rollerblades, dolls and accessories like strollers and baby bottles, dress-up clothes, coloring books, easel, crayons and markers, music, kiddie cassette player, swing sets, books, finger paint, mini basketball hoop, woodworking bench, kiddie swimming pool.

3–8 months old

❸ months old
Behavior Smiles often to others or while sleeping.
Interaction May cry differently when mother leaves the room than with other people. Begins to sort out who's who in his life. May prefer certain people.

❹ months old
Behavior Laughs while playing and may cry if playtime is interrupted. May still act passively, taking in whatever toy or face comes near.
Emotions Shows curiosity when inspecting rattle and dependency when wanting to be held. Moods may change rapidly.
Interaction Tries to get parent's attention by banging rattle or crying.

❺ months old
Behavior Child may become more assertive as he learns to reach for objects.
Emotions Shows anger when someone tries to take away his toy. May begin to handle stresses better because of maturing nervous system.
Tips Set clear rules if sibling tries to hurt baby. Give child responsibilities as big brother or sister.

❻ months old
Interaction May fear strangers. Responds positively to other children.
Tips When baby repeatedly puts an object in his mouth that he should not, gently pull his arm away, say no and distract with another activity.

❼ months old
Behavior May test parents' authority by refusing to follow their directions.
Emotions Shows humor and laughs at funny expressions or positions.
Interaction May give familiar people hugs and kisses. May raise his arms to be picked up.

❽ months old
Behavior Smiles at, pats or even kisses his mirror image. May distinguish between baby and image.
Interaction May reject being alone or confined in a crib or playpen. May fear being separated from parents as he learns to crawl. Buries head in parent's shoulder when meeting new people.

From *Newsweek*, Spring/Summer 1997, pp. 78-79. © 1997 by Newsweek, Inc. All rights reserved. Reprinted by permission.

🌐 Circles of Friends

A baby's first friends are his parents, and interaction with them prepares the child for future relationships in larger social circles:

AGE IN YEARS

4 — May have a best friend and participates in many social activities including preschool. Influenced by peer behavior and tests parental authority.

3 — Cooperates well with peers and realizes that not everyone thinks alike. Gradually stops competing for attention.

2 — Interacts in play groups but may resist sharing and fight over toys. Sees older siblings as heroes.

1 — Imitates others' actions and engages in parallel play with toddlers.

0 — Bonds with parents and recognizes their touch.

ℹ️ For More Information

Many organizations offer advice on parenting and child development. Check with your public school for local groups. A few notable programs:

Home Instruction Program for Preschool Youngsters (HIPPY USA): 212-678-3500

MELD (Minnesota Early Learning Design): 612-332-7563

Parents as Teachers National Center: 314-432-4330

Birth To Three: 800-680-7888

Family Resources: 800-641-4546

17–24 months old

17 months old
Interaction May respond correctly to what parents say. If scolded, child cries; if praised, she smiles.
Tips Some toddlers shy away from others. Give child time to adapt to new situations and hold her hand.

18 months old
Behavior Frustration may trigger tantrums. At this age, child acts on impulse due to limited understanding of good and bad, rules and warnings.
Interaction Communicates desire for closeness by plopping on parent's lap. Still has no sense of sharing with others.

19 months old
Behavior Enjoys getting out of the house and exploring new environments.
Interaction Some children will play among others in a group. May engage in parallel play.
Tips Praise will motivate child to obey the simple rules set. Give precedence to rules that keep her safe, as well as ones that prohibit hitting and kicking.

20 months old
Behavior During pretend play, child acts out what happens around her.
Emotions May fear thunder, lightning, big animals and the dark. Install night light if sleep is consistently disrupted.
Interaction Slowly warms to a new babysitter, but may still cling to mother around people she was comfortable with earlier.

21 months old
Emotions May sympathize with other people or recognize their feelings. Expresses love for parents by hugging and smiling.
Interaction Still possessive of toys but may give up objects that belong to someone else.

22 months old
Interaction Cooperates with others. Language development facilitates communication. Engages in parallel play with toddlers, often back to back.
Tips To build self-reliance, encourage child to separate from parents for short periods of time.

23 months old
Emotions May fear rejection and become frustrated with new activities.
Interaction May be willing to play alone. Likes to follow siblings and imitate their actions.
Tips Try to give siblings some privacy and designate a special time to spend with them.

24 months old
Behavior May become manipulative and bossy. Learns rules through trial and error.
Emotions Able to explain feelings and desires using gestures and simple phrases. Trusts adults.
Interaction Plays well with older children. May hand toy to another child. Imitates others through pretend play. May show signs of jealousy or revert to babyish actions when a new sibling arrives.

9–16 months old

9 months old
Interaction May perform tricks like "so big" and peekaboo for familiar people. May repeat act if applauded. Near the end of the first year, child may learn to assess moods and imitate them. If baby sees someone crying, he may cry too.

10 months old
Emotions Shows twinges of jealousy. May cry or whimper when sibling is at center of attention.
Interaction Starts to become aware of social approval and disapproval.

11 months old
Behavior May use a security blanket for comfort in strange places.
Interaction May assert himself among siblings. Likes to imitate gestures and sounds.

12 months old
Tips Try not to fuss when leaving child at home. Allow time for him to adjust to sitter. Distract baby with another activity and give a quick good-night kiss. Crying will pro-bably stop after parents depart.

13 months old
Behavior Laughs when chased. May become more demanding and seek constant attention.
Emotions After the first year, personality begins to emerge. May be an explorer, a tease, a showoff.

14 months old
Behavior Child may turn more aggressive as she learns to walk. May throw objects in anger.
Interaction May enjoy playing alone, but still likes to act for an audience (toy chart, above left).
Tips Time to baby-proof your house.

15 months old
Emotions May communicate feelings with a clear intent or purpose.
Interaction By midyear, some babies may recognize when familiar people are missing. May offer toys to others but will quickly want them back.

16 months old
Behavior Instead of using words, child flings arms or moves away to say no.
Interaction May hit parents in anger.

2–3 years old

25–29 months old
Behavior Sees the world almost exclusively through his needs. Assumes everyone thinks and acts like him. May throw tantrum when angry or frustrated.
Emotions May have frequent mood swings. May pout or feel guilty when scolded. Learns how to express sadness or stress.
Interaction May pull away from familiar children or adults. Siblings take on a greater role in daily life. May enjoy play groups; the concept of "friend" evolves.
Tips Do not give child an audience during a tirade. Try not to scream back or dwell on the tantrum after it's finished.

30–36 months old
Behavior Toddler slowly begins to realize what's acceptable and what's not. May find it difficult to concentrate on new tasks.
Interaction Child may be conscious of being a member of a family. May show pity or sympathy to familiar people. Sharing parent's attention with siblings can be dfficult. Insists on being at the center of play and may dislike sharing limelight with peers. May be ready for nursery school, which can create separation anxiety. In nursery school, child learns to follow rules, to cooperate with others and to spend a few hours away from home.
Tips Encourage child to act responsibly by setting limits on dangerous or antisocial behavior. Time-outs may help defuse anger. Be consistent with rules. Praise child when he plays well with others.

By Jennifer Lach

SOURCES: "THE EARLY CHILDHOOD YEARS: THE 2 TO 6 YEAR OLD," "THE SECOND TWELVE MONTHS OF LIFE," "THE FIRST TWELVE MONTHS OF LIFE" BY THERESA AND FRANK CAPLAN; "CARING FOR YOUR BABY AND YOUNG CHILD" BY STEVEN P. SHELOV, M.D.; "FIRST FEELINGS" BY STANLEY GREENSPAN; "YOUR BABY & CHILD" BY PENELOPE LEACH.

Prenatal Drug Exposure

Meeting the Challenge

Linda C. Sluder, Lloyd R.
Kinnison and Dennis Cates

*Linda C. Sluder is Associate Professor, Early Childhood and
Lloyd R. Kinnisonis Professor, Special Education, Texas Woman's University, Denton.
Dennis Cates is Associate Professor, Special Education, Cameron University, Lawton, Oklahoma.*

Educators and child care providers today face a challenging new community of children identified as one of the fastest growing at-risk populations in America (Poulsen, 1992). These children have been labeled as "crack babies," "prenatal drug exposed," "peri-natal cocaine addicted" or "substance exposed infants and children" (Kinnison, Sluder & Cates, 1995, p. 35).

The mainstream media first identified such children in the early 1990s, focusing on demographic projections and associated statistical implications. The pressing issue now, however, is that these children have reached school age. As these children enter early childhood programs, educators must be prepared to nurture and encourage them.

Children with prenatal drug exposure exhibit a complex range of cognitive abilities and behaviors (Chasnoff, 1992; Howard, Beckwith, Rodning & Kropenske, 1989). Wright (1994) emphasizes that identifying specific traits is difficult, however, because prenatal exposure has diverse effects.

From *Childhood Education,* Winter 1996/97, pp. 66-69. © 1996 by the Association for Childhood Education International, 17904 Georgia Avenue, Suite 215, Olney, MD. Reprinted by permission.

THE CASE OF TWO CHILDREN

Treavor

To the casual observer, Treavor appears to be a typical 5-year-old. He lives with his grandparents, who provide him with a caring and nurturing environment. His size is average for his age. Although his gross motor development appears to be age appropriate, he has some difficulty with fine motor tasks. In general, his physical responses are spasmodic, limiting his ability to independently accomplish directed activities, such as placing wooden pegs into specific holes.

Psychoeducational test evaluations (e.g., measures of cognitive ability and adaptive behavior) indicate that Treavor functions in the severe-profound range of mental retardation. He becomes excited and distracted when individuals enter the learning environment, often soiling his diaper or outer clothing.

Treavor's receptive language is adequate to deal with simple tasks. He is able to follow basic verbal directions and participate, to some extent, in classroom activities. Treavor usually responds during group language activities with gestures and grunts or by showing recognition through directed eye movements. He is able to identify size ("big" and "little"), pictures of his immediate family, and his teacher and classmates when their names are given as prompts. Over the past year, the teacher noticed that Treavor improved in receptive language, attempts at expressive language, motor skills and attention span. Treavor attends a half-day early childhood program for disabled children.

Melissa

Melissa, a 2nd-grader, participates in a special education resource room one hour each day. She is small for her age, but otherwise displays no physical indications of prenatal drug exposure. While pregnant, Melissa's birth mother ingested alcohol, marijuana and various other drugs, including, possibly, cocaine. Melissa lives with adoptive parents in what appears to be a positive environment.

Melissa suffered from seizures at an early age, for which anticonvulsive medications were prescribed. Additionally, she takes Ritalin daily to help control her attention deficit disorder with hyperactivity and possible obsessive conduct disorder. A psychoeducational assessment indicates that Melissa's cognitive ability is above average. Her reading skills range from one to two standard deviations above the mean. Melissa's math achievement is on grade level and her written language skills are one standard deviation above the mean. Assessments indicate that she has average oral language development. In contrast to the assessment scores, Melissa's classroom teacher reports extreme variations in her daily academic performance.

Melissa's teachers maintain daily logs that illustrate her erratic behavior. Her teachers say that Melissa "tries hard, [is] inattentive, lacks small muscle control, [is] slow, in constant motion and has extremes in emotions." She appears to work best in a relatively small space and in one-on-one teaching situations.

In the regular classroom, she is compulsive—always giving an answer. She can also be mentally inflexible, needs constant redirection and has limited attention. Her regular education teacher is frustrated and has threatened to resign if Melissa is not removed from her classroom.

Melissa's medication has been invaluable. Without prescriptive intervention, her behavior is unpredictable. Consequently, she does not seem to have control of her actions. Records document that prior to taking her medication, Melissa had, among other

---

Table 1

BEHAVIORAL INDICATORS OF PRENATAL DRUG EXPOSURE IN YOUNG CHILDREN

Motor Development

- Awkward eye and hand coordination
- Trembling arms and legs when reaching for objects
- Excessive fidgeting and/or hyperactivity
- Clumsy or immature use of tools such as spoons, crayons or small toys

Language Development

- Limited early vocalizations
- Prolonged articulation errors
- Difficulty in picture identification
- Problems following directions
- Limited vocabulary

Play Development

- Reluctance to initiate play activities
- Aimless wandering through the play area
- Inability to stack blocks
- Apparent confusion in some play situations
- Awkward understanding of and response to social cues
- Occasional aggressive behavior in group situations

Affective Development

- Avoidance of eye contact
- Low tolerance for change of environment or caregiver
- Difficulty in dealing with changes in routines
- Low ability to self-regulate own behavior
- Frequent limit testing
- Decreased response to verbal praise as a reinforcer
- Poor interactions with caregivers
- Increased frequency of temper tantrums
- Fearfulness of strangers

Cognitive Development

- Decreased imitative play
- Less pretend play or exploration of the environment
- Difficulty concentrating
- Disorganization
- Inability to structure work or play activities
- Diminished ability to stay on task
- Less goal-directed behavior
- Increasingly disruptive behavior
- Greater need for a more controlled learning environment

Adapted from: Kinnison, L., Sluder, L., & Cates, D. (1995). Prenatal drug exposure: Implications for teachers of young children. *Day Care & Early Education, 22*(3), 35–37.

things, threatened to beat her adoptive mother. After receiving treatment, Melissa was remorseful and expressed sorrow for such behavior.

COMPOUNDING ISSUES

Approximately 375,000 children are prenatally exposed to illicit drugs each year (Behrman, 1990; Feig 1990). A rapidly growing proportion of these children are exposed to crack cocaine. Feig (1990) estimates that 30,000 to 50,000 "crack babies" are born each year.

A survey by the National Institute on Drug Abuse (1989) revealed that approximately 9 percent of all women of child-bearing age admitted to using illicit drugs. The number of women in this age group testing positive for drug use increased from 25 percent in 1972 to 40 percent in 1988. Other data indicate that prenatal drug use has remained at a consistent level ("Children of Cocaine: Facing New Issues," 1990). Women who use drugs while pregnant come from all socioeconomic and ethnic backgrounds (Feig, 1990; Weston, Ivins, Zuckerman, Jones & Lopez, 1989).

The severity of cognitive, social, behavioral and motor deficiencies are compounded by the multiple ingestion of tobacco, alcohol and combined drugs. Table 1 offers some behavioral characteristics that may be associated with prenatal drug exposure.

COMPLICATIONS

Motor Development

Although a small number of drug-exposed children exhibit gross motor difficulties, the influences on fine motor development are far more apparent. Researchers report that cocaine-exposed infants and toddlers often avoid eye contact and negatively respond to multiple stimuli (Zuckerman, Jones, La Rue & Lopez, 1990). Other studies suggest that these infants appear to have underdeveloped muscle tone and poor reflexes, and that their arms and hands may tremble when they reach for objects (Daberczak, Shaner, Senie & Kendal, 1988; Feig, 1990). Behrman (1990) suggests that such visual-perceptual and fine motor problems persist as these children mature. Van Dyke and Fox (1990) suggest that fetal exposure to various types of illicit drugs (e.g., cocaine or cocaine used with other drugs) may cause other developmental problems. These complications' characteristics may be similar to those of hyperactivity.

Cognitive Development

Many factors related to prenatal drug exposure directly and indirectly influence cognitive development. Drugs such as cocaine may force blood vessels in an expectant woman to constrict, reducing the blood flow and decreasing the amount of oxygen delivered to the fetus's brain (Woods & Plessinger, 1990). Bellisimo (1990) emphasizes that the "high" brought on by drug use may cause the fetus to suffer small strokes or seizures. These findings suggest that central nervous system damage and subsequent learning problems are possible.

Children prenatally exposed to drugs tend to perform more poorly on tests designed to measure concentration, group interaction and the ability to cope within an instructional environment, according to Viadero (1990). Further studies suggest that these children are often disorganized, unstructured, irritable, less goal-directed and have problems processing information.

Language Development

Drug exposed infants and children are less likely to spontaneously vocalize or use gestures to communicate. In preschool, these children experience prolonged difficulty in articulating, identifying pictures and using expressive language (Chapman & Worthington, 1994).

Some children may have better success with receptive language (what is understood), as in Treavor's case. In this instance, receptive language may be superior to expressive language development. Treavor's behavior suggests he understands oral language, but cannot verbally communicate.

Affective-Behavioral Development

Children prenatally exposed to harmful substances may undergo a variety of emotional and behavioral swings, sometimes shifting rapidly from apathy to aggression. "A giggle becomes a scream, or a response to a question becomes an outburst" (Bellisimo, 1990, p. 25). Changes in environmental stimuli, such as visitors or minor disruptions in routines, may prompt the child to suddenly act uncontrollably. Melissa's behavior is characteristic of these extremes. It appears that prenatally drug exposed children commonly insist on addressing tasks in their own terms and persistently refuse to comply with requests.

These children interact poorly with others. Cocaine-exposed infants may become easily frustrated and throw temper tantrums when adults provide inconsistent directional cues (Bellisimo, 1990; Howard et al., 1989). Often, the children resist attachments to new adults or children. Some children actually avoid adult interactions.

Play Development

Howard, Beckwith, Rodning and Kropenske (1989) observed less representational play among drug exposed children. Instead, their play was characterized by randomly scattering toys, and then indiscriminately picking up and discarding them. These behaviors are in sharp contrast to children's typical play behavior.

Substance exposed infants and children often have difficulty initiating independent play activities. Consequently, they aimlessly wander through the learning environment. Many of these youngsters do not seem to have the necessary skills to spontaneously stack blocks or engage in representational play. They appear confused and unable to select a particular material for play or focus.

ACCEPTING THE CHILD

Children with suspected prenatal drug exposure need assurances from the adults in their lives. Educators who work with this population must understand the child's social, legal and educational needs. Unfortunately, accurate information about the extent of prenatal drug exposure is limited. Admitting that their child has been prenatally exposed to drugs places the mother or parents at risk for legal action. Moreover, as many states consider prenatal drug exposure to be child abuse, admission of such activity will be rare.

Other issues also prevent parents from fully disclosing their drug use. Increased public awareness of the effects of prenatal drug exposure places the parent in a precarious situation. Many fear the reactions of their families, friends, the community and their children. Fetal alcohol children interviewed in Michael Dorris's *The Broken Cord* (1989) expressed difficulty understanding their disability and their parents' reasons for engaging in drug use.

Often, these children come from chaotic and dangerous home environments where the potential for continued drug abuse is high. Their mothers may be estranged from the family because of their drug use, which perpetuates a lack of support systems for both mother and child. Careful consideration and effort must be given to ensure that extensive time and opportunity are provided for these children to develop bonds with the family or other caregivers.

IMPLICATIONS AND SUGGESTIONS

Children who are exposed prenatally to illicit drugs present myriad challenges for early childhood professionals. The cognitive and behavior extremes associated with prenatal exposure precludes drawing up an explicit list of "best practices" or pedagogical approaches.

Compounding the problem is researchers' inability to systematically identify children who have been exposed to illicit drugs. Many research studies have samples that are too small with poorly defined subjects or no control groups (Chapman & Worthington, 1994). Other studies have been narrowly defined and use highly selective strategies, offering limited general application.

The following suggestions for early childhood professionals are based on the most current review of research and experience. Educators should pay special attention to the learning environment, ensuring that programs are predictable and restricting the number of nonessential people who enter and leave the environment. Howard et al. (1989) reported that a small room or learning area is superior to large, open areas.

Education professionals must carefully consider these children's unique learning styles when determining the classroom environment and teacher-to-student ratios. Daily routines must allow the children to engage in self-directed exploration. The educator or care provider, however, must always be aware that these children do not tend to engage in spontaneous activities. Adult intervention may be necessary to direct the child toward cooperative play and work opportunities.

Many potentially volatile situations can be diffused by alerting children to transitions and providing time to adjust to new activities. When a child is cognitively and emotionally involved with a special activity, adults can reduce children's frustration by providing notice that the activity is about to end. A statement such as "We have five more minutes left in math before lunch" will alert the child that the activity is closing.

CONCLUSION

Educators and care providers must be aware that children may exhibit multiple disabilities—including physical, medical, emotional, social and/or educational. A team of professionals should work together to focus on individual children's needs. Community-based, family-centered solutions should be emphasized, as should confidentiality.

Early childhood education and care providers need to establish close working relationships with local and state agencies. Joint efforts should promote specific caregiver training, substance abuse counseling, activities to raise mothers' self-esteem and training in basic parenting skills. These efforts may be university-based or associated with community and state agencies. Only through such collaborative efforts can substantial help be given to children with prenatal drug exposure.

References

Behrman, J. (1990). Care for and educating the children of drug-using mothers: A challenge for society and schools in the 1990s. *Counterpoint, 11*(2), 15–16.

Bellisimo, V. (1990, January). Crack babies: The school's new high at risk student. *Thrust,* 23–26.

Chapman, J., & Worthington, L. (1994, April). *Illicit drug-exposed children: Four critical needs areas.* Paper presented at the annual convention of the Council for Exceptional Children, Denver, CO.

Chasnoff, I. (1992, October). *NAPARE today: People and programs. Update.* Chicago, IL: National Association for Perinatal Addiction Research and Education.

Children of cocaine: Facing new issues. (1990). (ERIC Document Reproduction Service No. ED 320 358)

Daberczak, T., Shanzer, S., Senie, T., & Kendal, S. (1988). Neonatal neurologic and electroencephalograms effects of intrauterine cocaine exposure. *Journal of Pediatrics, 113,* 354–358.

Dorris, M. (1989). *The broken cord.* New York: Harper.

Feig, L. (1990). *Drug-exposed infants and children: Service needs and policy questions.* Washington, DC: U.S. Department of Health and Human Services, Office of Human Services Policy, Division of Children and Youth.

Howard, J., Beckwith, L., Rodning, C., & Kropenske, Y. (1989). The development of young children of substance-abusing parents: Insights from seven years of intervention and research. *Zero to Three, 9*(5), 1–7.

Kinnison, L., Sluder, L., & Cates, D. (1995). Prenatal drug exposure: Implications for teachers of young children. *Day Care & Early Education, 22*(3), 35–37.

National Institute on Drug Abuse, Department of Health and Human Services. (1989). *National Institute of Drug Abuse: Household Survey on Drug Abuse 1988, Population Estimates.* Rockville, MD: Author. (DHHS Publication No. ADM 89-1636).

Poulsen, M. (1992). *Schools meet the challenge: Educational needs of children at risk due to prenatal substance exposure.* (ERIC Document Reproduction Service No. ED 348 800)

Van Dyke, D., & Fox, A. (1990). Fetal drug exposure and implications for learning in the preschool and school-age populations. *Journal of Learning Disabilities, 28*(3), 160–162.

Viadero, D. (1990). Drug exposed children pose special problems. *Education Week, 9*(8), 1–10.

Weston, D., Ivins, B., Zuckerman, B., Jones, C., & Lopez, R. (1989). Drug-exposed babies: Research and clinical issues. *Zero to Three, 9*(5), 1–7.

Woods, J., & Plessinger, M. (1990). Pregnancy increases cardiovascular toxicity to cocaine. *American Journal of Obstetrics-Gynecology, 162*(2), 529–535.

Wright, R. (1994). Drugged out. *Texas Monthly, 20*(11), 136, 150–154.

Zuckerman, B., Jones, C., LaRue, C., & Lopez, R. (1990). Effects of maternal marijuana and cocaine use on fetal growth. In J. R. Meratz & J. E. Thompson (Eds.), *Perspectives on prenatal care.* New York: Elsevier.

Families and Schools
Building Multicultural Values Together

Kevin J. Swick, Gloria Boutte
and Irma Van Scoy

Kevin Swick is Professor, Gloria Boutte is Assistant Professor and Irma Van Scoy is Assistant Professor, Early Childhood Education Program, College of Education, University of South Carolina, Columbia.

A society's culture encompasses its citizens' efforts to develop meaning about individual and collective values, beliefs and actions (Slonim, 1991). It serves as a continuing reference point through which people construct their perceptions about and reactions to the environment. Families and schools in a democratic, multicultural society must promote a positive climate in which children learn to appreciate not only their own culture, but also cultures of other people (Fu, Stremmel & Treppte, 1992).

Indeed, the current social context throughout the world suggests an urgent need for multicultural learning. The rise in hate groups, distorted perceptions of people of different cultures, ethnic-related crime and many other antisocial patterns must be countered by families and schools working together to build a social fabric that values cultural diversity (Swick, Van Scoy & Boutte, 1994). Before a proactive multicultural learning environment can be developed, parents and teachers must recognize both its importance, and the barriers that prevent its achievement.

The Rationale for
Multicultural Citizens
Csikszentmihalyi (1993) challenges the myopic view that multicultural learning is only important for minority populations. He notes that progressive societies succeed because their people can "transcend themselves" and relate to the environment in more sensitive and humane ways. This challenge is relevant to the growth and development of everyone in the global community. Pursuing unity through diversity calls for total involvement. Gary Howard (1993) stresses, "The future calls each of us to become partners in the dance of diversity, a dance in which everyone shares the lead" (p. 17). Multicultural learning must begin at birth and be continually nurtured through intentional family-school efforts.

Most important cultural understandings are shaped during the early childhood years. Thus, adult modeling of proactive multicultural values is critical for children. Hohensee and Derman-Sparks (1992) note that:

Numerous research studies about the process of identity and attitude development conclude that children learn by observing the differences and similarities among people and by absorbing the spoken and unspoken messages about these differences. The biases and negative stereotypes about various aspects of human diversity prevalent in our society under-cut all children's healthy development and ill-equip them to interact effectively with many people in the world. (p. 1)

Barriers to a Proactive Multicultural
Learning Framework
Many individual and cultural variables interact to impede the development of culturally sensitive individuals, including: cultural stereotypes, social isolation, tradition and excessive conformity. All of these factors have a powerful influence on children's understanding of racial, ethnic and cultural perspectives and behaviors (Banks, 1993).

Cultural stereotypes arise from incomplete and often distorted conceptions of people and events. They

From *Childhood Education,* Winter 1995/96, pp. 75-79. © 1995 by the Association for Childhood Education International, 17904 Georgia Avenue, Suite 215, Olney, MD. Reprinted by permission.

tend to emerge when people are insecure, have low self-esteem and are isolated from people of other cultures (Hilliard, 1992). Such contexts often create intergenerational racism and/or culturally destructive attitudes. Isolation and tradition often serve to reinforce ignorance and, thus, further exacerbate prejudices (Derman-Sparks, 1991). Social isolation reduces children's opportunities to learn about culturally different people. Tradition may actually even encourage the continuation of erroneous beliefs. Without understanding the need to become multicultural, many people conform to long-lasting beliefs that are racist, sexist or highly prejudicial.

Barriers of cultural conformity, tradition and related exclusionary practices daily convey a distorted and inequitable picture of people from different backgrounds and contexts. Men, for example, still hold most leadership positions while many women are subtly isolated from mainstream political life. Minorities still compose a disproportionate segment of low-paying positions. Television often presents incomplete and distorted views of minority cultures, offering prime-time programs filled with sexist humor, distorted ethnic characterizations and superficial presentations of illnesses like AIDS (Diaz, 1992).

These barriers are maintained and reinforced by individual, family, school and community patterns (Ramsey & Derman-Sparks, 1992). The family learning system, for example, may distort a child's images of people from other cultures (Slonim, 1991). Insecure adults pass on their distorted views to their children through the family socialization process. Insecure and fearful children are likely to form rigid conceptions of people different from themselves.

Schools also need to recognize the effect they have on children's multicultural development (Boutte, La Point & Davis, 1993). Some teachers have limited understanding of their students' cultural backgrounds. The resulting erroneous beliefs must be transcended through staff development, personal reading and enrichment, and through personal growth

What kind of citizens do we need to foster a truly proactive multicultural society?

experiences. Institutional practices of tracking, ability grouping and rigidly defined graded systems need to be replaced with more inclusionary strategies such as multiage grouping, cross-cultural peer learning and more personalized instruction. Unquestioned rituals and policies imprison culturally different children within an inequitable and insensitive environment (Swick, Van Scoy & Boutte, 1994). For example, the failure to use bilingual teaching strategies and resources can impede academic and social growth (Diaz, 1992). Inappropriate and inaccurate labeling has led many children to years of academic failure.

A Developmental Framework for Multicultural Learning

Learning new concepts, attitudes, skills and behaviors requires awareness, exploration and experimentation, systematic development, and integration of newly acquired knowledge (Hohensee & Derman-Sparks, 1992). Family-school collaboration is essential to actualizing these processes in ways that create meaningful multicultural learning.

Awareness. The initial step in this learning process is awareness of desired outcomes and potential barriers (Hohensee & Derman-Sparks, 1992). Critical questions to ask are: What kind of citizens do we need to foster a truly proactive multicultural society? And, what conditions support the development of this kind of person? We must be aware of the need for a multicultural learning vision and the strategies for achieving it (Gay, 1992).

Permeating this awareness process is our understanding of the cultural values and behaviors that we model for children and parents (Hilliard, 1992). Other important aspects of the awareness process include:

- *Examining how self-esteem is developed:*
  How do people feel about themselves?
  What do they know about their own culture?
- *Probing people's perceptions of different cultures, lifestyles and contexts:*
  What do people know about other cultures?
  What are their attitudes toward people from diverse cultures?
  What stereotypes and biases do people have about other cultures?
- *Examining the ingrained cultural habits of a society, particularly with regard to inequities in jobs, roles, salaries, status symbols and related rituals:*
  Are people from different cultures equitably represented in public roles?
  Do the housing and living patterns in our community reflect patterns of discrimination?
  Do employers, schools and business practice systematic discrimination?

■ *Analyzing the ways families socialize children about culture:*

Are parents educating children about their cultural heritage in appropriate ways?

Are parents modeling culturally sensitive and enriching behaviors and attitudes for children?

■ *Probing the substance of school and classroom practices relative to multicultural learning:*

Are staff exemplary models of multicultural learning?

Do school artifacts, policies and learning activities reflect equity and proactive multicultural learning?

■ *Studying the biases, inequities and related issues of cultural distortion that may pervade our daily lives:*

Are families providing equitable and respectful roles and relationships?

Are schools providing quality learning arrangements for all children?

Are communities actively seeking policies that support equity and justice for all citizens?

Awareness depends upon a climate of openness that can be created to strengthen attitudes, knowledge and skills that foster more sensitive and enriching interrelationships (Banks, 1993). Family and school frameworks need to encourage open discussion and analysis of cultural understanding, behavior patterns and relationship patterns.

Dialogue about how we live with and relate to each other should also include an assessment of specific family, school and community habits (Hilliard, 1992). For example, parent education could help adults assess the ways they teach their children to view themselves and others, especially people from different cultural contexts. Teach-

ers can enrich this process by using proactive multicultural teaching methods.

Exploration and experimentation. Exploration and experimentation with new ways of building multicultural learning environments is the second step in a multicultural learning process (Hohensee & Derman-Sparks, 1992). Attempts to gain everyone's involvement in culturally sensitive activities are typical of this effort. Parents and teachers can involve children in volunteer activities, for example, that broaden their cultural understanding and increase their self-efficacy. These activities might include service at a homeless shelter, participation in programs that serve special populations and social awareness field trips.

Teachers might develop regular activities that enrich children's perspectives, such as highlighting a "culture of the week," visiting community cultural events, involving parents and children in multicultural social and educational activities, hosting parent study groups that focus on multicultural issues, and offering teacher development programs on curriculum issues and community awareness activities that bring people of different cultures together in meaningful ways (Boutte & McCormick, 1992).

This exploratory phase of multicultural learning stimulates interest in learning about others in a positive and enjoyable way. The main focus in this effort is to help people realize the importance and enrichment possibilities of living in a multicultural environment (Banks, 1993).

Systematic development. Systematic multicultural development is the phase in which communities of people intentionally recognize and act on a transformational vision. The community focuses on building multicultural

learning communities in which beliefs, perceptions and actions create a flow of cultural habits that help people understand, value, support and learn from each other (Csikszentmihalyi, 1993). Formalized family and school collaboration incorporates planning, design and implementation of multicultural learning systems into daily life.

The initial step in this development phase is to review, refine and integrate proactive multicultural attitudes, knowledge and skills into all facets of the family-school-community learning system (Banks, 1993). Clearly, the major impediment to a fully functioning multicultural world is the lack of accurate representation and involvement of diverse peoples. Hilliard (1992) notes the pervasiveness of this impediment in global actions:

Those who have studied worldwide liberation struggles know that the manipulation of information, including propaganda and misinformation, are primary tactics employed in the domination process. Oppressive populations defame, stigmatize, stereotype and distort the reality of dominated populations. Ultimately, if the curriculum is centered in truth, it will be pluralistic, for the simple fact is that human culture is the product of the struggles of all humanity, not the possession of a single racial or ethnic group. (pp. 157-158)

In this context, it is critical that families and schools assess all aspects of their cultural functioning. For example, families need to examine how they relate to each other in terms of multicultural learning (Swick, Van Scoy & Boutte, 1994). At school, classroom content, teacher-child interactions and significant processes and rituals (such as grouping patterns, treatment of all children, involvement of families and the overall school culture) should be continuously reviewed for accuracy, cultural inclusion and degree of collaboration and individuality (Derman-Sparks, 1991).

Some specific actions that can promote this systematic effort include:

- Joint parent-teacher planning of activities and strategies that integrate multicultural learning into children's daily experiences
- Teacher assessment and refinement of instructional and curricular content, process and actions relative to providing accurate and comprehensive multicultural experiences
- School ecology team actions to develop policies that promote equity, cultural enrichment and individual sensitivity to cultural differences and commonalities.

Formalized planning brings systematic attention to all aspects of multicultural learning in order to promote accurate representations of culturally diverse people and promote a proactive multicultural orientation within family, school and community (Hilliard, 1992). Planners must develop goals, an action plan, strategies and tools for continually monitoring and refining the entire system. Nothing less than a comprehensive and collaborative approach to addressing multicultural learning needs can achieve the goal of a more sensitive and nurturing citizenry.

Swick, Van Scoy and Boutte (1994) suggest five "opportunities for multicultural learning" that can be initiated with children from birth through age 7: 1) educating parents about their role in building children's self-esteem, 2) helping children explore their own culture through family and school activities, 3) training parents and teachers to assess their multicultural competence, 4) supporting families' and schools' development of skills and strategies for promoting multicultural learning and 5) initiating intense teacher education about multicultural learning. The

*p*ositive multicultural learning relies upon a foundation of being valued within the family, meaningfully guided in school and engaged in helpful community rituals.

following sampling of strategies highlights the importance of a comprehensive approach:

- Teachers can share multicultural information with parents by lending them relevant books, articles and videos; posting information and suggestions on parent bulletin boards; offering monthly parenting programs; and publishing newsletters that report on multicultural activities within the school and community.
- Classroom displays should represent diverse ethnic, racial and cultural backgrounds. Also, these displays should include children's personal work. Parents can participate by helping to acquire materials and by volunteering in the classroom.
- Teachers can ask families to share pictures, family recipes, dramatic play props, family experiences,

books and other print materials, stories and other artifacts that reflect their cultures.

Integration of multicultural learning. This step is necessary to build a cooperative and proactive society (Byrnes & Kiger, 1992). This phase of multicultural development filters every aspect of social functioning through the lenses of equity, sensitivity, understanding and cultural enrichment. Families and schools will eventually internalize multicultural values so that these filtering actions become natural and sustaining behaviors. Four behavior patterns are essential: 1) nurturing authentic and positive self-esteem; 2) promoting a sharing, nurturing and positive self-other relationship syndrome; 3) nurturing the cultural strengths of all people and 4) promoting collaborative relationships among different cultures (Swick & Graves, 1993).

Low self-esteem is the most prevalent obstacle to building proactive multicultural communities (Slonim, 1991). Children and adults need contexts that build self-esteem. Positive multicultural learning relies upon a foundation of being valued within the family, meaningfully guided in school and engaged in helpful community rituals. The secure and valued "self" is the basis for cultural competence (Neugebauer, 1992).

Learning about others through nurturing, sharing and positive relationships can foster critical prosocial skills (Hilliard, 1992). Regular opportunities for people to meet, and learn from, culturally diverse people in positive ways must be available. Cooperative learning, cross-age grouping and networking activities are strategies that support this process.

Culturally different people are too often viewed from the perspective of the dominant culture, which is often deficit-focused (Neugebauer, 1992). An attitude of strength through diversity, by contrast, celebrates the multiple talents of all people. Likewise, collaborative relationships are critical to sustaining proactive multicultural learning (Oliver & Howley, 1992).

Systematic effort can facilitate integration of multicultural learning into family, school and community habits. This process must be revisited frequently to combat the often subtle forms of prejudice, racism, sexism and classism (Boutte, La Point & Davis, 1993).

Collaboration and Advocacy Is Essential

Every effort to promote a culturally sensitive and enriching world is empowering. Family-school collaboration, however, enables people to transform themselves in ways that can extend multicultural constructs toward full societal implementation. This collaboration process can occur in many ways: within the family, in collaboration between family and school and in societal planning and advocacy activities (Hilliard, 1992).

Collaborative schemes work best in small social units (e.g., teams of teachers, neighborhood action teams and community innovation groups). The power of small groups is evident in school events that focus on cultural celebrations, antibias committees and multicultural learning teams (Banks, 1993). Face-to-face interactions bring about the most powerful transformations and understandings. It is only through working together that we really come to understand one another. The important elements of these small social action units are: commitment to a common goal, continuous membership, specific roles for members, a detailed plan on how to achieve identified goals and a system for continued nurturance of the group's original mission (Csikszentmihalyi, 1993). Creating networks with like-minded groups can increase each group's influence, if system flexibility within the smaller units is maintained.

Advocacy is critical to the long-term promotion of multicultural values. Families, schools and communities need to monitor their systems to ensure cultural accuracy and to maintain supports that foster integrative multicultural learning habits. For example, education programs can highlight multicultural learning experiences that families can carry out on a regular basis. Schools and community groups can serve as anti-bias watchdogs. The best hope for cultural harmony that respects positive individuality is collaborative advocacy. We must be continually reminded of the urgency and need for attention to our cultural knowledge, attitudes and skills.

References

Banks, J. (1993). Multicultural education for young children: Racial and ethnic attitudes and their modification. In B. Spodek (Ed.), *Handbook of research on the education of young children* (pp. 236-251). New York: Macmillan.

Boutte, G. S., La Point, S., & Davis, B. (1993). Racial issues in education: Real or imagined? *Young Children, 49*(1), 19-22.

Boutte, G., & McCormick, C. (1992). Authentic multicultural activities: Avoiding pseudomulticulturalism. *Childhood Education, 68,* 140-144.

Byrnes, D., & Kiger, G. (Eds.). (1992). *Common bonds: Anti-bias teaching in a diverse society.* Wheaton, MD: Association for Childhood Education International.

Csikszentmihalyi, M. (1993). *The evolving self.* New York: HarperCollins.

Derman-Sparks, L. (Ed.). (1991). *Anti-bias curriculum: Tools for empowering young children.* Washington, DC: National Association for the Education of Young Children.

Diaz, C. (Ed.). (1992). *Multicultural education for the 21st century.* Washington, DC: National Education Association.

Fu, V., Stremmel, A., & Treppte, C. (Eds.). (1992). *Multiculturalism in early childhood programs.* Urbana, IL: ERIC Clearinghouse on Elementary and Early Childhood Education.

Gay, G. (1992). Effective teaching practices for multicultural classrooms. In C. Diaz (Ed.), *Multicultural education for the 21st century* (pp. 38-56). Washington, DC: National Education Association.

Hilliard, A. (1992). Why we must pluralize the curriculum. *Educational Leadership, 49*(4), 157-160.

Hohensee, J., & Derman-Sparks, L. (1992). *Implementing an anti-bias curriculum in early childhood classrooms.* Champaign, IL: ERIC Clearinghouse on Early Childhood Education. ED 351146.

Howard, G. (1993). Whites in multicultural education: Rethinking our role. *Phi Delta Kappan, 75*(1), 36-41.

Neugebauer, B. (Ed.). (1992). *Alike and different: Exploring our humanity with young children.* Washington, DC: National Association for the Education of Young Children.

Oliver, J.-P., & Howley, C. (1992). *Charting new maps: Multicultural education in rural schools.* Charleston, WV: ERIC Clearinghouse on Rural and Small Schools. ED 348196.

Ramsey, P., & Derman-Sparks, L. (1992). Multicultural education reaffirmed. *Young Children, 47*(2), 10-11.

Slonim, M. (1991). *Children, culture, and ethnicity.* New York: Garland.

Swick, K., Van Scoy, I., & Boutte, G. (1994). Multicultural learning through family involvement. *Dimensions of Early Childhood, 22*(4), 17-21.

Swick, K., & Graves, S. (1993). *Empowering at-risk families during the early childhood years.* Washington, DC: National Education Association.

Research in Review

The Education of Hispanics in Early Childhood: Of Roots and Wings

Eugene E. Garcia

As director of the Office of Bilingual Education and Minority Languages Affairs in the U.S. Department of Education, I sought to engage my *professional* experience and expertise as an educational researcher and my *personal* cultural and linguistic experience to address national education policy. The professional in me has been nurtured at some of the best educational institutions in the United States, while the nonprofessional has been nurtured in a large, rural, Mexican American family. Born in the United States and speaking Spanish as our first language for generations, our family included 10 children—four high school graduates and one college graduate.

Bringing these *personas* (Spanish for "persons") together was not as difficult as I had expected and the mixture was quite helpful to the wide variety of people I interacted with in my national role. Bringing together these personas, I communicated with individuals in ways not possible had I spoken only with one voice or separate voices.

This article presents my intersecting but distinct voices to help further our understanding of life in a diverse society—particularly of Hispanics growing up in the United States during their early childhood years. The historical pattern of the education of Hispanics in the United States is a continuous story of underachievement. It need not continue to be that way.

The three voices here address issues of the past, present, and future. They recognize the multiple selves that not only make up my own persona but those that are a reality for all of us. It is useful to recognize that we walk in varied and diverse cultures. There is great diversity within each individual, just as there is diversity among individuals and the many cultures they belong to or represent. We all live with diversity, some of us more than others. No one escapes this challenge or its advantages and disadvantages.

Eugene E. Garcia, *Ph.D., is professor and dean of the Graduate School of Education at the University of California in Berkeley. He continues to do research in areas related to language, culture, and schooling. He served as director of the Office of Bilingual Education and Minority Language Affairs in the U.S. Department of Education, 1993–95.*

*This is one of a regular series of Research in Review columns. The column in this issue was invited by **Carol Seefeldt,** Ph.D., professor at the University of Maryland, College Park.*

While English First, an organization committed to English as the official U.S. language, is passionately concerned that multilingualism will produce divisiveness and significant conflict, indigenous people whose roots in the Americas outdistance the "White man's" presence mourn just as passionately the loss of their languages and cultures. As this country and the world shrinks communicatively, economically, socially, and intellectually, diversity is becoming harder to hide, but it has always been there. In the following pages, I address issues related to the education of Hispanics in early childhood with the varied voices within me.

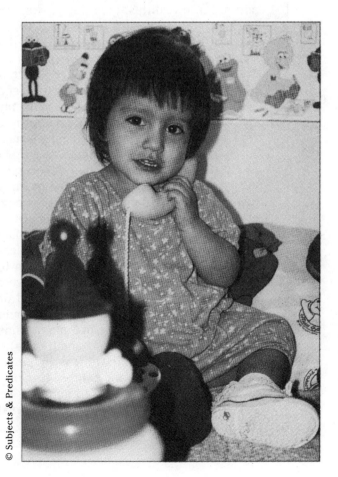

© Subjects & Predicates

From *Young Children*, March 1997, pp. 5-14. © 1997 by Eugene E. Garcia. Reprinted by permission.

The Voices

Eugene. This voice often represents my intellectual upbringing and is recognized primarily by my academic credentials—degrees received and where and when, how successful I was in those environments, academic positions I have held and their status in the academic world, the empirical research I have done, my teaching, and, of course, the articles and books I have written. This set of experiences and accomplishments, at its core, attempts to expand in critical and strategic ways our broader understanding of language acquisition, teaching, learning, and schooling, and the specific relevance of these to language-minority populations—learners who come to the educational enterprise not knowing the language of that formal enterprise and particularly for students like me who are classified as Hispanic in the present jargon of educators and demographers. I did not begin my academic pursuits with this specific population in mind but have naturally gravitated toward using my professional skills to address issues of relevance to it, but not *only* to it.

Gene. Other parts of me are more rooted in the nonacademic world, my social and cultural realities. I am a son, brother, husband, father, and so on. In such social and cultural roles, I have experienced a wonderful family environment, learning much from my father and mother—neither of whom ever had the opportunity to attend school. They taught me to respect them, my elders, my brothers and sisters, and others who were not members of my family—such as my teachers—or not like me, and, most of all, to respect myself. They never gave me a formal lesson about these things; they just lived them, in the harsh realities of poverty and the hard work any migrant or sharecropping family understands. This teaching and learning included experiences of outright racism and subtle institutional racism in which our language, color, and heritage were not always met with either individual or group respect. From these experiences and teachers emerged the voice of Gene (a name used most often by my family and friends).

This persona agreed to work as an undergraduate in the migrant camps, tutoring adults in English and related subjects so that they could earn the GED (general equivalency diploma). This persona realized early that he was different. I spoke primarily Spanish, my peers only English. I and my family worked in the fields; my peers and their families hired us to work in their fields. My peers enjoyed a much higher standard of living—I recall being embarrassed that my family did not take summer vacations or have running water and inside toilets. Quite honestly, most of the time, these differences did not weigh heavy on my mind or affect my behavior—I had lots of friends, some like me and others quite different from me.

It was likely more Gene than Eugene who accepted the invitation to join the Clinton administration and Secretary of Education Richard Riley in the Department of Education. In political/policy roles like this one, I realized that policymakers and practitioners of education do not always act based on the best theory, proven educational practices, or even promising educational innovations. They act mostly out of political interests. I realized the importance of the politics of education. Gene's voice is often dominated by these lessons, although Eugene is not totally unaffected by them.

Gino. Another voice within me is identified best by the endearing name that my mother used for me—Gino. In my large, quite Catholic family, to baptize a child is a distinct honor and, in recognition of that honor, *los padrinos,* the godparents, are given the authority to name the child. At my birth my parents selected my eldest sister and her husband to serve as my padrinos, and my sister was enchanted with the name Eugene. That is how I came to have a Greek name in a cohort of brothers and sisters named Antonio, Emelio, Cecelia, Ciprianita, Abel, Federico, Tiburcio, and Christina, and born of parents named Lorenzo and Juanita. My mother could not pronounce *Eugene,* so to her and my immediate family I became Gino.

Gino carries a distinct sense of cultural "Hispanic-ness," "Chicanismo," "Latino-ness," or "Raza-ness." These concepts reflect a deep regard for the linguistic and cultural roots that foster identity—best exemplified by a lesson from my father:

> For farmworkers and sharecroppers, winter was a time to prepare for work—there was not much work during this period. One winter in the high plains of Colorado where I was born and raised, my father pointed to an *árbol*—a cottonwood tree. He asked, *"Por qué puede vivir ese árbol en el frio del invierno y en el calor del verano?"* (How can that tree survive the bitter cold of winter and the harsh heat of summer?) My father was a man of few words—relatives often characterized him as quiet and shy—but when he spoke we all listened very carefully. I rambled on about how big and strong the tree was and how its limbs and trunk were like the strong arms and bodies of my elder brothers. Then he kindly provided a different perspective by referring to a common Spanish *dicho/consejo* (proverb): *El árbol fuerte tienen raíces maduros* (A strong tree has mature/strong roots).

In articulating this significant piece of the analysis that was absent from my youthful thoughts, my father made clear that without strong roots, strong trees are impossible–and we don't even see the roots! The roots of many Hispanics in this country have either been ignored or stripped away in the name of growing strong. Many have been directed to stop speaking Spanish, to perceive their culture as a "less-than" one, and to assimilate as quickly as possible so they can succeed in American society (Chavez 1991). Unfortunately, many have suffered the fate of the rootless tree—they have fallen socially, economically, academically, and culturally.

However, to Gino, my mother made it very clear: roots and their concomitant integrity and self-respect were not enough. She wanted the very best for all her children, certainly not the long and painful fieldwork that she had endured for a lifetime. She wanted us *bien educados*—to have a set of formal and marketable skills. She made very clear that children needed wings, like the wings she insisted we children grew every night upon falling asleep, so as to fly to heaven to be with God. "All children," she said, "are angels." In recent stories by Chicano author Victor Villaseñor, his mother elaborates further on this notion (Villaseñor 1991). She says that the children fly to God each night and station themselves as stars in His heaven. Both our mothers expressed a special regard for the sanctity of childhood and required children to have wings to perform their related roles. My mother emphasized that she could not provide the kind of wings that God and a good education could provide. She knew that the teachers and schools would have to take me further than she could personally. Education would need to provide the strong and elaborate wings for me to succeed where she often felt she had failed: "Go to school—strong wings like those of an eagle are also what you need in this world to raise your family and provide for them all that we have been unable to provide for you."

For Hispanics in this country, the emphasis on building wings in school has strategically focused on teaching English language skills: "Teach them English well and then they will succeed." Yet all educators realize that in today's information age, education must provide broad and strong intellectual wings related to fundamental linguistic, mathematical, scientific, and technological literacies. English literacy is important, but it is not enough. Gino feels that Hispanics, such as those he and his family represent, have been educationally shortchanged.

The "Hispanic" debate

Eugene, Gene, and Gino realize that their voices are not alone nor are their views held by all Hispanics in the United States. Most critical of such views of the interactive relationship of "roots and wings" for Hispanics are two well-regarded and influential Hispanic authors, each in her or his own way refuting the importance of roots and the relationship of those roots to the educational development of Hispanics.

Linda Chavez, an adviser in the Reagan White House, journalist commentator, and author of *Out of the Barrio: Toward a New Politics of Hispanic Assimilation,* suggests that

> Every previous group—Germans, Irish, Italians, Greeks, Jews, Poles—struggled to be accepted fully into the social, political and economic mainstream, sometimes against the opposition of a hostile majority. They learned the language, acquired education and skills, and adapted their own customs and traditions to fit an American context. (1991, 2)

The key for Hispanic success in America, Chavez argues, is minimizing the public/governmental recognition of Hispanic roots and the individual and governmental promotion of assimilation. She chides the federal government, particularly federal bilingual education programs, and Hispanic leaders for promoting permanent victim status and vying with Black Americans for the distinction of being the poorest, most segregated, and least educated minority, thereby entitling them to government handouts. These actions in turn, her conclusion advances, encourage Hispanics to maintain their language and culture and their specific identity in return for rewards handed out through affirmative action and federal, state, and local educational policies that thwart assimilation. This does not sound like my father's concern for the importance of roots or my mother's emphasis on wings.

Yet another Hispanic author, Richard Rodriguez, is very eloquent in his description of his upbringing in a Mexican home and a Catholic school where the English-speaking nuns literally beat the Spanish language and the "Hispanic-ness" out of him. His book *Hunger of Memory* (1982) describes this forced assimilation, painful as it was, that propelled him to new heights of educational achievement. Although he himself never articulates the conclusion, he leaves open the suggestion that such treatment of Hispanics is exactly what they need to get over their "problems." Eugene, Gene, and Gino reach a very different conclusion in this discussion. But you should know that the debate exists.

The following discussion indirectly addresses this debate but includes an expanded research-related discussion of vulnerability factors both within and outside the education arena along with data related to the "effective" treatment of this growing population of young children and families. The discussion addresses the following:

1. An overall demographic assessment of factors related to the schooling of culturally diverse populations, including issues of poverty, family stability, and immigrant status;

2. A particular analysis of the challenges associated with the growing number of language-minority students who are Hispanic—children who come to school with limited or no proficiency in English; and

3. A presentation of conceptual and empirical perspectives that sets the stage for a more informed approach to the education of Hispanics in early childhood.

The research

The demographic picture

The Census Bureau in its attempts to provide clarifying demographic information never fails in confusing us. In documenting the racial and ethnic heterogeneity of our country's population, it has arrived at a set of highly confusing terms that place individuals in separate exclusionary categories: White, White non-Hispanic, Black, Hispanic (with some five subcategories of Hispanics). Unfortunately, outside of the census meaning of these terms, they are for the most part highly ambiguous and nonrepresentative of the true heterogeneity which the Census Bureau diligently seeks to document. Therefore, it is important to note at the outset of this discussion that these categories are useful only as the most superficial reflection of our nation's true diversity. I do not know many census-identified "Whites," "Blacks," or "Hispanics" who believe they are "White," "Black," and so on, but given the forced-choice responses allowed them in census questionnaires, they are constrained by these choices.

Having consented to this significant restriction regarding efforts to document population diversity in this country, I still must conclude that an examination of the available data provides a fuzzy but useful portrait of our society and the specific circumstances of various groups within our nation's boundaries. That sketch is one of consummate vulnerability for non-White and Hispanic (usually referred to as "minority") families, children, and students. On almost every indicator, non-White and Hispanic families, children, and "at-risk" students are likely to fall

---

While English First, an organization committed to English as the official U.S. language, is passionately concerned that multilingualism will produce divisiveness and significant conflict, indigenous people whose roots in the Americas outdistance the "White man's" presence mourn just as passionately the loss of their languages and cultures.

Hispanic Demographics

General demographic character

• Of the approximately 22.7 million Hispanics in the continental United States, the following information characterizes the population's ethnic diversity.

Country/area of origin	Number (in millions)	%
Mexico	14.6	64.3
Puerto Rico	2.4	10.6
Central/South America	3.0	13.4
Cuba	1.1	4.7
Other Hispanic countries	1.6	7.0

• 89.5% of the total Hispanic population in the United States is concentrated in three states: California (26%), Texas (25.5%), and New Mexico (38%). Other states with significant Hispanic populations are Arizona (19%), Colorado (13%), Florida (12%), and New York (12%).

• Average age of the Hispanic population in 1993 was 26.7 years.

• 200,000 Hispanics immigrate legally to the United States annually; Hispanics are 40% of all legal immigrants. (An estimated 200,000 Hispanics immigrate illegally.)

• The Hispanic population grew by 53% from 1980 to 1990, compared to the 9.8% growth in the general U.S. population.

• 17 million Hispanics report speaking Spanish in the home.

• 90% of Hispanics live in metropolitan areas; 52% in central cities.

Indices of "vulnerability"

• Median family income has fluctuated for Hispanics (1982—$23,814; 1991—$24,614; 1992—$23,912), remaining below that of non-Hispanics (1982—$35,075; 1991—$38,127; 1992—$38,015).

• In 1992, 26.2% of Hispanic families lived below the poverty line, compared to 27.2% in 1982. (In 1992, 10.4% of non-Hispanic White families lived below the poverty line.)

• In 1993, 1,239,094 Hispanic families (23.3%) were maintained by a female head-of-household (an increase of .5% from 1983 when it was 22.8% or 827,184); 48.8% of these households lived below the poverty line.

• 72.9% of Hispanics hold unskilled and semiskilled jobs, compared to 50.8% of non-Hispanics.

Education

• Approximately 50% of Hispanics leave school prior to graduation (70% by 10th grade).

• 38% of Hispanics are held back at least one grade.

• 50% of Hispanics are overage at grade 12.

• 90% of Hispanic students are in urban districts.

• 82% of Hispanic students attend segregated schools.

• Hispanics are significantly below national norms on academic achievement tests of reading, math, science, social science, and writing at grades 3, 7, and 11, generally averaging one to two grade levels below the norm. At grade 11, Hispanics average a grade 8 achievement level on these tests.

• Hispanics are placed in special education services six times more often than the general student population.

Sources: U.S. Bureau of the Census, *The Hispanic Population in the United States: March 1993* (Washington DC: U.S. Government Printing Office, 1993); U.S. Bureau of the Census, *Social and Economic Characteristics in the U.S.: 1990 Census of the Population* (Washington DC: GPO, 1990); M.A. Reddy, *Statistical Record of Hispanic Americans* (Michigan: Gale Research, Inc., 1993); and U.S. Immigration and Naturalization Service, *Statistical Yearbook of the Immigration and Naturalization, 1993* (Washington DC: GPO, 1994).

into the lowest quartile on indicators of "well-being": family stability, family violence, family income, child health and development, and educational achievement. Yet this population has grown significantly in the last two decades and will grow substantially in the decades to come. The table on the previous page summarizes these factors for census-derived information on Hispanics.

Part of the current push for excellence and equity for all students has been increased attention to Hispanic children.

The demographic transformation that has become more evident in the last decade was easily foreseen at least that long ago. Our schools' future student profile is as predictable: in a mere 40 years, White students will be a minority in every category of public education as we know it today. Unfortunately, the emerging student majority of ethnic and racial background continues to be at risk in today's social institutions. The National Center for Children in Poverty (1995) provided a clear and alarming demographic window on these at-risk populations. Of the 21.9 million children under six years of age in 1990 who will move slowly through society's institutions—family, schools, the workplace—five million (25%) were living in poverty. Although less than 30% of all children under six years of age were non-White, more than 50% of the children in poverty were non-White. In addition, these children continued to live in racial/ethnic isolation. Some 56% lived in racially isolated neighborhoods in 1966; 72% resided in such neighborhoods in 1994; 61% of children in poverty live in concentrations of poverty where 20% of the population is poor.

High school or equivalent completion rates are alarming for these emerging majority student populations. In 1994 the high school completion rate for the U.S. population was 81.1% for 19-year-olds, 86.5% for 24-year-olds, and a very respectable 86% for 29-year-olds. For Blacks and Hispanics the rate of completion in all age groups was close to 60% (U.S. Department of Commerce 1990). With regard to academic achievement, in 1994, 30% of 13-year-old students were one grade level below the norm on standardized achievement measures. However, this differed significantly for emerging majority and White students: 27% for White students, 40% for Hispanic students, and 46% for Black students.

The qualitative description of education presented above is further affirmed for Hispanics by other quantitative descriptions. A recent study reported by de Leon Siantz (1996) uses descriptive data from the Hispanic Health and Nutrition Examination Survey, a national effort sampling stratified populations of Mexican American, Puerto Rican, and Cuban American families in three U.S. regions (southwest, northeast, and southeast). This study reports very small differences in family well-being and child well-being indicators across these groups and regions. The Hispanic population was described as growing, youthful, poor, lacking parental care, and at high risk for AIDS.

Moreover, recent national Head Start data (Phillips & Cabrera 1996) indicate that only one-third of the programs had an enrollment characterized by a single language, with a range of 1 to 32 languages represented in programs, while 72% of programs had enrollments of between 2 and 3 languages. The predominant languages represented in these programs were Spanish and English.

Combined with the contemporary educational zeitgeist that embraces excellence and equity for all students, attention to the Hispanic children, families, and students has been significant. Following this theme are recent analyses and recommendations: the California State Department of Education efforts to better train infant and toddler caregivers in state-supported programs (California State Department of Education 1992), the U.S. Department of Education reforms for federally funded education programs (Garcia & Gonzales 1995), the National Academy of Education discussion of standards-based reform (McLaughlin & Shepard 1995), the National Research Council's Roundtable on Head Start Research efforts to provide an issue analysis of research needed to produce a thriving future for Head Start for a highly diverse population of children and families (Phillips & Cabrera 1996), the National Council of Teachers of English and the International Reading Association's treatment of language arts standards (NCTE/IRA 1996), and NAEYC's position statement on linguistic and cultural diversity (NAEYC 1996). All of these publications have attended to the vulnerabilities of Hispanics and have addressed issues of language and culture in light of this country's past treatment of this population and the present conceptual and empirical understanding of the need for institutions to be more responsive. Much of this thinking about policy and practice is based on the issues and research findings that follow.

Our past approach: Americanization

Historically, Americanization has been a prime institutional education objective for Hispanic young children and their families (Elam 1972; Gonzales 1990; Garcia 1994). Schooling practices were adapted whenever the Hispanic student population rose to significant numbers in a community. This adaptation resulted in special programs applied to both children and adults in urban and rural schools and communities. The desired effect of Americanizing was to socialize and acculturate the targeted diverse community. In essence, if public efforts could teach these children and families English and American values, then social, economic, and educational failure could be averted. Ironically, social economists have argued that this effort was coupled with systematic efforts to maintain disparate conditions between Anglos and minority populations. Indeed, more than anything else, past attempts at addressing the Black, Hispanic, Indian, Asian, etc., "educational problem" have actually preserved the political and economic subordination of these communities (Spencer 1988). Coming from a sociological theory of assimilation, Americanization has traditionally been recognized as a solution to the problem of immigrants and ethnicity in the modern industrialized United States. Linda Chavez (1991) continues to champion this solution for Hispanics.

The Americanization solution has not worked. Moreover, it depends on the flawed notion of group culture. The Americanization solution presumes that culturally different children are, as a group, culturally flawed. To fix them individually, we must act on the individual as a member of a cultural group. By changing the values, language, and so forth of the group, we will have the solution to the educational underachievement of students representing these groups. The challenge facing educators regarding Hispanic students is not to Americanize them but to understand them and act responsively to the specific diversity they bring and the educational goal of academic success for all students.

Early childhood practices that meet the challenge

The debate regarding early childhood education of Hispanic students in the United States has centered on the role of cultural and developmental appropriateness of curriculum and pedagogy, along with Spanish language use and the development of English in these early childhood settings. Discussion of this issue has included cross-disciplinary dialogues involving psychology, linguistics, sociology, politics, and education. (For a more thorough discussion of these issues, see Cummins 1979, Troike 1981, Baker and deKanter 1983, Garcia 1983, Willig 1985, Rossell and Ross 1986, Hakuta and Gould 1987, August and Garcia 1988, Crawford 1989, Baker 1990, Kagan and Garcia 1991, Garcia 1994, Cole 1995, Garcia and Gonzalez 1995, and Rossell and Baker 1996.) The central theme of these discussions relates to the specific role of the native language.

Supporters of culturally sensitive and native language instruction are at one end in this debate. Proponents of this specially designed instructional strategy recommend the utilization of the child's native language and mastery of that language prior to the introduction of an English, more mainstream curriculum. This approach (Cardenas 1986; Fishman 1989) suggests that the competencies in the native culture and language, particularly about academic learning, provide important cognitive and social foundations for second-language learning and academic learning in general—you really only learn to read once. At the other end in this debate, introduction to the English curriculum is recommended at the onset of the student's schooling experience, with minimal use of the native language. This specially designed approach calls for English language "leveling" by instructional staff (to facilitate the understanding on behalf of the student with limited English proficiency) combined with an English-as-

a-second-language component. In essence, the earlier the student confronts English and the more times he or she is confronted, the greater the English linguistic advantage (Rossell 1992; Rossell & Baker 1996).

The native language debate has ignored the contributions of Friere (1970), Bernstein (1971), Cummins (1979, 1986), Heath (1986), Ogbu (1986), Trueba (1987), Levin (1988), Tharp (1989), Rose (1989), Moll (1991), Garcia (1995), and Krashen (1996), who have suggested that the schooling vulnerability of such students must be understood within the broader contexts of this society's treatment of these students and their families in and out of educational institutions. That is, no quick fix is likely under social and early education conditions that mark the Hispanic-language minority student for special treatment of his or her language difference without consideration for the psychological and social-cultural circumstances in which that student resides. This is not to suggest that the linguistic character of this student is insignificant. Instead, it warns us against the isolation of this single attribute as the only variable of importance. This more comprehensive view of the education, particularly early childhood education, includes an understanding of the relationship between home and school, the sociocultural incongruities between the two, and the resulting effects on learning and achievement (Kagan & Garcia 1991; Garcia 1994).

Recent research findings have redefined the nature of the educational vulnerability of Hispanic children, destroyed common stereotypes and myths, and laid a foundation on which to reconceptualize present educational practices and launch new initiatives. This foundation recognizes the homogeneity and heterogeneity within and between diverse student populations. No one set of descriptions or prescriptions will suffice; however, a set of commonalties deserves particular attention.

Research focusing on early childhood classrooms, teachers, administrators, and parents revealed an interesting set of perspectives on the treatment of children (Hakuta & Gould 1987; Rose 1989; Garcia 1991; Moll 1991; Ramirez et al. 1991; Wong Fillmore 1991; Garcia 1994; Cole 1995). Classroom teachers were highly committed to the educational success of their students; perceived themselves as instructional innovators utilizing "new" learning theories and instructional philosophies to guide their practice; continued to be involved in professional development activities, including participation in small-group support networks; had a strong, demonstrated commitment to student-home communication (several teachers were utilizing a weekly parent interaction format); and felt they had the autonomy to create or change the instruction and curriculum in their classrooms even if it did not meet the district guidelines exactly. Significantly, these teachers "adopted" their students. They had high academic expectations for all their students ("Everyone will learn to read in my classroom") and also served as advocates for their students. They rejected any conclusion that their students were intellectually or academically disadvantaged.

Parents expressed a high level of satisfaction and appreciation regarding their children's educational experience in these classrooms. All indicated or implied that academic success was tied to their children's future economic success. Anglo and Hispanic parents were both quite involved in the formal parent-supported activities of the schools. However, Anglo parents' attitudes were much more in line with a child advocacy view—somewhat distrustful of the school's specific interest in doing what was right for their child. Conversely, Hispanic parents expressed a high level of trust for the teaching and administrative staff.

This recent research addresses some significant practice questions regarding effective academic environments for Hispanic children:

1. *What role did native language instruction play?*

Teachers considered native language use in daily instruction as key. They implemented an articulated native language and literacy effort that recognized language as a tool for learning and not as a learning objective.

2. *Who were the key players in this effective schooling drama?*

Administrators and parents played important roles. However, teachers were the key players. They achieved the educational confidence of their peers and supervisors. They worked to organize instruction, create new instructional environments, assess effectiveness, and advocate for their students. They were proud of their students, reassuring but consistently demanding. They rejected any notion of linguis-

proficiency-as-a-problem approach to an asset inventory and native-language-as-a-resource approach.

Conclusion

Effective early education curriculum, instructional strategies, and teaching staffs recognize that development and learning have their roots in sharing expertise and experiences through multiple avenues of communication. Further, effective early childhood education for linguistically and culturally diverse children encourages them to take risks, construct meaning, and seek reinterpretation of knowledge within the compatible social contexts. Within this nurturing environment, skills are tools for acquiring knowledge, not ends in themselves, and the language of the child is an incredible resource. The curriculum recognizes that any attempt to address the needs of these students in a deficit or subtractive mode is counterproductive. Instead, this knowledge base recognizes, conceptually, that educators must be additive in an approach to these students.

Recent statements about these challenges reinforce this charge. The National Council of Teachers of English and the International Reading Association (NCTE/IRA) in their enunciation of standards for English language arts recognize that

> Be an advocate for our linguistically and culturally diverse children and families by nurturing, celebrating, and challenging them. They do not need our pity for what they do not have; they, like any individual and family, require our respect and the use of what they bring as a resource.

tic, cultural, or intellectual inferiority regarding their students. They were child advocates.

Imbedded in the activities of these educational enterprises for Hispanic students was the understanding that language, culture, and their accompanying values are acquired in the home and community environment; that children come to school with some knowledge about what language is, how it works, and what it is used for; that children learn higher-level metacognitive and metalinguistic skills as they engage in socially meaningful activities; and that children's development and learning are best understood in the interaction of linguistic, sociocultural, and cognitive knowledge and experiences. In particular for students who did not speak English, their native language was perceived as a resource instead of a problem. **In general terms, this research *suggests* moving away from a needs assessment and non-English-**

Students develop an understanding of and respect for diversity in language use, patterns, and dialects across cultures, ethnic groups, geographic regions, and social roles.

Students whose first language is not English make use of their first language to develop competency in the English language arts and to develop understanding of content across the curriculum.

Celebrating our shared beliefs and traditions are not enough; we also need to honor that which is distinctive in the many groups that make up our nation. (1996, 3)

NAEYC echoes these same concerns in its position statement related to educational practices regarding linguistic and cultural diversity in early childhood:

Early childhood educators can best help linguistically and culturally diverse children and their families by acknowledging and responding to the importance of the child's home language and culture. Administrative support for bilingualism as a goal is necessary within the educational setting. Educational practices should focus on educating children toward the "school culture" while preserving and respecting the diversity of the home language and culture that each child brings to the early learning setting. (1996, 12)

In the present era, this challenge must be met within the context of philosophical, ideological, and political debates surrounding our professional efforts to do things right and to do the right things for all children and families. Eugene, Gene, and Gino encourage you in these efforts, particularly for Hispanics, recognizing the significance of your role and regard for their roots and wings. Here are five practical applications that teachers can use to meet this challenge:

1. Know the linguistic and cultural diversity of your students. Like an ethnographer, be very observant and seek information regarding the languages and cultures represented by the children, families, and communities you serve. Learn to pronounce your student's name as the family pronounces it. For each student write down linguistic and cultural information so it becomes as important as the other things you write down.

2. Take on the new challenge of serving linguistic and culturally diverse children with resolve, commitment, and *ganas* (high motivation). Children and families will appreciate your willingness to learn their language—even small phrases of their language. They will also recognize paternalistic attitudes—attitudes that convey the notion that their children should negate their native language and culture.

3. Be up to date on the new knowledge base. We know so much more now about how better to deal with diversity. Most of us grew up or received our formal training in eras when diversity was not an issue. Incorporate personal and formal stories, games, songs, and poems from various cultures and languages into the curriculum.

4. Share the knowledge with the educational and noneducational community. There is so much strong feeling among educators and the general public that diversity is a problem and must be eliminated. Be clear about how you deal with diversity in ways that respect the need for common culture, shared culture, and individual integrity.

5. Above all else, care about and be an advocate for our linguistically and culturally diverse children and families by nurturing, celebrating, and challenging them. They do not need our pity or remorse for what they do not have; they, like any individual and family, require our respect and the use of what they bring as a resource.

References

August, D., & E. Garcia. 1988. *Language minority education in the United States: Research, policy and practice.* Chicago: Charles C. Thomas.

Baker, K.A. 1990. Bilingual education's 20-year failure to provide rights protection for language-minority students. In *Children at risk: Poverty, minority status and other issues in educational equity,* eds. A. Barona & E. Garcia, 29–52. Washington, DC: National Association of School Psychologists.

Baker, K.A., & A.A. deKanter. 1983. An answer from research on bilingual education. *American Education* 56: 157–69.

Bernstein, B. 1971. A sociolinguistic approach to socialization with some reference to educability. In *Class, codes and control: Theoretical studies towards a sociology of language,* ed. B. Bernstein, 146–71. London: Routledge & Kegan Paul.

California State Department of Education. 1992. *The program for infant/toddler caregivers: A guide to language development and communication.* Sacramento: Author.

Cardenas, J. 1986. The role of native-language instruction in bilingual education. *Phi Delta Kappan* 67: 359–63.

Chavez, L. 1991. *Out of the barrio: Toward a new politics of Hispanic assimilation.* New York: Basic.

Cole, R.W. 1995. *Educating everybody's children: What research and practice say about improving achievement.* Alexandria, VA: Association for Supervision and Curriculum Development.

Crawford, J. 1989. *Bilingual education: History, politics, theory, and practice.* Trenton, NJ: Crane.

Cummins, J. 1979. Linguistic independence and the educational development of biligual children. *Review of Educational Research* 19: 222–51,

Cummins, J. 1986. Empowering minority students: A framework for intervention. *Harvard Educational Review* 56 (I): 18–35.

de Leon Siantz, M. 1996. Profile of the Hispanic child. In *Hispanic voices: Hispanic health educators speak out,* ed. S. Torres, 134–49. New York: NLN Press.

Elam, S. 1972. Acculturation and learning problems of Puerto Rican children. In *The Puerto Rican community and its children on the mainland,* eds. F. Corradasco & E. Bucchini, 116–38. Metuchen, NJ: Scarecrow.

Fishman, J. 1989. Bias and anti-intellectualism: The frenzied fiction of "English only." In *Language and ethnicity in minority sociolinguistic perspective,* ed. Multilingual Matters, 214–37. London: Multilingual Matters.

Friere, P. 1970. *Pedagogy of the oppressed.* New York: Seabury.

Garcia, E. 1983. *Bilingualism in early childhood.* Albuquerque: University of New Mexico Press.

Garcia, E. 1991. *Education of linguistically and culturally diverse students: Effective instructional practices. Education Report #1.* Washington, DC: Center of Applied Linguistics and the National Center for Research on Cultural Diversity and Second Language Learning.

Garcia, E. 1993. Language, culture and education. In *Review of research in education,* ed. L. Darling-Hammond, 51–97. Washington, DC: American Educational Research Association.

Garcia, E. 1994. *Understanding and meeting the challenge of student diversity.* Boston: Houghton Mifflin.

Garcia, E. 1995. Educating Mexican American students: Past treatments and recent developments in theory, research, policy, and practice. In *Handbook of research on multicultural education,* eds. J. Banks & C.A. McGee Banks, 372–426. New York: Macmillan.

Garcia, E., & R. Gonzalez. 1995. Issues in systemic reform for culturally and linguistically diverse students. *College Record* 96 (3): 418–31.

Gonzalez, R. 1990. *Chicano education in the segregation era: 1915–1945.* Philadelphia: Balch Institute.

Hakuta, K., & L.J. Gould. 1987. Synthesis of research on bilingual education. *Educational Leadership* 44 (6): 39–45.

Heath, S.B. 1986. Sociocultural contexts of language development. In *Beyond language: Social and cultural factors in schooling language minority students,* ed. California Department of Education, 143–86. Los Angeles: Evaluation, Dissemination, and Assessment Center, California State University.

Kagan, S.L., & E. Garcia. 1991. Educating culturally and linguistically diverse preschoolers: moving the agenda. *Early Childhood Research Quarterly* 6: 427–43.

Krashen, S. 1996. *Under attack: The case against bilingual education.* Culver City, CA: Language Education Associates.

Levin, I. 1988. *Accelerated schools for at-risk students.* CPRE Research Report Series RR-010. New Brunswick, NJ: Rutgers University Center for Policy Research in Education.

McLaughlin, M.W., & L.A. Shepard. 1995. *Improving education through standard-based reform: A report by the national academy of education panel of standards-based education reform.* Stanford, CA: National Academy of Education.

Moll, L. 1991. *Funds of knowledge for change: Developing mediating connections between homes and classrooms.* Paper presented at the conference on "Literacy, Identity and Mind," University of Michigan, Ann Arbor.

NAEYC. 1996. NAEYC position statement: Responding to linguistic and cultural diversity—recommendations for effective early childhood education. *Young Children* 51 (2): 4–12.

National Center for Children in Poverty. 1995. *Welfare reform seen from a children's perspective.* New York: Columbia University School of Public Health.

NCTE/IRA (National Council of Teachers of English and International Reading Association). 1996. *Standards for the English language arts.* Urbana, IL: NCTE.

Ogbu, J. 1986. The consequences of the American caste system. In *The school achievement of minority children: New perspectives,* ed. U. Neisser, 73–114. Hillsdale, NJ: Erlbaum.

Phillips, D.A., & N.J. Cabrera. 1996. *Beyond the blueprint: Directions for research on Head Start's families.* Washington, DC: National Academy Press.

Ramirez, J.D., S.D. Yuen, D.R. Ramey, & D.J. Pasta. 1991. *Final Report: Longitudinal study of structured English immersion strategy, early-exit and late-exit transitional bilingual education programs for language-minority children.* San Mateo, CA: Aguirre International.

Rodriguez, R. 1982. *Hunger of memory.* New York: Bantam.

Rose, M. 1989 *Lives on the boundary.* New York: Free Press.

Rossell, C. 1992. Nothing matters? A critique of the Ramirez, et al. longitudinal study of instructional programs for language minority children. *Journal of the National Association for Bilingual Education* 16 (1–2): 159–86.

Rossell, C., & K. Baker. 1996. The education effectiveness of bilingual education. *Research in the Teaching of English* 30: 7–74.

Rossell, C., & J.M. Ross. 1986 *The social science evidence on bilingual education.* Boston: Boston University.

Spencer, D. 1988. Transitional bilingual education and the socialization of immigrants. *Harvard Educational Review* 58 (2): 133–53.

Tharp, R.G. 1989. *Challenging cultural minds.* London: Cambridge University Press.

Troike, R.C. 1981. Synthesis of research in bilingual education. *Educational Leadership* 38: 498–504.

Trueba, H.T. 1987. *Success or failure? Learning and the language minority student.* Scranton, PA: Harper & Row.

U.S. Department of Commerce. 1990. *The Hispanic population in the United States: March 1989.* Washington, DC: GPO.

Villaseñor, V. 1991. *Rain of gold.* New York: Delta.

Willig, A.C. 1985. A meta-analysis of selected studies on effectiveness of bilingual education. *Review of Educational Research* 55 (33): 269–317.

Wong Fillmore, L. 1991. When learning a second language means loosing a first. *Early Childhood Research Quarterly* 6 (3): 323–46.

Harvey Silver, Richard Strong,
and Matthew Perini

Integrating Learning Styles and Multiple Intelligences

What does it mean to express kinesthetic intelligence in an interpersonal way? Integrating styles and intelligences can help children learn in many ways—not just in the areas of their strengths.

*I*n the 20th century, two great theories have been put forward in an attempt to interpret human differences and to design educational models around these differences. Learning-style theory has its roots in the psychoanalytic community; multiple intelligences theory is the fruit of cognitive science and reflects an effort to rethink the theory of measurable intelligence embodied in intelligence testing.

Both, in fact, combine insights from biology, anthropology, psychology, medical case studies, and an examination of art and culture. But learning styles emphasize the different ways people think and feel as they solve problems, create products, and interact. The theory of multiple intelligences is an effort to understand how cultures and disciplines shape human potential. Though both theories claim that dominant ideologies of intelligence inhibit our understanding of human differences, learning styles are concerned with differences in the *process* of learning, whereas multiple intelligences center on the *content* and *products* of learning. Until now, neither theory has had much to do with the other.

Howard Gardner (1993) spells out the difference between the theories this way:

> In MI theory, I begin with a human organism that responds (or fails to respond) to different kinds of *contents* in the world. . . . Those who speak of learning styles are searching for approaches that ought to characterize *all* contents (p. 45).

We believe that the integration of learning styles and multiple intelligence theory may minimize their respective limitations and enhance their strengths, and we provide some practical suggestions for teachers to successfully integrate and apply learning styles and multiple intelligence theory in the classroom.

Learning Styles

Learning-style theory begins with Carl Jung (1927), who noted major differences in the way people perceived (sensation versus intuition), the way they made decisions (logical thinking versus imaginative feelings), and how active or reflective they were while interacting (extroversion versus introversion). Isabel Myers and Katherine Briggs (1977), who created the Myers-Briggs Type Indicator and founded the Association of Psychological Type, applied Jung's work and influenced a generation of researchers trying to understand specific differences in human learning. Key researchers in this area include Anthony Gregorc (1985), Kathleen Butler (1984), Bernice McCarthy (1982), and Harvey Silver and J. Robert Hanson (1995). Although learning-style theorists interpret the personality in various ways, nearly all models have two things in common:

■ *A focus on process.* Learning-style models tend to concern themselves with the process of learning: how individuals absorb information, think about information, and evaluate the results.

■ *An emphasis on personality.* Learning-style theorists generally believe that learning is the result of a personal, individualized act of thought and feeling.

Most learning-style theorists have settled on four basic styles. Our own model, for instance, describes the following four styles:

■ *The Mastery style learner* absorbs information concretely; processes information sequentially, in a step-by-step manner; and judges the value of learning in

From *Educational Leadership,* September 1997, pp. 22-27. © 1997 by the Association for Supervision and Curriculum Development. All rights reserved. Reprinted by permission.

terms of its clarity and practicality.

■ *The Understanding style learner* focuses more on ideas and abstractions; learns through a process of questioning, reasoning, and testing; and evaluates learning by standards of logic and the use of evidence.

■ *The Self-Expressive style learner* looks for images implied in learning; uses feelings and emotions to construct new ideas and products; and judges the learning process according to its originality, aesthetics, and capacity to surprise or delight.

■ *The Interpersonal style learner,*[1] like the Mastery learner, focuses on concrete, palpable information; prefers to learn socially; and judges learning in terms of its potential use in helping others.

Learning styles are not fixed throughout life, but develop as a person learns and grows. Our approximate breakdown of the percentages of people with strengths in each style is as follows: Mastery, 35 percent; Understanding, 18 percent; Self-Expressive, 12 percent; and Interpersonal, 35 percent (Silver and Strong 1997).

Most learning-style advocates would agree that all individuals develop and practice a mixture of styles as they live and learn. Most people's styles flex and adapt to various contexts, though to differing degrees. In fact, most people seek a sense of wholeness by practicing all four styles to some degree. Educators should help students discover their unique profiles, as well as a balance of styles.

Strengths and Limitations of a Learning-Style Model

The following are some *strengths* of learning-style models:

■ They tend to focus on how different individuals process information across many content areas.

■ They recognize the role of cognitive and affective processes in learning and, therefore, can significantly deepen our insights into issues related to motivation.

■ They tend to emphasize thought as a vital component of learning, thereby avoiding reliance on basic and lower-level learning activities.

Learning-styles models have a couple

Multiple intelligence theory is concerned with differences in the *content* of learning, whereas learning-styles theory centers on the *process* and *products* of learning.

of limitations. First, they may fail to recognize how styles vary in different content areas and disciplines.

Second, these models are sometimes less sensitive than they should be to the effects of context on learning. Emerging from a tradition that viewed style as relatively permanent, many learning-style advocates advised altering learning environments to match or challenge a learner's style. Either way, learning-style models have largely left unanswered the question of how context and purpose affect learning.

Multiple Intelligence Theory

Fourteen years after the publication of *Frames of Mind* (Gardner 1983), the clarity and comprehensiveness of Howard Gardner's design continue to dazzle the educational community. Who could have expected that a reconsideration of the word *intelligence* would profoundly affect the way we see ourselves and our students?

Gardner describes seven intelligences: linguistic, logical-mathematical, spatial, musical, bodily-kinesthetic, interpersonal, and intrapersonal.[2] The distinctions among these intelligences are supported by studies in child development, cognitive skills under conditions of brain damage, psychometrics, changes in cognition across history and within different cultures, and psychological transfer and generalization.

Thus, Gardner's model is backed by a rich research base that combines physiology, anthropology, and personal and cultural history. This theoretical depth is sadly lacking in most learning-style models. Moreover, Gardner's seven intelligences are not abstract concepts, but are recognizable through common life experiences. We all intuitively under-

stand the difference between musical and linguistic, or spatial and mathematical intelligences, for example. We all show different levels of aptitude in various content areas. In all cases, we know that no individual is universally intelligent; certain fields of knowledge engage or elude everyone. Gardner has taken this intuitive knowledge of human experience and shown us in a lucid, persuasive, and well-researched manner how it is true.

Yet, there are two gaps in multiple intelligence theory that limit its application to learning. First, the theory has grown out of cognitive science—a discipline that has not yet asked itself why we have a field called cognitive science but not one called affective science. Learning-style theory, on the other hand, has deep roots in psychoanalysis. Learning-style theorists, therefore, give psychological *affect* and individual personality central roles in understanding differences in learning.

Multiple intelligence theory looks where style does not: It focuses on the content of learning and its relation to the disciplines. Such a focus, however, means that it does not deal with the individualized process of learning. This is the second limitation of multiple intelligence theory, and it becomes clear if we consider variations within a particular intelligence.

Are conductors, performers, composers, and musical critics all using the same musical intelligence? What of the differing linguistic intelligences of a master of free verse like William Carlos Williams and a giant of literary criticism like Harold Bloom? How similar are the bodily-kinesthetic intelligences of dancers Martha Graham and Gene Kelly or football players Emmitt Smith and golfer Tiger Woods? How

Learning styles are not fixed throughout life, but develop as a person learns and grows.

can we explain the difference in the spatial intelligences of Picasso and Monet—both masters of modern art?

Most of us would likely agree that different types of intelligence are at work in these individuals. Perhaps one day, Gardner's work on the "jagged profile" of combined intelligences or, perhaps, his insistence on the importance of context will produce a new understanding of intelligence. But at the moment, Gardner's work does not provide adequate guidelines for dealing with these distinctions. Most of us, however, already have a way of explaining individual differences between Monet and Picasso, Martha Graham and Gene Kelly, or between different students in our classrooms: We refer to these individuals as having distinct *styles*.

Of course, as Gardner would insist, radically different histories and contexts go a long way in explaining distinctions between Monet and Picasso, for example. But how are teachers to respond to this explanation? As all teachers know, we must ultimately consider differences at the individual level. Learning styles, with their emphasis on differences in individual thought and feeling, are the tools we need to describe and teach to these differences.

Best of all, learning styles' emphasis on the individual learning process and Gardner's content-oriented model of multiple intelligences are surprisingly complementary. Without multiple intelligence theory, style is rather abstract, and it generally undervalues context. Without learning styles, multiple intelligence theory proves unable to describe different processes of thought and feeling. Each theory responds to the weaknesses of the other; together, they form an integrated picture of intelligence and difference.

Integrating Learning Styles and Multiple Intelligences

In integrating these major theories of knowledge, we moved through three steps. First, we attempted to describe, for each of Gardner's intelligences, a set of four learning processes or abilities, one for each of the four learning styles. For linguistic intelligence, for example, the *Mastery* style represents the ability to use language to describe events and sequence activities; the *Interpersonal* style, the ability to use language to build trust and rapport; the *Understanding* style, the ability to develop logical arguments and use rhetoric; and the *Self-expressive* style,

the ability to use metaphoric and expressive language.

Next, we listed samples of vocations that people are likely to choose, given particular intelligence and learning-style profiles. Working in this way, we devised a model that linked the process-centered approach of learning styles and the content and product-driven multiple intelligence theory.

Figure 2 shows how you might construct a classroom display of information about intelligences, styles, and possible vocations. Consider kinesthetic intelligence and the difference between a Tiger Woods and a Gene Kelly: People who excel in this intelligence, with an *Understanding* style, might be professional athletes (like Tiger Woods), dance critics, or sports analysts; people with a *Self-expressive* style might be sculptors, choreographers, dancers (like Gene Kelly), actors, mimes, or puppeteers.

The following outline shows how we categorized abilities and sample voca-

We all intuitively understand the difference between musical and linguistic, or spatial and mathematical intelligences.

FIGURE 1

Sample "Kinesthetic" Vocations by Style

Mastery	Interpersonal
The ability to use the body and tools to take effective action or to construct or repair *Mechanic, Trainer, Contractor, Craftsperson, Tool and Dye Maker*	The ability to use the body to build rapport, to console or persuade, and to support others *Coach, Counselor, Salesperson, Trainer*

Kinesthetic

Understanding	Self-Expressive
The ability to plan strategically or to critique the actions of the body *Physical Educator, Sports Analyst, Professional Athlete, Dance Critic*	The ability to appreciate the aesthetics of the body and to use those values to create new forms of expression *Sculptor, Choreographer, Actor, Dancer, Mime, Puppeteer*

tions for the seven intelligences, by learning style:

Linguistic

Mastery: The ability to use language to describe events and sequence activities (*journalist, technical writer, administrator, contractor*)

Interpersonal: The ability to use language to build trust and rapport (*salesperson, counselor, clergyperson, therapist*)

Understanding: The ability to develop logical arguments and use rhetoric (*lawyer, professor, orator, philosopher*)

Self-expressive: The ability to use metaphoric and expressive language (*playwright, poet, advertising copywriter, novelist*)

Logical-Mathematical:

Mastery: The ability to use numbers to compute, describe, and document (*accountant, bookkeeper, statistician*)

Interpersonal: The ability to apply mathematics in personal and daily life (*tradesperson, homemaker*)

Understanding: The ability to use mathematical concepts to make conjectures, establish proofs, and apply mathematics and data to construct arguments (*logician, computer programmer, scientist, quantitative problem solver*)

Self-expressive: The ability to be sensitive to the patterns, symmetry, logic, and aesthetics of mathematics and to solve problems in design and modeling (*composer, engineer, inventor, designer, qualitative problem solver*)

Spatial

Mastery: The ability to perceive and represent the visual-spatial world accurately (*illustrator, artist, guide, photographer*)

Interpersonal: The ability to arrange color, line, shape, form, and space to meet the needs of others (*interior decorator, painter, clothing designer, weaver, builder*)

Understanding: The ability to interpret and graphically represent visual or spatial ideas (*architect, iconographer, computer graphics designer, art critic*)

Self-expressive: The ability to transform visual or spatial ideas into imagina-

tive and expressive creations (*artist, inventor, model builder, cinematographer*)

Bodily-Kinesthetic

Mastery: The ability to use the body and tools to take effective action or to construct or repair (*mechanic, trainer, contractor, craftsperson, tool and dye maker*)

Interpersonal: The ability to use the body to build rapport, to console and persuade, and to support others (*coach, counselor, salesperson, trainer*)

Understanding: The ability to plan strategically or to critique the actions of the body (*physical educator, sports analyst, professional athlete, dance critic*)

Self-expressive: The ability to appreciate the aesthetics of the body and to use those values to create new forms of expression (*sculptor, choreographer, actor, dancer, mime, puppeteer*)

Musical

Mastery: The ability to understand and develop musical technique (*technician, music teacher, instrument maker*)

Interpersonal: The ability to respond emotionally to music and to work together to use music to meet the needs of others (*choral, band, and orchestral performer or conductor; public relations director in music*)

Understanding: The ability to interpret musical forms and ideas (*music critic, aficionado, music collector*)

Self-expressive: The ability to create imaginative and expressive performances and compositions (*composer, conductor, individual/small-group performer*)

Interpersonal

Mastery: The ability to organize people and to communicate clearly

what needs to be done (*administrator, manager, politician*)

Interpersonal: The ability to use empathy to help others and to solve problems (*social worker, doctor, nurse, therapist, teacher*)

Understanding: The ability to discriminate and interpret among different kinds of interpersonal clues (*sociologist, psychologist, psychotherapist, professor of psychology or sociology*)

Self-expressive: The ability to influence and inspire others to work toward

---

How similar are the kinesthetic intelligences of Martha Graham and Gene Kelly, or Emmitt Smith and Tiger Woods?

FIGURE 2

Student Choice: Assessment Products by Intelligence and Style

LINGUISTIC
Mastery
- Write an article
- Put together a magazine
- Develop a plan
- Develop a newscast
- Describe a complex procedure/object

Interpersonal
- Write a letter
- Make a pitch
- Conduct an interview
- Counsel a fictional character or a friend

Understanding
- Make a case
- Make/defend a decision
- Advance a theory
- Interpret a text
- Explain an artifact

Self-Expressive
- Write a play
- Develop a plan to direct
- Spin a tale
- Develop an advertising campaign

a common goal (*consultant, charismatic leader, politician, evangelist*)

Intrapersonal

Mastery: The ability to assess one's own strengths, weaknesses, talents, and interests and use them to set goals (*planner, small business owner*)

Interpersonal: The ability to use understanding of oneself to be of service to others (*counselor, social worker*)

Understanding: The ability to form and develop concepts and theories based on an examination of oneself (*psychologist*)

Self-expressive: The ability to reflect on one's inner moods, intuitions, and temperament and to use them to create or express a personal vision (*artist, religious leader, writer*)

As the final step in constructing the intelligence-learning style menus, we collected descriptions of products that a person with strengths in each intelligence and style might create. For example, in the linguistic intelligence domain, a person with the *Mastery* style might write an article, put a magazine together, develop a newscast, or describe a complex procedure. By contrast, a person with a *Self-expressive* style might write a play, spin a tale, or develop an advertising campaign (see fig. 2). In the kinesthetic intelligence domain, a person with an *Understanding* style might choreograph a concept or teach a physical education concept; a person with a *Self-expressive* style might create a diorama or act out emotional states or concepts. A class display of such lists might accompany charts like the sample shown in Figure 2.

How to Use the Integrated Intelligence Menus

Several years ago, Grant Wiggins reminded us that we can't teach every-thing. It is also quite obvious that we can't use every teaching method nor every form of assessment. Here are some ways to use the Integrated Intelligence Menus—particularly for performance assessment—without trying to do everything at once.

1. Use the menus as a compass. Keep a running record of the styles and intelligences you use regularly and of those you avoid. When a particular form of assessment doesn't work, offer the student another choice from another part of the menu.

2. Focus on one intelligence at a time. Offer your students a choice in one of the four styles, or urge them to do two assessments: one from a style they like and one from a style they would normally avoid.

3. Build on student interest. When students conduct research, either individually or in groups, show them the menus and allow them to choose the product or approach that appeals to them. They should choose the best product for communicating their understanding of the topic or text. Students thus discover not only the meaning of quality, but also something about the nature of their own interests, concerns, styles, and intelligences.

In developing assessments, teachers must devise their own standards and expectations. But we can judge the model itself by two powerful standards:

■ Does it help us develop every student's capacity to learn what we believe all students need to know?

■ Does it help each student discover and develop his or her unique abilities and interests?

In conjunction, both multiple intelligences and learning styles can work together to form a powerful and integrated model of human intelligence and learning—a model that respects and celebrates diversity and provides us with the tools to meet high standards.

[1]The term *interpersonal style* overlaps with Gardner's *interpersonal intelligence*. In Gardner's model, interpersonal intelligence is a category related to the content and products of knowledge. In our learning-style model, the interpersonal style refers to a way of processing knowledge.

[2]Gardner has recently introduced an eighth intelligence—*naturalist*. Although our integrated intelligence menus can easily accommodate this new category, we have chosen to work only with the classic seven intelligences.

References

Briggs, K.C., and I.B. Myers. (1977). *Myers-Briggs Type Indicator*. Palo Alto, Calif.: Consulting Psychologists Press.

Butler, K. (1984). *Learning and Teaching Style in Theory and Practice*. Columbia, Conn.: The Learner's Dimension.

Gardner, H. (1983). *Frames of Mind: The Theory of Multiple Intelligences*. New York: Basic Books.

Gardner, H. (1993). *Multiple Intelligences: The Theory in Practice*. New York: Basic Books.

Gregorc, A. (1985). *Inside Styles: Beyond the Basics*. Maynard, Mass.: Gabriel Systems, Inc.

Jung, C. (1927). *The Theory of Psychological Type*. Princeton, N.J.: Princeton University Press.

McCarthy, B. (1982). *The 4Mat System*. Arlington Heights, Ill.: Excel Publishing Co.

Silver, H.F., and J.R. Hanson. (1995). *Learning Styles and Strategies*. Woodbridge, N.J.: The Thoughtful Education Press.

Silver, H.F., and R.W. Strong. (1997). *Monographs for Learning Style Models and Profiles*. (Unpublished research).

Harvey Silver is President, **Richard Strong** is Vice President, and **Matthew Perini** is Director of Publishing at Silver Strong & Associates, Inc., Aspen Corporate Park, 1480 Route 9 North, Woodbridge, NJ 07095 (e-mail: silver_strong @msn.com).

Care and
Educational Practices

Educational practices with young children seem to be always changing, yet always the same. The notion of what is good practice in early childhood education seems to vary between two extremes. One approach is traditional, with an emphasis on skill and drill methods, segmented curriculum, and accuracy in work. The other approach, which includes curricular integration and an emphasis on play, is more constructive. These two approaches coexist in early childhood but are based in very different philosophies of how teaching and learning occur. So the dilemma is to determine which educational practice is most appropriate for children. Good practice can be found nationwide in very few countries. One place is Denmark, where the government and parents share responsibility for a comprehensive system of exceptionally high-quality child care. Valerie Polakow describes this unique public child-care model in her article, "Who Cares for the Children? Denmark's Unique Public Child-Care Model."

How does a person recognize good practice in a child care program or primary grade classroom? Basically, look for action in the learning environment. Children are busy constructing with blocks, working puzzles, and creating with multimedia. They invent, cook, and compose throughout the day. When children are interested and begin to experiment in the learning environment, they develop understanding. This process of active learning is described by Christine Chaillé and Steven Silvern in their article, "Understanding through Play."

Good practice is teachers in action. Teachers are busy holding conversations, guiding activities, and questioning children. They observe, draw conclusions, plan, and monitor the activities throughout the day. Learning how to teach well means knowing the children well. In "Nurturing Kids: Seven Ways of Being Smart," Kristen Nelson urges teachers to reinvent the curriculum by focusing on the children's wide range of learning styles. She emphasizes that teachers, like children, learn appropriate practice through doing—in this case, planning to foster multiple intelligences.

Good practice means teaching children, not curriculum. In their articles, Suzanne Winter, Kristyn Sheldon, and Jane Russell-Fox tackle ways to individualize teaching for children with special needs. A vital element of early childhood classroom work is to use a process approach to learning, with plenty of opportunities for open-ended projects based on integrated curriculum. To accomplish this approach, the teacher takes on the role of learning facilitator. Such a flexible role allows all children to engage in planning and carrying out their learning activities. Children with special needs can have a voice in their curriculum when teachers understand the basics of adaptation in the classroom.

This unit includes Ellen Booth Church's insightful "Your Learning Environment: A Look Back at Your Year." She recommends taking time to ask specific in-depth questions at the end of the year. This is a valuable way to get

an accurate evaluation of the entire learning environment. From the answers to questions about the centers and activities of the program, planning begins for the next year.

Good practice, appropriate for children's development and based on active play, has no shortcuts and cannot be trivialized. It takes careful thought and planning, using the latest knowledge of early childhood education, to make curriculum and practice choices. By working out specifics of routines and procedures, curriculum, and assessment suitable for young children, the early childhood professional strengthens skills in decision making. These are crucial tasks for a teacher interested in developmentally appropriate practice.

Looking Ahead: Challenge Questions

What countries provide high quality child care for all children, subsidized by the government?

Comment on the idea that there are multiple ways of being intelligent.

Analyze the ramifications of this statement: It's not what I as teacher *cover* that is important, it's what students *discover*.

What does inclusion mean?

What steps should educators take when labeling a young child for special education services?

Brainstorm three activities in a preschool classroom for children with limited motor abilities.

It may cause anxiety, but day care can benefit kids

Day care has small but significant effects on both cognitive development and the mother-child relationship, new research shows.

By Beth Azar
Monitor staff

High-quality day care may be good for a child's cognitive development, according to several new studies. In fact, some new research implies that children who spend their early years in center-based care perform better on tests of language and mathematics than children who stay home with their mothers.

Such studies are beginning to answer questions that have plagued parents since women started working outside the home: Does the amount of time spent in child care or the quality of child care affect a child's development?

Psychologists have tried to design studies to measure the effect of day care above and beyond other factors known to affect development, including a child's innate predispositions, aspects of parental care and socioeconomic status.

Although mounting evidence suggests that day care has had far less of an impact on child development than these factors, there also seem to be small but significant effects of day care on both cognitive development and the mother-child relationship.

© 1993 Ron Chapple/FPG.

A stimulating, interactive day-care setting can lead to good language and cognitive development.

The biggest and best designed study to date, funded by the National Institute on Child Health and Human Development (NICHD), released findings in April showing that:

• Children in high-quality day care—care that provides a stimulating environment—do as well on cognitive and language tests as children who stay home with their mothers, regardless of how many hours a day they spend in such care.

• Mothers are slightly more affectionate and attentive to their children the less time their children spend in day care.

• Mothers are slightly more affectionate and attentive to their children the higher quality the day care setting.

The study was conducted by a team of 29 researchers—mostly psy-

From APA Monitor, June 1997, p. 13. © 1997 by the American Psychological Association. Reprinted by permission.

chologists—who are funded by a 7-year grant from NICHD. They have been following 1,300 families and their children from 10 sites since 1991, beginning when the children were one month old. The results on cognitive development and mother-child interaction are from data collected when the children were 15 months, 24 months and 36 months old.

Stimulating conversation

The quality of the interaction between day-care providers and the children in their care is the most important aspect of day care for fostering children's cognitive skills, reported the NICHD researchers at the annual meeting of the Society for Research on Child Development in April.

Children whose care-givers asked them questions, engaged them in conversation and responded to them when they spoke, scored highest on measures of cognitive and language ability. These child-care variables contributed between 1.3 percent and 3.6 percent of the variance in cognitive and language development—a rather small, but significant effect, said Sarah Friedman, PhD, NICHD coordinator of the study and one of its investigators.

Another recent study conducted in Sweden found that children in center-based child care scored significantly higher on tests of language skill and math proficiency than children cared for by their mothers or in family-based day care.

The study, conducted by Swedish researchers Anders Broberg, PhD, and Philip Hwang, PhD, of Göteborgs University, and NICHD researchers Holger Wessels, PhD, and Michael Lamb, PhD, followed 146 children from age 16 months to age 8. The researchers regularly measured the quality of home and out-of-home care, child temperament and verbal abilities during the preschool years. And they measured cognitive ability when the children were in second grade.

As in the NICHD study, the researchers found that children who had more interaction with their caregivers scored better on tests of verbal ability.

The best predictor of mathematical ability were aspects of care such as small day-care groups, a small ratio of children to caregivers and a narrow range of ages within the child-care group.

The bottom line is that "child care *per se* is not placing children at a disadvantage," said Friedman. "And those are wonderful results."

Relationships with mom

Based on results released last year, the NICHD study concluded that child care did not damage the security of children's attachment to their mothers at age 15 months, provided the children received relatively sensitive care from their mothers. In the most recent analysis, the study found a small link between the amount of time children spend in day care and how affectionate and attentive their mothers were when the children were age 3.

In particular, mothers were slightly less attentive, less responsive and less positively affectionate with their children, the more time their children spent in out-of-home care when they were very young, said University of Virginia psychologist Robert Pianta, PhD, one of the study investigators. But of all the possible predictors of the mother-child relationship, day care only accounted for about 1 percent, he added.

As for quality of day care, the more positive the relationship between children and their day-care providers, the more involved and sensitive mothers were to their children.

"Both quantity and quality of child care has a significant but small effect on maternal attachment," said Pianta.

One flaw in the NICHD study is the fact that the researchers did not systematically measure the quality of home-based care for children who received full-time care from their mothers, said Pianta. So there is no way to compare low-quality mother care with high-quality mother care or low-quality out-of-home care.

The researchers did, however, look to see if high-quality care could act as a buffer for children at high risk of

poor development because of home factors such as poverty or mothers' depressive symptoms. For example, they looked to see if poor children in high-quality care had a better relationship with their mothers than poor children in low-quality care.

"We found slim to no buffer effects of high quality care for these children," said Pianta.

They also found that low-quality care did not put high-risk children at significantly more risk than high-risk children in high-quality care, he said. The NICHD research group is conducting the same types of analyses for cognitive and language development, said Friedman.

In an analysis from the study now in press, the researchers found that at age 15 months, poor children in home-based day care received lower quality care than children from more affluent homes who were in home-based day care. However, of the children in child-care centers, those from the most affluent and the poorest homes received higher-quality care than children from homes just above the poverty level. This implies that government day-care subsidies provide a safety net for the poorest families while the near-poor must settle for less-expensive, lower quality care, said the researchers.

The next phase of the study will look at how training and experience of day-care providers affect child development, said Pianta. And they still have several years worth of data to analyze before they make any final conclusions about the long-term effect of child care on children.

More complex analyses will be welcome, said Harvard University psychologist Jerome Kag[a]n, PhD. This kind of research has therapeutic value for parents who are worried about how child care influences their children.

But it also highlights the need for more research on the complex interactions between social class, temperament and quality of care and the impact of those interactions on a child's behavior, anxiety level, and language and cognitive abilities, he added.

Infants and Toddlers

Meeting Basic Needs: Health and Safety Practices in Feeding and Diapering Infants

Janis Warrick[1,3] **and Mary Kay Helling**[2]

INTRODUCTION

The number of infants in group care settings continues to increase. According to the National Child Care Staffing Study (1989), 14% of the children in child care centers in 1977 were infants and toddlers, 2 years old or younger. By 1988, this increased dramatically to 30%. Along with the increase in center care, nearly 60% of the infants in out-of-home care are in family child care homes, while 40% are in centers (Committee for Economic Development, 1993).

Providing high quality care for infants is one of the priority areas in early childhood education. A key component of quality child care for children generally and infants in particular is attending to their basic needs for a healthy and safe environment. Based on findings from a four-state study, the quality of infant care was judged to be poor to mediocre. Almost half of the infants in the study were in rooms that were rated as having less than minimal quality (Helbrun *et al.*, 1995). What this means for infants is that they may not be in environments that meet their needs for health and safety. As reported in the study, infants in the poor quality centers are more susceptible to illness due to lack of sanitary conditions and are in danger due to lack of safe environments.

Child care providers and educators may at times wonder about the appropriateness of the routine procedures used in meeting the basic needs of infants within their programs. Information about health and safety changes rapidly in response to new research findings and suggestions for best practices.

Moreover, informal observations of students in pre-service programs as well as of providers in the field point out the need, in some cases, for opportunities to build on the knowledge base of infant basic care. Results from an exploratory survey of childcare providers and pre-service early childhood professionals also pointed out the need for better dissemination of information about infant basic care. For example, only 35.5% of the 170 students and caregivers who responded to the Infant Care Survey indicated they would wash a baby's hands after diapering (Warrick, 1994). At times, babies may touch their genitals or other areas within the diapering space; therefore it is important to wash their hands.

As this example illustrates, proper procedures for infant basic care may not be common knowledge among early childhood personnel. Also, the procedures used may work well from an efficiency standpoint, yet not be recommended from a health and safety perspective.

It is generally assumed that individuals learn these skills from their personal experiences in caring for children or from observing others caring for children. At times, a person may perform daily routines within the child care and education context without much thought. But the practices observed in the field are not always the ones necessary or recommended for maintaining a safe and healthy environment.

The purpose of this article is to encourage those who are responsible for the care and education of young children to periodically reassess the procedures used when involved in the daily routines of caring for infant basic needs. Basic needs include: diapering, sanitation, safety, feeding, handling infants, and caring for children not feeling well. This article provides an overview of two of the most basic care areas—diapering and feeding.

HEALTHY AND SAFE FEEDING PRACTICES

Feeding practices which are healthy and safe is a key element in providing quality care for infants. Recommendations for best practices in feeding infants are included in this section.

It is not necessary to heat formula but many care-

---

[1]Lake Area Technical Institute, Watertown, South Dakota.

[2]South Dakota State University, Brookings, South Dakota.

[3]Correspondence should be directed to Jan Warrick, Box 730, Lake Area Technical Institute, Watertown, South Dakota 57201.

From *Early Childhood Education Journal*, Vol. 24, No. 3, 1997, pp. 195-199. © 1997 by Human Sciences Press, Inc. Reprinted by permission.

givers prefer to do so. It is also likely that a microwave will be used to heat the formula. Because of this, it is important to follow the protocol developed by Sigman-Grant, Bush, and Anantheswaran (1992):

Prior to Heating:

1. Heat only bottles containing 4 oz. or more without the nipples.
2. Heat only refrigerated formula.
3. Always stand the bottle up.
4. Always leave bottle top uncovered to allow heat to escape.

Heating Instructions (with microwave set on full power).

1. 4 oz bottles: Heat for no more than 30 seconds.
2. 8 oz bottles: Heat for no more than 45 seconds.

Serving instructions

1. Always replace nipple assembly: then invert ten times (vigorous shaking is unnecessary).
2. Formula should be cool to the touch; formula warm to the touch may be too hot to serve.
3. Always test formula; place several drops on tongue or on top of the hand (not the inside wrist) (p. 414).

When heating formula in the microwave avoid using glass bottles because they absorb microwave energy, whereas plastic bottles do not (Sigman-Grant *et al.*, 1992).

Discard any formula or breast milk left in the bottle and not consumed by the baby during each feeding (Deitch, 1987). Do not be tempted to save and reheat the milk again for a later feeding. This is because germs or salivary enzymes may mix in from the baby's sucking according to Dr. Madeleine Rose, Assistant Professor, Nutrition and Food Science Department, South Dakota State University (personal communication, June 8, 1994).

Avoid feeding an infant directly out of the jar of commercially prepared baby food if the remaining contents will be fed to the baby at another time or to another child. Cover the remaining contents and label with the baby's name and date. Store the jar in the refrigerator and discard the contents if not used within 36 hours (Deitch, 1987).

To further assure safe handling of infant foods (Deitch, 1987; Martin & Lewis, 1994):

1. Require parents who bring their infant's food into your home or center to only bring unopened containers. Ready to serve formula should be in unopened containers as well.
2. Wash your hands with soap and water before preparing baby's formula and bottles to prevent infection.
3. Use bottles, caps, and nipples that have been washed in clean water and dishwashing detergent, or in the dishwasher. If you wash them by hand, use a bottle brush. Squeeze water through nipple holes to make sure they are open. Rinse well and let them stand in a rack to dry. Disinfect the rack frequently.
4. With canned formula, clean the top of the can with soap and water. Rinse. Use a clean punch-type can opener to open.
5. Use only fresh water from the tap or distilled water if you are mixing a concentrate or powder formula. If you use well water rather than water from a community water supply, have it tested before using it for an infant. High nitrate levels could harm the baby. Boiling the well water does not assure its safety.
6. Store prepared formula, tightly covered, in the refrigerator for no more than 48 hours after opening. Refrigerate formula you prepare from powder and use within 24 hours. Tightly cover the remaining powder. Store in a cool, dry place and use within 1 month. Label and date each bottle.
7. Discard any formula or milk left in an infant's bottle or cup after each feeding. Once the baby nurses from a bottle, microorganisms from the baby's mouth are introduced into the formula. Neither refrigeration nor reheating the milk will prevent microorganisms from growing.
8. You may safely keep breast milk in the refrigerator for 24–48 hours or keep frozen for several months. Do not defrost the milk until just before you intend to use it. At this time, remove the container from the freezer and run under cold water, then warmer water. Shake the contents gently. Set the container of milk in a pan of water until the milk reaches room temperature.

Because formula, milk, juices, and sweetened drinks (soda, Kool-Aid, Hi-C, Hawaiian Punch, Tang, etc.) contain sugar, infants should not be given these liquids when they are laid down to sleep. Existing or erupting teeth may decay creating a condition known as nursing bottle syndrome. This especially affects the front teeth, leading to an early loss of these teeth. Because of this, the child may not be able to chew food properly and the permanent teeth may be crowded as a result (Kendrick *et al.*, 1991). Dr. Robert A. Arnold, orthodontist (personal communication, May 19, 1994) explains that the primary teeth maintain space for the developing permanent teeth. An infant's permanent teeth begin developing on the average at age 6 months and take 4–6 years to develop. If the primary teeth are lost, so is the arch length needed for the permanent teeth.

Always try to have the child drink his/her bottle before lying down in bed. Children who drink their bottles lying down are prone to ear infections because the fluid may drain into the ear. If an infant wants to take a bottle to bed, fill it with plain water (Kendrick *et al.*, 1991). Explain this possible harm so the infant's parents will understand the importance for the baby to not drink while lying down.

Because an infant's digestive system and the skills for self-feeding and swallowing are not well-developed, experts recommend infants be 4- to 6- months-old before semisolid foods (for example, rice cereal) are introduced. Add vegetables and fruit between 6 and 8 months of age. At about 8 or 9 months, offer food that is lumpy or cut into one-quarter inch cubes. This would include table food that the infant can easily chew, mash, or swallow whole. By the time the child is 1 year old, most of their food should be table food (Kendrick *et al.*, 1991). Continue giving the infant breast milk or formula up to age one (Frankie & Owen, 1993). Neither whole milk nor skim milk is suitable for the first year (Robinson, Lawler, Chenoweth, & Garwick,1990).

Some things to remember (Kendrick *et al.*, 1991):

1. Offer the baby water from a cup between meals, beginning at about 6 months of age when the baby is eating solid foods.
2. Avoid infant cereals that are premixed with formula, fruit, or honey. Dr. Madeleine Rose (personal communication, June 29, 1994) recommends starting with rice cereal because it does not cause as many allergies as wheat.
3. Use a baby-sized spoon to feed baby.
4. A baby's bottle is for water, formula, or diluted (one part juice to one part water) 100% juice only. Dr. Madeleine Rose (personal communication, June 29, 1994) says that very young infants (less than 6 months of age) do not need water. They get enough from the breast milk or formula. If they get too much water or juice, they may not get enough protein, calories, vitamins, and minerals that the milk provides.
5. Add one new food at a time. Wait 3–5 days before introducing another one. This will give the baby time to get used to the new food and to identify if the baby has an allergic reaction to it.
6. Sugar, salt, and butter should not be added to baby's food.
7. The best foods are: plain fruits, plain vegetables, plain meats, eggs (only 2–3 per week and after the child is 10 months of age), 100% fruit juice, unsalted crackers, rice, noodles, spaghetti, whole-wheat bread, hot or cold unsweetened cereals, plain yogurt, cottage cheese, and water.
8. Foods to avoid are: mixed dinners, bacon, luncheon meats, hot dogs, ham, creamed vegetables, corn, fruit desserts, puddings, cookies, candy, cakes, nuts, popcorn, whole grapes, and sweetened drinks. Food objects such as hot dogs, candies, nuts, and grapes pose a threat for death by choking (Ryan, Yacoub, Paton, & Avard, 1990). Other listed foods contain high amounts of sugar or fat.
9. Continue giving whole milk until the child is 2 years old. Infants need the nutrients and calories whole milk provides. Skim and low fat milk contain too few calories and too much protein.
10. Every baby is different. Encourage parents to consult their physicians for advice.

Parents may also choose to consult a dietitian, community health nurse, physician's assistant, or other professional for advice.

HEALTHY AND SAFE DIAPERING PROCEDURES

Anyone who cares for infants knows that the need to change diapers may seem like an endless yet necessary task. Caregivers are encouraged to give careful thought to the diapering routine to prevent the spread of illnesses and diseases.

For many, the floor seems like a likely place for safe diapering, but is not recommended due to the possibility of spreading infectious diseases. The preferred surface is at least 3 feet above the floor (Kendrick, Kaufmann, & Messenger, 1991).

Diapering needs to be done on a surface used only to change diapers. This surface should be as far away from any food-handling area as possible. Running water needs to be nearby, preferably within arm's reach (Kendrick *et al.*, 1991). Other children should not be in the diaper-changing area (American Academy of Pediatrics and American Public Health Association, 1992). Never leave the child, even for a second. Always keep one hand on the baby even if using a strap on the changing table (Kendrick *et al.*, 1991).

Cover fecal material by folding the soiled diaper inward (Yamauchi, 1991). Keep diapers in containers separate from other waste receptacles. Locate such containers near the diaper changing area. Line waste containers with plastic garbage bags and cover with a tight-fitting lid. Keep soiled clothing in a separate plastic bag. Frequently clean containers to prevent odors and the spread of disease (American Academy of Pediatrics and American Public Health Association, 1992). Empty diaper disposal containers at least daily, more often as needed (Kendrick *et al.*, 1991).

When using cloth diapers, store clean diapers away from the area where soiled diapers are kept. Doing so prevents contamination (Yamauchi, 1991). Put the soiled diaper and/or soiled training pants into a labeled, sealed bag. Fecal contents of diapers can be emptied into the toilet. It is recommended to not rinse diapers in the toilet due to possible contamination of the toilet area for the next use (American Academy of Pediatrics and American Public Health Association, 1992). Store the bag out of children's reach. Send it home with the parent for proper laundering (Kendrick *et al.*, 1991).

Caregivers may often give the baby something to play with to occupy the child during the diapering routine. Whatever the toy, disinfect it before using it again. Avoid giving a bottle of lotion or a container with talcum powder. These substances are dangerous to swallow or inhale, and an infant mouthing the container might eat some of the contents (Kendrick *et al.*, 1991). Discourage routine use of talcum powder since the powder can cause severe respiratory problems (Pairaudeau, Wilson, Hall, & Milne, 1991).

Research indicates that when children wear clothing over diapers, there is a significant decrease in the likelihood of contamination (Van, Morrow, Reves, & Pickering, 1992). Therefore, make sure that you require parents to send extra changes of clothing for added protection. During summer months make sure that infants wear shorts over their diapers. Children also need to wear clothing over training pants as well.

In sum, the Centers for Disease Control (1984, pp. 10-11) recommends the following steps when changing diapers:

1. Check to make sure you have supplies ready.
2. Place roll paper or disposable towel on the part of the changing area where the infant's bottom will be.
3. Hold the infant away from your body as you carry them to the changing area. Lay the baby on the paper or towel.
4. Remove diaper. Put the diaper in a plastic bag or plastic-lined waste receptacle.
5. Clean the baby's bottom with a premoistened towelette or dampened paper towel. Dispose of the towelette in the same container as the soiled disposable diaper.
6. Remove the paper or towel from under the infant and dispose of it in the same way as the diaper.
7. Wipe your hands with a fresh premoistened towelette or a damp paper towel and dispose of it in the plastic bag or receptacle with the diaper. If you wear disposable gloves, discard now.

8. Diaper the infant.
9. Wash the baby's hands.
10. Return the child to play area.
11. Clean and disinfect the diapering area and any supplies that were touched.
12. Wash your hands.
13. Record the time of the diaper change and whether the baby was wet, dry, or had a bowel movement.

Recorded information provides valuable documentation for monitoring infant's activities. For example, the caregiver can easily scan the record sheet and note the frequency of loose stools. This, in turn, alerts the caregiver of the possibility the infant may be ill. Such a record is also important for the parents to have at the end of the child's day. The caregiver should feel comfortable recording such information so it is accurate for that infant and not confused or mixed up with another child's activity record.

To disinfect the diapering area, use a bleach solution of 1 tablespoon of bleach (5.25% sodium hypochlorite) to 1 quart of water (1/4 cup of bleach per 1 gallon of water) (Deitch, 1987). Look closely at the label found on the side of the bleach bottle to make sure the percentage of sodium hypochlorite is 5.25.

Mix a fresh solution of bleach each day because it deteriorates rapidly (Deitch, 1987). Put it in a labeled spray bottle to be used exclusively for cleaning and sanitizing the area. Keep out of children's reach (Kendrick *et al.*, 1991). Safely dispose the unused portions of the bleach solution at the end of the day. Do this by discarding the bleach solution in the sanitary sewer drain (Deitch, 1987).

SUMMARY

Diapering and feeding are two vitally important routines in meeting basic needs of infants. Such routine times provide opportunities for enhancing infants' development through interaction with others. Feeding and diapering times are ideal for one-to-one interaction with infants. Caregivers are encouraged to speak directly with children, asking questions and responding to infant vocalizations with verbal and nonverbal (e.g., smile, head nod) communications. Adults can also label infant body parts as well as the items used in the process of feeding and diapering. Singing simple songs and reciting rhymes can also be incorporated into routine times.

Early childhood professionals educating and caring for infants are encouraged to review the procedures used in diapering and feeding. Assessing whether procedures assure safe and healthy conditions for infants is an important component of quality care.

REFERENCES

American Academy of Pediatrics and American Public Health Association (1992). *Caring for our children—National health and safety performance standards: Guidelines for out-of-home child care programs*. Washington, DC: Author.

Centers for Disease Control (1984). *What you can do to stop disease in the child day care center* (Stock #017-023-00172-8). Washington, DC: U.S. Government Printing Office.

Committee for Economic Development (1993). *Why child care matters: Preparing young children for a more productive America*. New York: Author.

Deitch, S. (Ed.). (1987). *Health in day care: A manual for health professionals*. Elk Grove Village, IL: American Academy of Pediatrics.

Frankie, R. T., & Owen, A. L. (1993). *Nutrition in the community: The art of delivering services*. St. Louis, MO: Mosby.

Helbrun, S., Culkin, M., Howes, C., Bryant, D., Clifford, R., Cryer, D., Peisner-Fenberg, & Kagan, S. (1995). *Cost, quality, and child outcomes in child care centers* (executive summary). Denver, CO: University of Colorado, Economics Department.

Kendrick, A. B., Kaufman, R., & Messenger, K. P. (Eds.). (1991). *Healthy young children: A manual for programs*. Washington, DC: National Association of the Education of Young Children.

Martin, H. D., & Lewis, N. M. (1994). *Guidelines for bottlefeeding* (Report G94-1203-A). University of Nebraska, Lincoln: Cooperative Extension, Institute of Agriculture and Natural Resources.

Pairaudeau, P. W., Wilson, R. G., Hall, M. A., & Milne, M. (1991). Inhalation of baby powder: An unappreciated hazard. *British Medical Journal, 302*, 1200-1201.

Robinson, C. H., Lawler, M. R., Chenoweth, W. L., & Garwick, A. E. (1990). *Normal and therapeutic nutrition* (17th ed.). New York: Macmillan.

Ryan, A., Yacoub, W., Paton, B., & Avard, D. (1990). Childhood deaths from toy balloons. *American Journal of Diseases of Children, 144*, 1221-1224.

Sigman-Grant, M., Bush, G., & Anantheswaran, R. (1992). Microwave heating of infant formula: A dilemma resolved. *Pediatrics, 90*, 412-415.

Van, R., Morrow, A. L., Reves, R. R., & Pickering, L. K. (1991). Environmental contamination in child day-care centers. *American Journal of Epidemiology, 133*, 460-470.

Warrick, J. C. (1994). *Infant Care Survey*. Unpublished survey.

Whitebook, M., Howes C., & Phillips, D. (1989). *Who Cares? Child Care Teachers and the Quality of Care in America*. Final Report of the National Child Care Staffing Study, Child Care Employee Project, Oakland, CA.

Yamauchi, T. (1991). Guidelines for attendees and personnel. In L. G. Donositz (Eds.), *Infection control in the child care center and preschool* (pp. 9-19). Baltimore, MD: Williams and Wilkins.

Who Cares for the Children?
Denmark's Unique Public Child-Care Model

BY VALERIE POLAKOW

While anti-tax discourse pervades public consciousness in the U.S. and has assumed the status of natural law, we might do well to pause and think about what we have lost by failing to create a publicly subsidized day-care system and a generous set of family support policies, Ms. Polakow reminds us.

The public authorities have an overall responsibility to create sound social frameworks and the best possible conditions for families with children. Furthermore, the public sector shall protect children and young persons against injustice and lack of care and, through guidelines and supportive measures, make it possible for parents to assume [their] responsibility as parents.[1]

Illustration by Brenda Grannan

WHO CARES FOR the children is a politically charged question in the United States in 1997 — a question that confronts all working parents and particularly single mothers working in low-wage employment. The chronic lack of affordable, licensed, high-quality child care has a long tradition in this society, rooted in ideologies about motherhood, the family, and

VALERIE POLAKOW is a professsor in the College of Education, Eastern Michigan University, Ypsilanti.

the role of government. However, it is instructive to consider an alternative tradition — one in which government and parents share responsibility for child care and public funding for the care of young children receives widespread support among citizens of all socioeconomic classes. In Denmark it is laid down by law that day-care facilities must be available to all children, and the government has assumed the cost of subsidizing a high-quality, comprehensive child-care system for infants and children from 6 months to 7 years of age, as well as an extensive after-school child-care system for school-age

From *Phi Delta Kappan*, April 1997, pp. 604-610. © 1997 by Phi Delta Kappa International, Inc. Reprinted by permission.

In Denmark high-quality child care is guaranteed for every child, regardless of economic status.

• •

children.

During 1995-96 I lived in Denmark and spent many fascinating months researching Danish family and child-care policies, conducting interviews and observations from the top down and from the bottom up in order to develop an "in vivo" understanding of the strong public policies that support families and children. In this article I present a portrait of Denmark's unique national model of public child care.

Child Care and Universal Entitlements

In order for readers to understand the current success and popularity of the Danish child-care system, it is necessary to place the widespread support for child care within the context of the social democratic infrastructure of the Danish welfare state. Denmark has a long tradition of public family support policies and egalitarian values resulting in social policies that aim at uniting rather than dividing the population. Universalism is promoted as a goal for all entitlement programs. Public support and social services are seen as rights because the welfare of all citizens is seen as a collective social responsibility. Together with the other Nordic countries, Denmark has developed an impressive multi-tiered system of universal support policies for families, thereby removing chronic family and child poverty.[2] A comprehensive national child-care policy is seen as a vital component of this system, which is intended to sustain family life and parenting, irrespective of family form.

There is a statutory paid maternity leave (four weeks before birth and 14 weeks after) followed by a paid parental leave for one or both parents for an additional 10 weeks. When the infant is 6 months old, another 26-week parental leave, which is paid at a flat rate (about 80% of the level for maternity and initial parental leave), may be taken by one or both parents. This leave may be extended to 52 weeks with an employer's agreement. In addition, the system includes universal child and family allowances, a single-parent allowance, and a monthly social assistance stipend, as well as housing subsidies, generous unemployment benefits, and universal health care.

While working mothers in the United States, particularly low-income single mothers, wrestle daily with a child-care crisis involving unavailable infant care, high costs, lack of access, and lack of regulation,[3] in Denmark high-quality child care is a guaranteed entitlement for every child, regardless of economic status. The Danish day-care system has for decades been internationally recognized for its extensive, high-quality services,[4] and there is increasing demand for those services. A comprehensive, subsidized public day-care system serves infants from the age of 6 months, and each local *kommune* (municipality) guarantees a child-care slot for all 1-year-olds, with single parents frequently receiving priority placement. Because day care is available, accessible, and widely supported by all

segments of the population, mothers — both single and married — are able to work and become economically self-sufficient.

The Organization of the Public Day-Care System

The subsidized public day-care system, under the jurisdiction of the Ministry of Social Affairs, offers both professional center-based care for children from infancy through age 6 and paraprofessional home-based family day care for infants and toddlers up to age 3. With the maternity and parental leave policies, infants generally do not enter day care before the age of 6 months. Since formal schooling begins only at age 7, most Danish children are in day care for approximately six years.

Paraprofessional family day care. The *Dagpleje* (family day care) is a neighborhood-based system administered by the local *kommune*. The caregivers, known as *dagplejemødre* (day-care mothers), receive three weeks of child development training during their first year and are supervised by a certified early childhood *pædagog* (teacher). Family day-care homes are inspected prior to licensing, and complete background and police checks are completed for all adult household members. If the day-care mother is selected as a potential applicant, other family members living at home are also screened by an early childhood supervisor. According to Eva Halse, director of the Copenhagen Østerbro Family Day Care Services, only about 25% of eligible applicants actually make it through the rigorous selection process. After the initial one-year period, early childhood supervisors visit "experienced" family day-care homes on a monthly basis and are on call to discuss any problems and offer ongoing professional support.

While official regulations permit a 1:5 caregiver-to-infant/toddler ratio,[5] I never found this arrangement in any of the sites I visited in metropolitan Copenhagen. The family day-care mothers there are regularly assigned three children, unless two are infants, in which case the ratio is 1:2. The day-care homes are grouped in neighborhood clusters of six or seven, and once a week each cluster of day-care mothers and their respective children spend the day together at a *legestue* (a three-room mini-day-care center fully equipped by the *kommune*), which is used on a rotating basis by five different neighborhood cluster groups. In this way the day-care mothers are not isolated in their homes and develop relationships with other caregivers and with the other children in their cluster. If a day-care mother falls ill or goes on vacation, she has back-up substitutes, each of whom is permitted to take on an extra child in her care. Once a month the cluster is also visited by its early childhood supervisor, who observes and meets with the caregivers during nap time. As unionized municipal employees, all family day-care mothers receive five weeks of paid vacation a year, full pensions, and a monthly salary of approximately

11,418 Dkr (U.S. equivalent: $2,003).

Day-care centers. There are several types of day-care centers serving infants and preschool children and providing after-school care. All the centers are run by certified *pædagoger* (teachers), assisted by paraprofessionals.[6] Both the teachers and the assistants are unionized municipal employees, with salaries for teachers in metropolitan Copenhagen ranging from 15,600 Dkr to 18,500 Dkr per month (U.S. equivalent: $2,736 to $3,245) and for assistants from 12,000 Dkr to 14,000 Dkr per month (U.S. equivalent: $2,105 to $2,456). All staff members receive pensions, get five weeks of paid vacation per year, and work between 30 and 37 hours a week.

• The *vuggestuer* are infant/toddler centers serving children between the ages of 6 months and 3 years. There are usually 30 to 40 children at a center, divided into smaller family groupings of eight to 10 children. The average ratio is one adult per 2.7 children,[7] and the staff members usually work in teams made up of one certified early childhood *pædagog* and one or two paraprofessional assistants.

• The *børnehaver* are preschool centers serving children from 3 to 6 years of age. They enroll from 20 to 80 children, usually divided into smaller family groups of 10 to 20 children, with an average ratio of one adult to 5.5 children.[8] The staff organization is similar to that of the infant/toddler centers, with teams of one certified early childhood *pædagog* and one assistant.

• The *aldersintegrerede institutioner* (age-integrated centers) have become more widespread since the first experimental ones were established during the 1970s. These centers enroll children from 6 months to 14 years of age and account for about 20% of enrolled day-care children.[9] Philosophically, these centers promote play and social interactions across early and middle childhood, fostering responsibility on the part of older children (who attend the centers after school) and continuity and stability of adult/child and child/child relations, since the children may remain in these centers until early adolescence. Size and staffing ratios depend on the age of the children and follow the patterns of the *vuggestuer* and *børnehaver.*

In addition to the three types of centers described above, there are also after-school centers for elementary children between the ages of 6 and 9 and new experimental "forest schools" for children from 4 to 6 years of age, who spend the entire year experiencing intensive outdoor/environmental education. These "forest schools" have become increasingly popular among parents, particularly those living in the cities.

It is significant to note that the public day-care system is supported by government funds but is decentralized and run by each local *kommune,* which decides fees and ratios within the broad mandates of the Danish government, to which it is accountable for providing high-quality care for all children irrespective of their families' economic status. There is also a small private day-care sector run by private associations, but the private centers too receive approximately 80% of their funds from their local *kommune* and must follow the same operating guidelines.

While day-care costs exhibit slight variations from *kommune* to *kommune,* the tuition costs overall are fairly standardized (with $5 to $15 differences in monthly costs, depending on the area). In Copenhagen, for example, full-time care for an infant at either a family day-care home or an infant/toddler center in 1995-96 cost a maximum of 1,525 Dkr per month (U.S. equivalent: $267), and maximum full-time preschool costs were 1,325 Dkr (U.S. equivalent: $232). Fees are set on a sliding scale, with tuition waived for the lowest-income parents and then rising from approximately $11.60 per month to full tuition rates for those with annual incomes of more than $33,560.

The family day-care system is widely used in areas where there is high demand for infant care and in rural areas of the country, where centers are not as readily available. In some areas family day-care costs are a little lower than the center-based care (approximately $15 to $20 per month lower), with slightly longer hours. By combining a well-supervised paraprofessional system with a national public day-care center system, the Danes are attempting to meet working parents' increasing demand for day-care slots. While there is not yet full coverage, Danish family policy objectives aim toward that goal. It is significant to note that, in 1995, 60% of infants and over 80% of 3- to 6-year-olds were in public day care.[10]

While the structure, organization, and public financing of the day-care system are impressive, so too is the quality of infant and preschool care. During the fall of 1995, I visited five family day-care homes, attended the weekly cluster group meetings of family day-care mothers, and observed at seven different day-care centers. While the bulk of my observations took place in metropolitan Copenhagen, I also visited several sites in rural areas and interviewed staff members at all the day-care sites. In the following sections I present some brief snapshots of day care in action.

Stepping Inside: Family Day Care in Action

Jytte[11] is a single mother in her late twenties with two children. Her 5-year-old attends a nearby preschool, and she takes care of her own 15-month-old daughter and two other toddlers, explaining that she chose to become a family day-care mother so that she could spend more time with her children.

I visited Jytte's home in the Nordhavn area — a lovely old neighborhood of flats and small shops near the harbor. Jytte's flat was on the second floor, comfortably furnished, with two bedrooms and a large living-room area. Jytte was returning from a morning outing with her daughter, Lise; Per,18 months; and Bo, 12 months. All three toddlers were sitting in the large baby carriage supplied by her local *kommune.* Jytte lifted the

> *The public day-care system is funded by the government but is run by each local kommune.*

Danish teachers uniformly reacted with horror at such an unthinkable practice as "time outs."

two older ones out first and then picked up Bo, who had fallen asleep. After locking up the baby carriage outside, we entered the building, and the two toddlers clambered up the steps as Jytte unlocked the door, still holding Bo. As they entered the flat, Bo woke, and she took off his coat and mittens (it was a cold October morning) while the two toddlers peeled off their jackets and mittens and ran to take their slippers from the bedroom.

Jytte was calm and efficient, talking to the two toddlers softly while undressing Bo and eventually changing his diaper in the bedroom on a changing table. All three children then moved to the living-room area, where large blocks were set out, and Jytte went to prepare a snack in the kitchen. Milk and crackers and bananas were placed on the table, and when the children caught sight of the snack they went to fetch their bibs — including Bo, who crawled over to reach his. Jytte smiled as I remarked on how they each knew their own bibs (and earlier their slippers), telling me, "They are so clever — they always remind me if I forget to do anything." She lifted Bo into his high chair while Lise and Per climbed up onto theirs. Jytte began to sing a song while clapping her hands, and the toddlers followed suit, shouting out different sounds. Bo tried to pour his own milk, following the example of the two older toddlers, but he missed and the milk fell on the plastic cloth under the table. Jytte promptly produced a sponge and wiped it up, then held Bo's arm and encouraged him to pour again.

She cuddled all three children on the couch after the snack and then put Bo down for a nap in one of the three cribs in the bedroom, while the two older ones were playing on the couch. The atmosphere was warm and nurturing, and Jytte remained calm and unruffled as the children became cranky later in the morning. After their morning play period, when Jytte also read them several stories, she prepared lunch — milk and finger foods with fruit. Then she changed all three babies. Both Per and Lise went to fetch their own diapers from a large box, to which she smilingly replied *tak* (thank you); after they were changed and down in their cribs with pacifiers, Jytte relaxed in the living room, telling me, "This is my one hour of quiet! I treasure it."

Jytte has been a family day-care mother for more than four years, beginning when her older son was a baby. She appreciates the fact that she is able to count her own child as one of her day-care clients and speaks warmly of her supervisor as "always ready to help if there are any problems." As a family day-care mother, Jytte receives an allowance for food, diapers, and equipment, and one-third of her salary is tax free to compensate for the use of her home. All family day-care mothers are supplied with a large baby carriage, which seats up to four children. All the day-care mothers use these carriages as their main mode of transportation, and indeed it is a common sight on Copenhagen streets around 10 a.m. to see day-care moth-

ers wheeling their young charges onto buses, off trains, through the downtown area, in parks, through wind and rain and fog. Even as the icy winds of November blew in, there was no decrease of activity, as exercise and fresh air are considered an essential part of Danish child care at all ages. All the caregivers I interviewed, including Jytte, expressed satisfaction with their occupation. In addition, the other day-care mothers told me how important their weekly cluster meeting was: "We can share our problems and talk with each other as adults. If you are always alone talking to small children every day without a break, it can make you feel crazy."

Stepping Inside: Day-Care Centers in Action

I visited seven day-care centers: three infant/toddler centers, three preschools, and one age-integrated institution. The diverse early childhood centers I observed in Copenhagen, Frederiksberg, and Herlev were all high-quality programs, providing flexible, play-based, developmental early education, with a strong focus on child-centered, child-initiated learning. Expressive group-oriented activities were fostered, and symbolic representation (as in the Reggio Emilia approach) was seen as a key to intellectual learning. Music and movement were central features of the morning, and the rest of the day was loosely and flexibly structured according to the children's play desires. Field trips took place several times a week — the preschoolers were taken via trains and buses to visit monuments, art galleries, outdoor theaters, libraries, parks, the harbor, and the forests. The programs were characterized by an open and flexible structure with an absence of teacher-directed learning. Autonomy and independence were fostered (4-year-olds were permitted to play alone in small groups with no adults present, both inside and outside), and cooperative play and socially inclusive group activities were emphasized.

There was a strong bias against any form of exclusion. When asked about the use of "time outs" with "difficult" children, Danish teachers uniformly reacted with horror at such an unthinkable practice, and one director told me, "No, never. We would never isolate a child — maybe that is one thing we in Denmark would get sued over!" Another head teacher remarked, "Often it is us. We have to look at how we are. Often we must change the way we are with the child or the way we say something, or sometimes we must look together with the parents at what is making the child angry or sad. But we should never isolate or punish the child who is having trouble." These perceptions about discipline and child management techniques were expressed by both directors and teachers at all the sites. In fact, the consistent responses across seven different centers serving diverse groups of children revealed key Danish educational tenets, influenced by N. F. S. Grundtvig (the Danish John Dewey): equality, social solidarity, cooperation, and gentle teaching. There were also strong injunctions against any formal "teaching" of reading or math readiness. All forms of early childhood intervention for vulnerable "at-risk" children were conducted within the child's center, where the services of a social worker and a psychologist were regularly available.

The following observations capture the flavor of a typical day at an age-integrated center.

I walked in to observe a lunch time with the youngest group of children. The cook, also a salaried municipal employee, was serving the food. Eleven babies and toddlers (ranging in age from 10 to 23 months) and three teachers were seated around a long table. The teachers tied on the children's feeding bibs and passed out forks (actual silverware) and china plates — even the youngest there picked up his fork, as the lox and ham and liverwurst spread on *smorrebrød* (open-faced sandwiches) were passed around. Bjarne (about 18 months old) poured his own milk with a great flourish, and others followed suit. The teachers moved quietly around, wiping up splashes of milk with wet washcloths.

Next came the second course: mini-quiche pieces with strong Danish cheese and slices of tomato. A 1-year-old ladled a piece onto her plate and then tried to stab it with her fork; on the third try she successfully speared the piece and put it in her mouth. She lunged for the pitcher and poured herself more milk, laughing as some splashed on her bib. The small pitchers were now empty, and a "*mere maelk*" (more milk) chant began. The toddlers banged with their forks, laughing uproariously, and the smiling teachers refilled the pitchers. Then the toddlers reached for them again, taking turns, amid many wild splashes. As the eating, pouring, and serving continued, no child fussed to come down from his or her high chair, and all valiantly ate with their forks, using chubby little fingers to collect what didn't quite make it to their mouths.

After about 25 minutes, Bjarne, the eldest, made a move to get down. A teacher gently told him to wait, and she brought out warm washcloths and passed them around. The toddlers wiped their faces with some help from the adults, who intervened only after the children had first tried to do it themselves. The teachers said "*tak for mad*" (thank you for the meal), which the toddlers repeated.

After lunch three toddlers went alone into the arts-and-crafts room, with a teacher watching from the open doorway. One toddler climbed onto a low table and, laughing, pulled a furry mobile down. A teacher looked in and told him "*nej*" (no) but left him on the table. He jumped down, picked up a puzzle piece, and threw it across the room. An older child (about 5 or 6 years of age) came in, told him "*nej*" sternly, and picked up the piece. As the older girl fit the piece into the puzzle, a teacher came in and took the toddler for a diaper change before putting him down for his outside nap in a *kommune*-supplied baby carriage. (I later learned that all babies and toddlers sleep outside unless the temperature drops below 0 degrees centigrade!)

The relaxed atmosphere at lunch was a common occurrence that I observed at different centers. The staff members were attentive but intentionally allowed the toddlers to experiment and rarely intervened. I was surprised to see the toddlers eat so competently and sit for such an extended period of time, but it was clear that autonomy and independence were being fostered —

amid an acceptance of milky messes and many a miss — and that these young children were being socialized effectively for their future Danish dinners, which, I subsequently discovered, often extended to midnight and beyond, with elaborate multiple courses of delectable and elegant cuisine!

The following description is drawn from a preschool I visited outside Copenhagen.

Four 3-year-olds were playing in the large activity room, which was essentially a free space until lunch, when tables were set up. The four were running together, colliding, and dissolving into gales of laughter. One began jumping on the couch, and the other three followed suit. Therese (the leader) jumped from the couch and pulled several large wooden blocks (which doubled as high chairs) to make "steps," and the children began a pattern of follow the leader on the couch and then balancing on the "steps." Suddenly Morten shouted to the other three to wait as he transformed the blocks into a "train," leaving one step to climb. He now assumed the lead, and the other three followed a new pattern of jumping on the couch, climbing onto the "step," and then riding the train. They all cooperated in the game, making train noises, and several others joined in so that there were now seven riding the train, with one serving as ticket collector for make-believe tickets. Several teachers walked by, smiling but not interfering, and the game continued for about half an hour.

I was fascinated by the cooperative nature of their play. No conflicts ensued, and several children inventively extended the initial game so that there were multidimensional forms of representation involving many symbols and artifacts. The key was that the children had complete autonomy; they had taken over the space and made it their own. Both children and adults looked on, respecting the world of the train riders. As one of the teachers commented, explaining her philosophy of early childhood education: "Never, never interrupt their play. We have an absolute emphasis on always respecting their play!"

In the arts-and-crafts room an extensive assortment of materials was arranged around the perimeter of the room, with Lego blocks in profusion, as well as books, pattern blocks, drawing/cutting/painting supplies, dozens of little plastic farm animals, farm people, and other miniatures. Three children, ranging in age from 3 to 6, were playing with the farm animals and different miniature flowers, sorting them into sets. One 4-year-old, Kresten, began building a symmetrical horizontal and vertical structure using the Lego blocks. I watched him; he was completely engrossed for about 20 minutes. Next to Kresten, Julie began to build a "garden." Inge entered the building area, picked up a Lego block, and threw it at Julie's garden, and Julie began to cry. A teacher walked over and immediately comforted Julie, but before the teacher could talk to Inge, Inge threw another block. Several of the adjacent children shouted "*nej, nej*" at Inge, and two repaired Julie's garden, saying "*så*" (a common exclamation equivalent to "there you go").

Inge stopped and watched as the teacher moved over and began to play with farm animals, telling a story in Danish about a duck who quacked loudly and who met other animals in Julie's garden, all of which made different sounds. The children were entranced, and all sat listening, including Inge. Meanwhile, the little builder, Kresten, who was both listening and building, now tried to fit the farm animals under an overturned box, next to his elaborate structure. But the large animals wouldn't fit. A little girl moved out of the story circle, came over and looked, and tried to lift the box. Together they figured out that Kresten needed to lift up the box and tilt it in order to fit the larger animals inside. As the story ended, the teacher took Inge on her lap. Two new children joined Kresten and his helper, who had now created a working farm with different tasks for the animals; all four children developed roles for themselves and continued their farm play for another 20 minutes. At lunch time they built a fence and left it standing as they moved to the lunchroom.

In this center, as in others I visited, the children had an autonomy of action that led to inventive transformational play. The respect accorded to children's expressive activities was in clear contrast to the approach that I have observed over the years in many child-care centers in the U.S., which are overly regimented and highly structured (despite guidelines embracing developmentally appropriate practice). In these Danish centers, gentle, respectful teaching à la Martin Haberman and Stacie Goffin[12] appeared to be the norm. Most impressive was the social/cooperative nature of group play, which clearly dominated daily experience. The above incidents of children intervening both to reprimand and to assist one another were not atypical. In fact, I observed such incidents at all seven sites.

What Can We Learn from the Danes?

While there were local differences between the various centers I visited — four had two or more male early childhood teachers on site, and two were ethnically diverse, with large numbers of immigrant children (particularly Turkish, Pakistani, and Bosnian) — all seven centers were nurturing, flexibly structured, and developmentally supportive, with a strong emphasis on social cooperation, expressive activity, child-initiated learning, and the "sacred" nature of play. These Danish day-care centers were part of a high-quality day-care system run by trained early childhood professionals with good paraprofessional assistance, and they were supported and appreciated by working parents. The family day-care homes, offering alternative infant care to parents, were well-organized, well-regulated, and carefully supervised by early childhood professionals. Clearly, the design of this paraprofessional system could be seen as one model for increasing access to and quality of infant- and toddler-care services in the U.S.

The Danish public day-care system is popular, and the status and respect accorded to early childhood teachers reflect the central place of day care in Danish family life. Day care is both accessible and affordable, and the operating costs and teacher salaries are subsidized by the local government; hence it is possible to run a high-quality system in which staff turnover is low. The widespread social support and the public economic base for a strong universal child-care system are phenomena from which we in the U.S. could learn a great deal; particularly impressive is the way in which a universal day-care system promotes equality of early educational opportunities for young children, because access to services does not depend on economic or family status. The families who are potentially most

vulnerable — low-income single mothers and children, families experiencing domestic violence, immigrant families, refugee families, and "socially disabled" families — are given priority placement, because public day care is seen as both an equalizer and a potent force for the successful integration of the young into Danish society.

Contrast the Danish day-care system, which serves all children irrespective of their parents' economic status, with the current realities for poor families in the U.S. Head Start reached only 36% of income-eligible children in 1995 and remains underfunded.[13] There is also a national crisis of affordable child care for all American children whose parents are low-wage earners. The recent report released by the General Accounting Office, reviewing federally funded early childhood centers in different states across the nation, found severe health and safety violations in each of the states investigated and concluded that lack of regulation and monitoring was a critical cause.[14] Nancy Ebb also raised urgent concerns about the quality and availability of federally subsidized child care for families collecting AFDC (Aid for Families with Dependent Children) and for the working poor.[15] Meanwhile, with the dismantling of the federal welfare system, increasing numbers of poor single mothers will be forced into the workplace without adequate or affordable child care. The level of care is particularly inadequate for infants and toddlers, and findings from the *Cost, Quality, and Child Outcomes* study indicate that care for this age group may be even worse than previously documented.[16] In this study, child care at most centers in the U.S. was rated poor to mediocre. Only 8% of the infant/toddler rooms received a rating of "good" quality, and 40% received a rating of less than "minimal" quality.

Furthermore, in the absence of a nationally subsidized child-care system, private child-care costs are prohibitive — not only for poor parents but for middle-income families as well. Frequently costs run $800 a month for high-quality center-based infant care. In Michigan, for example, high-quality full-time infant care in Washtenaw County has risen to $10,000 a year — 40% more than undergraduate tuition costs at the University of Michigan.

While participation in the labor force by mothers of young children in the U.S. is high — 59.7% of women with children under 6[17] — there is a dearth of family-support policies to assist them. We have no paid maternity or parental leave, and the usual unpaid parental leave means that many mothers reenter the labor force when their infants are 12 weeks old or younger. We are the only country in the industrialized democratic world that fails its mothers and infants so abysmally in terms of family support and parental leave policies.

Denmark not only has generous maternity and parental leave policies, but its public day-care system has made a very different family life possible for working parents, particularly working and single mothers. Of all European Community (EC) countries, Denmark has the highest rate of working mothers with young children, approximately 79%.[18] The striking integration of day care into the fabric of society — there is literally a small center on almost every block in the city of Copenhagen — has created multilevel support from government and citizens and has become a part of the sacred universal system of benefits supported by high public taxes. While anti-tax discourse pervades public consciousness in the U.S. and has assumed the status of natural law, we might do well to pause and think about what we have lost by failing to create a publicly subsidized day-care system and a generous set of family support policies. "Who cares for the children?" is the perennial question. Clearly, in Denmark there is a sound partnership between parents and government, and their young children are the visible beneficiaries.

1. *Social Policy in Denmark: Child and Family Policies* (Copenhagen: Danish Ministry of Social Affairs, 1995), p. 4.

2. Sheila B. Kamerman and Alfred J. Kahn, eds., *Child Care, Parental Leave, and the Under 3's: Policy Innovation in Europe* (New York: Auburn House, 1991); idem, *Starting Right: How America Neglects Its Youngest Children and What We Can Do About It* (New York: Oxford University Press, 1995); and Valerie Polakow, *Lives on the Edge: Single Mothers and Their Children in the Other America* (Chicago: University of Chicago Press, 1993).

3. Nancy Ebb, *Child Care Tradeoffs: States Make Painful Choices* (Washington, D.C.: Children's Defense Fund, 1994); U.S. General Accounting Office, *Review of Health and Safety Standards at Child Care Facilities* (Washington, D.C.: Department of Health and Human Services, 1993); and Suzanne Helburn, ed., *Cost, Quality, and Child Outcomes in Child Care Centers* (ERIC ED 386 297, 1995).

4. Marsden Wagner and Mary Wagner, *The Danish National Child-Care System* (Boulder, Colo.: Westview Press, 1976); David A. Corsini, "Family Day Care in Denmark: A Model for the United States?," *Young Children*, July 1991, pp. 10-15; and *Employment Equality and Caring for Children: Annual Report* (Brussels: European Commission Network on Child Care, 1993).

5. Jacob Vedel-Petersen, *Day Care for Children Under School Age in Denmark* (Copenhagen: Danish National Institute of Social Research, 1992), p. 18.

6. Teacher certification for *pædagoger* is a unique and separate 3½-year training program for early childhood teachers, special needs teachers, and recreation specialists offered at 32 colleges of social education in Denmark.

7. Vedel-Petersen, p. 17.

8. Ibid.

9. Jytte Juul Jensen, "Age-Integrated Centres in Denmark," in *Employment Equality and Caring for Children: Annual Report* (European Commission Network on Child Care, 1992), pp. 35-38.

10. *Social Policy in Denmark.*

11. All names have been changed to protect confidentiality.

12. Martin Haberman, "Gentle Teaching in a Violent Society," *Educational Horizons*, vol. 72, 1994, pp. 131-35; and Stacie G. Goffin, "How Well Do We Respect the Children in Our Care?," *Childhood Education*, vol. 66, 1989, pp. 68-74.

13. *The State of America's Children 1996* (Washington, D.C.: Children's Defense Fund, 1996).

14. U.S. General Accounting Office, op. cit.

15. Ebb, op. cit.

16. Helburn, op. cit.

17. *The State of America's Children*, p. 93.

18. Bodil Stenvig, John Andersen, and Lisbeth Laursen, "Statistics for Work and the Family in Denmark and the EC," in Søren Carlsen and Jørgen E. Larsen, eds., *The Equality Dilemma: Reconciling Working Life and Family Life, Viewed in an Equality Perspective* (Copenhagen: Danish Equal Status Council, 1994).

NURTURING KIDS'
Seven Ways *of Being* Smart

How to develop your students' multiple intelligences

Kristen Nelson

KRISTEN NELSON *is a sixth-grade teacher at Ambuel Elementary in the Capistrano unified school district in Orange County, California. She is also a mentor teacher and consultant on multiple intelligences in the classroom.*

Throughout my teaching career I've been perplexed and fascinated by students who perform poorly in math and language activities, and appear unmotivated—yet thrive outside of the classroom. I'd see these "underachievers" in the streets after school, their faces lit with laughter and enthusiasm for whatever they were doing. They were engaged, expert, joyful—why couldn't I bring this out of them in class? Dr. Howard Gardner's Multiple Intelligences Theory nudged me toward the answer: I could reach many of these turned-off kids if I discovered their special ways of being smart.

You're probably familiar with Gardner's theory, but here's a refresher of his basic premise: Individuals don't have one fixed intelligence, but at least seven distinct ones that can be developed over time—linguistic, logical-mathematical, spatial, musical-rhythmic, bodily-kinesthetic, interpersonal, and intrapersonal. See the box ("The Seven Intelligences") and the clip-and-save chart [in this article] for more details about these seven kinds of smarts.

HOW MY TEACHING CHANGED

Gardner's theory is a dream come true for teachers—because it means intelligences can be nurtured. And with that in mind, I reinvented my curriculum and the way I taught it so that it met the needs of a wider range of learning styles—which, as educator Thomas Armstrong says, are "the intelligences put to work."

The strategies you can use to put the Multiple Intelligences Theory into play in your own classroom are limitless. To add to your thinking, here are two approaches that have had a big impact on my students' achievement: one is a focused unit that introduces kids to the concept of diverse strengths; the other is an open-ended exploration of the seven intelligences through classroom flow areas, which are similar to learning centers.

7 Smarts: An 8-Day Unit

Think a kindergartner will have trouble grasping the theory of Harvard psychologist Gardner? Think again. As a mentor teacher on multiple intelligences, I work with children throughout grades K–6, and even the youngest students naturally take to the idea that there are multiple ways of being intelligent.

I begin the unit by asking students what being smart

From *Instructor,* July/August 1995, pp. 26-30, 34. © 1995 by Scholastic, Inc. Reprinted by permission.

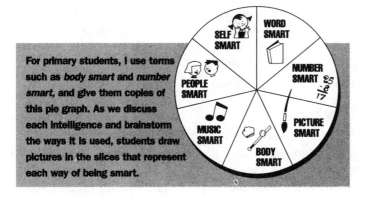

For primary students, I use terms such as *body smart* and *number smart,* and give them copies of this pie graph. As we discuss each intelligence and brainstorm the ways it is used, students draw pictures in the slices that represent each way of being smart.

means to them, and then list their replies on the board. Since their answers usually revolve around reading, writing, and math, we discuss the importance of these subjects in school success.

Next, I ask them to brainstorm other ways a person can be smart, conveying the idea that humans have proven time and again that although having strong math and language skills is important, it is not the only predictor of success in life. With grades 3 to 6, I discuss famous people who performed poorly in school but were smart in other ways. Albert Einstein and Pablo Picasso—who both disliked

school rules and dropped out to study under experts—are two good examples to use. With younger students, we talk about the fact that not everyone likes school all of the time.

As we continue our discussion, I give kids lots of examples of skills, activities, and professions that make use of each intelligence area.

EXAMINING STRENGTHS

After the introductory lesson, I focus on a different intelligence area for each of the next seven days. For example, on a spatial intelligence day with fourth graders, I might have students draw

floor plans of the Spanish mission we are studying and have them practice picturing numbers in their minds as we do oral calculations in math. On body-kinesthetic day, we role-play a scene from a novel we're reading, and learn a new sport. Each day, I also devote 45 minutes to exploring the famous people, book characters, and historical figures who are good role models in that intelligence.

By now, students are not only familiar with the different ways they're smart, but they are now ready and usually very willing to use their intelligences in daily work.

NURTURING KIDS ALL YEAR

After the opening unit, I integrate Multiple Intelligences Theory into my lesson plans for the rest of the year, adapting activities to meet various learning styles. For example, a child who is strong in spatial intelligence and is a visual learner can strengthen her reading and writing skills by drawing a picture before writing about a book she's reading. See the chart Draw Out Your Students' Strengths for

The Seven Intelligences

As you explore these seven intelligences with your students, keep in mind that Gardner's theory should not be used as another way to pigeonhole students as "spatial," "musical," and so forth. Students need to perceive themselves as having a combination of these intelligences, capable of growth in all areas.

Bodily-Kinesthetic: involves using the body to solve problems, create products, and convey ideas and emotions.

Interpersonal-Social: refers to the ability to work effectively with others; to understand them; and to notice their goals, motivations, and intentions.

Intrapersonal-Introspective: involves the ability to be deeply aware of inner feelings, intentions, and goals.

Logical-Mathematical: involves the ability to reason deductively or inductively and to recognize and manipulate abstract patterns and relationships.

Musical-Rhythmic: includes sensitivity to pitch, timbre, and rhythm of sounds, and responsiveness to music.

Verbal-Linguistic: involves ease with reading and writing skills, and sensitivity to the nuances, order, and rhythm of words.

Visual-Spatial: involves the ability to create visual-spatial representations of the world and to transfer those representations mentally or concretely—to think in pictures.

Adapted from "Seven Ways of Knowing" by David Lazear; *If Minds Matter: A Forward to the Future,* Vol. II (IRI/Skylight Publishing)

more ideas on how to build on your kids' multiple intelligences.

Flow Areas Foster Intelligence

Using multiple intelligences in your teaching has to go beyond detecting strengths in students and flexing just those intellectual muscles. You need to give students the opportunity to explore all seven domains. Setting up flow areas—which are centers organized around the seven intelligences—will help you accomplish this.

The concept of *flow* was developed by Mihaly Csikszentmihalyi, Ph.D., professor of human development at the University of Chicago, who describes flow as a state of complete absorption in something, to the point where one loses track of time. Csikszentmihalyi first observed flow when studying artists; he then looked for and found it in dancers, athletes, scientists, musicians, and talented people in many other fields.

In the classroom, flow areas provide students with the space, materials, time, and challenging activities that spark deep involvement while strengthening children's intelligences.

GO WITH THE FLOW

The very nature of flow areas is flexible, and they can be designed in numerous ways. Sometimes you'll want to set up flow areas for four to six weeks, and at other times just for a week or two. How you guide students to use them will vary, too. You'll want children to work in them solo, with partners, and in small groups; you can have children use them only when they're finished with their class work, or you can rotate students through the areas on a regular schedule. Try to block out a period of at least 30 minutes for kids, so they have a chance to get lost in their endeavor.

You can set up flow areas as centers independent of what students are studying, or you can link them to your curriculum.

21 FLOW-AREA IDEAS
Verbal-Linguistic

1. Set up a language lab with a cassette player, cassettes, earphones, and talking books. Invite students to tape themselves reading a story or poem they've written, to share with others.
2. Establish a writing center with a computer, writing supplies, and examples of different types of writing. A fourth grader I taught used this area to write letters to local land developers to discuss her environmental concerns.
3. Organize a tutoring station where older children volunteer to help younger students with reading and writing. One sixth grader who lacked confidence in his reading gained more self-assurance when he helped a first grader learn to read.

CLIP AND SAVE

Draw Out Your Students' Strengths

Intelligence Area:	Is Strong In:	Likes to:	Learns Best Through:	Famous Examples:	Common Misbehaviors:
Verbal/ Linguistic	Reading, writing, telling stories, memorizing dates, thinking in words	Read, write, tell stories, talk, memorize, do word puzzles	Reading, hearing, and seeing words; speaking; writing; discussions	T. S. Eliot, Maya Angelou, Abraham Lincoln	Passing notes, reading during lessons
Logical/ Mathematical	Math, reasoning, logic, problem-solving, patterns	Solve problems, question, reason, work with numbers, experiment, use computers	Working with patterns and relationships, classifying, abstract thinking	Albert Einstein, John Dewey, Susanne Langer	Working on math or building things during lessons
Visual/ Spatial	Reading, maps, charts, drawing, puzzles, imagining things, visualization	Design, draw, build, create, daydream, look at pictures	Working with pictures and colors, visualizing, drawing	Pablo Picasso, Frank Lloyd Wright, Georgia O'Keeffe, Bobby Fischer	Doodling, drawing, daydreaming
Bodily/ Kinesthetic	Athletics, dancing, acting, crafts, using tools	Play sports, dance, move around, touch and talk, use body language	Touching, moving, processing knowledge through bodily sensations	Charlie Chaplin, Michael Jordan, Martha Graham	Fidgeting, wandering around the room
Musical/ Rhythmic	Singing, picking up sounds, remembering melodies, rhythms	Sing, hum, play an instrument, listen to music	Rhythm, melody, singing, listening to music and melodies	Leonard Bernstein, Mozart, Ella Fitzgerald	Tapping pencil or feet
Interpersonal/ Social	Understanding people, leading, organizing, communicating, resolving conflicts	Have friends, talk to people, join groups	Sharing, comparing, relating, interviewing, cooperating	Mohandas Gandhi, Ronald Reagan, Mother Teresa	Talking, passing notes
Intrapersonal/ Introspective	Understanding self, recognizing strengths and weaknesses, setting goals	Work alone, reflect, pursue interests	Working alone, self-paced projects, reflecting	Eleanor Roosevelt, Sigmund Freud, Thomas Merton	Conflicting with others

How to Enhance Your Teaching Smarts

☑ **Invite guest speakers.** Show students the relevance of each intelligence by inviting parents and community members as guest speakers—their professions can highlight specific intelligences. For example, a local architect described to my students how he designed a building they pass every day on their way to school—the kids were fascinated.

☑ **Create a video.** Have your students plan and execute a video to inform parents or other classes about the many ways of being smart.

☑ **Encourage individual projects.** Have students choose an intelligence area in which they would like to complete a one- to two-week project.

☑ **Honor overlooked intelligences.** Remember to recognize students that excel in bodily-kinesthetic, interpersonal, and intrapersonal intelligences.

☑ **Assess your own intelligences.** Think about how your strengths and weaknesses in the seven intelligences influence your teaching. Look at your lesson plans. Beside each activity, write the initials of the intelligences exercised—you will be able to see your dominant intelligence areas as well as the areas you need to enhance. Share your strengths and weaknesses with students.

☑ **Stretch yourself.** Instead of accepting the belief that you don't excel in certain areas, attend workshops and read books that can help strengthen these skills.

☑ **Team teach.** Use fellow teachers who have different intelligence strengths to plan lessons and activities. Rotating students can allow you to teach to your strengths and loves, while providing students with different styles of teaching and learning.

☑ **Update your professional portfolio.** Set your sights on having a portfolio that contains examples of lessons that use each intelligence area.

Math-Logic

4. Make a math lab with manipulatives, calculators, objects to measure and graph, and so on. My younger students love to use the area to classify pattern blocks, buttons, and coins. One older student calculated the expenses of an upcoming family trip and planned an itinerary.

5. Put together a science lab with simple hands-on experiments and science books. A flower-dissection lab—which I set up when we're learning about plant reproduction—is a favorite of my students.

6. Create a logic-challenge center. For example, I invited my fifth graders to develop a mystery-based board game. When I challenged my sixth graders to design a way to teach a blind person geometric shapes, they collected yardsticks and made giant squares, triangles, and parallelograms on the playground.

Spatial

7. Enrich an art area with paints, pencils, different types of paper, clay, and various objects students can use as models for still-life drawings. Display examples of famous artists' work for students to study. My students loved it when I brought in a large shell and invited them to do a painting of it in the style of Georgia O'Keeffe.

8. Stock a visual media center with a video camera, VCR, and videotapes. Invite groups of students to make a short classroom documentary. My students chose topics of concern to them, like getting along with parents.

9. Fill an architecture center with pencils, rulers, and large sheets of paper. Invite students to draw the floor plan of anything. A fourth grader planned, designed, and built a futuristic mission for space exploration.

Bodily-Kinesthetic

10. Put together a hands-on center with materials such as clay, blocks, and craft materials. While studying Michelangelo's sculpting style, my students decided to make chess sets out of clay.

11. Enrich a drama center with play books and ideas for student performances or puppet theater. One student wrote his own version of a Greek tragedy, selected his cast, and performed it for other classes.

12. Create an open space for creative movement (mini-trampoline, juggling equipment, drama area, and so on). Or set up an outside flow area that can be monitored by a parent volunteer. I've seen students use this area to learn how to juggle (which increases eye-hand coordination) and teach jazz and country dances to their peers.

Musical

13. Set up a music lab with cassettes, earphones, and various tapes to compare and contrast. For example, students can compare Mozart's "Symphony No. 39" with Garth Brooks's "The Thunder Rolls" and the Beatles' "Paperback Writer."

14. Display lyrics for students to analyze. Fill a listening lab with sound-related items such as a stethoscope, walkie-talkies, and a conch shell.

15. Invite students to compose their own songs and write the lyrics. A fourth grader composed a song for the violin that represented the tone

and feeling of the book *Where the Red Fern Grows* by Wilson Rawls.

Interpersonal

16. Create a flow area with a round table—to encourage group discussions. You can write curriculum-based discussion ideas on cards and place them in the center, or let students choose their own topics.

17. Establish a debate center where students form teams and choose a subject to debate. Give kids ten minutes to prepare for the debate. Rain-forest preservation versus local economic needs, and whether or not kids should be allowed to ride in-line skates to school are two topics that sparked heated discussions among students.

18. Give students an index card stating a common school-related problem. Challenge them to work together to come up with solutions. A group of second graders discussed how to resolve arguments that developed in their handball games. They wrote rules to share with other students.

Intrapersonal

19. Create a selection of self-esteem activities. For example, ask students to list ten of their strengths or have them write out specific ways they are a good friend to others. Encourage journal writing.

20. Invite kids to draw a picture that describes a mood or feeling. I've found this really helps older students to become aware of their fluctuating moods and to reflect on how their moods affect their daily lives.

21. Design study nooks for individual work. Use beanbag chairs to make them cozy spaces. A third grader who had difficulty controlling his anger used this nook often as a cooling-off location.

Personalized Learning

The biggest impact that the Multiple Intelligences Theory has had in my classroom is that it has helped me create an individualized learning environment. I no longer expect students to think exactly alike in order to be *right*. I am more comfortable with my students' individualistic thinking—and my own. In personalizing each student's education experience, I find that an increasing percentage of students discover their own strengths, put more effort into improving their weaker areas, and feel better about themselves.

Teaching nursery school is not about formal lessons. It's about listening and guiding, helping little children to make sense of the big world they're entering.

The New Preschool

BY LYNNELL HANCOCK
AND PAT WINGERT

LISTEN TO THE SNAP, crackle, pop of baby neurons. Teacher Martha Rodriguez crouches near the 2-year-old sand diggers at Manhattan's Bank Street Family Center, gently negotiating the rights to a suddenly special yellow rake. As Rodriguez bargains, the toddlers spin new connections to the brain area that controls "gimme now" impulses, connections that could very well later be used to ratchet up their SAT scores or their job-interviewing skills. Head teacher Lisa Farrell explains that the doll in Cammy's hot grip is really Caroline's from home, hence her classmate's avalanche of tears. Cammy's brain is wiring up to read other people's feelings, a skill she'll need to navigate through future relationships. A third teacher leads the diaper-dependent kids, one by one, to the changing table, exchanging coo for coo, babble for babble. Each child's neural circuits are carving highways in the brain where future vocabulary words will later travel with ease.

In the "superbaby" '80s, the preschool debate centered on how soon was too soon for children to be coached in the ABCs or one-two-threes. Now the discussion has become more about nurturing neurons, less about drilling for facts. Brain research underscores what educators have long argued: early social and emotional experiences are the seeds of human intelligence. Time spent flipping flashcards—at the age of 1 or 3—is precious time wasted. Instead, teachers need to tune in to each child's

33% of all parents say that they plan to start sending their child to school by the age of 3; an additional 30% say their child will start by age 4

daily experiences and needs, helping them feel safe and loved while encouraging them to explore and experiment. "Children are born hard-wired," says Sue Bredekamp of the National Association for the Education of Young Children. "Experience provides the software."

Is this nation's haphazard collection of nurseries and day-care centers—which accommodate nearly half the 15 million infants and toddlers whose parents are working—up to such a task? According to a 1995 national study conducted by the University of Colorado Economics Department, the answer is clearly no. Many programs are unlicensed. Most are staffed with untrained, poorly paid adults. Ninety-one percent don't have basic toys, books, hygiene, or enough adults to respond to each child. A full 40 percent are downright hazardous, both to a child's health and safety

as well as to her social and intellectual development.

The formula for preschool success mirrors a child's upbringing in a good home. Whether in pricey private preschools or Head Start–like programs, American educators agree on the simple elements that add up to quality: one trained, well-paid teacher assigned to every three to four infants or half-dozen toddlers; safe, stimulating surroundings and strong ties between staff and families, so children know there is loving continuity in their lives. This is neuroscience, not rocket science. The well-regarded Bank Street Family Center, for children 6 months to 4 years, has been perfecting this family-friendly formula for nearly three decades. There is no Mozart training, no foreign-language tapes, no work sheets to ponder. Instead, its unassuming rooms are filled with big, lumpy armchairs for reading, a kitchen for cooking, tables for drawing, blocks for building forts, stairs for building muscles. Children (about 12 per class) are free to visit other classrooms, as they would go from bedroom to den at home.

Education at this age is not about imparting facts and imposing strict schedules. It's about listening, guiding, helping individual children to make sense of the real world. The "curriculum" is learning to say goodbye to Mom, forming relationships to others, feeling competent exploring their world. With these emotional skills reinforced, says director Margot Hammond, reading, writing and physics will come more easily when kids are ready. And,

From *Newsweek*, Spring/Summer 1997, pp. 36-37. © 1997 by Newsweek, Inc. All rights reserved. Reprinted by permission.

since children's brains are so malleable at this age, supportive care can even repair neurological damage created by depressed, distracted or abusive parents. Heavy doses of love, attention and proper signaling between caregiver and toddler forge new connections.

Parents are known to scramble for a spot on Bank Street's lengthy waiting list while their children are still in utero. They start saving then, too: tuition is $16,000 a year for an all-day program. The vast majority of families can't afford such sticker prices. The new Early Head Start for children under 3 only has 22,000 slots for 2.9 million eligible children. With federal welfare reform pushing more mothers of young children into the work force, demand is expected to reach record levels. More parents will have to patch together a makeshift sitter system. "There is too much freelancing with these kids already," says Ron Lally, director of the Center for Child and Family Studies in San Francisco.

Although some child-development experts believe the best solution would be for more parents to stay home with young kids, that clearly isn't a reality for many families, especially since many women bring home half the family income. Unlike families in Germany or Sweden, American parents do not receive government subsidies to replace one parent's paycheck. Instead, we rely on the kindness of strangers.

Who's Watching the Kids?

Parents rely on relatives or paid sitters to help mind even their smallest children. With 1-year-olds, 50 percent of families use some nonparental arrangement. By the time they are 5, just 16 percent of children are watched only by their parents.

PERCENTAGE OF CHILDREN IN EACH AGE GROUP*						
	less than 1	1 year old	2 years old	3 years old	4 years old	5 years old
Children in relative care	24%	24%	19%	21%	18%	15%
Children in non-relative care	17%	19%	20%	19%	15%	17%
In center-based program	7%	11%	19%	41%	65%	75%

*COLUMNS DO NOT ADD UP TO 100 BECAUSE SOME CHILDREN PARTICIPATED IN MORE THAN ONE TYPE OF DAY CARE. SOURCES: U.S. DEPARTMENT OF EDUCATION, NATIONAL CENTER FOR EDUCATION STATISTICS

"We require licenses for beauticians and caterers," says Sharon Lynn Kagan, author of "Reinventing Early Care and Education." "It's ludicrous that we don't require licenses for child-care workers."

Licenses will not rescue Washington, D.C.'s Model Early Learning Center, home away from home to 20 children and their pudgy cat, Coco. The richly outfitted preschool, modeled after the pioneering Reggio Emilia nurseries in northern Italy, has served some of the capital's poorest children for the past four years. But last year local public funding shriveled, and the

school may close in June.

Still, the Model Center children go about their projects, oblivious to the school's fate. A small group recently hatched a plan for a "flying machine" for the peripatetic Coco. The cat's contraption would have a magic button to convert it into a submarine, and wings made of dried leaves and feathers. Whether or not this ambitious plan is ever completed, it already has produced enough brainstorming to electrify the minds of its young designers. These tots are wired for ideas, the ultimate head start.

Understanding Through Play

Christine Chaillé and
Steven B. Silvern

*Christine Chaillé is Professor, Curriculum and Instruction,
Portland State University, Portland, Oregon. Steven B. Silvern is Professor,
Early Childhood Education, Auburn University, Auburn, Alabama.*

A visitor walks into a kindergarten classroom and observes the children scattered about the room, playing in various areas. In one area a child is playing with a magnetic toy. The toy consists of four magnets embedded in a plastic base and hundreds of tiny metal parallelograms that can be formed into larger forms above the magnets in the base. The child has constructed an arch between two of the magnets. He then takes one tiny parallelogram and tries to stick it onto another one that he holds in his hand. When he tries to stick the combination onto the arch with one hand, one parallelogram falls to the floor. He picks it up and then presses the two objects together harder, as though trying to make them stick together by the force of his hand pressure.

This child is displaying *understanding*. When we speak of "understanding" we are referring to the active construction of meaning. Children arrive at understanding by creating hypotheses about items and events that they find interesting. They test hypotheses as they actively interact with the materials and events in their environment (Chaillé & Britain, 1991). The child in the above scenario was testing his hypothesis that each individual metal piece would stick to any other one.

The idea that these understandings *belong* to each child, individually, is important when discussing children's understanding. While the actions described above are familiar to teachers, not every child will act with the same understandings. As the child acts, familiar tools are applied to unfamiliar ideas. In the above example, when the two pieces did not stick together, the child attempted to make them stick in the same way that he would try to make a piece of paper stick with glue.

Sometimes these familiar tools do not *work* in the way that an adult would consider to be correct. Once the two pieces did not stick together, for example, an adult would not consider trying to use more force to try and make them stick. Nevertheless, some tools may work for the child. That is, although the hypothesis may not be totally correct, it has enough correctness to be satisfying to the child. Therefore, the child has an understanding; in this case, an understanding about things sticking together. It is not completely correct, but it is correct enough that the child is satisfied with the result. Only if the child sees a discrepancy in his reasoning will he be motivated to modify his reasoning, and ultimately his answer. Thus, when the piece fell a second time, the child abandoned his strategy and placed the individual pieces one at a time on the arch.

Piaget refers to the intentional social process of constructing understanding (partially described above) as active education (DeVries & Kohlberg, 1987). Active education involves four elements: interest, play, genuine experimentation and cooperation. In this article, the authors contend that interest, experimentation and cooperation are joined within the context of play. They first examine the kinds of play and the relation of these kinds of play to active education. Then, they place these kinds of play into particular learning contexts, intending to show that through play, children achieve all the elements of active education through play.

It is important to remember, however, that play may take two different forms, one of which is not active learning. When children are interested and applying attention to their play, they are engaging in active education. If, however, their play involves a simple manipulation of materials, without applying mental activity, it is unlikely that knowledge construction will take place. This is why constructivists caution against simply giving children materials to manipulate. Little understanding can occur without interest, experimentation and cooperation.

Play and Active Education

Piaget (1962) identified four kinds of play: practice play, symbolic play, games with rules and constructions. (Piaget, in fact, separates constructions as a unique form of play that leads to adapted behaviors.) Opportunities for active education exist within each of these kinds of play.

■ *Practice play.* Practice play is the "... exercise [of] structures for no other purpose than the pleasure of functioning" (Piaget, 1962, p. 110). This definition stresses the importance of pleasure over the learning of a new behavior. According to this definition, learning does not necessarily take place in practice play. We can imagine, however, many instances of adult play in which the same ability is exercised and we do construct a "new" behavior. While we ski to get pleasure from the activity, for example, each time we do so we attempt to gain more control or, perhaps, more speed. So, too, as we watch our children and their friends jump rope or use a pogo stick, we can see them attempting to gain more control as they exercise their ability. They seem to ask the implicit questions: Can I jump longer? Can I jump farther? Can I jump two ropes going in different directions? Some intent to learn appears present even in practice play.

Other elements of active education, certainly interest, are present in practice play. Children will not continue to jump without an interest evidenced either internally or through peer relations. Active experimentation occurs as children attempt to go beyond what they can already do, even if that is only an attempt to maintain "social position" (by jumping longer, for example). Interestingly, children often

adapt rules during practice play. When jumping rope, for example, they may decree that children cannot monopolize the jump rope longer than the jump rope chant permits. The social negotiation that occurs around the act of jumping then involves the cooperation necessary for further understanding. In this case, it may not be further understanding of jumping, but instead an understanding of interactions that allows everyone to jump without becoming bored with turning the rope or waiting one's turn.

■ *Symbolic play.* As the children in one kindergarten class prepared to act out "Little Red Riding Hood," Shuwan said, "I'll be the chopper and this is my ax, OK? Pretend my hand is the ax." This is an example of symbolic play. Such play "...impl[ies] representation of an absent object ... [and] make-believe representation ..." (Piaget, 1962, p. 111). It is impossible to represent or make believe without applying active thought. Therefore, symbolic play would seem to be the epitome of active interest. Children cannot simply manipulate something that is not present, nor can an object be substituted for another without some mental effort. Interest, then, is implied when children engage in symbolic play.

Ample opportunity for genuine experimentation exists during symbolic play, although it does not always occur. Experimentation is possible whenever children construct props for their symbolic play. Granny's house in "Little Red Riding Hood," for example, had to be built tall enough for the wolf to hide behind, yet be stable enough that it would not topple easily. Another kind of experimentation involves modes of communication. Whenever children seek alternate means for communicating their intent, as with Shuwan and his hand/ax, they are experimenting to find out if their actions/representations communicate.

Cooperation among children lies at the core of the negotiations that must occur whenever symbolic play occurs in groups of children. Rubin (1980) and Williamson and Silvern (1992) identify the discussions that occur within symbolic play as the impetus for thinking. During symbolic play children disagree, discuss the problem and come to agreement so that the play can continue. Children come to see other points of

> *A*ctive experimentation occurs as children attempt to go beyond what they can already do, even if that is only an attempt to maintain "social position."

view during this exchange and learn to understand the others' reasoning.

■ *Games with rules.* Games with rules are defined as "... prescribed acts, subject to rules, generally penalties for the infringement of rules and the action proceeds in a formal evolution until it culminates in a given climax ..." (*Encyclopedia Americana*, 1957, p. 266, cited in DeVries, 1980, p. 1). In games with rules, children willingly submit themselves to the rules so that the game can continue. Interest and cooperation are evident within this context for, without either, the game cannot continue. The concept of genuine experimentation is not as commonplace. Children do experiment in games with rules when they try alternate means of achieving an end. In marbles, for example, the child may ask himself, "Can I make my marble skip over another? Can I hit one marble hard enough so that it will hit into other marbles?"

■ *Constructions.* While not identified by Piaget as a kind of play itself, constructions are seen as a midway point between play and work. Children might use materials to represent reality, for example, by carving wood to represent a boat, instead of simply taking a block of wood and pretending it is a boat (Piaget, 1962). It is perhaps easiest for teachers to see active education in constructions. Clearly, when a child is engaged in making something for the pleasure of making it, he or she is active and engaged in genuine experimentation. When the constructions take on a group form (e.g., block constructions), cooperation is also present.

Play and Content

Although play is one of the richest contexts for observing children's construction of understanding, it is important for teachers to be able to recognize the different types of knowledge that are being constructed through play. Teachers will then be able to identify the "content" that children are understanding through play, and relate it to the curricular goals of the classroom.

■ *Play and physical knowledge.* Numerous interesting problems arise in the context of play that lead to experimentation, creative problem solving and cooperation; all these behaviors contribute to the construction of understanding. When two preschool children are devising a drawbridge at the entry to their pretend castle, for example, they must figure out how to connect the drawbridge on each end, and be able to move one end up and down over the "moat." They may draw on a range of possible solutions, use a variety of materials and engage in substantial trial-and-error as they

seek a solution. Highly motivated children will work on the problem for longer periods of time and with less frustration than if the task were part of a decontextualized problem.

Similarly, 2nd-graders constructing marble roll-ways using cardboard tubes will encounter numerous situationally determined tasks, or problem-solving situations, that will lead to active experimentation and, ultimately, the construction of understanding. The idea that the steeper the ramp, the faster the marble will roll, becomes concrete as children try to get the marble to roll up a hill at the other end.

■ *Play and logico-mathematical knowledge.* Play also helps children construct understanding of relationships, which is the heart of logico-mathematical knowledge. Think of children constructing a tower from unit blocks. If they run out of big blocks, they must eventually figure out that two of the smaller blocks together will match one of the larger ones. Or think of older children trying to figure out how many weights to put on top of a pendulum to make it swing far enough to knock down a target. After each weight is placed on the pendulum bob, they swing it to see how it moves. They then add one weight at a time until the target is reached. Here, children are demonstrating their interest and cooperation in play.

The motivated construction of relationships that occurs in the context of play is also evident when children are sharing materials: dividing up the play dough and comparing amounts, sorting through the crayons or serving up the "dinner" at the pretend restaurant. And it is in the context of games that children, particularly older children, are challenged to incorporate scoring systems that provide a meaningful context for the use of arithmetic (Kamii & DeVries, 1980).

■ *Play and language.* Some of the most interesting developments

in relation to both oral and written language happen in the context of play. In the arena of oral language, children have an opportunity to explore language without the fear of correction or constraint. One of the characteristics of play is the "suspension of belief" (Garvey, 1977), which makes it possible for a 5-year-old girl to "become" an old man in speech and mannerisms. We see much experimentation with language patterns and sounds through dramatic play, both in solitary and in social dramatic play.

It is in the context of social dramatic play, however, that we observe the role of communicative competence and the instrumental use of language to accomplish shared goals. Collaboration in an imaginary context requires a good deal of language use to establish the scene, verify the pretend context and guide each other's actions. "You be the doctor, okay? And this is the blood pressure thing, right?" Language takes on the important role of marking pretense, as well as labeling objects and actions.

Similarly, in other types of play oral language use, though not as necessary as in the pretend mode, becomes important as children function together (e.g., in the building of a model). Older children in particular use language for planning play actions. The 2nd-graders working on the marble roll-way may "talk out" their predictions about whether and how a particular structure will work; preschoolers might talk less and do more.

Construction of understanding through written language also occurs in the play context. Print can be incorporated into younger children's play in many ways. "Stop" and "Go" signs used with toy cars, for example, can signify for young children the basic idea that print has meaning. Older children may use written language to codify the rules of a game and introduce modifications. In addition, many games themselves directly involve language, including numerous board games such as Scrabble™. Many in the field of language arts (Wilde, 1991) view invented spelling as the best way of learning to become a good speller. This practice can be viewed as a playful approach to the act of writing itself.

■ *Play and curricular integration.* Segmenting the curriculum according to what children are learning, and monitoring that learning in the classroom, leads us to analyze play and understanding in terms of separable content areas: language, mathematics and science. One of the most salient characteristics of the play environment, however, is that it facilitates the cross-fertilization of ideas and connections across content areas. Literacy and spatial relations come together in play when a child builds a set of gears and labels each part to keep track of where they belong. Mathematics and oral communication occur simultaneously as children play an exciting card game and debate the ways to keep score.

The separations of curricular domains fade when children are actively engaged, self-directed and highly motivated—as they are when they play. As we move toward projects and integrated themes in preschool and elementary curriculum development, we need to keep in mind that in play, projects and curriculum integration happen as a matter of course. We can facilitate the construction of understanding by encouraging children to engage in all forms of play.

■ *Play and the sociomoral environment.* The elements of interest, experimentation and cooperation must be present in order for active learning, or understanding, to occur through play. An appropriate sociomoral environment is essential if these elements are to come together. The classroom's culture needs to be one in which children feel ownership and responsibility

for their own actions. They must feel a sense of community and safety in having their own ideas and trying them out, and they must feel good and caring about each other and share ideas in collaborative activity. Without such a classroom culture, the children will not manifest experimentation, engagement and interest.

Why is the classroom climate or the sociomoral environment so necessary for these elements to come together in constructing understanding? Children need to feel the safety and confidence that permits them to take risks, as they do in their play. Children's understandings (everyone's new understandings, for that matter) are tentative and fragile. Conflict must be experienced in order for learning and growth to take place. Children need to feel safe enough to go out on a limb and confident that falling will not matter. The role of sociocognitive conflict, so necessary for cognitive growth and learning, can seamlessly occur without affective disturbance, in large part because of the framework of play.

Think of the child rolling play dough out with a roller, making a smooth flat surface. He announces that he wants to make a line across it, "to make a road." A girl offers him a roller with spokes in it that, if rolled across a surface, would leave dots and indentations, not a line. He rolls it across, and the two children declare that they have made a "bumpy road." They have changed their "task" based on the outcome of their incorrect prediction. The play context allows the conflict between the prediction, the spoke will make a road when you roll it across the play dough, and the reality, the spoke makes bumps across the play dough, to be assimilated into a new goal. Because the goal is of their choosing to begin with, and because the play context allows for self-directed flexibility, it truly does not matter. Nonetheless, the chil-

dren have acquired a deeper understanding of the relationship between the marks on the roller and the action of rolling it on play dough—a relationship they can build on in their future hypotheses.

Play, then, offers the child the opportunity to make sense out of the world by using available tools. Understanding is created by doing, by doing with others and by being completely involved in that doing. Through play, the child comes to understand the world and the adult comes to understand the child.

◆

References

Chaillé, C., & Britain, L. (1991). *The young child as scientist.* New York: HarperCollins.

DeVries, R. (1980). Good group games: What are they? In C. Kamii & R. DeVries (Eds.), *Group games in early education: Implications of Piaget's theory* (pp. 1-9). Washington, DC: National Association for the Education of Young Children.

DeVries, R., & Kohlberg L. (1987). *Programs of early education: The constructivist view.* White Plains, NY: Longman.

Garvey, C. (1977). *Play.* Cambridge, MA: Harvard University Press.

Kamii, C. K. (1985). *Young children reinvent arithmetic: Implications of Piaget's theory.* New York: Teachers College Press.

Kamii, C., & DeVries, R. (Eds.). (1980). *Group games in early education: Implications of Piaget's theory.* Washington, DC: National Association for the Education of Young Children.

Piaget, J. (1962). *Play, dreams and imitation in childhood.* New York: Norton.

Rubin, K. H. (1980). Fantasy play: Its role in the development of social skills and social cognition. In K. H. Rubin (Ed.), *Children's play* (pp. 69-84). San Francisco: Jossey-Bass.

Wilde, S. (1991). *You kan red this! Spelling and punctuation for whole language classrooms K-6.* Portsmouth, NH: Heinemann.

Williamson, P. A., & Silvern, S. B. (1992). "You can't be grandma; you're a boy": Events within the thematic fantasy play context that contribute to story comprehension. *Early Childhood Research Quarterly, 7,* 75-93.

Your Learning Environment

A look back at your year

by Ellen Booth Church When you assess your children's growth and learning, set aside some time to also evaluate your learning environment. You'll find that an end-of-year review is a great tool — one you can use to plan an even better classroom and curriculum for next year.

GETTING STARTED On the following pages you'll find questions to get you started in evaluating five key classroom learning centers. You probably have other learning centers to look at, and you may wish to generate additional questions that refer to specific learning goals for your children. So use the questions that follow as a framework, which you can customize for your classroom.

Make use of all the tools you have available to help you in your evaluation. These include your own thoughts and memories and also the documentation you have collected, such as your anecdotal notes, portfolios, and other records of children's work. You might even want to make use of a video camera to get an accurate look at what's really happening in your centers.

Also, seek out feedback from people who know your classroom well, including, if appropriate, your director or principal, parents, and colleagues. Finally, don't forget your children! Their perspectives offer valuable information and can serve as a barometer of how well your learning centers worked this year. Ask them questions such as these: *What was your favorite center and why? What didn't you like about school this year? What suggestions do you have for next year's children? What new things do you think we need in the classroom?*

Now, let's take an in-depth tour through your learning environment.

From *Early Childhood Today*, May/June 1996, pp. 28-35. © 1996 by Scholastic, Inc. Reprinted by permission.

Literacy: Bringing Language to Life

Your language and literacy activities may be integrated in one place or consist of a separate library corner, writing center, listening center, and/or group-meeting area. But however the literacy center is designed, it should help children understand the forms and functions of spoken and written language; give them meaningful experiences with reading, writing, speaking, and listening; help them master early-literacy skills; and foster a love of books.

■ How many opportunities did children have every day to read? To write? Was there enough time and enough materials every day to accommodate all children who were interested?

■ How many opportunities did children have to make use of environmental print? Was the print meaningful to them? What percentage of the words that surrounded children were written or dictated by them?

■ How did your center resources demonstrate the connections between reading and writing and all the other areas of your curriculum? Did you use, for example, song charts, science vocabulary, or books about current themes?

■ What was the balance of large-group, small-group, and individual reading activities?

■ Were activities readily available in the classroom to reinforce specific age-appropriate literacy skills, such as sequencing picture stories for younger children and matching sounds with letters for kindergartners?

■ How would you describe your book collection in terms of quality, quantity, and variety? Are the books age-appropriate? Do they reflect the cultures of your children?

■ How did your environment communicate to parents and visitors information about children's literacy experiences? Were samples of individual children's writing displayed? What about class books and experience charts?

■ Did you offer materials to reinforce literacy at home? How did families respond?

■ Did children have frequent opportunities to see their ideas written down through dictation and invented spelling?

■ Was there a place for children to record and read back new vocabulary words of interest to them?

■ Were children free to play with language, its sounds and meaning?

PLANNING TIPS

● Make sure there is enough room for children to access all needed materials.

● Avoid clutter by using hanging storage pockets (such as clear shoe or clothing bags) for writing, listening, and language-game materials.

A LOOK AT SYSTEMS

Your management systems allow your learning centers to operate smoothly. In a child-centered environment, they also enable children to manage themselves as much as possible.

Did children feel empowered by your systems and routines? Could they independently check in to learning centers, choose their own activities, and take out and put away materials by themselves?

Were systems easy to follow? If you had to explain procedures repeatedly, your systems need work. Review procedures that were difficult, and think about ways to simplify them or to alter the environment to help.

Did your environment provide visual or tactile cues? If children were confused, mark shelves and materials with matching symbols. Post pictorial daily schedules and signs in each center so that children know what to expect.

● Augment your literacy space (and reinforce the connections between literacy and other learning) by adding paper and writing materials to other areas.

● Use bins to store books in other learning centers — books about building in the block area, for example.

● Check that all children in your room can see themselves respectfully represented in books, songs, and discussions.

Manipulatives: Making Math Work

Your math and manipulative center is where children use materials to explore and discover concepts that help them organize their world. Because math is integral to many other activities — art, music, science — your math center also functions as a storehouse for portable materials that can be used around the room.

■ What range of materials did you have that could be used for sorting and classifying? For seriating? For measuring weight and dimensions? For making patterns? For exploring number and spatial concepts? Did you have materials that could be used in a variety of ways?

■ What was the balance of teacher-directed and child-directed math activities?

■ How did your activities in this center encourage children to use math to reason, communicate ideas, make connections, and solve problems?

■ How did the environment facilitate bringing math materials to other areas of the room for activities like measuring and making patterns?

■ How did your environment help children learn the language of math, such as the terms *more* and *less* for younger children, and *add* and *plus* for kindergartners?

■ What opportunities did children have to record and review the results of their problem solving?

PLANNING TIPS

● Limit materials and games to those related to math concepts, such as links, cubes, and objects for sorting. Keep non-math-related games elsewhere.

● Supply multiples of manipulatives that are particularly popular or are necessary for developing particular skills, especially for kindergartners.

● Keep tabletops orderly by offering children trays or mats to work on.

● Rotate manipulatives and materials often enough to spark children's interest.

● Offer basic information and structure so that children understand some ways they can use the materials. Then encourage and accept children's own innovations.

Art: An Invitation to Creativity

Art is one of many languages children use to express their feelings and ideas. Your art area can support children's developing creativity by offering the materials, time, and space for them to explore freely. Activities should be open-ended and emphasize process rather than just product.

■ How many open-ended materials (paper, crayons and markers, wood, recycled objects) were available to children on a daily basis? Was there a wide variety of each?

■ How often did you introduce new or innovative materials to the art area? How much time did children have to fully explore these items?

■ How did you help children learn specific art skills, such as printing or using scissors?

■ Did behavior problems arise in your art area due to children's boredom with the materials, frustration over scarcity of materials, or insufficient space?

■ Which of your children visited the art area frequently? Occasionally? Not at all?

■ Was there freedom to create on a variety of surfaces, like easels and the floor?

■ Was there space to store works-in-progress? To continue projects over time?

■ How did you provide space

to display two- and three-dimensional creations?

PLANNING TIPS

● Check your art area regularly to make sure it is well-stocked and orderly.

● Try integrating curriculum themes and activities based on raw art materials — paper, paint, or string — into all your learning centers.

● Stock materials such as fabrics, buttons, beads from many cultures, and crayons and paints in different skin tones, to help all children feel at home in the art area. Encourage donations from families.

● Engage the interest of children who rarely choose art by offering activities such as driving toy cars through paint to make tire prints.

● Have smocks and extra play clothes available so children who are not dressed for messy play can feel free to participate.

A LOOK AT FLOW

Traffic problems can undermine an engaging curriculum and well-planned routines.

Was there too much running in your classroom? There may be too large an open space or a runway through your room. Expand your learning centers to incorporate some of the extra space.

Were children in quiet work areas disturbed by children in other areas? Group quieter centers, such as literacy and math away from noisier activities like blocks, dramatic play, and music. Define the centers' borders clearly with rugs, shelving, or tape.

Dramatic Play: Acting Out of the World

In your dramatic-play area, children have an opportunity to explore their imaginations and practice language and social skills by playacting meaningful events and characters in their lives.

■ Were play themes and props age-appropriate, focusing on home, families, and friends for preschoolers, and expanding to include community, adventure, and fantasy themes for older fours, fives, and kindergartners?

■ What was the balance of child-initiated and teacher-initiated play themes? How successfully did each one work?

■ Did you change themes or props often enough to sustain children's interest? Too often to allow for in-depth exploration by children?

■ Were social conflicts caused by too little space? By arguments over sharing props?

■ How did children apply literacy and math concepts in their dramatic play? What props in the area encouraged these behaviors?

■ What did you do to make sure your dramatic-play area reflected the home environments of all your children? What more might you do next year?

PLANNING TIPS

● Provide enough space and materials for children to freely interact and recreate meaningful experiences.

● Expand your supply of props by enlisting the help of families and visiting tag sales and flea markets.

● Assemble dramatic-play "prop boxes" for different themes children have enjoyed.

● Store large blocks near the dramatic-play area so that children can create their own play structures.

● Look for meaningful ways to foster age-appropriate skills. Include literacy props such as books, telephones, message pads, and markers. Offer props that promote math skills, including a clock, a cash register with play money, and a balance scale.

Science: Making New Discoveries

In a child-centered program, science is individualized to accommodate all learning styles and enable children to explore their interests in their own way. Yet, the goal for all children is to practice using basic science skills and processes — observation, prediction, experimentation, and evaluation — to help understand the world around them.

■ What specific materials and activities in your science area encouraged children to observe, predict, experiment, and evaluate?

■ Did children have many opportunities to record their science findings through drawing, writing, or creating charts and graphs? Did opportunities match your children's varying literacy and math abilities?

■ Did you adequately introduce new concepts and techniques in mini-lessons to help children who needed more structure? Did you then allow everyone plenty of opportunity for free exploration?

■ How often could you accommodate children's desires to test out their ideas? Were you able to provide them with the necessary materials and time?

■ How did you use your observations of children's experiments in this center and around the room to offer activities that built on their natural curiosity?

■ Did you provide activities in this center that responded to a specific experience of children's — for example, seeing "cracks" (erosion) produced by rain on the playground?

■ Did your science tools and materials support a range of scientific experiences, from physics to plant and animal studies to chemical reactions?

■ Did your science center seem more like just a museum than a laboratory for active learning? How could you change this?

PLANNING TIPS

● Provide bins of materials for children to use in creating self-directed explorations and experiments.

● Make sure that your science center includes things to *do*, not just to look at. Stock it with science tools such as magnifying glasses and magnets. Prepare discovery trays of materials and tools like metal and nonmetal objects and a magnet. Add pictorial cards that present problem-solving experiments children can conduct.

● Set up your science area so that it invites several children to actually sit, spend time, and work there together.

● Watch for children using materials inappropriately — as pretend weapons, for example. To redirect children, spark their interest by interacting with them in the activities you've set out.

● Consider other science-related areas and activities when planning your science-center curriculum. These can include the outdoors, your sand and water tables, cooking, and art.

A LOOK AT TONE

Children's emotions, behavior, and interactions are strongly influenced by your program and space, and can indicate aspects of your learning environment that need improvement. Your answers to the questions below can serve as a barometer of your classroom's tone.

• Was the general tone of the classroom happy, balanced, energetic, or chaotic?

• Were most children excited about activities and school in general?

• Were many children anxious to go home throughout the day?

• Were children generally focused or were they easily distracted?

• What was the quality of children's interactions? Was there a great deal of fighting or shouting?

• What was the quality and quantity of adult-child interactions?

• Were children relatively independent or always needing assistance?

As you assess your learning environment, make note of the things that worked really well, even as you look at the things that you could (or should) do better. Then set realistic goals that will keep you moving forward, and look for fun things that you can do over the summer to enrich your program next year. And remember, a classroom environment with your own personal touches will make for a more successful, exciting year to come for you and your children!

Ellen Booth Church is an early childhood consultant for the New York State Department of Education and for early childhood programs across the country.

Your Environment for
CHILDREN WITH SPECIAL NEEDS

Children with special needs may be included in your classroom along with those who do not require special accommodation. Take some time to look at how your room has specifically enabled children with disabilities to meet the following special challenges:

Visual Challenges: Well-planned learning centers with clearly defined borders can do wonders to make the classroom more navigable. In each learning center, ask yourself how you can add texture to items to make them identifiable through more than one sense.

Hearing Challenges: Do your planned activities and materials enable hearing-impaired children to manage independently? Place simple drawings and symbols in centers, bathrooms, and hallways to remind them and all children about procedures and routines.

Physical Challenges: Are your learning areas arranged for comfort and support? Heavy, stable furniture placed on a carpet that won't slide is a must.

Cognitive/Intellectual Challenges: Did you design activities that complement children's various developmental stages? Look for more ways to develop your learning centers and your curriculum to provide repetition. Present new information and materials in manageable pieces so that children can experience frequent success.

Social/Emotional Challenges: Did some children get overstimulated or confused? Consider making aspects of your environment less stimulating, limiting some choices, and varying the length of time for activities. Make sure your environment accommodates your spending one-on-one time with children who need extra support.

Talented and Gifted: Restlessness and misbehavior can be signs of boredom. Increase individual responsibility and adjust the complexity of projects and materials to motivate children who have special gifts.

Labeled for life?

Over two million kids are termed **"learning disabled."** But this and other tags are often **inaccurate** and always **damaging.**

BY NAOMI BARKO

Naomi Barko writes frequently on education.

Vicki LaFarge was devastated when a preschool psychologist suggested that her 4-year-old daughter, Adrienne, had Asperger's disorder, a mild form of autism. She had taken the child for independent testing after a nursery-school teacher said she wasn't interacting normally with other kids. "If the autism label wasn't scary enough," says Vicki, "the tests said she was acting at a low-normal level of intelligence!"

Terrified, Vicki took her daughter to the Developmental Consultation Services at the Harvard Community Health Plan, in Somerville, Massachusetts, for a second opinion. "They took one look at her and said, 'She does not have autism or low-normal intelligence. It may be a subtle learning disorder. Or it may

be that she is just developing socially at a different rate. We won't know until she's in regular school and is faced with more learning challenges.'" Happily, Vicki reports, "We are working on Adrienne's social skills and she's doing much better."

At age 5, Kenny Ridenour, of Bellflower, California, was diagnosed with attention deficit/hyperactivity disorder (ADHD), and his pediatrician prescribed Dexedrine. Always a good student, Kenny had never had learning problems. But when he was around 8 his school began to complain that he refused to complete writing assignments, and began labeling him "noncompliant."

"Kenny would cry and say that he hated school, even though he had always loved it before," says his mother, Phyllis. Then she transferred him to the Child Development Center of the University of California, Irvine.

He was taken off Dexedrine and taught how to work and interact by employing behavior-modification techniques. Now 9, Kenny is flourishing and doing work above his grade level.

Are we treating kids for disorders they don't have?

Welcome to the era of psychological evaluations, where schools, psychologists, and physicians freely attach such labels to small children, with potentially grave consequences. Yet parents need to be aware that in many cases, the methods used to make these evaluations are not definitive, which leaves them in a quandary. While it's damaging to have a problem misdiagnosed, it's equally tragic not to seek specialized help for a child who is truly struggling, since early treatment can make all the difference in school success.

No one is suggesting that these problems don't exist, but experts are admitting that detecting them is an inexact science, and warning parents to be vigilant before letting anyone label their child.

"The evaluations children are getting throughout the United States are often problematic," says Mel Levine, M.D., professor of pediatrics at the University of North Carolina at Chapel Hill and president of All Kinds of Minds, a nonprofit institute for the understanding of differences in learning. "Some of the most misleading testing is done for preschoolers. I can say this because I've developed some of those tests myself. They're not fine-grained enough. There are some kids who look as if they're in trouble at age 4 and they're great at 8 or 9. It's difficult to evaluate learning disabilities in preschoolers because they are not faced with complex language and conceptual challenges until later in school."

"Our testing instruments are simply not refined enough to differentiate slow learners and low achievers from the truly learning disabled," says James Ysseldyke, Ph.D., professor of educational psychology at the University of Minnesota.

If preschoolers are so difficult to diagnose accurately, why all the interest in having them evaluated? "Labels are convenient for schools, or for getting reimbursements from managed-care or insurance companies," explains Levine. "But in no way do they fit all kids." By school age, he says, "kids are reduced to a test score or a simplistic label, without focusing on their strengths and weaknesses."

Learning and behavior problems can be misread

The sheer number of "problem kids" is staggering. Some 2.5 million children—about 5 percent of the school population—are labeled as having learning disabilities, a loose term for a group of disorders that cause significant difficulty in listening, speaking, reading, writing, reasoning, or mathematical abilities.

LDs often overlap with attentional dysfunctions, though they are two separate problems. ADD (attention deficit disorder) is a neurological disorder characterized by an inability to focus attention and a tendency to be easily distracted; ADHD is the same as ADD, but with hyperactivity nd impulsivity.

The number of ADD and ADHD diagnoses has grown so dramatically that since 1990, production of Ritalin—a brain stimulant used to treat ADHD—has increased sixfold. It is now estimated that some 1.3 million American children be-

tween ages 5 and 14 are taking it.

Experts fear that many kids are being medicated for a disorder they may not have. ADHD is especially difficult to diagnose because doctors haven't successfully defined hyperactivity. So a common error that professionals make is "turning normal variations of temperament into abnormalities," says William Carey, M.D., clinical professor of pediatrics at the Children's Hospital of Philadelphia. "In fact, half of normal children are more or less active than average, but that doesn't mean they have something wrong with their brain."

"Forty percent of the so-called ADHD cases I see are kids who are suffering from anxiety caused by family tensions," adds Boston child psychiatrist Arnold Kerzner, M.D. He recalls an 8-year-old whose pediatrician put him on Ritalin after his teacher said he had sudden outbursts of anger.

"I found he was suffering from severe anxiety caused by his parents' marital problems," says Kerzner. "I took him off Ritalin and counseled the family. After six months the symptoms disappeared."

The biggest problem is the evaluation process itself. "Most ADHD diagnoses are not made by psychologists or other mental-health professionals," reports Russell Barkley, Ph.D., professor of psychiatry and neurology at the University of Massachusetts Medical Center, in Worcester. "They are made mainly on the basis of a brief interview with parents by a pediatrician. And rarely is there any contact between the doctor and the teacher."

Our health-care system may be contributing to these quick diagnoses, which may become even more common as doctors join HMOs, warns Barkley: "Managed care can demand that a pediatrician spend less than 20 minutes with a patient."

"Spending time with a family, counseling them and educating them, is expensive," adds Levine. Unfortunately, the most efficient and "most reimbursable thing you can do is put a child on drugs."

Is it really dyslexia or just poor teaching?

There is more controversy over a common LD, dyslexia, a disorder characterized by inaccuracy and slowness in reading. "Sixty to 80 percent of children identified as learning disabled in school have reading as their primary difficulty," says Reid Lyon, Ph.D., director of research programs on learning disabilities at the National Institute of Child Health and Human Development, in Washington, D.C.

But not all reading difficulties mean dyslexia. "It seems that any kid who has a reading problem is labeled as dyslexic," says Frank Vellu-

tino, Ph.D., director of the Child Research and Study Center at the State University of New York, Albany. "If what you mean by 'dyslexic' is a basic neurological or genetic inadequacy, then only 3 to 5 percent of children are truly dyslexic."

In a six-year study involving 1,400 children, Vellutino selected a group of 76 of his worst first-grade readers, some of whom had already been labeled dyslexic. With intensive one-on-one teaching for half an hour a day, about 70 percent of the children were brought up to an average reading range in just one semester. "These children are not dyslexic," he claims. "You might say they just got off to a poor start."

Are some kids more likely to be labeled? There are indicators, says Ysseldyke. "A kid who bothers the teacher will get referred for testing, yet another kid who may

How reliable are IQ tests?

Tests for giftedness can be as misleading as tests for learning disabilities. According to current estimates, 5 percent of children (preschoolers through high school)—roughly 2.5 million—are gifted and talented. But experts believe many of them are never identified.

Though IQ tests were once viewed as an absolute measure of intelligence, many educators have questioned their validity and fairness. Still, most schools use tests (such as the Stanford-Binet or Wechsler scale) as part of the screening process for gifted-and-talented programs, says Ellen Winner, Ph.D., author of *Gifted Children: Myths and Realities*

(Basic Books) and a professor of psychology at Boston College.

"IQ measures verbal, numerical, and some spatial ability," says Winner. "But it's narrow because it doesn't take into account visual, musical, athletic, leadership, or social ability."

"The IQ test is not in itself an indication of giftedness; it is only one of a series in the identification process," adds Peter D. Rosenstein, executive director of the National Association for Gifted Children (NAGC), in Washington.

Other gifted kids may fall through

the cracks because they don't fit the "bookworm" stereotype.

"A precocious child who is not being challenged may act up in class and show behavior problems associated with ADHD," says Rosenstein. (Many bright kids can also have LDs, and their giftedness can often be overlooked.)

If you think your child may be gifted, experts recommend getting an individual evaluation by a trained professional who will administer a series of tests beyond the IQ measurement. For more information, call the NAGC at 202-785-4268.

have real problems won't get referred because she's quieter." These "troublesome" kids usually turn out to be boys, who until recently were reported to have four times the reading problems of girls. However, says Lyon, "NIH has found that girls have almost as many reading problems as boys."

Still, schools alone can't be blamed for rampant misdiagnosis, say critics. Ironically, the problem may be the federal law that was designed to help children. The Individuals With Disabilities Education Act (IDEA), enacted in 1975 to assure a free, appropriate public education for kids with physical and learning disabilities, distributes about $2 billion nationally each year for special education.

"Public schools aren't getting money for smaller classes, better-trained teachers, or aides to help kids who fall behind," says Ysseldyke. "But they can get money for special education, and the only way they can get it under federal law is to test a child and label him—and 'learning disabled' is the most convenient."

IDEA has fueled the learning-disabilities issue. "The law defines an LD as a 'significant discrepancy' between a child's IQ and achievement as measured on a test or shown by his performance in school," says Susan Vess, Ph.D., president of the National Association of School Psychologists. This discrepancy or gap between how capable a child seems and how he is performing is what school psychologists are looking for when they test. "But that difference can vary from state to state," adds Vess. "So a child who is borderline could be learning disabled in one state, but not in another."

Why your pediatrician's opinion isn't enough

If you think you see early signs of learning problems, start by discussing them with your child's pediatrician and preschool teachers, advises Betty Osman, Ph.D., a psychologist affiliated with the White Plains Medical Center, in White Plains, New York. "Parents are often the first to notice these things, and in most cases they and their child's teachers can intervene to resolve many social or learning problems." However, in severe cases—if there is a significant language delay by age 3 or difficulties with motor skills—she advises consulting a speech or physical therapist.

School-age kids (and some preschoolers, depending on the problem) should be evaluated by a multidisciplinary team—a school psychologist, a speech therapist, a teacher, and sometimes a developmental pediatrician.

"What's crucial is to get a picture of the whole child," says Claire Wurtzel, chair of special education at the Bank Street College of Education, in New York, and a member of the advisory board of the National Center for Learning Disabilities. "A child should be seen over a period of time to study his development. The parents should always be involved. And you need a teacher's assessment: If you change the method of teaching, does the problem persist, change, or even disappear?"

Christine Lord, of Washington, D.C., knows the value of getting other opinions. When her daughter, Elicia, was entering fourth grade, she was diagnosed with ADD and put on Ritalin. But Christine decided to see a new doctor, who found the real problem: a mild form of epilepsy. "Elicia was having trouble paying attention because she was having seizures," says Christine. "Now she's getting the proper medication, and she's doing great."

Christine's advice? "Don't be afraid to be a pushy parent. If you don't believe the experts, get more opinions. You know your child better than anyone else."

"SMART" Planning for Inclusion

Suzanne M. Winter

Suzanne M. Winter is Assistant Professor, Division of Education, The University of Texas at San Antonio.

eachers across the nation are facing the need to meet a wider range of abilities in the classroom. The Rehabilitation Act of 1973 (Section 504), the Americans with Disabilities Act (ADA) of 1990, and the Individuals with Disabilities Education Act Amendments of 1991 (IDEA) require the inclusion of children with disabilities in general child care and education programs when it is in their best interests (Deiner, 1993; Salisbury, 1991; Underwood & Mead, 1995).

In 1993, the U.S. Department of Education, Office of Special Education Programs, reported that nearly five million children with disabilities received special education services during the 1991-1992 school year (U.S. Department of Education, 1993). Sixty-nine percent of these children were enrolled in general education classrooms over 40 percent of the time. More than half of the total children with disabilities represented by this report ranged in age from 3 to 11 years. Thus, one can assume that general early childhood and elementary programs went to great lengths to include this marginalized population.

In 1995, the Joint Committee on Teacher Planning for Students with Disabilities reported that new instructional techniques implemented by trained teachers benefited all children (Joint Committee on Teacher Planning for Students with Disabilities, 1995). Unfortunately, general education teachers typically have few opportunities for training or collaboration with specialists (Joint Committee, 1995; Schloss, 1992; Wolery et al., 1994). General education teachers, who generally do not have sufficient instructional planning time during the school day, also face increasing pressures to raise student performance, teach larger classes and cover more curriculum content (Joint Committee, 1995). Given the need for streamlining the instructional planning cycle, this article will propose a practical, five-point system designed to guide teachers through the process of instructional planning for inclusive education programs.

THE "SMART" PLANNING SYSTEM

SMART is an acronym for: Select, Match, Adapt, Relevant and Test. Rather than indicating a sequence of steps, the acronym is meant to remind teachers of five key planning components that, both singly and in combination, influence instructional power. A graphic depiction of these dynamics as geometrical rays underscores how effective planning must be a continuous process (see Figure 1). The triangle formed by the intersection of these rays represents the strong foundation for instruction that interplay of these five dynamics can create.

Select Curriculum and Approaches

Teachers practicing inclusion must carefully select curricula and instructional approaches. All routines and learning activities must be consistent with the chosen curricular framework. The inclusion movement lacks an accumulated research base to provide definitive answers regarding the best inclusion curriculum models. The following tentative strategies can help guide teachers through this selection process.

Compare characteristics of individuals and curricula. How curricula mesh with the characteristics of individual children with disabilities may determine

From *Childhood Education*, Summer 1997, pp. 212-218. © 1997 by the Association for Childhood Education International, 17904 Georgia Avenue, Suite 215, Olney, MD. Reprinted by permission.

children's success (Cole, Dale, Mills & Jenkins, 1993; Cole, Mills, Dale & Jenkins, 1991; Scruggs & Mastropieri, 1993) and the extent of their integration into a program (Bricker, 1995). A major shift in emphasis is occurring. Rather than determining the "best practices" for inclusion, researchers are examining the appropriateness of specific practices for individual children with disabilities (Carta, 1994; Johnson & Johnson, 1994; Salisbury et al., 1994; Wolery & Bredekamp, 1994). Therefore, teachers should select curricula and approaches that fit a specific child's characteristics and cultural contexts (Carta, 1994; Johnson & Johnson, 1994; Scruggs & Mastropieri, 1993). An emphasis on the individual, however, should not be considered synonymous with one-to-one instruction. Through assiduous planning and a willingness to accommodate individuals, a common curriculum can be implemented for all children attending an inclusive program (Richarz, 1993; Wolery & Flemming, 1993).

Involve families in the selection process. Interaction with families is critical when selecting a curriculum appropriate for each child. A teacher should use an "ecological perspective" (Bronfenbrenner, 1979) and consider the multiple contexts related to the child's family, culture and community (Peck, 1993). In addition to providing information, families can evaluate the chosen curriculum model (Wolery & Bredekamp, 1994) or participate in the actual decision-making process (Johnson & Johnson, 1994; Odom, McLean, Johnson & LaMontagne, 1995).

Choose a flexible curriculum model. Selecting flexible curriculum models and instructional approaches is also critical (National Association of State Boards of Education, 1992). In accordance with federal mandates, teachers must make whatever reasonable accommodations are possible to allow individual children with disabilities to fully participate in general education or child care programs (Deiner, 1993; Grubb, 1993; Surr, 1992; Underwood & Mead, 1995). Teachers should select a curriculum that allows such accommodations without jeopardizing the curriculum's overall integrity.

The selected curriculum and approaches should also be flexible enough to accommodate various arrangements for planning and teaching. Sharing responsibilities with a special education teacher or other professionals may require a teacher to team teach, tutor individual children or teach alternately with others (Roach, 1995; Salisbury, 1991).

View from a constructivist perspective. While Richarz (1993) cautions against using a single curriculum model for all inclusive education programs, designing program models from a constructivist curricular base appears promising. A constructivist perspective permits children to create their own knowl-edge through interactive experiences with their physical and social environment (Piaget, 1952; Vygotsky, 1978). Educators for children of all age levels have showed increased interest in using a constructivist approach.

The inclusion movement has sparked debate concerning the merits of traditional practices in the early childhood and early childhood special education fields (Carta, 1994; Carta, Schwartz, Atwater & McConnell, 1991; Fox, Hanline, Vail & Galant, 1994; Johnson & Johnson, 1994; Wolery & Bredekamp, 1994). Wolery and Bredekamp (1994) found that constructivism was a common plank underlying the theory and practices of both fields. Cook, Tessier and Klein (1996), Miller (1996) and others recommend using constructivist elements such as an interdisciplinary curriculum, holistic approaches, "hands-on" experiences and play for inclusive early childhood programs.

Inclusive programs serving elementary through secondary level children are increasingly using constructivist approaches (Mastropieri & Scruggs, 1995; Sapona & Phillips, 1993; Scruggs & Mastropieri, 1993; Udvari-Solner & Thousand, 1995). Recent research studies suggest that active participation in holistic learning experiences enhances learning of all children, including those with disabilities. Rather than teaching concepts piecemeal, a holistic approach engages children in meaningful experiences that illustrate how

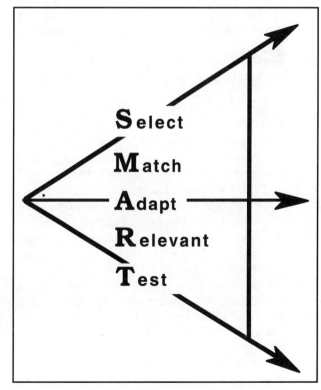

Figure 1

concepts are related (Eichinger & Woltman, 1993; Patton, 1995; Scruggs & Mastropieri, 1993; Sears, Carpenter & Burstein, 1994).

Some educators fear that constructivist approaches may not benefit children whose learning style is passive and disorganized (Carta et al., 1991). Countering this argument, McIntosh, Vaughn, Schumm, Haager and Lee (1994) suggest that passivity may be associated with insufficient accommodation for individual learning differences. A child with special needs may participate more actively in journal writing, for example, if allowed to use a computer with an adaptive keyboard that accommodates for his lack of fine motor control.

For certain children, a teacher may want to supplement a constructivist approach with more direct intervention. A whole language approach combined with explicit teaching, for example, can advance the language and literacy development of children with hearing loss (Kelly, 1995) and children with learning disabilities (Sears et al., 1994).

Special education teachers, physical therapists and other professionals on a multidisciplinary team can help a classroom teacher implement the principles of SMART planning. Most teachers present lessons to the entire class at the same time, using the chalkboard to provide examples. Children read a textbook for each subject and answer chapter questions or completed worksheets for practice.

Using the SMART planning approach, team members record the children's responses to instruction. Conversations with parents also provide valuable insights into how children with special needs learn best.

Match Instruction to the Child

Children's individual characteristics can cause them to respond differently to learning experiences in inclusive classrooms (Cole, Dale, Mills & Jenkins, 1993; Cole, Mills, Dale & Jenkins, 1991). An emerging trend is to create a match between learning opportunities and children by identifying individual strengths rather than focusing on children's deficits (Allen, 1992; Richarz, 1993; Sapona & Phillips, 1993).

Plan for different learning styles and preferences. All children have individual learning styles that favor different types of sensory input. Some children learn more efficiently when they receive information orally, while others require tactile, kinesthetic learning provided by manipulation of materials (Dunn, Dunn & Perrin, 1994). Identifying the learning styles of children with disabilities can help teachers plan for successful inclusion (Richarz, 1993).

In addition to sensory modalities, other preferences also influence a child's learning style. Ford, Riggs, Nissenbaum and LaRaia (1994) found that preschool children with autism learned more efficiently when

given tasks that provided a high degree of structure with few opportunities for choice. Conversely, Rose and Rose (1994) found that allowing greater responsibility and choice in learning increased cognitive effort and self-esteem of school-age children with learning disabilities.

Match facilitation strategies to suit each child. Matching the kind and amount of assistance offered to each child can be critical to learning (Sears et al., 1994). Lev Vygotsky explained that teaching strategies influence the knowledge a child constructs (Bodrova & Leong, 1996). Therefore, such strategies as modeling, giving directions and breaking the task into smaller steps can facilitate learning (Richarz, 1993). The child's response should guide the amount and type of teacher intervention offered (Bodrova & Leong, 1996; Wolery, 1991).

Peer-mediated strategies can also be successful, provided the teacher matches children for compatibility and monitors the activity to prevent over-direction by the peer-tutor (Krogh, 1994). Teachers must consider any disparity between the functioning levels of children in the tutoring pair. Children with marked disabilities appear to benefit less from language and social stimulation by highly skilled peers (Cole et al., 1991). Certain activities may call for pairing a child with disabilities with an average learner, rather than a gifted one.

Learning centers that give children a choice of multisensory materials and activities at different levels of challenge are useful. Children with special needs can work on concepts and skills at their own level while interacting socially with their peers. The teacher should facilitate children's learning by posing problems, asking questions and conversing with children about their work.

Adapt When Necessary

The next dynamic of the SMART planning system guides teachers in deciding whether modifications of the curriculum, learning environment, teaching styles or evaluation practices are warranted. Teachers must determine the type and extent of accommodation needed for each child.

Plan for differentiated instruction. Teachers must become well informed about the range of adaptations possible, and their implementation (Baker & Zigmond, 1990; Leister, 1993; Schumm & Vaughn, 1991). Research suggests that few teachers change their teaching style or make adaptations for children with special needs in inclusive classrooms. Undifferentiated instruction for the entire class is common, often resulting in children with learning disabilities assuming passive roles (Baker & Zigmond, 1990; McIntosh et al., 1994). A wider range of instructional strategies, such as additional interactive tasks, varied groupings and increased time for engagement in learning activities, may lead to more effective instruction (Baker & Zigmond, 1990). Programs that give accommodation a high priority experience no loss of instructional time, even when children with severe disabilities are present (Hollowood, Salisbury, Rainforth & Palombaro, 1995). Teachers and caregivers may need a network of professional support to effectively plan and implement a wider range of instructional strategies and adaptations (Fuchs, Fuchs, Hamlett, Phillips & Karns, 1995; Salisbury et al., 1994). Therefore, a multidisciplinary team should receive regular training and establish affiliations with other professionals within the school district and community.

Plan for the success of each child. While some children may need contextual supports, teachers should not assume that every child with disabilities will need accommodations for each learning activity (Barone, 1994; Salisbury, 1991). Instead, teachers should scrutinize instructional plans to detect situations that might warrant accommodations (Schumm & Vaughn, 1991). Whether the modifications are simple or sophisticated, the key is to identify options that focus on a child's strengths in order to promote success.

Assistive technology, such as computers, may allow a child to circumvent his weaknesses. Carefully selected technology can enhance certain children's independence and encourage their active participation (Holder-Brown & Parette, 1992; Holzberg, 1994; Prickett, Higgins & Boone, 1994).

Effective adaptations need not be complex. Simple options, such as identifying equivalent stimuli, can be very effective (Wolery, 1991). If a child has difficulty interpreting numerical representations of fractions, for example, the teacher could use an equivalent representation of fractions using pictures of objects divided into fractional parts.

Share decisions and plan in advance. Multidisciplinary teams that include the teacher should examine the increasing range of possible adaptations for individual children. By planning in advance, teachers will need to improvise less and will have sufficient intensity to ensure the instruction's effectiveness (Salisbury et al., 1994). The team will need to monitor the results of instructional accommodations for individual children on a continual basis (Salisbury, 1991; Salisbury et al., 1994). Several adaptations that may be tried include using electronic auditory enhancement systems to improve communications, adjusting tables for wheelchair height and moving furniture to widen pathways throughout the room.

Relevant Skills Targeted

When planning instruction, teachers must evaluate the meaningfulness and importance of learning opportunities for individual children. To make decisions about curricular relevance, teachers must take a child-centered approach by comparing each child's interests, strengths and goals to the curriculum and instruction (Brown & Lehr, 1993).

Estimate the immediate and long-term significance. Together, teachers and families should evaluate the immediate and future impact of the instructional activities (Beck, Broers, Hogue, Shipstead & Knowlton, 1994). Meaningful daily routines and activities can immediately encourage children's social interactions and participation in the program (Bricker, 1995; Brown & Lehr, 1993).

Use functional and community-based instruction. Functional curricula focus on developing concepts and skills needed in real life. Authentic learning experiences can help generalize a child's learning to current or future real life situations (Beck et al., 1994; Notari-Syverson & Shuster, 1995). Cook, Tessier and Klein (1996) recommend using real objects in the classroom and taking frequent field trips. Teachers should plan community-based or community-referenced instruction that requires children to apply functional knowledge and skills in actual on-site situations (Beck et al., 1994; Udvari-Solner & Thousand, 1995). Teachers can create more authentic environments in schools by using modern technological advances, such as videodiscs, laserdiscs and CD-ROMs (Duttweiler, 1992; Means & Olson, 1994). Assistive technology can enable certain children with disabilities to participate more fully in functional learning activities conducted in community settings (Gelman, 1993). Functional curricula and community-based instructional approaches have been successful in inclusive programs serving children from infancy through adolescence (Beck et al., 1994; Field, LeRoy & Rivera, 1994; Helmke, Havekost, Patton & Polloway, 1994; Notari-Syverson & Shuster, 1995).

Assistive technology, such as computers, may allow a child to circumvent his weaknesses.

Test To Inform Instruction

Inclusive education models must include a comprehensive system of tests and continuous assessment to determine children's progress, teacher effectiveness and program outcomes (Miller, 1996). Unfortunately, a classroom teacher's instructional planning is more likely to be influenced by the teacher's impressions of student ability, the curricular materials available and the goals set by local or state education agencies (Zigmond & Miller, 1986). Training is essential to prepare teachers for gathering and using actual data to inform curriculum and instruction in inclusive education settings (Miller, 1996).

Evaluate the whole child. Multiple assessment measures provide an accurate view of individual children in inclusive education settings (Fox, Hanline, Vail & Galant, 1994). Computers, for example, make it easier to aggregate multiple assessments (Irvin & Walker, 1994).

Teachers must monitor a child's progress in each developmental domain. Individualized assessments of a child's natural performance during learning activities (Fox et al., 1994) or multidomain criterion-referenced assessments provide valuable information. Of the latter, some instruments link directly with intervention planning options (Benner, 1992). Evaluation that recognizes children's multiple intelligences (Gardner, 1983) can help identify the strengths of children with disabilities (Mindes, Ireton & Mardell-Czudnowski, 1996; Udvari-Solner & Thousand, 1995).

Use alternative assessment. Alternative assessment tools, such as play-based measures, systematic observation, portfolios, curriculum-based tests and authentic assessment, are rapidly gaining favor (Benner, 1992; Bergen, 1993/94; Kindsvatter, Wilen & Ishler, 1996; Miller, 1996; Mindes et al., 1996). In contrast to standardized tests, alternative assessments are sensitive to individual variations in performance and developmental changes over time. Curriculum-based assessments evaluate a child's progress relative to the program's curriculum content. Alternative assessment measures are especially advantageous for programs that are limited in time and personnel (Mindes et al., 1996).

Embed authentic assessment into the curriculum. Authentic assessments evaluate a child's performance in real life contexts or situations that are contrived to simulate genuine circumstances. This form of alternative assessment is performance-based, meaning that the child demonstrates application and integration of knowledge through actual performance. Teachers can embed authentic assessment tasks into the curriculum by engaging children in thematic units, projects, play and other active learning experiences. Overlapping instruction and assessment eliminates the necessity to schedule time solely for testing (Kindsvatter, Wilen & Ishler, 1996; Linn & Gronlund, 1995; Miller, 1996; Mindes et al., 1996). Teachers can observe and record samples of students' language usage and problem-solving skills during cooperative learning activities, for example.

Explore technology-based assessment. Exciting new technology-based assessment options offer greater convenience, increased accuracy, immediate feedback and higher reliability (Greenwood, 1994). As technology-based assessments remove barriers to the participation of children with disabilities (Greenwood & Rieth, 1994), inclusive assessment is becoming more common. Technology can enable teachers to identify optimal learning conditions, present multimedia problem-solving simulations and use expert diagnostic systems (Fuchs, Fuchs & Hamlett, 1994; Gerber, Semmel, Semmel & Semmel, 1994; Greenwood & Rieth, 1994; Woodward & Howard, 1994). Recording and analyzing teacher observations is also easier to accomplish using technology (Greenwood, Carta, Kamps, Terry & Delquadri, 1994). Technology-based assessment appears to have the potential to greatly improve planning for inclusive programs.

CLIP 'N SAVE

S   *Select curriculum & approaches*

M   *Match instruction to child*

A   *Adapt when necessary*

R   *Relevant skills targeted*

T   *Test to inform instruction*

CONCLUSION

Implementing inclusion requires meticulous attention to instructional planning. Teachers can focus on those elements likely to influence the successful inclusion of children with disabilities by considering each of the dynamics highlighted in the SMART planning system. By streamlining the instructional planning process, teachers implementing inclusion may experience less stress, greater confidence and more success.

References

Allen, K. (1992). *The exceptional child: Mainstreaming in early childhood education* (2nd ed.). Albany, NY: Delmar.

Baker, J., & Zigmond, N. (1990). Are regular education classes equipped to accommodate students with learning disabilities? *Exceptional Children, 56*(6), 515-526.

Barone, D. (1994). Myths about "crack babies." *Educational Leadership, 52*(2), 67-68.

Beck, J., Broers, J., Hogue, E., Shipstead, J., & Knowlton, E. (1994). Strategies for functional community-based instruction and inclusion for children with mental retardation. *Teaching Exceptional Children, 26*(2), 44-48.

Benner, S. (1992). *Assessing young children with special needs: An ecological perspective.* White Plains, NY: Longman.

Bergen, D. (1993/94). Authentic performance assessments. *Childhood Education, 70*, 99-102.

Bodrova, E., & Leong, D. (1996). *Tools of the mind: The Vygotskian approach to early childhood education.* Englewood Cliffs, NJ: Merrill/Prentice-Hall.

Bricker, D. (1995). The challenge of inclusion. *Journal of Early Intervention, 19*(3), 179-194.

Bronfenbrenner, U. (1979). *The ecology of human development.* Cambridge, MA: Harvard University Press.

Brown, F., & Lehr, D. (1993). Making activities meaningful for students with severe multiple disabilities. *Teaching Exceptional Children, 25*(4), 12-16.

Carta, J. (1994). Developmentally appropriate practices: Shifting the emphasis to individual appropriateness. *Journal of Early Intervention, 18*(4), 342-343.

Carta, J., Schwartz, I., Atwater, J., & McConnell, S. (1991). Developmentally appropriate practice: Appraising its usefulness for young children with disabilities. *Topics in Early Childhood Special Education, 11*(1), 1-20.

Cole, K., Dale, P., Mills, P., & Jenkins, J. (1993). Interaction between early intervention curricula and student characteristics. *Exceptional Children, 60*(1), 17-28.

Cole, K., Mills, P., Dale, P., & Jenkins, J. (1991). Effects of preschool integration for children with disabilities. *Exceptional Children, 58*(1), 36-45.

Cook, R., Tessier, A., & Klein, M. D. (1996). *Adapting early childhood curricula for children in inclusive settings* (4th ed.). Englewood Cliffs, NJ: Merrill/Prentice-Hall.

Deiner, P. (1993). *Resources for teaching children with diverse abilities* (2nd ed.). Fort Worth, TX: Harcourt Brace College Publishers.

Dunn, R., Dunn, K., & Perrin, J. (1994). *Teaching young children through their individual learning styles: Practical approaches for grades K-2.* Boston: Allyn and Bacon.

Duttweiler, P. (1992). Engaging at-risk students with technology. *Media and Methods, 12*, 6-8.

Eichinger, J., & Woltman, S. (1993). Integration strategies for learners with severe multiple disabilities. *Teaching Exceptional Children, 26*(1), 18-21.

Field, S., LeRoy, B., & Rivera, S. (1994). Meeting functional curriculum needs in middle school general education classrooms. *Teaching Exceptional Children, 26*(2), 40-43.

Ford, L., Riggs, K., Nissenbaum, M., & LaRaia, J. (1994). Facilitating desired behavior in the preschool child with autism: A case study. *Contemporary Education, 65*(3), 148-151.

Fox, L., Hanline, M., Vail, C., & Galant, K. (1994). Developmentally appropriate practice: Applications for young children with disabilities. *Journal of Early Intervention, 18*(3), 243-257.

Fuchs, L., Fuchs, D., & Hamlett, C. (1994). Strengthening the connection between assessment and instructional planning with expert systems. *Exceptional Children, 61*(2), 138-146.

Fuchs, L., Fuchs, D., Hamlett, C., Phillips, N., & Karns, K. (1995). General educator's specialized adaptation for students with learning disabilities. *Exceptional Children, 61*(5), 440-459.

Gardner, H. (1983). *Frames of mind: The theory of multiple intelligences.* New York: Basic Books.

Gelman, S. (1993). Innovative technology for students with disabilities. *Principal, 73*(2), 52-53.

Gerber, M., Semmel, D., & Semmel, M. (1994). Computer-based dynamic assessment of multidigit multiplication. *Exceptional Children, 61*(2), 114-125.

Greenwood, C. (1994). Advances in technology-based assessment within special education. *Exceptional Children, 61*(2), 102-104.

Greenwood, C., Carta, J., Kamps, D., Terry, B., & Delquadri, J. (1994). Development and validation of standard classroom observation systems for school practitioners: Ecobehavioral assessment systems software (EBASS). *Exceptional Children, 61*(2), 197-210.

Greenwood, C., & Rieth, H. (1994). Current dimensions of technology-based assessment in special education. *Exceptional Children, 61*(2), 105-113.

Grubb, B. (1993). The Americans with Disabilities Act and learning disabilities. *LDA Newsbriefs, 28*(4), 3-4.

Helmke, L., Havekost, D., Patton, J., & Polloway, E. (1994). Life skills programming: Development of a high school science course. *Teaching Exceptional Children, 26*(2), 49-53.

Holder-Brown, L., & Parette, H., Jr. (1992). Children with disabilities who use assistive technology: Ethical considerations. *Young Children, 47*(6), 73-77.

Hollowood, T., Salisbury, C., Rainforth, B., & Palombaro, M. (1995). Use of instructional time in classrooms serving students with and without severe disabilities. *Exceptional Children, 61*(3), 242-252.

Holzberg, C. (1994). Technology in special education. *Technology & Learning, 14*(7), 18-21.

Irvin, L., & Walker, H. (1994). Assessing children's social skills using video-based microcomputer technology. *Exceptional Children, 61*(2), 182-196.

Johnson, J., & Johnson, K. (1994). The applicability of developmentally appropriate practice for children with diverse abilities. *Journal of Early Intervention, 18*(4), 343-346.

Joint Committee on Teacher Planning for Students with Disabilities. (1995). *Planning for academic diversity in America's classrooms: Windows on reality, research, change, and practice.* Lawrence, KS: The University of Kansas Center for Research on Learning.

Kelly, L. (1995). Processing of bottom-up and top-down information by skilled and average deaf readers and implications for whole language instruction. *Exceptional Children, 61*(4), 318-334.

Kindsvatter, R., Wilen, W., & Ishler, M. (1996). *Dynamics of effective teaching* (3rd ed.). White Plains, NY: Longman Publishers USA.

Krogh, S. (1994). *Educating young children: Infancy to grade three.* New York: McGraw-Hill.

Leister, C. (1993). Innovative teaching in the 1990's: Technology competencies needed by teachers of preschool age children with severe disabilities. *Reading Improvement, 30,* 134-139.

Linn, R., & Gronlund, N. (1995). *Measurement and assessment in teaching* (7th ed.). Englewood Cliffs, NJ: Merrill/Prentice Hall, Inc.

Mastropieri, M., & Scruggs, T. (1995). Teaching science to students with disabilities in general education settings: Practical and proven strategies. *Teaching Exceptional Children, 27*(4), 10-13.

Means, B., & Olson, K. (1994). Tomorrow's schools: Technology and reform in partnership. In B. Means (Ed.), *Technology and education reform: The reality behind the promise* (pp. 191-222). San Francisco: Jossey-Bass Publishers.

McIntosh, R., Vaughn, S., Schumm, J., Haager, D., & Lee, O. (1994). Observations of students with learning disabilities in general education classrooms. *Exceptional Children, 60*(3), 249-261.

Miller, R. (1996). *The developmentally appropriate inclusive classroom in early education.* Albany, NY: Delmar.

Mindes, G., Ireton, H., & Mardell-Czudnowski, C. (1996). *Assessing young children.* Albany, NY: Delmar.

National Association of State Boards of Education. (1992). *Winners all: A call for inclusive schools.* Alexandria, VA: Author.

Notari-Syverson, A., & Shuster, S. (1995). Putting real-life skills into IEP/IFSPs for infants and young children. *Teaching Exceptional Children, 27*(2), 29-32.

Odom, S., McLean, M., Johnson, L., & LaMontagne, M. (1995). Recommended practices in early childhood special education: Validation and current use. *Journal of Early Intervention, 19*(1), 1-17.

Patton, J. (1995). Teaching science to students with special needs. *Teaching Exceptional Children, 27*(4), 4-6.

Peck, C. (1993). Ecological perspectives on the implementation of integrated early childhood programs. In C. Peck, S. Odom & D. Bricker (Eds.), *Integrating young children with disabilities into community programs: Ecological perspectives on research and implementation* (pp. 3-15). Baltimore, MD: Paul H. Brookes.

Piaget, J. (1952). *The origins of intelligence in children.* New York: W. W. Norton.

Prickett, E., Higgins, K., & Boone, R. (1994). Technology for learning . . . not learning about technology. *Teaching Exceptional Children, 26*(4), 56-60.

Richarz, S. (1993). Innovations in early childhood education: Models that support the integration of children of varied developmental levels. In C. Peck, S. Odom & D. Bricker (Eds.), *Integrating young children with disabilities into community programs: Ecological perspectives on research and implementation* (pp. 83-107). Baltimore, MD: Paul H. Brookes.

Roach, V. (1995). Supporting inclusion: Beyond the rhetoric. *Phi Delta Kappan, 77*(4), 295-299.

Rose, D., & Rose, C. (1994). Students' adaptation to task environments in resource room and regular class setting. *The Journal of Special Education, 28*(1), 3-26.

Salisbury, C. (1991). Mainstreaming during the early childhood years. *Exceptional Children, 58*(2), 146-155.

Salisbury, C., Mangino, M., Petrigala, M., Rainforth, B., Syryca, S., & Palombaro, M. (1994). Innovative practices: Promoting the instructional inclusion of young children with disabilities in the primary grades. *Journal of Early Invention, 18*(3), 311-322.

Sapona, R., & Phillips, L. (1993). Classrooms as communities of learners: Sharing responsibility for learning. In A. Bauer & E. Lynch (Eds.), *Children who challenge the system* (pp. 63-87). Norwood, NJ: Ablex Publishing Corporation.

Schloss, P. (1992). Mainstreaming revisited. *The Elementary School Journal, 92*(3), 233-44.

Schumm, J., & Vaughn, S. (1991). Making adaptations for mainstreamed students: General classroom teachers' perspectives. *Remedial and Special Education, 12*(4), 18-27.

Scruggs, T., & Mastropieri, M. (1993). Current approaches to science education: Implications for mainstream instruction of students with disabilities. *Remedial and Special Education, 14*(1), 15-24.

Sears, S., Carpenter, C., & Burstein, N. (1994). Meaningful reading instruction for learners with special needs. *The Reading Teacher, 47*(8), 632-638.

Surr, J. (1992). Early childhood programs and the Americans with Disabilities Act (ADA). *Young Children, 47*(5), 18-21.

Udvari-Solner, A., & Thousand, J. (1995). *Promising practices that foster inclusive education. Creating an inclusive school.* Alexandria, VA: Association for Supervision and Curriculum Development.

Underwood, J., & Mead, J. (1995). *Legal aspects of special education and pupil services.* Boston: Allyn and Bacon.

U.S. Department of Education, Office of Special Education Programs. (1993). *Fifteenth annual report to Congress on the implementation of the Individuals with Disabilities Education Act.* Washington, DC: Author.

Vygotsky, L. (1978). *Mind in society: The development of higher psychological processes.* Cambridge, MA: Harvard University Press.

Wolery, M. (1991). Instruction in early childhood special education: "Seeing through a glass darkly . . . knowing in part." *Exceptional Children, 58*(2), 127-135.

Wolery, M., & Bredekamp, S. (1994). Developmentally appropriate practices and young children with disabilities: Contextual issues in the discussion. *Journal of Early Intervention, 18*(4), 331-341.

Wolery, M., & Flemming, L. (1993). Implementing individualized curricula in integrated settings. In C. Peck, S. Odom & D. Bricker (Eds.), *Integrating young children with disabilities into community programs: Ecological perspectives on research and implementation* (pp. 109-132). Baltimore, MD: Paul H. Brookes.

Wolery, M., Huffman, K., Holcombe, A., Martin, C., Brookfield, J., Schroeder, C., & Venn, M. (1994). Preschool mainstreaming: Perceptions of barriers and benefits by faculty in general early childhood education. *Teacher Education and Special Education, 17*(1), 1-9.

Woodward, J., & Howard, L. (1994). The misconceptions of youth: Errors and their mathematical meaning. *Exceptional Children, 61*(2), 126-136.

Zigmond, N., & Miller, S. (1986). Assessment for instructional planning. *Exceptional Children, 52,* 501-509.

Early Childhood Special Education

"Can I Play Too?" Adapting Common Classroom Activities for Young Children with Limited Motor Abilities

Kristyn Sheldon[1,2]

This paper offers suggestions on adapting common classroom activities found in early childhood classrooms to increase participation of young children with limited motor abilities. It stresses the importance of de-emphasizing differences among children and highlighting that all children, even those with severe disabilities, can benefit from the same activities.

KEY WORDS: adapting activities; inclusion; limited motor abilities.

INTRODUCTION

Amber, eager to attend her first day of school in her new classroom, enters the room ready to play. The art easel looks like a good place to start, but she discovers she cannot reach the paint. Amber tries the dramatic play area next, but her wheelchair will not fit in the space and she accidently bumps toys and shelves everywhere. She would like to play with puzzles, but is unable to manipulate the small pieces. Amber attempts to play at the sensory table, but it is too high and her wheelchair gets in the way. Circle time is no better. There is nowhere for her to sit and she is unable to participate in the group activities.

Many children with special needs are enrolled in early childhood programs. Such enrollment is a wonderful learning opportunity for all, but it involves more than placing children together in the same program (Odom & McEvoy, 1990). Many early childhood educators are open to the inclusion of preschoolers with mild to moderate disabilities, but may be hesitant to include children with severe disabilities because they believe extensive modifications will be needed (Demchak & Drinkwater, 1992). Teachers are constantly challenged with arranging the environment to allow young children with physical impairments to participate and engage in the environment. These special challenges include increasing the amount and quality of participation for young children with limited motor abilities (Bigge, 1991).

Although there are an increasing number of children with motor difficulties integrated into early childhood classrooms, many early childhood teachers have limited experience and training in working with these children. Existing day care services and preschool settings provide natural and rich environments for early education experiences with only minor modifications or adaptations needed in daily activities to accommodate children with limited motor ability (Klein & Sheehan, 1987). This article provides suggestions on adapting common classroom activities found in early childhood classrooms to increase participation of young children with limited motor abilities.

DEFINITION OF LIMITED MOTOR ABILITY

The term, limited motor ability, is used in this article to define any movement difficulty that negatively affects a child's participation in an activity (Bigge, 1991). For example, Randy, age 4, has cerebral palsy that affects his equilibrium and ability to control his movement. Jamar, age 5, has cerebral palsy which has limited his ability to walk, run, or even sit up by himself. Kelly, a 3-year old girl, has spina bifida and no sensation below

[1]Department of Educationial Services and Research, The Ohio State University, Columbus, Ohio.
[2]Correspondence should be directed to Kristyn Sheldon, Department of Educational Services and Research, 356 Arps Hall, 1945 North High Street, Columbus, Ohio 43210-1172.

From *Early Childhood Education Journal,* Winter 1996, pp. 115-120. © 1996 by Human Sciences Press, Inc. Reprinted by permission.

her waist. She wears braces on her legs, uses a walker for mobility, and depends on her upper body for engaging in most activities. Sara uses a wheelchair, has only minimal use of her left arm, and needs support to sit upright in her chair. What is important to remember about children with special needs such as Randy, Jamar, and Kelly is not their physical limitations but their abilities.

Neisworth and Madle (1975) stressed the importance of de-emphasizing differences and highlighting that all children, even those with severe disabilities, can benefit from the same activities. Developmentally Appropriate Practice guidelines currently followed in early childhood classrooms are also appropriate for children with disabilities (Bredekamp, 1987). The guidelines for developmentally appropriate practice (Bredekamp, 1987) and the curriculum and assessment guidelines with NAEYC and NAECS/SDE (1991) clearly recognize the importance of individual differences and the need to adapt the curriculum to those differences (Wolery, Strain, & Baily, 1992). The guidelines are the context in which appropriate early education of children with special needs should occur; however, a program based on the guidelines alone is not likely to be sufficient for many children with special needs. Programs that use the guidelines may be good places for children with special needs to receive early education, but those programs must be adjusted to be maximally beneficial to those children (Wolery et al. 1992). Adaptations are usually needed so children with special needs, especially children with limited motor abilities, can participate.

It is not always necessary for children to participate in an activity to the same degree as children without disabilities for the activity to be enjoyed. Partial participation is a valid goal as long as meaningful participation is encouraged. The principle of partial participation states that, regardless of severity of disability, individuals can be taught to participate in variety of activities to some degree, or activities can be adapted to allow participation (Baumgart, Brown, Pumpian, Nisbet, Ford, Sweet, Messina, & Schroeder, 1982). Activities and materials should be adapted or modified, and/or personal assistance strategies used. Have a child with a disability and a peer without a disability play together to allow the child with a disability to participate in the activity to the maximum extent appropriate.

SPECIAL ADAPTATIONS

In planning activities for children with limited motor ability, start with typical activities planned for all children. When special adaptations are needed, they should be designed to include other children whenever possible (Chandler, 1994). Special activities such as speech or physical therapy, if needed, should be provided in addition to, not instead of, typical program activities. In successfully integrated preschools, teachers strive to use the least intrusive, natural prompts, and contingencies needed to help children participate actively and menaingfully in the routines of the preschool (Drinkwater & Demchak, 1995). Encourage and assist the child to participate as fully as possible in activities such as circle time, art, books, sensory play, fine motor activities, dramatic play, snack, and gross motor activities. Some suggestions are provided below.

Circle Time

Circle time is a popular activity in early childhood classrooms, but certain environmental adaptations may be needed during circle to ensure that everyone can participate. Some problems children with limited motor abilities experience at circle time are difficulties in finding a place to sit, a difference in eye level from other children, and the possibility of being unable to communicate with the other children or the teacher. During circle time, children often sit on the floor or on carpet squares. This can become a problem for children in a wheelchair or children unable to sit independently on the floor. They may not be able to physically fit in the circle area or the children with limited motor abilities may not be comfortable. Remember children in a wheelchair will be at a different eye level than the rest of the group. It is important to recognize this when presenting circle time activities or reading books. Children with limited motor abilities often have communication difficulties, so adaptations must be used to ensure all children are able to communicate with the teacher and their peers.

Suggestions for Circle Time

- To facilitate the integration of children in wheelchairs have the children and teacher sit in chairs at circle time. This will allow all children's eye level to more similar and make children in wheelchair "less different."
- Include modalities of communication other than verbal language. For example, a song board can be incorporated for all of the children to select what songs they want to sing. The board can have pictures of the songs the children sing during circle and both children with limited motor abilities and typical peers can use this board to choose a song.
- Use songs that can involve the children interacting with one another. For example, "If you're happy and you know it, hug a friend, give them five."

- Use books which talk about and include children with disabilities.
- Seat children with disabilities next to their peers to provide natural opportunities for interaction (Hanline, 1985).

Art

Children with physical disabilities have difficulties coloring and painting for many reasons. Some children with limited motor ability have problems because they cannot grasp and hold the tools or they are unable to maintain their arms and hands in the necessary angle or position to draw, color, or paint (Bigge, 1991). Others cannot reach the materials or enter the art area. A common problem for children who are nonambulatory is their inability to reach the standard art easel typically used in classrooms.

Suggestions for Art

- Provide a variety of areas and surfaces for children to paint. For example, place the paper on the floor or more easily accessible surfaces such as a window, wall, refrigerator, etc.
- Cut off the legs of an art easel so children can crawl to or kneel at the easel.
- Use adaptations such as velcro or yarn to fasten a paint brush to the child's hand or wrist.
- Encourage children to paint using their fingers, feet, and other body parts.
- Use edible paint for those who engage in hand mouthing. For example, paint with jello and water, marshmallow whip, or pudding. Food coloring can be added with many edible painting mediums.
- Assign a buddy to be paired with a child with disabilities to encourage meaningful participation (Drinkwater & Demchak, 1995).
- Use age appropriate clothing for activities. For example, use a paint shirt as a cover-up and not a bib (Drinkwater & Demchak, 1995).

Specific Art Activity Suggestions

- *Funnel painting.* Place a large funnel made of paper over a table and allow the children to push the funnel back and forth, dripping paint out of the funnel onto a large piece of paper.
- *Record player art.* Place a piece of paper on a record player and have the children hold a crayon, pencil, or paint brush on the paper as the record player turns.

- *Swing art.* This activity allows a child with limited motor ability to color or paint a large piece of paper. The child is placed in a seater swing and a crayon or paint brush is attached to the swing. As the child is slowly pushed back and forth a drawing is created.
- *Contact paper collages.* This activity is appropriate for children with limited motor movement because they do not have to manipulate any tools, they simply drop or place items onto the sticky surface of the contact paper. A piece of contact paper is taped on a flat surface and the child is given different materials to drop onto the sticky side of the contact paper. Contact paper collages can be made with a variety of different materials such as, feathers, torn colored paper, uncooked macaroni or beans, cotton balls, etc.
- *Glue activities.* Glue activities can be challenging for children with limited hand movement and control. In order to increase the participation of children in these activities, have the children brush the glue onto the paper or materials instead of using squeeze bottles. The glue can be provided in foil pie dishes or bowls.

Sensory Play

The use of sensory play (water, sand, cornmeal, shaving cream, cotton, etc.) is a wonderful activity for young children with limited motor abilities. Many times children are unable to reach the sensory table where the items are commonly placed or are hesitant to explore a sensory activity because of the textures involved. When adaptations for this activity are implemented, children with limited motor abilities can actively participate and engage in sensory play.

Suggestions for Sensory Play

- Arrange some of the sensory items in a messy tray on the floor or use a sensory table that is wheelchair accessible.
- Place sensory items in a zip lock bag and tape it to the table or tray on the children's wheelchairs for exploration.
- Place sensory items directly on the children's tray.
- Encourage children to touch the sensory items with their feet or rub it on their arms or legs.
- Use large mirrors to increase engagement in the activity. For example, place a mirror on the table, spray shaving cream on the mirror, and allow children to explore with their fingers or toys (small cars, paint brushes, etc.).

- Encourage the children to explore the object with a variety of senses.

Specific Sensory Activity Suggestions

- *Tactile stimulation.* Provide sponges, honey, peanut butter, marshmallow fluff, mashed bananas, cotton candy, snow, whipped gelatin, etc. for children to experience various textures.
- *Visual stimulation.* Blow bubbles, play with bubble wands, or use automatic blowers for children who may have difficulty in blowing. Paint on black paper with fluorescent paint and use lights to show off the child's art.
- *Auditory stimulation.* Play music with regular classroom activity or help children make shakers with uncooked beans and macaroni.
- *Aromatic stimulation.* Let the class feel and smell cut fruit, flowers, and spices. For example, oranges, lemons, fresh flowers, herbs, spices in jars, etc.

Books

Children with limited motor abilities often have difficulty engaging in book time or playing in the book area. The books may be too difficult to manipulate, out of their reach, or not stimulating enough. Some books have very thin pages which are difficult for young children with limited motor abilities to manipulate. High and unstable book shelves are often found in an early childhood classroom. This arrangement makes it difficult for children to have access to books and the area.

Suggestions for Book Area

- Arrange shelves at different levels so the materials are accessible to everyone.
- Provide headphones and tapes so children can listen to the stories.
- Add a bookstand to hold the book for children unable to hold the book.
- Incorporate textured books (homemade or commercial) to book selection.
- Encourage the use of musical books that include individual sounds, songs, and voices.
- Provide books in several areas of the classroom, especially if the book area is in a loft.

Fine Motor

Fine motor activities are often difficult for young children with limited motor movement because many of the fine motor activities involve the manipulation of small pieces and materials. Puzzles are usually a fun activity for young children, but sometimes the pieces are too small or there are too many. Also, if the activity is done on a table top, items may slip around on the table causing difficulties for children with limited motor abilities to complete the task.

Suggestions for Fine Motor Area

- Select puzzles that have large knobs on the tops of the pieces and only three to four pieces per puzzle.
- Provide puzzles with auditory stimulation. For example, puzzles that play music when children place the puzzle piece in the correct place or take it out.
- Select musical shape sorters with auditory stimulation. For example, a song plays when the child places the correct shape into the holder.
- Try to keep the fine motor items large enough for the children to manipulate. The size can be changed as the children progress with the activity. For example, large chalk, crayons, pencils, and pegs can be used.
- Use Velcro to prevent materials from sliding around on the table or their tray. Velcro can be placed under the toy or puzzle.

Dramatic Play

Some problems young children with limited motor abilities may experience in the dramatic play area of a preschool classroom are difficulties in participating in the social games, the area may not be wheelchair accessible, and the toys may be too difficult to manipulate. Social interactions typically occur during dramatic play. However, children with limited motor abilities often also have language and communication delays which make social interactions more difficult. Also, the dramatic play area often contains many pieces of furniture which limits space and accessibility for children with limited motor abilities. If a child needs additional or different type of space modifications, they should be made only if necessary. This is so attention is not called to the child's disability and opportunities for children to move around in and accommodate to physical barriers in the natural environment are not lost (McCormick & Feeney, 1985).

Suggestions for Dramatic Play Area

- Make this section of the room accessible to children with limited motor abilities.
- Incorporate items such as hats, dishes, and utensils that are large and easy to manipulate.

- Label shelves with pictures as well as words so children do not have to be able to read to participate in clean up.
- Encourage peers to include and play with the children with limited motor ability. For example, plan integration experiences and activities for the children (Chandler, 1994).
- Allow children to use adaptive equipment on the dolls and their peers in the dramatic play area. For example, the children can explore and play with wheelchairs, walkers, and braces. Monitor this activity so equipment is not damaged (Chandler, 1994). Children can gain a sense of what equipment feels like and will likely be less fearful or anxious about the apparatus and the child who uses it.
- Create opportunities for children with motor impairments to interact with their normally developing peers. For example, provide materials and toys that promote play, engagement, and learning (Sainato & Carta, 1992).
- Structure the social dimensions of the environment to include peer and adult models.
- Facilitate proximity to responsive and imitative adults (Odom, McConnell, & McEvoy 1992b).

Snack

Some problems children with limited motor abilities encounter during snack are cups that easily tip, bowls that slide on the table, difficulty finding a seat, communicating their needs and overall inclusion in the activity. Regular cups and bowls can cause frequent spills. Also, children with limited motor ability are sometimes unable to communicate their wants and needs.

Suggestions for Snack

- Encourage peers to help the children with limited motor ability. For example, peers can help the child communicate or eat.
- Use bowls with suctions to avoid table sliding and sipper cups to avoid spills.
- Design a job board to include jobs for all children. For example, include children with limited motor ability by allowing them to pass out the cups, napkins, or bowls at snack.
- Include all of the children at the table during snack, even if not all the children are eating.

Gym and Playground

Playground and gym time can be very difficult for children with physical impairments. Most children are running, jumping, and climbing during this time. Children with limited motor abilities may become frustrated at not being able to perform these skills. Young children with limited motor abilities may not be able to sit safely in a swing, have access to the sand box, or engage in social games.

Suggestions for Gym and Playground

- Provide scooter boards for the children to sit on. The children can either push themselves around or be pulled by a peer.
- Include a pool of balls for the children to sit in and explore.
- Encourage wagon, blanket, and sheet pulls. The child with limited motor ability can be in the wagon, blanket or sheet while the peer pulls them around.
- Provide adaptive tricycles (adaptive pedals or hand cycles) and/or roller sakes.
- Make sand tables and swings accessible for everyone.

Computers and Technology

Computers and related technology can help provide the means to adapt classroom areas and activities in order to provide for children's diverse needs. Technology can provide young children with and without disabilities the opportunity for maximum participation in the social and educational environment of the early childhood setting. Young children with limited motor abilities who have difficulty communicating, playing, and/or interacting with their environment can benefit from technology in a number of ways (Brett, 1995).

Suggestions for Computer Use

- Use battery-operated toys, switches, and computer games to provide children with and without disabilities to play together.
- Use alternative keyboards or switches with speech output for children who are nonverbal to participate in language development activities.
- Provide children with exploratory and open-ended computer programs to provide children the opportunity to play together.
- Include modifications of the standard keyboard, alternative keyboards, touchsensitive screens, hand-held devices, switches, and voice input (Brett, 1995).

Modifications for the Standard Keyboard

- Place stickers on keys for a particular program to help children locate them more easily.
- Set a template or overlay over a keyboard so that only certain keys show.
- Place a keyguard over a standard keyboard to allow only one key to be hit at a time (Brett, 1995).

Alternative Keyboards

- Muppet Learning Keys feature large keys in alphabetical order with pictures that designate functions
- The PowerPad is a large touch-sensitive board which can be divided into squares of various sizes. Each square can be easily programmed to generate voice and visual output.
- Condensed keyboards or minikeyboards are small enough so children with a limited range of motion can reach the keys.
- Unicorn Keyboard is a touch-sensitive membrane keyboard which has 128 squares that can be programmed to operate in several different ways, including imitation of the standard keyboard.
- A touch-sensitive screen such as Touch Window is an input device which allows children to point to their selections on the screen.
- Hand-held devices, such as the mouse and the joystick, are input devices which require less fine motor skill than a keyboard.
- Switches are on–off devices that are activated by contact or by detection of motion, sound, or light.
- Voice input allows an individual to speak commands into the computer and have the computer carry out these commands (Brett, 1995).

CONCLUSION

Teachers in typical early childhood settings need to provide an effective learning environment for children who exhibit a wide range of abilities within the context of the naturally occurring activities. Adaptations to activities can enhance opportunities for interactions and increase the quality of participation among children with limited motor ability. As part of a developmentally appropriate program, these adaptations can be integrated into the curriculum to make the preschool environment stimulating and interesting for all children.

ACKNOWLEDGMENTS

Support for this research was provided by a Leadership Training Grant (H029D10054) from the Office of Special Education and Rehabilitation Services, U.S. Department of Education.

REFERENCES

Baumgart, D., Brown, L., Pumpian, I., Nisbet, J., Ford, A., Sweet, M., Messina, R., & Schroeder, J. (1982). Principle of partial participation and individualized adaptations in educational programs for severely handicapped students. *Journal of the Association for the Severely Handicapped, 7*(2),17-27.

Bigge, J. L. (1991). *Teaching individuals with physical and multiple disabilities* (3rd Ed.). New York: Macmillian Publishing Company.

Bredekamp, S. (Ed.) (1987). *Developmentally appropriate practice in early childhood programs serving children from birth through age 8.* Washington, D.C.: National Association for the Education of Young Children.

Brett, A. (1995). Technology in inclusive early childhood settings. *Day Care and Early Education, 10,* 8-11.

Chandler, P. A. (1994). *A place for me.* Washington, D.C.: National Association for the Education of Young Children.

Demchak, M., & Drinkwater, S. (1992). Preschoolers with severe disabilities: The case against segregation. *Topics in Early Childhood Special Education, 11*(4), 70-83.

Drinkwater, S., & Demchak, M. (1995). The preschool checklist integration of children with disabilities. *Teaching Exceptional Children, 28*(1), 4-8.

Diamond, K., Hestenes, L., & O'Conner, C. (1994). Integrating young children with disabilities in preschool: Problems and promises. *Young Children, 49*(2), 68-75.

Hanline, M. F. (1985). Integrating disabled children. *Young Children, 40*(2), 45-48.

Janney, R. E., Snell, M. E., Beers, M. K., & Raynes, M. (1995). Integrating students with moderate and severe disabilities into general education classes. *Exceptional Children, 61* (5), 425-439.

Klein, N., & Scheehan, R. (1987). Staff development. A key issue in meeting the needs of young handicapped children in day care settings. *Topics in Early Childhood Special Education, 7* (1), 13-27.

McCormick, L., & Feeney, S. (1995). Modifying and expanding activities for children with disabilities. *Young Children, 50*(4), 10-17.

Newsworth, J. T., & Madle, R. A. (1975). Normalized day care: A philosophy and approach to integrating exceptional and normal children. *Child Care Quarterly, 4,* 163-171.

Odom, S. L., & McEvoy, M. A. (1990). Mainstreaming at the preschool level: Potential barriers and tasks for the field. *Topics in Early Childhood Special Education, 10*(2), 48-61.

Odom, S. l., McConnell, S. R., & McEvoy; M. A. (1992). *Social competence of young children with disabilities: Issues and strategies for intervention.* Baltimore, MD: Paul H. Brooks.

Sainato, D. M., & Carta, J. J. (1992). Classroom influences on the development of social competence in young children with disabilities. In S. L. Odom, S. R. McConnell, & M. A. McEvoy, (Eds.) Social competence of young children with disabilities: Issues and strategies for intervention (pp. 93-109). Baltimore: Paul H. Brookes.

Snell, M. E. (1993). *Instruction of students with severe disabilities* (4th ed.). New York: Merrill/Macmilan.

Wolery, M., Holcombe, A., Venn, M., Brookfield, J., Huffman, K., Schroeder, C., Martin, C., & Flemming, L (1993). Mainstreaming in early childhood programs: Current status and relevant issues. *Young Children, 49*(1), 78-94.

Wolery, M., & Wilbers, J. S. (1994). *Including children with special needs in early childhood programs.* Washington, D.C.: National Association for the Education of Young Children.

Wolery, M., Strain, P., & Baily D. (1992). *Reaching potentials: Appropriate curriculum and assessment for young children.* Washington, D.C.: National Association for the Education of Young Children.

Together Is Better:

Specific Tips on How to Include Children with Various Types of Disabilities

Develop a professional relationship with the child's parents. Keep communication lines open among all involved—parents, physicians, special education teachers, and other relevant people.

Jane Russell-Fox

M y experiences with both inclusive and noninclusive environments has led me to conclude that "together is better." I believe that early childhood professionals who are including children with special needs in their classrooms can set up the environment so that it accommodates these children as well as typically developing children. In doing this the professional takes the first steps toward successful inclusion.

While working in several different self-contained settings, I spent most of my time negotiating with my peers and administrators to plan for inclusion of the special needs children in my group. Usu-

Jane Russell-Fox, M.Ed., is a preschool teacher for the inclusive "Wee Wildcat" program for the Eastmont School District in East Wenatchee, Washington.

Photographs © The Growth Program.

ally my plan was for inclusion that would operate 15 to 20 minutes of the school day to give my children a chance at least to hear others model language, involve themselves in cooperative play, and establish friendships.

Staff members who knew I was a strong supporter of inclusive classrooms tended continually to say to me, "That sounds like a good idea; we should try that next week." Next week always came, and we were no closer to the beginning of an inclusive environment than we were the week before.

After my experiences in inclusive environments, I know now that everyone has to be sold on inclusion before it can work successfully. After one is sold on inclusion, it's the job of the team to set up the environment and offer choices to all children at a variety of levels so that all can learn together in the same room.

It is also the job of the team to continue updating skills and working to improve the effectiveness of the program. Children with special needs do need specialized services based on individual needs, including predictable routines, accurate record keeping of goals, effective teaching strategies, all performed in a developmentally appropriate environment. There is no blueprint to follow—each person is an individual.

The following ideas are only a way to get you started. A range of services needs to be provided to most children with special needs. You can't do it all by yourself. Expect your team members to be there for you. Team members can include everyone from a child care provider to an occupational therapist.

The following processes are adaptations that are easy and use many commonsense ideas and readily available materials. For example, Jennifer has a vision impairment and is not able to see some of the books you read during circle time. What can you do? Try storytelling, enlarging the books, using flannel-board characters, or giving Jennifer a designated spot toward the front during circle time.

From *Young Children*, May 1997, pp. 81-83. © 1997 by the National Association for the Education of Young Children. Reprinted by permission.

Working with a child who has exceptional health needs

• Develop a professional relationship with the child's parents and physician, and in some cases with other care providers who may come in contact with the child.

• Keep communication lines open among all.

• Get informed about the child's health needs, including medicine and diet.

• Invite the school nurse to become a part of the team.

• Develop a program plan for the child who may be out of the classroom for long periods of time. Home visits, telephone calls, classmate phone lists, and care packages from classmates or activity packets from the teacher can assist the child and his or her family in continuing to be a part of the classroom.*

Working with a child who has exceptional hearing needs

• Develop a professional relationship with the child's parents, audiologist, hearing specialist, sign language interpreter, and speech and language therapist.

• Keep communication lines open with them.

• Learn to change a hearing aid battery and cord.

• Use visual and tactile aids as much as you can.

• Use the child's name when seeking the child's attention.

• Make sure you have the child's attention before beginning the activity, giving directions, or introducing additional material.

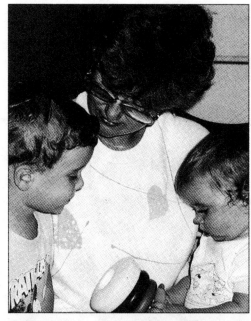

Facilitating social skills is an essential part of facilitating true inclusion. Teachers will want to keep groups relatively small so children can interact as children typically do.

• Speak at normal speed and volume without exaggerating lip movements.

• Make certain the child sits up close for good visibility of the teacher, activity, and other children.

• Encourage language in group activities by allowing time for the child to start and finish speaking.*

Working with a child who has exceptional learning needs

• Concentrate on the child's strengths, not weaknesses.

• Present content in short segments using a multisensory approach (audio, visual, manipulative). Provide for as much overlearning or repeated practice as necessary.

• Praise the child's progress.

• Use task analysis.

• Be patient when it is necessary to show a child how to do something many times.

• Give directions one at a time until a child can handle more than one.

• Help parents to recognize their children's small successes.

• Plan for modeling and imitation.

• Provide clear transitions; try to avoid abrupt changes in activities.

• Present developmental-level challenges.

• Allow time and opportunity to practice new skills needed for activities.

Specific intervention strategies for working with a child with visual impairments

• Consult with the child's parents and vision specialists to determine what the child can see and what play materials would be most appropriate.

• Orient the child to the classroom layout and locations of materials. Give a new orientation whenever changes are made.

• Provide the child with a rich variety of tactile, manipulative, and auditory experiences.

• Encourage independence both by your actions and in the way the room is arranged.

• Be alert to the need for physical prompts.

• Before beginning a new activity, explain what is going to happen.*

Working with a child who has exceptional communication needs

• Be a good listener.

• Use parallel talk. Broadcasting play-by-play action of the child's

---

Source: Adapted by permission, from R.E. Cook, A. Tessier, and M.D. Klein, *Adapting Early Childhood Curricula for Children with Special Needs,* 3d ed. New York: Merrill/Macmillan, 1992. 206-07, 209.

activity helps to stimulate the acquisition of language (e.g., "You're putting the ball in the basket").

• Use alternative communications as needed (e.g., sign language, augmentative communication).

• Have everyone in the classroom model good language by talking about and labeling what they are doing.

• Promote specific reasons for expressing language (i.e., giving information, requesting and getting attention, protesting, and commenting).

Working with a child who has exceptional physical needs

• Get input from the physical therapist on the proper handling and positioning of the child. Get specific directions on the length of time the child should be in a given position. Seek suggestions from the occupational therapist on adapting fine-motor materials so that the child participates in all of the classroom projects. (Of course parents must be included in all planning for the child.)

• Make sure materials and toys are accessible to the child.

• Remember that physical delays don't always have an accompanying mental disability.

• Become familiar with adaptive

equipment and know how to use and care for it.

• Arrange the environment to accommodate adaptive equipment.

• Allow extra time for making transitions.

• Support and encourage that which the child can do physically.

• Foster independence by focusing on the child's nonphysical abilities.

*   *   *

Facilitating social skills is an essential part of facilitating true inclusion. Teachers will want to keep groups relatively small so children can interact as children typically do. Rewarding remarks reinforce specific desired behaviors. Materials appropriate to the skills of interaction desired need to be provided. For example, if your desired outcome is cooperation, set up situations in the classroom to encourage teamwork—"After we pick up the blocks, then we can get ready for snack." Making sufficient materials available helps promote cooperation and imitation.

With each new child with special needs, a few accommodations can be made to a classroom environment and the instruction to allow these children to be included. Placing children with special needs in a learning environment with their typical peers offers many challenges for families and staff, but the rewards reaped and the teamwork accom-

plished are well worth the effort.

Coming into a work environment that is already sold on inclusion and is *practicing* it has been one of the greatest rewards of my professional career. I strongly urge you to develop inclusive classrooms in *your* setting!

For further reading

Allen, K.E. 1980. *Mainstreaming in early childhood education.* Albany, NY: Delmar.

Barnes, E., C. Berrigan, & D. Biklen. 1978. *What's the difference: Teaching positive attitudes toward people with disabilities.* Syracuse, NY: Human Policy Press.

Buscaglia, L. 1983. *The disabled and their parents: A counseling challenge.* New York: Holt, Rinehart, & Winston.

Chandler, P.A. 1994. *A place for me: Including children with special needs in early care and education settings.* Washington, DC: NAEYC.

Cook, R.E., A. Tessier, & M.D. Klein. 1987. *Adapting early childhood curricula for children with special needs.* 3d ed. New York: Harcourt Brace Jovanovich.

Deiner, P.L. 1983. *Resources for teaching young children with special needs.* New York: Harcourt Brace Jovanovich.

Debelak, M., J. Herr, & M. Jacobson. 1981. *Creative innovative classroom materials for teaching young children.* New York: Harcourt Brace Jovanovich.

Froschl, M., L. Colon, E. Rubin, & B. Sprung. 1984. *Including all of us—An early childhood curriculum about disabilities.* New York: Project Educational Equity Concepts.

Fullwood, D. 1990. *Chances and choices: Making integration work.* Baltimore: Paul H. Brookes.

Trainer, M. 1991. *Differences in common. Straight talk on mental retardation, Down syndrome and life.* Bethesda, MD: Woodbine House.

Supporting Young Children and Their Families

No subject in early childhood education seems to attract the attention of teachers and parents more than how to guide behavior. New teachers are concerned that they will not be able to keep the children "under control." Mature teachers wrestle with the finer points of how to guide behavior positively and effectively. Parents have strong feelings on the subject of behavior, often based on their own childhood experiences. Teachers spend many hours thinking and talking about the best ways to guide young children's behavior: *What should I do about the child who is out of bounds? What do I say to parents who want their child punished? Is punishment the same as discipline? How do I guide a child who has experienced violence and now acts out violently?*

Schools that include families in significant ways find that problems decrease and academic performance increases. With the diversity of family-school environments across the nation, family involvement means many different things. The most successful family involvement programs are based on careful planning and an underlying philosphy. This is the premise of the report by Mick Coleman and Susan Churchill, "Challenges to Family Involvement." Teachers and families both benefit from an open communication of themes to guide family-school interactions. The authors outline excellent strategies for family life educators to use with teachers, communities, and parents.

In "Beyond Discipline to Guidance," Dan Gartrell clearly defines and applies the approach to working with children called guidance. He gives us a thorough history of the guidance approach, including the contributions of international leaders such as Friedrich Froebel, Maria Montessori, and John Dewey. They all believed the goal of guidance was self-control and self-discipline. Gartrell sorts out five misunderstandings about guidance and provides six key guidance practices. He believes that "the objective is to teach children to solve problems rather than punish them for having problems they cannot solve."

Kristen Kemple and Lynn Hartle, in "Getting Along: How Teachers Can Support Children's Peer Relationships," provide vignettes illustrating how teachers foster peer competence by shaping the classroom both physically and emotionally. Once that foundation is laid, teachers can assist children in resolving disputes and conflicts.

The rise of homelessness in America is causing teachers to be concerned for children who move between shelters or migrate across the nation. Teachers who deal with homeless children are considering the climate and obstacles of schooling. Experiences of homelessness can hinder children's progress and affect their behavior. Ralph da Costa Nunez and Kate Collignon give us insight into the specialized education such children need in their essay "Creating a Community of Learning for Homeless Children." Their goal for working with these children is to lower barriers to school attendance and participation. Model programs offer intensive services, ranging from tutoring children and parent literacy to health and nutrition care. Da Costa Nunez and Collignon emphasize the necessity of community and school partnerships. They illustrate this with examples of programs around the nation that share the goal of ensuring children's continuous ac-

cess to schooling. While in child care or primary grades, homeless children should feel school is a safe, stable place. They need affectionate, supportive teachers who refrain from labeling or excluding them.

As with all areas of early childhood education, a high-quality, effective plan for guiding behavior does not arrive prepackaged for the teacher's immediate use. Guiding and disciplining are hard work, requiring careful attention to individual children and differing situations. The work is not complete until teachers examine their own sense of control and feelings about children's behavior. Anger and disrespect have no place in a positive environment. When feelings are brought out into the open and discussed calmly, teachers create an atmosphere where everyone is able to speak and act responsibly. This is the basis for a caring, helping environment for young children.

Looking Ahead: Challenge Questions

What does family involvement mean in a child care program, a preschool, and a primary grades school?

What is the difference between guidance and punishment? How is that difference reflected in a teacher's approach to classroom management?

Brainstorm five ways teachers can support peer relationships in setting up the classroom.

What classroom rituals or routines have you observed that create a climate of caring and affirmation?

In what ways are young children jeopardized when they are homeless?

Challenges to Family Involvement

Mick Coleman and Susan Churchill

Mick Coleman is Associate Professor and Susan Churchill is a doctoral student in the Department of Child and Family Development, University of Georgia, Athens.

The percentage of 3- and 4-year-olds enrolled in early childhood education programs has risen more than threefold since the mid-1960s (U.S. General Accounting Office, 1990). Public schools increasingly provide child care, preschool education and before- and after-school care for young children. Such school-based early childhood programs reflect a growing interest in early educational enrichment experiences for children in general, as well as an expansion of compensatory education programs for children who are judged to be at risk for school failure because of poverty, lack of proper health care, inadequate home-learning environments and a lack of adult protection (Swick & Graves, 1993, pp. 26, 93).

Recognizing the mutuality of families' and schools' concerns about children's growth and development, educators are seeking new ways to involve families in their children's education (Boyer, 1991; Silvern, 1988; U.S. Department of Education, 1991). While family involvement is a concept that has wide appeal, only limited institutional support exists (Epstein & Dauber, 1991; Greenberg, 1989; Swick & McKnight, 1989).

Challenges to Family Involvement

No conclusive evidence exists that family involvement programs are uniformly effective (White, Taylor & Moss, 1992), despite the many positive ways families can affect their children's academic efforts (see, for review, Henderson, 1988; Hess & Holloway, 1984; Peters, 1988; Rutter, 1985; White et al., 1992), and the many positive ways quality early childhood programs can affect families (see Pence, 1988; Powell, 1989; Schorr & Schorr, 1988). Family involvement efforts face two challenges aside from the difficulties associated with the diverse methodologies used in family involvement studies (White et al., 1992).

■ *Ambiguous definitions of family involvement.* It is hard to find consensus on the meaning of family involvement (Haseloff, 1990; White et al., 1992). Family involvement may include the following elements, among others: providing parents with facts about their child's development, teaching parents to become effective change agents for their child, providing parents with emotional support, training parents to guide and teach their child, exchanging information about a child between parents and teachers, hosting joint parent/teacher activities like childhood assessments or program planning, and helping parents get access to community services (McConachie, 1986; Peterson & Cooper, 1989).

Ambiguous definitions of family involvement can result in programs that are merely a series of disconnected activities with little relevance to family or classroom environments. To be effective, family involvement planners must address the ambiguous boundaries that exist between home and school (Johnston, 1990), and the resulting sense of intrusion and power imbalance that can occur when parents and teachers attempt to coordinate their interactions with children (Haseloff, 1990).

In practice, family involvement planning must include the formulation of a family involvement philosophy and supportive goals. In the course of conducting inservice workshops on family involvement, the authors have discovered that sufficient attention is not always paid to this conceptual process. Subsequent discussions about the meaning and purpose of family involvement, however, often uncover a common set of philosophical themes (see Table 1). Teachers can use the themes in Table 1 as an aid to beginning the reflective process. Teachers should delete from, or add to, the list so that it meets their schools' particular concerns and interests.

The list of themes is used as a planning device so that teachers can prioritize their family involvement goals while thinking about past family involvement experiences. In most cases, teachers can select one theme that best reflects their family involvement goal for the upcoming year. They can then develop specific family in-

 From *Childhood Education*, Spring 1997, pp. 144-148. © 1997 by the Association for Childhood Education International, 17904 Georgia Avenue, Suite 215, Olney, MD. Reprinted by permission.

volvement objectives that reflect their school's diverse family-school environments.

■ *Diversity of family-school environments.* The call for greater collaboration between families and schools is admirable in that it recognizes the different contexts in which children learn. Nevertheless, the discontinuities between a young child's home and school lives can pose numerous challenges (Hess & Holloway, 1984; Peters, 1988; Silvern, 1988). A school's customs, schedules, spaces, resources, expectations, experiences, languages and values, for example, may not be reflected in the same way or to the same degree at home. This may be especially true for children from racial and cultural minority families, as well as those from lower socioeconomic families.

In particular, school environments may fit better with the family environments of children from middle-class families because public schools are often staffed with middle-class administrators and teachers. Middle-class families subsequently may be more responsive to school policies and family involvement programs than lower socioeconomic families.

Parent education and family socioeconomic status are two factors that may create discontinuity between schools and families. Although it is true that parents with higher levels of education and from higher socioeconomic backgrounds show greater family involvement, this trend does not necessarily indicate differential *interest* in family involvement (Epstein & Dauber, 1991;

Stevenson & Baker, 1987). In fact, parents from low-income families are as supportive of the family involvement concept as parents with higher incomes (Chavkin & Williams, 1989).

One way parents from lower and higher income families may differ is where they are willing or able to be involved in their children's education. Researchers have found a positive relationship between socioeconomic status and school-based family involvement activities such as parent conferences and volunteering, as well as teacher perceptions of parent support; socioeconomic status, however, has not been associated with home-based activities like tutoring (Hoover-Dempsey, Bassler & Brissie, 1987). This finding may reflect the difficulty or hesitancy parents from lower socioeconomic backgrounds may experience when directly interacting with schools. Some parents may have conflicting work and family demands. Others may limit their involvement with schools because of their own negative school experiences and feelings of academic inadequacy.

Parents with higher levels of education tend to be more involved in school activities, and their children are more likely to be doing well in school (Stevenson & Baker, 1987). These findings may reflect parental attitudes, work schedules and lifestyle priorities that are congruent with those found in schools. Parents with more education may have more positive attitudes toward school, resulting in more frequent and positive interactions with teachers and more reinforcement of classroom activities in the home. Parents with higher levels of education also may have more flexible work schedules, allowing them to assist with homework projects and attend school functions. Also, these families' adult-child interactions and childhood behavioral expectations may resemble more closely those found in the school.

To develop strategies that link the early learning experiences in home and school settings, planners must address the discontinuities between those environments. The authors have summarized in Table 2 some of the themes that they have found useful in helping family-school coordinators and teachers link family and school environments.

Teachers can use Table 2's themes to further expand their family involvement philosophies. Using the guides, for example, can facilitate the planning and implementation of enrollment interviews, home visits, parent-teacher meetings and classroom activities. Some teachers use the themes to formulate questions and possible explanations about family-school disagreements (e.g., home-school differences in behavior

---

Table 1

THEMES FOR GUIDING FAMILY INVOLVEMENT PHILOSOPHIES[*]

Theme	Goal
Empowerment	To provide families with the information and support they need to actively participate in school-related discussions regarding their children's education
Parenting	To support parents in nurturing and guiding their children
Family Strengths	To assist families in identifying and developing strengths and coping mechanisms as a means of managing family life stressors
Child-Siblings	To prepare school-age children and their younger siblings for schooling
Community Resources	To provide parents with the information, support and skills necessary to identify and manage community services
Educational Modeling	To involve parents in identifying education objectives and providing supportive in-home learning opportunities for their children
Family-Teacher Relations	To improve the quality of interpersonal relations between teachers and children's families

The purpose of the themes is to help structure ideas about family involvement and their implications for planning practical family involvement strategies. Some overlap is expected.

management and self-help expectations). Or, the themes can be used to structure classroom activities that build upon children's home experiences (e.g., childhood interests, home routines, family relationships). The themes in Table 2, like those in Table 1, are only a beginning point. Teachers can add themes that reflect their school's individual concerns.

Working with Family Professionals

Stamp and Groves (1994) suggested that family involvement be viewed as a "third institution" whose primary purpose is to strengthen family-school linkages. As we already have noted, the diversity of family structures and lifestyles can present barriers to creating such a "third institution."

On the other hand, a conclusion that families and schools cannot be linked would be based on too narrow an interpretation of family and school goals regarding early childhood education. The traditionally stated goals of child care (protection, nurturing and socialization) and school (education and socialization) always have been interdependent (Caldwell, 1990). Today, more than ever, academic education (learning to read and write) and life-skills education (learning self-help and social responsibilities) are mutually supportive endeavors that occur across family and school settings. Likewise, parents and teachers, although sometimes depicted as adversarial, have similar educational goals (Epstein, 1991) and philosophies (Stipek, Milburn, Clements & Daniels, 1992).

Thus, creating a "third institution" of family involvement is not impossible, although greater attention must be given to devising practical strategies for linking families and schools (Sexton, Aldridge & Snyder, 1994). The authors will now examine some ways in which three types of family professionals can work with schools to develop practical strategies for strengthening family involvement.

■ *Teacher training: Family life educators.* Teachers whose training in family relations is limited have only their own family experiences to guide them when developing a family involvement program. Family life educators can help address teachers' questions about potential barriers to family involvement. During inservice training, teachers should brainstorm questions. Some common questions regarding family involvement follow:

- What are the challenges that confront families from different socioeconomic backgrounds, and how do they influence families' involvement with schools and other social institutions?
- What concerns do families from different ethnic, religious, racial and sexual orientation backgrounds have regarding how their families are depicted in school?
- What are the potential stressors associated with divorce, death and remarriage in relation to child-teacher and parent-teacher relations?
- What strategies can be used to acknowledge the roles of foster parents, grandparents and other extended family guardians?

Barriers to family involvement go beyond school-based issues. Family life educators can help coordinate and facilitate the following professional learning experiences:

- Selected teachers might receive release time for social service internships in order to better understand the diversity of family life within a community context.
- Teachers might be asked to develop a family involvement program that is tied to a youth program, or that is based at a work site, community center or church.
- Inservice training can be provided to highlight the different roles that parents can play in supporting their children's development and education within and outside school and home settings.

One of the most popular topics in education today is diversity (Jacob & Jordan, 1993; McCracken, 1993; Neugebauer, 1992). Teachers need opportunities to explore their own respective cultures, as well as

Table 2	
THEMES FOR GUIDING FAMILY-SCHOOL INTERACTIONS	
Theme	**Example**
Home Routines	Child's typical daily schedule and activities
Child's Interests	Child's favorite toys, television programs, foods, games, books, etc.
Behavior Management	Types of encouragement, reinforcements, limits and consequences used by parents to guide child's behavior
Communication	Verbal and nonverbal strategies used by parents to instruct
Child's Fears	Objects, events and situations feared by a child
Community Involvement	Community events, activities and institutions that families attend (e.g., church, library, recreational, cultural)
Relationships	Child's most important interpersonal relationships within and outside the home setting
Self-Help Expectations	Self-help skills relating to personal hygiene and home chores that parents expect child to perform
Instructional Strategies	Strategies used by parents to teach a child (e.g., instruction, demonstrations, play)

those of others, in relation to curriculum issues. They should be careful, however, not to overgeneralize or stereotype, since all families are unique regarding their rates of cultural assimilation or their racial, ethnic, religious, socioeconomic and sexual orientation backgrounds. Family life educators can facilitate the following activities:

- Keep personal journals related to positive and negative family-school interactions to encourage reflective thought on teaching practices involving children from different family backgrounds.
- Discuss the meaning of "family diversity" and its implications for classroom practices to facilitate group creativity and problem-solving. The authors have found it useful to ask teachers to reflect upon their own meaning of "family" as a beginning reference point.
- Ask teachers to develop parent workshops on topics of their choosing that take into account the different family backgrounds represented in their respective classrooms.

■ *Community education: Family life advocates.* Early childhood advocates warn that educators must not promise more than early childhood programs can deliver, since legislators tend to view early childhood programs as a means by which to achieve sweeping education and social reforms (Morado, 1986). Family life advocates can work with teachers to ensure that family involvement expectations are kept realistic.

- Form task forces to identify barriers and recommend strategies for strengthening family-school-community linkages. School-community linkages may be needed, for example, to ensure the efficient delivery of social services to families who are recent immigrants and/or who have limited means of transportation or income.
- Encourage school administrators to make family life education an integral part of the curriculum. The concept of "families" rather than "family" should be stressed in order to reflect the diversity of family structures and lifestyles in contemporary society.
- Provide training to expand parents' child advocacy efforts. Such training might include establishing parent advisory boards, arranging co-teaching experiences and informing parents of child advocacy efforts in the community.

■ *Family involvement research: Family researchers.* Although the effectiveness of family involvement programs has not been adequately documented, parents and teachers continue to search for meaningful ways to support each other. Teachers can work with family and education researchers to clarify the importance of family involvement through examination of the following questions:

- Are parents better able to understand and implement information regarding child guidance and education when it is presented in parent-led support groups as opposed to teacher-led educational groups? A study about strategies for coordinating family-school expectations and practices regarding children's guidance and education would be useful.
- Do children from certain family backgrounds (e.g., well-established versus recently immigrated; different socioeconomic levels) perform better in the classroom when classroom activities include materials found in their homes, rather than standard classroom materials? Teachers could benefit from learning how to use home materials to support and expand the classroom curriculum.
- Are community-based programs that link families with human services agencies more effective than similar school-based programs? This question could be answered by comparing the joint efforts of teachers and family service workers with those of schools and human service agencies.
- In what ways does family involvement serve as a mediating variable in children's short- and long-term academic and social adjustment? Educators could benefit from studies about family involvement programs' timing, structure and content.
- What are the secondary effects of family involvement programs? Research is needed, for example, on how family involvement programs may benefit younger siblings still at home and the ability of parents to advocate for their children across community settings.

Conclusion

Understanding family lives is central to building a meaningful family involvement program. Family professionals can work with school administrators and teachers to meet the challenges associated with family involvement by helping to develop a family involvement plan that is both practical and relevant to community needs.

References

Boyer, E. L. (1991). *Ready to learn: A mandate for the nation.* Lawrenceville, NJ: Princeton University Press.

Caldwell, B. M. (1990). Educare: A new professional identity. *Dimensions, 18,* 3–6.

Chavkin, N. F., & Williams, D. L. (1989). Low-income parents' attitudes toward parent involvement in education. *Journal of Sociology and Social Welfare, 16,* 17–28.

Epstein, J. L. (1991). Paths to partnership: What we can learn from federal, state, district, and school initiatives. *Phi Delta Kappan, 72,* 344–349.

Epstein, J. L., & Dauber, S. L. (1991). School programs and teacher practices of parent involvement in inner-city elementary and middle schools. *The Elementary School Journal, 91,* 289–305.

Greenberg, P. (1989). Parents as partners in young children's development and education: A new American fad? Why does it matter? *Young Children, 44,* 61–75.

Haseloff, W. (1990). The efficacy of the parent-teacher partnership of the 1990s. *Early Child Development and Care, 58,* 51–55.

Henderson, A. T. (1988). Parents are a school's best friends. *Phi Delta Kappan, 70,* 148–153.

Hess, R. D., & Holloway, S. D. (1984). Family and school as educational institutions. In R. D. Parke, R. N. Emde, H. P. McAdoo, & G. P. Sackett (Eds.), *Review of child development research: The family* (Vol. 7) (pp. 179–222). Chicago: University of Chicago Press.

Hoover-Dempsey, K. V., Bassler, O. C., & Brissie, J. S. (1987). Parent involvement: Contributions of teacher efficacy, school socioeconomic status, and other school characteristics. *American Educational Research Journal, 24,* 417–435.

Jacob, E., & Jordan, C. (1993). *Minority education: Anthropological perspectives.* Norwood, NJ: Ablex.

Johnston, J. H. (1990). *The new American family and the school.* Columbus, OH: National Middle School Association.

McConachie, H. (1986). *Parents and young mentally handicapped children: A review of research issues.* Cambridge, MA: Brookline Books.

McCracken, J. B. (1993). *Valuing diversity: The primary years.* Washington, DC: National Association for the Education of Young Children.

Morado, C. (1986). Prekindergarten programs for 4-year-olds: Some key issues. *Young Children, 41,* 61–63.

Neugebauer, B. (1992). *Alike and different: Exploring our humanity with young children.* Washington, DC: National Association for the Education of Young Children.

Pence, A. (1988). *Ecological research with children and families.* New York: Teachers College Press.

Peters, D. L. (1988). Head Start's influence on parental and child competence. In S. K. Steinmetz (Ed.), *Family and support systems across the life span* (pp. 73–97). New York: Plenum.

Peterson, N. L., & Cooper, C. S. (1989). Parent education and involvement in early intervention programs for handicapped children. In M. J. Fine (Ed.), *The second handbook on parent education: Contemporary perspectives* (pp. 197–233). New York: Academic.

Powell, D. (1989). *Families and early childhood programs.* Washington, DC: National Association for the Education of Young Children.

Rutter, M. (1985). Family and school influences on cognitive development. *Journal of Child Psychology and Psychiatry, 26,* 683–704.

Schorr, D., & Schorr, L. (1988). *Within our reach: Breaking the cycle of disadvantage.* New York: Doubleday.

Sexton, D., Aldridge, J., & Snyder, P. (1994). Family-driven early intervention. *Dimensions, 22,* 14–18.

Silvern, S. (1988). Continuity/discontinuity between home and early childhood education environments. *The Elementary School Journal, 89,* 147–159.

Stamp, L. N., & Groves, M. M. (1994). Strengthening the ethic of care: Planning and supporting family involvement. *Dimensions of Early Childhood, 22,* 5–9.

Stevenson, D. L., & Baker, D. P. (1987). The family-school relation and the child's school performance. *Child Development, 58,* 1348–1357.

Stipek, D., Milburn, S., Clements, D., & Daniels, D. H. (1992). Parents' beliefs about appropriate education for young children. *Journal of Applied Developmental Psychology, 13,* 293–310.

Swick, K., & Graves, S. B. (1993). *Empowering at-risk families during the early childhood years.* Washington, DC: National Education Association.

Swick, K., & McKnight, S. (1989). Characteristics of kindergarten teachers who promote parent involvement. *Early Childhood Research Quarterly, 4,* 19–29.

U.S. Department of Education. (1991). *Preparing young children for success: Guideposts for achieving our first national educational goal.* Washington, DC: Author.

U.S. General Accounting Office. (1990). *Early childhood education: What are the costs of high-quality programs?* (GAO/HRD-90-43BR). Washington, DC: Author.

White, K. R., Taylor, M. J., & Moss, V. D. (1992). Does research support claims about the benefits of involving parents in early intervention programs? *Review of Educational Research, 62,* 91–125.

Beyond Discipline to Guidance

Dan Gartrell

A student teacher in a Head Start classroom recorded—in her journal an anecdotal observation of two children involved in a confrontation (printed with permission); the children here are named Charissa and Carlos.

Observation: Charissa and Carlos were building with blocks. Charissa reached for a block, and Carlos decided he wanted the same one. They both tugged on the block, and then Carlos hit Charissa on the back. Charissa fought back tears and said, "Carlos, you're not s'posed to hit—you're s'posed to use the 'talking stick.'"

Carlos said yeah and got the stick. I couldn't hear what they said, but they took turns holding the stick and talking while the other one listened. After only a minute, the two were playing again, and Charissa was using the block. Later I asked her what the talking stick helped them decide. She said, "That I use the block first this time. Carlos uses it next time."

Reflection: I really got concerned when Carlos hit Charissa, and I was just about to get involved. I couldn't believe it when Charissa

---

Dan Gartrell, Ed.D., is professor of early childhood education at Bemidji State University in Minnesota. This article is based on his forthcoming text, titled A Guidance Approach for the Encouraging Classroom, and the writings of many other early childhood educators and developmental psychologists over the years.

didn't hit back but told Carlos to get the talking stick—and he did! Then they solved the problem so quickly. DeeAnn [the teacher] told me she has been teaching the kids since September [it was now April] to solve their problems by using the talking stick. Usually she has to mediate, but this time two children solved a problem on their own. It really worked!

Firm guidance and calm coaching help children solve social problems.

Preschoolers do not typically solve a problem like this, on their own, by using a prop like a talking stick! But DeeAnn had been working with the children all year to teach them this conflict management skill. To ensure consistency, she had persuaded the other adults in the room to also use the talking stick (even once themselves!). Utilizing the ideas of Wichert (1989), the adults started by using a lot of coaching (high-level mediation) but over time encouraged the children to take the initiative to solve their problems themselves.

Conflict management—in this case through the technique of a decorated, venerable talking stick—is an important strategy in the overall approach to working with children called *guidance*

(Janke & Penshorn Peterson 1995). By now guidance is a familiar term in early childhood education, as is its companion term, *developmentally appropriate practice* (DAP). However, like the misinterpretations of DAP that have surfaced in recent years, some interpretations of guidance show a misunderstanding of what the approach is about. Erroneous interpretations have led to the misapplication of guidance ideas: some teachers may think they are using guidance when they are not.

This article is an effort to amplify the concept of guidance. It defines guidance, traces the guidance tradition in early childhood education, examines the present trend toward guidance, explains what guidance is not, and illustrates key practices in classrooms where teachers use guidance.

Guidance defined

Teachers who practice guidance believe in the positive potential of children, manifest through a dynamic process of development (Greenberg 1988). For this reason, teachers who use guidance think beyond conventional classroom discipline—the intent of which is to keep children (literally and figuratively) in line. Rather than simply being a reaction to crises, guidance involves developmentally appropriate, cul-

---

turally responsive education to reduce the occurrence of classroom problems. Guidance means creating a positive learning environment for each child in the group.

Guidance teaches children the life skills they need as citizens of a democracy (Wittmer & Honig 1994): respecting others and one's self, working together in groups, solving problems using words, expressing strong emotions in acceptable ways, making decisions ethically and intelligently. Teachers who use guidance realize that it takes well into adulthood to master these skills and that, in learning them, children—like all of us—make mistakes. Therefore, because children are just beginning this personal development, teachers regard behaviors traditionally considered *mis*behaviors as *mistaken* behaviors (Gartrell 1987b, 1995). The interventions teachers make to address mistaken behaviors are firm but friendly, instructive and solution oriented but not punitive. The teacher helps children learn from their mistakes rather than punishing them for the mistakes they make; empowers children to solve problems rather than punishing them for having

problems they cannot solve; helps children accept consequences but consequences that leave self-esteem intact.

Guidance teaching is character education in its truest, least political sense—guiding children to develop the empathy, self-esteem, and self-control needed for *autonomy,* Piaget's term for the capacity to make intelligent, ethical decisions (Kamii 1984). In contrast to the notion that the teacher handles all problem situations alone, guidance involves teamwork with professionals and partnerships with parents on behalf of the child.

The guidance tradition

The only task harder than learning democratic living skills is teaching them to others. Guidance has always been practiced by the kind of teacher whom, if we were fortunate, we had ourselves; whom we would want our children to have; whom we would like to emulate. From time immemorial there probably have been "guidance teachers." A

rich guidance tradition spanning more than 150 years has been documented in the early childhood field.

The pioneers

Educators interested in social reform long have viewed children as being in a state of dynamic development and adults as patterning effective education and guidance practices responsive to the developmental pattern of the child. During the nineteenth century the European educators Herbart, Pestalozzi, and Froebel began fundamental educational reform, in no small part as a result of their views on the child's dynamic nature (Osborn 1980). Herbart and Pestalozzi recognized that children learn best through activities they can tie to their own experiences rather than through a strictly enforced recitation of facts.

© Blakely Fetridge Bundy

© Bob Loveland

Often, friendly adult intervention and assistance can help children work through a seemingly insoluble social problem themselves. Most of the time, children want to solve what they perceive as the problem.

German born Friedrich Froebel was the originator of the kindergarten, at the time intended for children aged three to six. Froebel incorporated such practices as manipulatives-based instruction, circle time, home visits, "mothers' meetings," and the use of women teachers (Lilley 1967). (In the 1870s, his kindergartens were barred in Germany for being "too democratic.") For Froebel the whole purpose of education was guidance so that the "innate impulses of the child" could be developed harmoniously through creative activity. As part of his early developmental orientation, Froebel believed that the nature of the child was essentially good and that "faults" were the product of negative experiences, sometimes at the hand of the educator (Lilley 1967).

Similarly, Maria Montessori took a developmental viewpoint, maintaining that "the child is in a continual state of growth and metamorphosis, whereas the adult has reached the norm of the species" (cited in Standing 1962, 106). Montessori's remarkable vision included not only the innovations of the "prepared environment" and a child-oriented teaching process but also the idea that intelligence is greatly influenced by early experience. It interesting to note that Montessori's early theory of "sensitive periods" of learning is supported in graphic fashion by the brain research of today.

Montessori—as well as her American contemporary, John Dewey—abhorred the traditional schooling of the day, which failed to consider children's development. She criticized didactic teaching practices with children planted behind desks, expected to recite lessons of little meaning in their lives, and kept in line by systematic rewards and punishments (Montessori 1964). Her approach made the child an active agent in the education process; through this responsibility children would learn *self*-discipline.

Like Montessori, Dewey viewed discipline as differing in method depending on the curriculum followed. The "preprimary" level in Dewey's University of Chicago Laboratory School featured project-based learning activities that built from the everyday experience of the young learners. Dewey saw the connection between school and society, postulating that our democratic ideals need to be sustained through the microcosm of the classroom. In his 1900 monograph *The School and Society*, Dewey states,

> If you have the end in view of forty or fifty children learning certain set lessons, to be recited to the teacher, your discipline must be devoted to securing that result. But if the end in view is the development of a spirit of social co-operation and community life, discipline must grow out of and be relative to such an aim. There is a certain disorder in any busy workshop; there is not silence; persons are not engaged in maintaining certain fixed physical postures; their arms are not folded; they are not holding their books thus and so. They are doing a variety of things, and there is the confusion, the bustle that results from activity. Out of the occupation, out of doing things that are to produce results, and out of doing these in a social and co-operative way, there is born a discipline of its own kind and type. Our whole conception of discipline changes when we get this point of view. (1969, 16–17)

Dewey, of course, was not just speaking of early childhood education but of schooling at all levels. Almost 100 years later, his words still challenge America's educators and eloquently capture the "guidance difference."

Midcentury influences

In the first half of the twentieth century, progressive educators and psychologists increasingly viewed children not in traditional moralistic terms (good and bad) but in terms responsive to a positive developmental potential. The nursery school movement in Britain and the United States was imbued with these progressive ideas and influenced the writings of two midcentury early childhood educators, James L. Hymes Jr. (1949, 1955) and Katherine Read (1950).

Katherine Read Baker was a nursery education leader. Her classic *The Nursery School: A Human Relations Laboratory* is currently reprinted under a new title in a ninth edition. For Read, the classroom is a supportive environment for both children and adults to gain understanding in the challenging area of human relationships. Read speaks clearly of the child's need for understandable, consistent limits and of the use of authority to encourage self-control:

> Our goal is self-control, the only sound control. But self-control can be sound only when there is a stable mature self. Our responsibility is to help the child develop maturity through giving him the security of limits maintained by responsible adults while he is growing. (Read [1950] 1993, 233)

Hymes distinguished himself as director of the noted Kaiser Day Care Centers during World War II and later as one of the people who strongly influenced the educational approach basic to Head

One of the major areas in which kindergarten and nursery education historically have distinguished themselves from elementary and secondary education is in the area of "behavior education." The former advocates guidance rather than punishment.

Start. Hymes wrote frequently about early childhood education matters, including the landmark *Effective Home-School Relations* (1953). His *Discipline* (1949) and *Behavior and Misbehavior* (1955) stressed the importance of understanding the reasons for children's behavior. He argued that the causes of problems often are not in the child alone but a result of the program placing inappropriate developmental expectations on the child.

Hymes and Read both stressed the need for teachers to have high expectations of children— but expectations in line with each child's development. They articulated a key guidance premise, that the teacher must be willing to modify the daily program for the benefit of children, not just hold the program as a fixed commodity, against which the behavior of the child is to be judged.

The basic educational and child guidance philosophy of Head Start, which was created as a nationwide program by War on Poverty leaders in 1965, was the nursery school/kindergarten philosophy developed long before and taught to several generations of teachers by Read, Hymes, and others of like persuasion.

Jean Piaget, often considered the preeminent developmental psychologist of the twentieth century, discussed implications of his work for the classroom in *The Moral Judgment of the Child* ([1932] 1960). The Swiss psychologist shared with Montessori the precept that children learn through constructing knowledge by interacting with the environment. Further, he shared with Dewey and leaders of nursery school and kindergarten

© BmPorter/Don Franklin

Comfort the hurt child first, then have a conversation with others involved. The objective is to increase empathy and interpersonal problem-solving skills.

education a high regard for the social context of learning—insisting that peer interaction is essential for healthy development. He maintained that education must be an interactive endeavor and that discipline must respect and respond to this fact. Speaking directly about the uses of conventional classroom discipline, Piaget points out,

> If one thinks of the systematic resistance offered by pupils to the authoritarian method, and the admirable ingenuity employed by children the world over to evade disciplinary constraint, one cannot help regarding as defective a system which allows so much effort to be wasted instead of using it in cooperation. ([1932] 1960, 366–67)

Like Dewey, Read, and Hymes, Piaget saw the classroom as a "laboratory" in which the practice of democracy was to be modeled, taught, and learned. For these writers, the means to social, personal, *and* intellectual development was guidance practiced in the classroom by a responsible adult.

As Piaget's work demonstrates, midcentury psychologists as well as educators have enhanced guidance ideas. Important names that readers may have encountered in college educational psychology classes are Erikson, Adler, Maslow, Rogers, Combs, Purkey, and Jersild, among others (Hamacheck 1971).

Two such psychologists who have greatly influenced guidance views are Dreikurs (1968) and Ginott (1972). In line with Adler's theory about personality development, Dreikurs's construct of Mistaken Goals of Behavior has contributed to the present concept of mistaken behavior. Ginott, a particular influence on my writing, has contributed much to the language of guidance, illustrated by one of his more famous quotes: "To reach a child's mind, a teacher must capture his heart. Only if a child feels right can he think right" (1972, 69). Across the middle of the century, a broad array of educators and psychologists nurtured and sustained the guidance tradition.

The 1980s

Through the 1970s the guidance tradition was sustained by writers such as Jeannette Galambos Stone (1978) and Rita Warren (1977), who authored widely read monographs for the National Association for the Education of Young Children (NAEYC), along with many other well-known early childhood educators. While guidance was becoming important in preschool programs, a new trend in the public schools threatened to stop the percolating up of guidance ideas, a long-sought goal of early childhood educators. "Back to the basics" became the call of public school educators, and curriculum and teaching methods grew more proscribed. During this time academic and disciplinary constraints were even put on kindergarten and preschool children. With disregard for young children's development, teachers were pressured to "get students ready" for the academics of the next level—a pressure still felt by some early childhood teachers today.

During these years, the interactive nature of the guidance approach did not fit the regiment of the academic classroom. New "obedience-driven" discipline systems, such as assertive discipline, came into widespread use at all levels of public education—and even in some preschool programs (Gartrell 1987a; Hitz 1988). In *Discipline with Dignity*, Curwin and Mendler lamented the widespread adoption of obedience models of discipline by public schools:

It is ironic that the current mood of education is in some ways behind the past. The 1980s might someday be remembered as the decade when admiration was reserved for principals, cast as folk heroes walking around schools with baseball bats, and for teachers and whole schools that systematically embarrassed students by writing their names on the chalkboard. But we do have hope that the pendulum will once again swing to the rational position of treating children as people with needs and feelings that are not that different from adults. Once we begin to understand how obedience is contrary to the goals of our culture and education, the momentum will begin to shift. Our view is that the highest virtue of education is to teach students to be self-responsible and fully functional. In all but extreme cases, obedience contradicts these goals. (1988, 24)

The guidance trend

Throughout the 1980s and up to the present, educators and writers at the early childhood level maintained their independence from the obedience emphasis in conventional discipline. In 1987 NAEYC published its expanded *Developmentally Appropriate Practice in Early Childhood Programs Serving Children from Birth through Age 8* (Bredekamp).

Now in its revised edition (Bredekamp & Copple 1997), the position statement and document advocate the interactive teaching practices responsive to the development of each child that our profession always has. In relation to behavior management, the document reflects the guidance approach and draws a sharp distinction with conventional elementary school classroom discipline. In *appropriate* teaching practice,

Teachers facilitate the development of social skills, self-control, and self-regulation in children by using positive guidance techniques, such as modeling and encouraging expected behavior, redirecting children to more acceptable activities, setting clear limits, and intervening to enforce consequences for unacceptable, harmful behavior. Teachers' expectations respect children's developing capabilities. Teachers are patient, realizing that not every minor infraction warrants a response. (Bredekamp & Copple 1997, 129)

Inappropriate practices are those in which

Teachers spend a great deal of time punishing unacceptable behavior, demeaning children who misbehave, repeatedly putting the same children who misbehave in time-out or some other punishment unrelated to the action . . . . Teachers do not set clear limits and do not hold children accountable to standards of acceptable behavior. The environment is chaotic, and teachers do not help children set and learn important rules of group behavior and responsibility. (Bredekamp & Copple 1997, 129)

At both the preprimary and primary-grade levels, these NAEYC documents illustrate the ambiguous distinction between conventional discipline techniques and the use of punishment (Bredekamp & Copple 1997. In fact, a growing number of early childhood professionals have become dissatisfied in recent years with the very term "discipline" (MnNAEYC 1991; Reynolds 1996). The reason is that teachers have a hard time telling where discipline ends and punishment begins. Other educators argue that discipline is a "neutral" term and does not have to mean punishment (Marion 1995). However, when most teachers use discipline, they tend to include acts of punishment; they mix up discipline and punishment out of anger or because they feel the child "deserves it." The very idea of "disciplining" a child suggests punishment, illustrating the easy semantic slide of the one into the other.

Teachers who go beyond discipline do so because of the baggage of punishment that discipline carries. These teachers reject punishment for what it is by definition: the infliction of "pain, loss, or suffering for a crime or wrongdoing."

For many years educators and psychologists have recognized the harmful effects of punishment on children (Dewey [1900] 1969; Piaget [1932] 1960; Montessori 1964; Slaby et al. 1995). Some of the effects of punishment are

• low self-esteem (feeling like a "failure"),

• negative self-concept (not liking one's self),

• angry feelings (sometimes under the surface) toward others, and

• a feeling of disengagement from school and the learning process.

A teacher who uses guidance knows that children learn little when the words they frequently hear are "Don't do that" or "You're naughty" or "You know better than that." When discipline includes punishment, young children have difficulty understanding how to improve their behavior

The ideas in this article are not new, but many teachers are not yet putting them into practice.

(Greenberg 1988). Instead of being shamed into "being good," they are likely to internalize the negative personal message that punishment carries (Gartrell 1995).

Experts now recognize that through punishment children lose their trust in adults (Clewett 1988; Slaby et al. 1995). Over time young people come to accept doing negative things and being punished for them as a natural part of life. By contrast, the increasing use of conflict management (teaching children to solve their problems with words) fosters children's faith in social processes. Conflict management and other guidance methods are being used more now because they work better than punishment (Carlsson-Paige & Levin 1992). These methods teach children how to solve problems without violence and help children to feel good about themselves, the class, and the teacher (Levin 1994). Young children need to learn how to know better and do better. The guidance approach is positive teaching, with the teacher having faith in the young child's ability to learn (Marion 1995).

Guidance: What it isn't

The term "discipline" remains in wide use at the elementary, middle-school, and secondary levels. Whether educators embrace the term "guidance" or attach a positive qualifier to "discipline," new notions about classroom management can be expected that claim the use of guidance principles. With the never-ending parade of new information, it is important for us to recognize what guidance is not—so as to better understand what it is.

Five misunderstandings about guidance

1. Guidance is *not* just reacting to problems.

Many problems are caused when a teacher uses practices that are not appropriate for the age, stage, and needs of the individual child. Long group times, for instance, cause young children to become bored and restless. (They will sit in large groups more easily when they are older.) The teacher changes practices—such as reducing the number and length of group activities—to reduce the need for misbehaviors. Changes to other parts of the education program—including room layout, daily schedule, and adult-to-child ratios—also help reduce the need for misbehavior. Guidance prevents problems; it does not just react to them.

2. Guidance does *not* mean that the program won't be educational.

When activities are developmentally appropriate, *all* children succeed at them, and *all* children are learning to be successful students. The Three *R*s are a part of the education program, but they are integrated into the rest of the day and made meaningful so that children want to learn. This "basic" of Progressive Education, the parent of what we now call developmentally appropriate practice, is well explained in the original and revised editions of *Developmentally Appropriate Practice in Early Childhood Programs* and both volumes of *Reaching Potentials* (Bredekamp 1987; Bredekamp and Rosegrant 1992, 1995; Bredekamp & Copple 1997). When teachers use guidance, however, the Three *R*s are not all there is.

The importance of guidance, according to Lilian Katz, means that the teacher makes *relationships* the first *R* (cited in Kantrowitz & Wingert 1989). The social skills that are learned through positive relationships come first in the education program. Children need to know how to relate with others in all parts of their lives. Beginning to learn social skills in early childhood will help children in their years of school and in adult life (Wittmer & Honig 1994). (Social skills, after all, are really social studies skills and language arts skills.)

3. Guidance is *not* a "sometimes thing."

Some teachers think that it is natural to use "guidance" in one set of circumstances and "discipline" in another. Yet nonpunitive guidance techniques exist for all situations and, once learned, are effective (Carlsson-Paige & Levin 1992; Reynolds 1996). For example, a common discipline technique is the time-out chair, but the time-out chair usually embarrasses the child, seldom teaches a positive lesson, and is almost always punishment (Clewett 1988). The teacher can cut down on the use of this punishment by reducing the need for mistaken behavior and helping children to use words to solve their problems.

If a child does lose control and needs to be removed, the teacher can stay with the child for a cooling-down time. The teacher then talks with the child about how the other child felt, helps the child find a way to help the other child feel better (make restitution), and teaches a positive alternative for next time. Guidance encompasses a full spectrum of methods, from prevention to conflict resolution to crisis intervention to long-term management strategies.

Teamwork with parents and other adults is frequently part of the overall approach.

4. Guidance is *not* permissive discipline.

Teachers who use guidance are active leaders who do not let situations get out of hand. They do not make children struggle with boundaries that may not be there (Gartrell 1995). Guidance teachers tend to rely on guidelines—positive statements that remind children of classroom conduct—rather than rules which are usually stated in the negative, as though the adult expects the child to break them. When they intervene, teachers direct their responses to the behavior and respect the personality of the child (Ginott 1972). They avoid embarrassment, which tends to leave lasting emotional scars. They make sure that their responses are friendly as well as firm.

The objective is to teach children to solve problems rather than to punish children for having problems they cannot solve. The outcomes of guidance—the ability to get along with others, solve problems using words, express strong feelings in acceptable ways—are the goals for citizens of a democratic society. For this reason, guidance has a meaning that goes beyond traditional discipline. Guidance is not just keeping children in line; it is actively teaching them skills they will need for their entire lives (Wittmer & Honig 1994).

5. Guidance is *not* reducible to a commercial program.

The guidance tradition is part of the child-sensitive educational practice of the last two decades. Guidance is part of the movement toward developmentally appropriate and culturally responsive

> **The objective is to teach children to solve problems rather than to punish children for having problems they cannot solve. The outcomes of guidance—the ability to get along with others, solve problems using words, express strong feelings in acceptable ways—are the goals for citizens of a democratic society.**

education. Teachers who use guidance rely on a teaching team (adults in the classroom working together) and positive parent-teacher relations. Guidance involves more than a workshop or a program on paper; it requires reflective commitment by the teacher, teamwork by the staff, and cooperation with families and the community.

© Blakely Fetridge Bundy

One-on-one guidance works better than scolding.

Six key guidance practices

Teachers who use guidance have classrooms that are encouraging places to be in. In the words of one teacher, when guidance is present, children want to come to school even when they are sick. Both children and adults feel welcome in guidance classrooms. An informed observer who visits such a classroom quickly sees that "guidance

is practiced here." Six key guidance practices follow. When they are evident in a classroom, the teacher is using guidance.

1. The teacher realizes that social skills are complicated and take into adulthood to fully learn.

In the process of learning social skills, children—like all of us—make mistakes. That's why behaviors traditionally considered to be "misbehaviors" are regarded as "mistaken behaviors" (Gartrell 1987a, b; 1995). The teacher believes in the positive potential of each child. He recognizes that mistaken behaviors are caused by inexperience in social situations, the influence of others on the child, or by deep, unmet physical or emotional needs. Understanding why children show mistaken behavior permits the teacher to teach social skills with a minimum of moral judgment about the child. He takes the attitude that "we all make mistakes; we just need to learn from them."

The teacher shows this understanding even when the children demonstrate "strong-needs" (serious) mistaken behavior (Gartrell 1987b, 1995). Such children are sometimes regarded as "bad" children, but the teacher using guidance knows that they are children with bad problems that they cannot solve on their own. In working with strong-needs mistaken behavior, the teacher takes a comprehensive approach. He seeks to understand the problem, modifies the child's program to reduce crises, intervenes consistently but nonpunitively, builds the relationship with the child, involves the parents, teams with staff and other professionals, and develops, implements, and monitors a long-term plan.

2. The teacher reduces the need for mistaken behavior.

One major cause of mistaken behavior is a poor match between the child and the educational program (the program expects either too much or too little from the child). The teacher improves the match by using teaching practices that are developmentally appropriate and culturally sensitive (Bredekamp 1987; Bredekamp & Copple 1997). She reduces wait times by offering many activities in learning centers and small groups. She gives children choices so they can work at their own levels in activities. To avoid problems, she anticipates when particular children will need support and encouragement. She changes activities, adjusts the schedule, and modifies the room arrangement as circumstances warrant. She uses adults in the classroom to increase individual attention and expand opportunities for positive adult-child attachments. When children's development, learning styles, and family backgrounds become the main priorities of a program, children become positively involved and feel less need to show mistaken behavior.

3. The teacher practices positive teacher-child relations.

The teacher works to accept each child as a welcome member of the class (Warren 1977). To prevent embarrassment and unnecessary competition, the teacher avoids singling out children either for criticism or praise. Instead, she uses private feedback with the individual and group-focused encouragement with the class (Hitz & Driscoll 1988).

Even if children are preschoolers, the teacher holds class meetings both for regular business and for problems that arise (Brewer 1992). The teacher relies more on guidelines—positive statements of expected behaviors—than on rules with negative wording and implied threats. She models and teaches cooperation and empathy-building skills. She models and teaches acceptance of children who might be singled out negatively for physical, cultural, or behavioral reasons. She teaches that differing human qualities and circumstances are natural, to be appreciated and learned from. She understands that children who feel accepted in the classroom have less need to show mistaken behavior.

4. The teacher uses intervention methods that are solution oriented.

The teacher creates an environment in which problems can be solved peaceably (Levin 1994). He intervenes by modeling and teaching conflict management—initially using high-level mediation and continually encouraging the children to negotiate for themselves. He avoids public embarrassment and rarely uses removal (redirection and cooling-down times) or physical restraint, and then only as methods of last resort. After intervention, the teacher assists the child with regaining composure, under-standing the other's feelings, learning more acceptable behaviors, and making amends and reconciling with the other child or group.

The teacher recognizes that, at times, he too shows human frailties. The teacher works at monitoring and managing his own feelings. The teacher learns even as he teaches. As a developing professional, the teacher models the effort to learn from mistakes.

5. The teacher builds partnerships with parents.

The teacher recognizes that mistaken behavior occurs less often when parents and teachers work together. The teacher also recognizes that being a parent is a difficult job and that many parents, for personal and cultural reasons, feel uncomfortable meeting with educators (Gestwicki 1992). The teacher starts building partnerships at the beginning of the year. Through positive notes home, phone calls, visits, meetings, and conferences, she builds relationships. It is her job to build partnerships even with hard-to-reach parents. When the invitations are sincere, many parents gradually do become involved.

6. The teacher uses teamwork with adults.

The teacher recognizes that it is a myth that she can handle all situations alone. She creates a teaching team of fellow staff and volunteers (especially parents), who work together in the classroom. She understands that children gain trust in their world when they see adults of differing backgrounds working together. When there is serious mistaken behavior, the teacher meets with parents and other adults to develop and use a coordinated plan. Through coordinated assistance, children can be helped to overcome serious problems and build self-esteem and social skills. The teacher knows that effective communication among adults builds a bridge between school and community. Though working together, teachers accomplish what they cannot do alone.

* * *

In summary, guidance goes beyond the traditional goal of classroom discipline: enforcing children's compliance to the teacher's will. On a day-to-day basis in the classroom, guidance teaches children the life skills they need as citizens of a democracy. Teachers encourage children to take pride in their developing personalities and cultural identities. Guidance teaches children to view differing human qualities as sources of affirmation and learning.

Guidance involves creating a successful learning environment for each child. The teacher plans and implements an educational program that is developmentally appropriate and culturally responsive. She serves as leader of a classroom community and helps all children to find a place and to learn. The teacher uses nonpunitive intervention techniques, in firm but friendly ways, to establish guidelines and guide children's behavior. She uses conflict resolution as a regular and important tool.

The guidance approach involves teamwork on the part of adults, especially in the face of serious mistaken behavior. Guidance links together teacher, parent, and child on a single team. Success in the use of guidance is measured not in test scores or "obedient" classes but in positive attitudes in the classroom community toward living and learning.

References

Bredekamp, S., ed. 1987. *Developmentally appropriate practice in early childhood programs serving children from birth through age 8.* Exp. ed. Washington, DC: NAEYC.

Bredekamp, S., & C. Copple, eds. 1997. *Developmentally appropriate practice in early childhood programs.* Rev. ed. Washington, DC: NAEYC.

Bredekamp, S., & T. Rosegrant, eds. 1992. *Reaching potentials: Appropriate curriculum and assessment for young children—volume 1.* Washington, DC: NAEYC.

Bredekamp, S., & T. Rosegrant, eds. 1995. *Reaching potentials: Transforming early childhood curriculum and assessment—volume 2.* Washington, DC: NAEYC.

Brewer, J.A. 1992. Where does it all begin? Teaching the principles of democracy in the early years. *Young Children* 47 (3): 51–53.

Carlsson-Paige, N., & D.E. Levin. 1992. Making peace in violent times: A constructivist approach to conflict resolution. *Young Children* 48 (1): 4–13.*

Clewett, A.S. 1988. Guidance and discipline: Teaching young children appropriate behavior. *Young Children* 43 (4): 22–36.*

Curwin, R.L., & A.N. Mendler. 1988. *Discipline with dignity.* Alexandria, VA: Association for Supervision and Curriculum Development.

Dewey, J. [1900] 1969. *The school and society.* Chicago: University of Chicago Press.

Dreikurs, R. 1968. *Psychology in the classroom.* New York: Harper & Row.

Gartrell, D.J. 1987a. Assertive discipline: Unhealthy for children and other living things. *Young Children* 42 (2): 10–11.

Gartrell, D.J. 1987b. Punishment or guidance. *Young Children* 42 (3): 55–61.

Gartrell, D.J. 1995. Misbehavior or mistaken behavior? *Young Children* 50 (5): 27–34.

Gestwicki, C. 1992. *Home, school and community relations.* Albany, NY: Delmar.

Ginott, H. 1972. *Teacher and child.* New York: Avon.

Greenberg, P. 1988. Avoiding 'me against you' discipline. *Young Children* 43 (1): 24–25.*

Hamacheck, D.E. 1971. *Encounters with the self.* New York: Holt, Rinehart, & Winston.

Hitz, R. 1988. Viewpoint. Assertive discipline: A response to Lee Canter. *Young Children* 43 (2): 25–26.

Hitz, R., & A. Driscoll. 1988. Praise or encouragement? New insights into praise: Implications for early childhood teachers. *Young Children* 43 (4): 6–13.

Hymes, J.L. 1949. *Discipline.* New York: Bureau of Publications, Columbia University.

Hymes, J.L. 1953. *Effective home-school relations.* Englewood Cliffs, NJ: Prentice Hall.

Hymes, J.L. 1955. *Behavior and misbehavior.* Englewood Cliffs, NJ: Prentice Hall.

Janke, A.J., & J. Penshorn Peterson. 1995. *Peacemaker's A,B,Cs for young children.* S. Marine on St. Croix, MN: Growing Communities for Peace.*

Kamii, C. 1984. Autonomy: The aim of education envisioned by Piaget. *Phi Delta Kappan* 65 (6): 410–15.

Kantrowitz, B., & P. Wingert. 1989. How kids learn, *Newsweek,* 17 July, 50–56.

Levin, D.E. 1994. *Teaching young children in violent times.* Cambridge, MA: Educators for Social Responsibility.

Lilley, I.M., ed. 1967. *Friedrich Froebel: A selection from his writings.* London: Cambridge University Press.

———
* Recommended reading.

Marion, M. 1995. *Guidance of young children.* 5th ed. Columbus, OH: Merrill.

Minnesota Association for the Education of Young Children (MnAEYC). 1991. *Developmentally appropriate guidance of children birth to eight.* Rev. ed. St. Paul: Author.

Montessori, M. 1964. *The Montessori method.* New York: Schocken.

Osborn, D.K. 1980. *Early childhood education in historical perspective.* Athens, GA: Education Associates.

Piaget, J. [1932] 1960. *The moral judgment of the child.* Glencoe, IL: Free Press.

Read, K.H. [1950] 1993. *Early childhood programs: Human relations and learning.* 9th ed. Fort Worth, TX: Harcourt Brace.

Reynolds, E. 1996. *Guiding young children: A child-centered approach.* 2d ed. Mountain View, CA: Mayfield.

Slaby, R.G., W.C. Roedell, D. Arezzo, & K. Hendrix. 1995. *Early violence prevention: Tools for teachers of young children.* Washington, DC: NAEYC.

Standing, E.M. 1962. *Maria Montessori: Her life and work.* New York: New American Library.

Stone, J.G. 1978. *A guide to discipline.* Rev. ed. Washington, DC: NAEYC.

Warren, R.M. 1977. *Caring: Supporting children's growth.* Washington, DC: NAEYC.

Wichert, S. 1989. *Keeping the peace: Practicing cooperation and conflict resolution with preschoolers.* Philadelphia: New Society.*

Wittmer, D.S., & A.S. Honig. 1994. Encouraging positive social development in young children. *Young Children* 49 (5): 61–75.*

For further reading

Gartrell, D.J. 1994. *A guidance approach to discipline.* Albany, NY: Delmar.

Greenberg, P. 1990. Ideas that work with young children. Why not academic preschool? (Part 1). *Young Children* 45 (2): 70–80.

Greenberg, P. 1992. Why not academic preschool? (Part 2) Autocracy or democracy in the classroom? *Young Children* 47 (3): 54–64.

Greenberg, P. 1992. Ideas that work with young children. How to institute some simple democratic practices pertaining to respect, rights, roots, and responsibilities in any classroom (Without losing your leadership position). *Young Children* 47 (5): 10–17.

Hendrick, J. 1992. Where does it all begin? Teaching the principles of democracy in the early years. *Young Children* 47 (3): 51–64.

Getting Along: How Teachers Can Support Children's Peer Relationships

Kristen M. Kemple[1,2] and Lynn Hartle[1]

Peer relationships provide an important context for the young child's social development. Teachers can influence children's developing social competence in a variety of ways. This article describes how teachers can support children's peer relationships by intentionally shaping the classroom's physical and emotional context. With these basic supports in place, teachers can effectively use planned activities and on-the-spot guidance to help children learn to interact competently and form satisfying relationships.

KEY WORDS: peer relationships; social competence; teachers' roles.

INTRODUCTION

It is Friday afternoon, and Mr. Casey is preparing his kindergarten classroom for the following week. He equips the block area with construction hats, rubber tools, and construction vehicles. He makes a note to himself to read *Mike Mulligan and his Steam Shovel* at story time on Monday, and to provide books related to building construction in the literature corner. He has planned a short field trip to observe a nearby construction site on Tuesday. Mr. Casey has found that certain children in his class, like Terrance, are more successful in interacting with peers in the block area when a theme is suggested and supported by props, literature, and some common experience.

In Ms. Morrison's classroom, 3-year-old Marta responds to Carmen's suggestion that they play "mommies" with a curt and emphatic "no." Hearing this, and sensing Carmen's feeling of rejection, Ms. Morrison says to Marta, "You don't want to play mommies with Carmen. Is there something else you would like to play with her?" When Marta suggests, "Hey, want to be kitty cats?" Carmen nods a happy "yes," and the two girls

begin to mew and drink pretend milk. Ms. Morrison is pleased by this outcome. Marta's frequent rejections of peers' play ideas are seldom followed up with an alternative suggestion by Marta, with the result that her peers feel rejected while Marta is left alone.

Mrs. Talbot's second grade class will be gaining a new member next week. The new child, Carson, has multiple disabilities and uses a wheelchair. The girl's parents have expressed concern that she will have difficulty making friends in her new classroom. Mrs. Talbot has already consulted with the special education liaison teacher about ways to help Carson become socially integrated into her new peer group. A willing and sociable child, Janine, will be Carson's "host" for the first week of school, helping her to "learn the ropes." Carson has been appointed "snack assistant," which means she will pass out placemats bearing classmates' names. This will allow her a special opportunity to interact with peers and learn their names.

Mr. Casey, Ms. Morrison, and Mrs. Talbot have several things in common. They are early childhood teachers who recognize the importance of young children's peer relationships. They hold the development of peer competence as an important goal for the children in their classrooms. They believe that they, as teachers, can have a positive influence on children's peer interactions, and they act planfully and intentionally to promote peer competence in their classrooms.

[1]Department of Instruction and Curriculum, College of Education, University of Florida, Gainesville, Florida.

[2]Correspondence should be directed to Kristen M. Kemple, Department of Instruction and Curriculum, College of Education, Norman Hall, University of Florida, Gainesville, Florida 32611.

From *Early Childhood Education Journal*, Vol. 24, No. 3, 1997, pp. 139-146. © 1997 by Human Sciences Press, Inc. Reprinted by permission.

IMPORTANCE OF PEER COMPETENCE IN EARLY CHILDHOOD

Peer relationships provide an important context for the young child's social development. Peer interactions present children with different challenges and different opportunities than do interactions with adults. The research literature suggests that peer relationships contribute to children's long term development in unique and important ways (Hartup & Moore, 1991; Kupersmidt, Coie, & Dodge, 1990; Parker & Asher, 1987). It has often been suggested that the early childhood years may be an ideal time to assist children who are experiencing difficulty in peer relationships (Katz & McClellan, 1991; Ramsey, 1991; Rubin & Everett, 1982). Furthermore, the developmental significance of competence in peer interaction is becoming increasingly recognized by early interventionists concerned with children with disabilities (Guralnick, 1990; Odom, McConnell, & McEvoy, 1992). These early years may comprise a time when all young children are particularly sensitive to experiences which contribute to the development of social competence (Katz & McClellan, 1991).

TEACHERS' ROLES

In most cases, positive and satisfying peer relationships do not magically occur simply because young children are in close and frequent proximity in a classroom or on a playground. The development of social competence in the peer group setting requires the attention of an adult who understands the social needs and capabilities of young children and who knows how to provide appropriate support and intervention when needed. Teachers can support children's developing social competence in a variety of ways. Practices which help children learn how to interact with one another may be as indirect as setting up the physical environment in a way that subtly encourages interaction. At times, practices may be as direct as taking a child aside and coaching him or her in skills to use to gain entry into a play situation, or stepping in to guide children step-by-step through the process of resolving a conflict. One of the most useful sets of tools an excellent teacher of young children may possess is her skill in facilitating children's interactions as they are occurring, in the least intrusive way that is effective for a particular situation, for a particular child, at a particular time.

The Emotional Climate

The emotional climate of the classroom influences children's disposition to interact positively and peacefully with one another. A *democratic style of discipline* is exemplified by adults who set firm limits on inappropriate behavior, and rely largely on explanations and other-oriented reasoning to help children learn appropriate behavior. This style of discipline allows children to feel listened to, to understand the rules and the reasons behind the rules, and to feel confident that they will be protected. This is in contrast to a chaotic environment produced by a laissez-faire, highly permissive approach, or the inhibited feeling of a classroom characterized by harsh, punitive authoritarian discipline (see Kostelnik, Stein, Whiren, & Soderman, 1993; Greenberg, 1992a, for descriptions of practices associated with positive discipline). Children who feel safe, cherished, and respected are able to focus their attention on peers. Children who are frightened (of the harshly punitive teacher, or of out-of-control peers) are consumed with protecting themselves. This may significantly influence the amount and quality of energy children have available to interact competently and enjoyably with peers.

A classroom in which children are viewed and *respected as individuals* can provide the basic foundation for a caring community of children. Teachers who use children's names frequently help children learn and use one another's names. Teachers who elicit discussion of individual likes, dislikes, abilities, and experiences give children further opportunities to get to know one another and to identify commonalities and shared interests. For example, teachers who openly facilitate discussions reflecting classmates' questions and concerns about a child with a disability can help peers to understand the disability and to accept the child. Teachers can guide such conversations to encourage children to notice ways in which they are different as well as ways in which they are the same: Samir and Tony both like to read books about sharks. Samir walks, and Tony uses a wheelchair. Samir brings tabouleh in his lunch box, and Tony brings potato salad. The Anti-Bias Curriculum (Derman-Sparks and the A.B.C. Task Force, 1989) is a good source of information which can help teachers develop a classroom climate in which children recognize their similarities and respect one another's differences.

Arrangement of Physical Space

Although we sometimes overlook, forget, or are unaware of some of the most subtle influences on the quality of children's interactions with one another, subtle influences may be the most powerful in setting the stage for social competence. The way the classroom is arranged may influence both the amount and the nature of children's interactions. For example, the presence and the quality of a *dramatic play center* (sometimes called a "housekeeping corner") and a *block center* can influence the kinds of interactions in the classroom. Young children carry on a great deal of interaction within the context of sociodramatic play (pretend play that involves more than one child engaged in the pretense). If the classroom does not provide children with spaces and materials designed to encourage and support engagement in sociodramatic play, children miss out on one of their most natural avenues for interaction. A cramped block play area does not invite children to engage in extended periods of social play, and sends the message "one or two at a time." A dramatic play corner which is large enough to comfortably accommodate several children can encourage the kind of cooperative pretend that gives children practice in negotiating roles and enacting mutually developed pretend sequences. The benefits of dramatic play and block building areas are not limited to preschool and kindergarten. The benefits of such centers continue through the primary years (Wasserman, 1990).

Teachers can encourage social interaction by arranging the classroom into *interest areas that accommodate small groups*. Children naturally spread themselves out if teachers prepare areas with adequate arrangement of chairs and tables or floor space. Children have more opportunities for developing positive peer relationships in well-defined spaces for four children, than if teachers call children individually to come to the art center, for example. A well stocked writing center with a table and four chairs can be a great place for children to initiate or maintain peer relationships by creating letters and presents to give to new and old friends (Babcock, Hartle, & Lamme, 1995).

Teachers can help to avoid recurring conflicts by organizing the placement of classroom centers with careful attention to *traffic pathways*. A construction area situated near a path where children are often coming and going will be the frequent site of mishaps, as children's creations are damaged or destroyed by passersby. Although children must experience conflicts in order to learn to resolve them, a room arranged in a manner that precipitates a multitude of unnecessary clashes is likely to feel unsafe to the young child. Pathways can also be important in the outdoor environment for encouraging social experiences. On the playground, children often use pathways for running, chasing, and pretend scenarios. Pathways can be designed to keep the action going: around the swings so children can spot an open seat by a friend and past the dramatic playhouse to check in on the activity there (Hartle & Johnson, 1993). In a class which includes a child with a disability that affects his or her gross motor movement, adequate traffic pathways are especially important.

Provision of Materials and Equipment

Materials affect the social dimensions of play and work. Availability of a balance of types of materials that support individual, pair and group play allow children choices of social grouping throughout the day (Trawick-Smith, 1992). For example, John arrived one day and wanted to be alone, so he chose to do a puzzle. Later, during activity time, he chose to go to the writers' workshop area to help two other children edit the stories they wrote yesterday. In the afternoon, he and a partner built a skyscraper with the blocks. The availability of social options allowed John to follow his own rhythms.

Teachers can display materials with ready access for selection and use. Materials which are intended for children to choose and to put away independently should be readily accessible to all children. For the child with a motor disability, this may require some reorganization of classroom shelf space. For the child whose movement and communication are affected by a disability, a special system of communicating choices of activities and materials may be developed in the form of a communication board (cf. Bailey & McWilliams, 1990).

Teachers can support children's peer interactions by changing the available materials. Dress-up clothes for the dramatic play corner should be changed periodically. Take care that you don't include only traditionally feminine attire; boys and girls like to dress up in construction hats, too. Another kind of block can be added to fit the unit theme. New clothes or fresh blocks may precipitate new peer relationships. Two children who have never played together before might find some common interest in the hospital dress-up clothes. Two others who never before collaborated on an activity might be anxious to try out the new bristle blocks together. These partners may help each other share new perspectives and ideas that might not otherwise have been realized.

Tying dramatic play props to a unit theme, or to a favorite book which children enjoy during circle time, can be helpful in giving children something to play about. This provides children with some common foundation from which to play, allowing an entree to sociodramatic play for those children who are unfamiliar with many popular play "scripts." Children who "don't get it" with regard to a particular play theme may be left out of play.

Teachers can also set up situations that encourage more complex social interactions. Setting up an art table activity for four children and providing two glue bottles and two pairs of scissors sets the stage for sharing. If this is a new and/or challenging experience for some or all of the children, the teacher should be available to facilitate the process as needed. When planning this kind of an activity, wise teachers pay attention to individual developmental level. The above is not likely to work for most 2-year-olds. To facilitate toddlers' sharing, it is best not to rely on them to share attractive or popular toys, but to have two of these available instead of just one (e.g., two firetrucks, two shopping carts). Redirection is an especially valuable guidance tool with toddlers.

Schedules and Routines

Teachers can help to nurture children's growing social competence by allowing *adequate time for free choice*. Free play is a prime opportunity for peer interaction. To learn social competence with peers, children need opportunities to interact through the medium of play. When adequate time is provided for free choice, children are less likely to feel in competition to get a turn at a favored activity. The stakes are not quite as high (or anxiety as sharp) when children know they will get a turn. Another reason teachers plan the daily schedule to include large blocks of time is to allow children opportunities to work through positive peer interactions without interruptions. Frequent changes of activities do not allow children time to collaborate on the completion of tasks (Gareau & Kennedy, 1991), or to engage in complex and satisfying play (Christie & Wardle, 1992).

Snack time can be a time to enjoy and practice conversation in an atmosphere that is not mediated by toys, pretend, materials, or projects. Conversational turn-taking, attending, making requests, sharing experiences are all important competencies which children can practice during a "family style" snack time. Snack times in which children do not eat together (the "fast-food" model) or snack times in which children are required to eat in silence eliminate an important opportunity for peer interaction.

Snack time during which a teacher does *not* sit down and participate with the children limits the opportunity for the teacher to guide peer interaction when needed. Teachers can join snack time intending to model, guide, and encourage polite conversation. If children are given the responsibilities to pass and serve food, opportunities will arise to use proper etiquette as modeled by teachers.

Planned Activities

As teachers observe children's social interaction and note areas in need of further development, they may plan activities specifically designed to enhance children's ability to think about and solve the social dilemmas they encounter in the classroom. Puppets and literature are common vehicles used for this purpose. In the primary grades, teachers may also plan cooperative learning experiences as opportunities for enhancing social skills (cf. Johnson & Johnson, 1991).

Puppets can serve as a good medium for fostering group discussion about social problems and potential solutions. For example, Ms. Johnson has observed that many of the children in her classroom of 4- and 5-year-olds are experiencing conflicts over who gets to play with the rubber animals which she has placed in the block area. The children are especially interested in the lion and the elephant. To help children think about how they can solve such conflicts, she plans an interactive puppet "show" to elicit children's ideas. During large group time, she introduces Harry the Hippo (a puppet on her left hand) and Frieda the Fox (on her right hand). Using the piano bench as a stage, Ms. Johnson enacts a conflict between Frieda and Harry using real props from the block area (blocks and the rubber elephant). Frieda and Harry wind up tugging on the elephant and crying "Its mine! My turn!" Frieda the Fox then turns slowly and purposefully toward the children and declares, "I think we have a problem." Harry the Hippo turns to the children and adds, "Can you tell us what our problem is?" The chorus of voices from the children reply, "You're fighting" and "You're being mean!" Harry the Hippo guides the children to more clearly identify the root of the problem, probing with "What are we fighting about?" One child says, "The elephant!" Frieda asks, "What is our problem about the elephant?" A child replies, "You both want it!" Frieda sums up and extends, saying, "We both want the elephant. But there is only one! Oh, help us out! What can we do to solve this problem?" Through the puppets, Ms. Johnson can guide the children through the process of generating alternative solutions to the problem, and evaluating the merits of suggested solutions. Some teachers make such "problem puppet" experiences a regular part of their large group times (cf. Kreidler, 1984; Shure, 1992).

Children's literature can also serve as a springboard for discussions about social skills. For example, in *Lets be Enemies* (Udry, 1961), a boy tells us, "James used to be my friend. But today he is my enemy" (pp. 2-3). He goes on to describe James' behavior: James throws sand, always wants to be the boss, grabs the best digging spoon, etc. Teachers can use such literature as a tool for interactive book sharing, stopping to ask children, "has that ever happened to you?" or "I wonder what this boy could do when James takes all the crayons." "What did you do when that happened to you?" "How did that make you feel?" A short list of children's books that deal with children's peer relationships immediately precedes the references section of this article (cf. Krogh & Lamme, 1985; Lamme & McKinley 1992; Ramsey, 1991). An advantage of using literature in this way is that, while a teacher may have to wait all day to witness a real example of a child who shares or reaches out to a friend in need, books are ready at any time to introduce and stimulate discussions about getting along with others (Lamme & McKinley, 1992).

Actual social dilemmas which children experience in the classroom can be brought into a circle time session for *class discussion*. A first grade teacher asks his class if anyone would like to describe something fun they did with some friends during recess. He then asks, "Did anyone have a problem during recess that they would like to talk about?" One child volunteers, "They wouldn't let me play with them at the monkey bars." Questions like "How did that make you feel?" "What did you say to them, to let them know you wanted to play?" What could she do, of she wants to play with those children?" or "...if she wants to play on the monkey bars?" can be used to guide the discussion.

Based on problem-solving discussions generated by puppets, books, actual situations, or hypothetical role play, teachers and children can maintain a poster-sized list of ideas for dealing with social dilemmas. As children continue to discuss social dilemmas, new ideas can be added to the list. The list can be used as a resource during group discussion, or can be referred to as the teacher steps in to assist children with a problematic situation.

On-the-Spot Support

One of the most important means by which teachers can help children learn to interact effectively with one another is to provide spontaneous, on-the-spot support for children when they are in the midst of experiencing a difficult or challenging interaction (Hazen, Black, & Fleming-Johnson, 1984; Katz & McClellan, 1991; Kemple, 1991; Ramsey, 1991). Consider the following example: Leah and Max are in the block area. Max has been using a plastic steam shovel to construct a freeway. He puts the steam shovel down as he scoots over to the shelf to get more blocks. Leah notices the steam shovel on the floor, and picks it up. When Max sees this, he darts over to Leah and grabs the steam shovel. A tug-of-war begins, with both children angry, shouting, and very soon they are in tears. This is when the teacher arrives. How might she respond to this situation? "Leah, you

need to give it back to Max and say you're sorry" might solve the problem for the moment, but would not help the children learn how to cope with a similar situation in the future. "You two need to work this out" might be an adequate prompt for children who are already skilled in the process of social problem-solving, just as "You need to use your words" would likely only work for children who already know which words to use and how to use them!

Max and Leah could be guided through the process of resolving their dispute as follows. First children are guided in defining the problem, by allowing each to state his/her perspective of the situation. Next, the teacher helps to ensure that the children understand each other by paraphrasing each child's view to the other and by defining the problem in mutual terms. The teacher lets the children know that they have some responsibility for finding a mutually acceptable solution, and then guides them through the process of generating alternative solutions, offering her own ideas when needed, and facilitating children's discussion of the merits of suggested solutions until one is mutually agreed upon. When a solution is agreed upon, the teacher acknowledges the emotional investment each child had in the conflict and the effort that went into finding a solution (cf. Oken-Wright, 1992; Carlsson-Paige & Levin, 1992b).

Teachers may wonder, "But where would I find the time to do this? And what might happen with the other children while I am attending to these two?" Stein and Kostelnik (1984) found that, during the first 5 weeks of using a conflict mediation process like that described above, the average session lasted 7–10 minutes. That time decreased to a little more than 4 minutes per session by the end of 10 weeks. Extra time invested early in the year can pay off later, as children eventually become skilled in handling their own problems without a teacher's assistance. Teachers often find that, when they are involved in helping two or three children resolve a dispute, other children become interested observers or sideline participants. As a result, problems can be less likely to erupt in other parts of the classroom during this time.

While much attention has been devoted recently to the role the teacher can play in supporting children through the process of resolving conflicts which occur naturally in the classroom (cf. Bernat, 1993; Carlsson-Paige & Levin, 1992a,b; Dinwiddie, 1994; Edwards, 1992; Oken-Wright, 1992) conflicts are by no means the only situations in which teachers can provide on-the-spot scaffolding of children's social competence. Three important areas of peer competence for young children are their ability to resolve conflicts, initiate interaction, and maintain interaction (Kostelnik *et al.*, 1993).

Consider the following situation: Three children are at the play-dough table. You have provided a variety of cookie cutters, small baking pans, and a box with this activity. The children are forming what they call "cookies" and "birthday cakes," baking them in the "oven" and talking among themselves about who should bake which products. Jo has stood by the group for the last couple of minutes, watching them. You sense that he wants to play with this group. How might you respond in such a situation? Would you stand by without intervening? Would you suggest to the other children that Jo might want to play? Would you provide Jo with appropriate words to use to gain entry into the situation? Any of these approaches might be appropriate depending on the needs and capabilities of the individual children involved, as well as on further details of the immediate situation.

It is important to tailor such interventions to the needs and abilities of the individual child. A teacher's suggestions should depend not only on the situation, but also on the competencies of the child or children involved (Katz & McClellan, 1991). Adjusting facilitation to be individually appropriate implies that effective facilitation strategies fall along a continuum from highly direct to indirect. In the following example, a teacher works to help a child gain entry into play by first providing very indirect support, and then becoming more directly supportive as she believes is needed. A group of children are pretending to be sharks, putting their hands on their heads as fins in the block area. Fred wants to enter. Fred approaches the group wearing a mail carrier's hat and carrying a bag, calling out "Mailman! Here's your mail!" Dan says, "No, we're sharks. We're not playing mailman." Fred leaves dejectedly, and watches from a distance. Fred's teacher approaches him and says, "You look like you'd like to play with them" to which Fred replies, "Yes, but they won't." "Let's watch and see what they are playing. What do you think they are playing?" she asks. Fred offers "Sharks," his teacher says, "Sharks. Hmmm. Can you think of something you could do to help them with that?" Fred protests, " No, I don't want to play that. I want to be the mailman." His teacher paraphrases Fred's sentiments by saying, "You want to be the mail carrier, but they want to be sharks. Can you think of a way to play so you can both be what you want?" Fred says adamantly, "No, I want some people to take their mail." When his teacher ventures, "Maybe you could be a shark-mail carrier and deliver mail to other sharks." Fred perks up, and says "Yeah!" Then he approaches the group of "sharks," putting his hand on his head like a fin, over his mail hat, while calling out, "Here's the shark-mailman! I've got mail for the sharks." Dan says, "Oh good! Where's mine?" The sharks read their letters, then pretend to write letters to other sharks which Fred, the shark-mail carrier, delivers (thanks to Nancy Hazen, the teacher in this example). In this illustration, notice that the teacher helped Fred define the problem, helped him to view the situation from the group's perspective and identify both his own needs and those of the other children. She then guided him through problem-solving by encouraging him to generate potential solutions, and ultimately suggested to him a specific solution which combined the interests of all involved in the situation. Of course, things won't always work out this neatly, and many children need numerous supported experiences of this nature before they can begin to solve social problems independently!

By paying careful attention to children's social interactions, a teacher can learn to identify opportunities to scaffold children's conversational exchanges and help them to maintain interaction. If a teacher notices that one child has not acknowledged another child's comment about what they might do on the playground in the afternoon, she might turn to the first child and say, "I think she is talking to you." Alternatively, she might turn to the second child and say, "Maybe he doesn't know you are talking to him. How could you get his attention?" The teacher's decision about what to say would depend on her interpretation of the situation, as well as her knowledge of each child. Perhaps she has previously noticed that one child seems unaware of the need to get another person's attention when she wants to communicate with them or perhaps another child has a recurring tendency to ignore or to be unaware of comments that are intended for him.

Teachers and researchers have identified a variety of social competencies that are associated with being liked or disliked by peers (Katz, 1991; Kemple, 1991; Hazen et al., 1984). Knowledge of behaviors that are related to acceptance can guide a teacher's observations of children and can help the teacher to decide what to look for in assessing individual children's social strengths and needs. A child who doesn't seem to be proficient at "reading" other children's emotional responses could be guided by such teacher interventions as "Look at Chandra's face, Carolyn. What is her face telling you?" or "Do you think that Chandra likes it when you push her that way? Look at the unhappy look on her face." A more directive approach by the teacher might consist of gently turning Carolyn's face toward Chandra's and saying "Chandra looks angry. I think she doesn't like being pushed." Teachers can assist children by indicating ways in which they can state their feelings, ideas, and desires clearly. For example, a teacher's suggestion might be, "Say to Thomas, 'Please pass me that long block,' or 'Let

Mary know that it bothers you when she makes the easel shake.'"

Generally speaking, it is best to support a child in the least directive way that is appropriate for that child. Some children require more direct guidance than others and each child requires different types of guidance on different days and in different situations. A common misconception is to assume that a child with a disability will require highly direct and structured social interventions. Yet it is true that a substantial proportion of young children with disabilities experience significant problems in peer-related social competence (Guralnick & Groom, 1985, 1987; Peterson & McConnell, 1993). There is growing sentiment among professionals in early childhood special education that naturalistic strategies be tried before considering more teacher-directed approaches such as social skills training groups and direct teacher reinforcement of desired social behaviors (Conroy, Langenbrunner, & Burleson, 1996). Highly structured interventions may, however, be a helpful "next step" for some children (whether typically-developing or not) when less intrusive strategies have not been successful. Odom and Brown (1993) have described a variety of strategies which have been successful in promoting social integration of young children with disabilities. It has been cautioned that such interventions are not necessary for all children with disabilities, and neither should they necessarily be limited to children with disabilities. Some typically-developing children might benefit from social intervention strategies described in the early intervention literature (Odom & Brown, 1993). McGinnis and Goldstein (1990), for example, describe a program called "skill streaming" which involves modeling, role playing, performance feedback, and transfer training, and which can be used with a variety of young children, either individually or in groups.

CONCLUSIONS

When teachers arrange aspects of classroom environment, provide materials and props which encourage social interaction and social play, schedule sufficient free play, establish routines that allow children to be as independent and competent as they can be, and institute a positive system of management and discipline, they help to support children's peer relationships. When these basic supports are in place, teachers have set the stage for using on-the-spot facilitation of children's naturally occurring interactions. The support of a high quality program, well-honed skills of observation and a sound understanding of developmentally appropriate practice appear to be important foundations for the teacher who values and strives to nurture the growth of young children's social competence with peers.

CHILDREN'S BOOKS RELEVANT TO PEER RELATIONSHIPS

Berry, J. (1988). *A children's book about teasing.* Connecticut: Grolier Enterprises.
Boeghold, B. D. (1993). *The fight.* New York: Bryon Press.
Bulla, C. R. (1989). *The Christmas coat.* New York: Alfred A Knopf.
Crary, E. (1982). *I can't wait.* (Also, *I want it* and *I want to play*). Seattle, WA: Parenting Press.
Crary, E. (1983). *My name's not Dummy.* Seattle, WA: Parenting Press.
Everitt, B. (1992). *Mean soup.* San Diego, CA: Harcourt Brace Jovanovich.
Griffin, J. (1992). *Who is the boss.* New York: Houghton Mifflin.
Havill, J. (1993). *Jamaica and Brianna.* Boston, MA: Houghton Mifflin Company.
Joosse, B. M. (1989). *Dinah's mad, bad wishes.* New York: Dial Books.
Mayer, G., & Mayer, M. (1992). *A very special critter.* New York: Goldenbooks.
Naylor, P. R. (1991). *King of the playground.* New York: Atheneum.
O'Shaughnessy, E. (1992). *Somebody called me a retard today. . . and my heart felt sad.* New York: Walker Publishing Company.
Pfister, M. (1995). *Rainbow fish to the rescue.* New York: North-South Books.
Polacco, P. (1992). *Chicken Sunday.* New York: Philomel Books.
Rabe, B. (1981). *The balancing girl.* New York: Dutton.
Rogers, F. (1987). *Making friends.* New York: G.P. Putnam & Sons.
Seuss, Dr. (1985). *The butter battle book.* New York: Random House.
Seuss, Dr. (1961). *The Sneetches and other stories.* London: Random House.
Steig, B. (1971). *Amos and Boris.* New York: Farrar, Straus, and Giroux.
Steig, W. (1990). *Shrek!* Toronto: Harper Collins.
Stevens, J. (1993). *Coyote steals the blanket: A Ute tale.* New York: Holiday House.
Waber, B. (1988). *Ira says goodbye.* Boston, MA: Houghton Mifflin Company.
Zolotow, C. (1969). *The hating book.* New York, NY: Harper and Row.

REFERENCES

Babcock, F., Hartle, L., & Lamme, L. (1995). Prosocial behaviors of five-year-old children in sixteen learning/activity centers. *Journal of Research in Childhood Education, 9*(2), 113-127.
Bailey, D. B., & McWilliams, R. A. (1990). Normalizing early intervention. *Topics in Early Childhood Special Education, 10*(2), 33-47.
Bernat, V. (1993). Teaching peace. *Young Children, 48*(3), 36-39.
Carlsson-Paige, N., & Levin, D. E. (1992a). Moving children from time-out to win–win. *Child Care Information Exchange, 84,* 38-42.
Carlsson-Paige, N., & Levin, D. E. (1992b). Making peace in violent times: A constructivist approach to conflict resolution. *Young Children, 48*(1), 4-12.
Christie, J. F., & Wardle, F. (1992). How much time is needed for play? *Young Children, 47*(2), 28-32.
Conroy, M. A., Langenbrunner, M. R., & Burleson, R. B. (1996). Suggestions for enhancing the social behaviors of preschoolers with disabilities using developmentally appropriate practices. *Dimensions of Early Childhood,* Winter, 9-15.
Derman-Sparks, L., & the A.B.C. Task Force (1989). *Anti-bias curriculum: Tools for empowering young children.* Washington, DC: National Association for the Education of Young Children.
Dinwiddie, S. A. (1994). The saga of Sally, Sammy, and the red pen: Facilitating children's social problem-solving. *Young Children, 49*(5), 13-19.

Edwards, C. (1992). Creating safe places for conflict resolution to happen. *Child Care Information Exchange, 84,* 43-45.

Gareau, M., & Kennedy, C. (1991). Structure time and space to promote pursuit of learning in the primary grades. *Young Children, 46*(4), 46-51.

Greenberg. P. (1992a). How to initiate some simple democratic practices pertaining to respect, rights, responsibilities, and roots in any classroom (without losing your leadership position). *Young Children, 47*(5), 10-17.

Greenberg, P. (1992b). Why not academic preschool? Part 2. Autocracy or democracy in the classroom? *Young Children, 47*(3), 54-64.

Guralnick, M. J. (1990). Social competence and early intervention. *Journal of Early Intervention, 14*(1), 3-14.

Guralnick, M. J., & Groom, J. M. (1985). Correlates of peer-related social competence of developmentally delayed preschool children. *America Journal of Mental Deficiency, 90,* 140-150.

Guralnick, M. J., & Groom, J. M. (1987). The peer relations of mildly delayed and non handicapped preschool children in mainstream education play groups. *Child Development, 58*(6), 1156-1575.

Hartle, L., & Johnson, J. E. (1993). Historical and contemporary influences of outdoor play environments. In C. Hart (Ed.), *Children on playgrounds: Research perspectives and applications* (pp. 14-42). Albany, NY: SUNY Press.

Hartup, W., & Moore, S. G. (1991). Early peer relations: Developmental significance and prognostic implications. *Early Childhood Research Quarterly, 5,* 1-7.

Hazen, N. L., Black, B., & Fleming-Johnson, F. (1984). Social acceptance: Strategies children use and how teachers can help children learn them. *Young Children, 39*(6), 26-36.

Johnson, D., & Johnson, R. (1991). *Learning together and alone: Cooperative, competitive, and individualistic learning.* Englewood Cliffs, NJ: Prentice Hall.

Katz, L. G., & McClellan, D. E. (1991). *The teacher's role in the social development of young children.* Urbana, IL: ERIC Clearinghouse on Elementary and Early Childhood Education.

Kemple, K. M. (1991). Preschool children's peer acceptance and social interaction. *Young Children, 46*(5), 47-54.

Kostelnik, M. J., Stein, L.C., Whiren, A. P., & Soderman, A. K. (1993). *Guiding children's social development.* Cincinnati, OH: South-Western.

Kreidler, W.J. (1984). *Creative conflict resolution: More than 200 activities for keeping peace in the classroom.* Glencoe, IL: Scott, Foresman & Company.

Krogh, S. L., & Lamme, L. L. (1985). "But what about sharing?":

Children's literature and moral development. *Young Children, 40*(4), 48-51.

Kupersmidt, J. B., Coie, J. D., & Dodge, K. A. (1990). The role of poor peer relationships in the development of disorder. In S. R. Asher & J. D. Coie (Eds.), *Peer rejection in childhood* (pp. 274-305). New York, NY: Cambridge University Press.

Lamme, L. L., & McKinley, L. (1992). Creating a caring classroom with children's literature. *Young Children, 48*(1), 65-71.

McGinnis, E., & Goldstein, A. P. (1990). *Skill-streaming in early childhood: Teaching prosocial skills to the preschool and kindergarten child.* Champaign, IL: Research Press.

Odom, S. L., & Brown, W. H. (1993). Social interaction skill interventions for young children with disabilities in integrated settings. In C. Peck, S. Odom, & D. Bricker, (Eds.), *Integrating young children with disabilities into community programs* (pp. 39-64). Baltimore, MD: Paul H. Brookes.

Odom, S. L., McConnell, S. R., & McEvoy, M. A. (Eds.). (1992). *Social competence of young children with disabilities: Nature, development, and intervention.* Baltimore, MD: Paul H. Brookes.

Oken-Wright, P. (1992). From tug of war to let's make a deal: The teacher's role. *Young Children, 48*(1), 15-20.

Parker, J. G., & Asher, S. R. (1987). Peer relations and later personal adjustment: Are low accepted children at risk? *Psychological Bulletin, 102,* 357-389.

Peterson, C. A., & McConnell, S. R. (1993). Factors affecting the impact of social interaction skills interventions in early childhood special education. *Topics in Early Childhood Special Education, 13,* 38-56.

Ramsey, P. G. (1991). *Making friends in school: Promoting peer relationships in early childhood.* New York: Teachers College Press.

Rubin, K., & Everett, B. (1982). Social perspective-taking in young children. In S. G. Moore & C. R. Cooper (Eds.), *The young child: Reviews of research,* Vol. III (pp. 97-113). Washington, DC: National Association for the Education of Young Children.

Shure, M. (1992). *I can problem-solve: An interpersonal cognitive problem solving program.* Champaign, IL: Research Press.

Stein, L. C., & Kostelnik, M. J. (1984). A practical problem-solving model for conflict resolution in the classroom. *Child Care Quarterly, 13*(1), 5-20.

Trawick-Smith, J. (1992). The classroom affects children's play and development. *Dimensions of Early Childhood, 20*(2), 27-30, 40.

Udry, J. M. (1961). *Let's be enemies.* New York: Harper and Row.

Wasserman, S. (1990). *Serious players in the primary classroom.* New York: Teachers College Press.

The Caring Classroom's Academic Edge

Catherine C. Lewis, Eric Schaps, and Marilyn S. Watson

The Child Development Project has shown that when kids care about one another—and are motivated by important, challenging work—they're more apt to care about learning.

At Hazelwood School in Louisville, Kentucky, pairs of students are scattered around a 2nd–3rd grade classroom. Heads bent together, students brainstorm with their partners why Widower Muldie, of the book *Wagon Wheels*, left his three sons behind when he set off across the wilderness in search of a home site. Although this story of an African-American pioneer family is set in the rural America of more than 100 years ago, these inner-city students have little trouble diving into the assignment: Write a dialogue between Johnnie and Willie Muldie, ages 11 and 8, who are left in charge of their 3-year-old brother.

Teacher Laura Ecken sets the stage:

> Let's imagine that we're Johnny and Willie. It's the first night all alone without daddy. We've put little brother to bed, and we're just sitting up talking to each other.

Before students launch into their work, Ecken asks the class to discuss "ways we can help our partners." The children demonstrate remarkable forethought about how to work together: "Disagree without being mean." "If your partner says something that don't fit, then work it into another part." "Let your partner say all they want to say."

Over the next hour, students become intensely interested in figuring out what the Muldie boys might have said to each other. The teacher offers no grade or behavioral reward for this task, nor is any needed.

Students are friendly, helpful, and tactful, but also determined to write the best dialogue they know how. In one partnership, John says, "We could talk about how much we miss daddy." Cynthia counters: "But daddy's only been gone for a day." After a few exchanges on this point, John and Cynthia agree to talk about "how much we're *going* to miss daddy." In another partnership, Barry makes use of a strategy suggested by a classmate in the preceding discussion: "How about if we use your idea to 'help me hunt for food' later, because right now we're talking about how the boys feel." Students seem remarkably comfortable questioning and expressing disagreement; the easy camaraderie extends to the many partnerships that cross racial and gender lines.

Fruits of Community

That children at Hazelwood School care about learning and about one another seems perfectly natural. But it didn't just happen. The school's staff has worked very hard over the past five years to create what they call "a caring community of learners"—a community whose members feel valued, personally connected to one another, and committed to everyone's growth and learning. Hazelwood's staff—and educators at other

Do students view their classmates primarily as collaborators in learning, or as competitors in the quest for grades and recognition?

 From *Educational Leadership*, September 1996, pp. 16-21. © 1996 by Catherine C. Lewis, Eric Schaps, and Marilyn S. Watson. Reprinted by permission.

Child Development Project (CDP) schools across the country—believe that creating such a community is crucial to children's learning and citizenship. A growing body of research suggests they are right.

At schools high in "community"—measured by the degree of students' agreement with statements such as "My school is like a family" and "Students really care about each other"—students show a host of positive outcomes. These include higher educational expectations and academic performance, stronger motivation to learn, greater liking for school, less absenteeism, greater social competence, fewer conduct problems, reduced drug use and delinquency, and greater commitment to democratic values (Battistich et al., in press; Bryk and Driscoll 1988; Hom and Battistich 1995).

Our approach in the Child Development Project is to take research findings about how children learn and develop—ethically, socially, and intellectually—and translate them into a comprehensive, practical program with three facets: (1) a classroom program that concentrates on literature-based reading instruction, cooperative learning, and a problem-solving approach to discipline; (2) a school-wide program of community building and service activities; and (3) a family involvement program.

We originally developed these approaches in collaboration with teachers in California's San Ramon and Hayward school districts. We then extended them, beginning in 1991, to six additional districts nationwide (Cupertino, San Francisco, and Salinas in California; Dade County, Florida.; Jefferson County, Kentucky; and White Plains, New York). In both the original and extension sites, students in CDP schools were studied and compared with students in matched non-project schools (Solomon et al. 1992).

Five Principles to Practice

How exactly do Child Development Project schools become "caring communities of learners"? They adhere

to five interdependent principles, striving for the following.

1. Warm, supportive, stable relationships. Do all members of a school community—students, teachers, staff, parents—know one another as people? Do students view their classmates primarily as collaborators in learning, or as competitors in the quest for grades and recognition? Teachers at our CDP schools carefully examine their approaches, asking, "What kind of human relationships are we fostering?" They recast many old activities.

For example, at one California elementary school, the competitive science fair has become a hands-on family science night that draws hundreds of parents. With awards eliminated, parents are free to focus on the pleasures of learning science with their children. A Dade County, Florida, elementary school removed the competitive costume contest from its Halloween celebration, so that children could enjoy the event without worrying about winners and losers. Other schools took the competition out of PTA membership drives, refocusing them to emphasize participation and celebration of the school's progress.

Teachers also added or redesigned many academic and nonacademic activities so that students could get to know one another and develop a feeling of unity and shared purpose as a class and school. "A big change for me is that on the first morning of school, the classroom walls are blank—no decorations, no rules," explains a teacher from California. Like many of her Child Development Project colleagues, she involves students in interviewing classmates and creating wall displays about "our class" that bring children closer together.

In the first class meetings of the year, students discuss "how we want to be treated by others," and "what kind of class we want to be." From these discussions emerge a few simple principles—"be kind," "show respect," "do our best"—that are remarkably similar across diverse schools.

Says one teacher,

> When you invest time up front in having the kids get to know one

another, the picked-on child never has a chance to emerge. Kids find out that they share the same favorite food, hobby, or whatever; they see one another as human beings. The child who might have been the nerd in previous years never gets seen that way because classmates remember that that child's favorite food is McDonald's hamburgers, too.

2. Constructive learning. Children naturally try to make sense of the world—to figure out how magnets work or why friends help. Good teaching fosters these efforts to understand, but also hones them, helping children become ever more skillful, reflective, and self-critical in their pursuit of knowledge. How can teachers support and extend children's natural efforts to learn?

First, educators can provide a coherent curriculum, organized around important concepts, rather than a potpourri of isolated facts. Second, educators can connect the curriculum with children's own natural efforts to make sense of the world. Children should see mathematics, for example, as a powerful means for understanding the world, not as arbitrary principles that apply only within classroom walls. When children see how the ideas and skills of school help them understand and act upon the world—how they are genuinely useful—they begin to practice these academic skills throughout their home and school lives.

Third, lessons can be set up so that children must weigh new information against what they already know, work through discrepancies, and construct a new understanding. When children make discoveries, struggle to find explanations, and grapple with evidence and views that differ from their own, they are likely to reach more profound levels of understanding than they can achieve through simple rote learning. The students at Hazelwood School who wrote a dialogue between the Muldie boys were constructive learners in all these senses.

Like other books in our project's literature-based program, *Wagon Wheels* pursues important issues: What experiences have shaped the lives of diverse Americans? How have acts of principle, courage, and responsibility shaped history, and how do they shape our own daily lives? These issues are explored not just in literature and social studies, but in class meetings, problem solving, and in many other ways.

In addition, to make sense of an experience that happened long ago, Ecken's students needed to draw on both school learning and their own experiences. Would being left without parents and in charge of a younger brother feel any different in 1878 than in 1994? Finally, the task of writing a dialogue challenged students to take the perspective of the boys in the story and to reconcile their thinking with their partner's perspective.

3. An important, challenging curriculum. In an era of rapid technological change, certain skills and habits are likely to remain important—thoughtful reading, self-critical reflection, clear communication, asking productive questions. But the de facto curriculum defined by commercial textbooks and standardized tests often emphasizes something much less enduring—isolated subskills and piecemeal knowledge. Like Jere Brophy and Janet Alleman (1991), we believe that curriculum development must "be driven by major long-term goals, not just short-term coverage concerns." These goals should be broadly conceived to include children's development as principled, humane citizens.

Numerous critiques of the curriculum in this country argue that it sells children short by presenting material that is too simple and too easily mastered—for example, basal readers whose barren language and shallow ideas offer little reason to read. That a more challenging curriculum is more compelling to children, even so-called slow learners, is a tenet underlying some recent interventions (Hopfenberg 1993).

4. Intrinsic motivation. What kind of schooling produces eager, lifelong learners? Certainly not schooling that relies on the power of extrinsic rewards—prizes, honors, grades, and so forth. In fact, studies show that these can actually undermine children's interest in learning (Lepper and Greene

1978). Awarding prizes for creating science projects, reading books, running laps, or a host of other worthwhile ends can diminish interest in the activity itself by focusing children's attention on the reward, and by implying that the task is not inherently worthwhile (Kohn 1993). As one sage commentator quipped, "If we want children to read books, we should offer them books as a reward for eating pizzas, not pizzas for reading books."

To minimize extrinsic rewards, educators need a curriculum that is worth learning and a pedagogy that helps students see why it is worth learning. The students writing a dialogue between the Muldie boys were motivated by the task itself. *Wagon Wheels* raised issues of timeless importance, and the teacher took care to introduce the book in a way that piqued students' curiosity and helped them make personal connections to the book.

5. Attention to social and ethical dimensions of learning. Everything about schooling—curriculum, teaching method, discipline, interpersonal relationships—teaches children about the human qualities that we value. As students discuss the experiences of African-American families like the Muldies, they grow ethically and socially. This growth stems from the content they encounter, the experience of working with classmates, and the reflection following partner work on their difficulties and successes working with others.

Child Development Project teachers scrutinize disciplinary approaches not just for whether they help children behave in the short run, under an adult's surveillance, but whether they promote children's responsible behavior in the long run. Teachers engage children in shaping the norms of their class and school, so that they see that these norms are not arbitrary standards set by powerful adults, but necessary standards for the well-being of everyone. Teachers also help children develop collaborative approaches to resolving conflicts, guiding them to think about the values needed for humane life in a group. Playground disputes become

opportunities for students to learn about the needs and perspectives of other students, and to practice skills of nonviolent problem solving.

Finally, teachers look at the many programs, special events, parent-supported activities, and policies of the school through the lens of social and ethical development. Do these activities help children understand the values that sustain democratic society? Do they give students many opportunities to develop and practice qualities that we want them to have as adults—responsibility, collaboration, tolerance, commitment to the common good, courage to stand up for their beliefs, and so on?

Synergy of Academic and Social Goals

It is common to think of the academic and social goals of schooling as a hydraulic—to imagine that fostering one undermines the other. But when schools attend to all five elements described above, they create environments where children care about one another and about learning.

For example, students work harder, achieve more, and attribute more importance to schoolwork in classes in which they feel liked, accepted, and respected by the teacher and fellow students. Warm, supportive relationships also enable students to risk the new ideas and mistakes so critical to intellectual growth. It is no coincidence that, to create an environment in which students can discuss classmates' incorrect solutions to math problems, Japanese teachers spend a great deal of time building friendships among children and a feeling of classroom unity.

Schools that provide an important, challenging curriculum, and help children connect it to their own efforts to understand the world, become allies in children's quest for competence—and teachers in those schools have a head start in being seen as supportive, valued adults.

A shift away from competition, rewards, and punishments helps all students—not just the high-achievers—feel like valued members of the classroom community. Faced with a competitive, skill-and-drill curriculum, educationally less-prepared children may preserve their self-esteem by reducing their efforts. They may psychologically withdraw from the classroom or school community, leaving it powerless to influence their social, ethical, or intellectual development (Nicholls 1989).

The caring classroom is not one that avoids criticism, challenge, or mistakes. Parker J. Palmer (1983) has written:

> A learning space needs to be hospitable not to make learning painless but to make the painful things possible... things like exposing ignorance, testing tentative hypotheses, challenging false or partial information, and mutual criticism of thought. [None of these] can happen in an atmosphere where people feel threatened and judged.

Like a family, the caring classroom provides a sense of belonging that allows lively, critical discussions and risk-taking.

Countering Conventional Wisdom

We think relatively few American schools have managed to sustain a simultaneous focus on students' social, ethical, and intellectual development. What will it take to achieve this on a much broader scale? First, it will take changes in thinking; the agenda we have proposed runs counter to much current conventional wisdom in education.

Such changes cannot be expected to come quickly or easily. Because adults, too, are constructive learners, they need the same five conditions that children do. School improvement hinges on a sense of community and collaboration among teachers, conditions that

enable teachers to risk changing practice and to admit and learn from mistakes.

At the schools participating in the Child Development Project, teachers spend up to 30 days over three years in staff development. The schools have worked consciously to build strong personal connections among staff members. They do this through social events, shared planning and reflection, and often by meeting regularly in "learning partnerships" of two to four teachers to discuss their efforts to reshape practice. In an era of tight budgets, such time for adult learning is difficult to obtain.

Finally, we need to recognize that community and learning are interdependent and must be pursued in context. This means that it is not enough to ask whether a new science curriculum increases students' mastery of important scientific concepts; we must also ask whether it fosters their capacity to work with fellow students, their intrinsic interest in science, and their recognition that science depends upon both collaboration and honesty. This is a big picture to keep in focus. Educators who have traditionally worked in isolation from one another—specialists in subject matter, pedagogy, school climate, motivation—must help one another to keep it in perspective.

References

Battistich, V., D. Solomon, D. Kim, M. Watson, and E. Schaps. (In press). "Schools as Communities, Poverty Levels of Student Populations, and Students' Attitudes, Motives, and Performance." *American Education Research Journal.*

Brophy, J., and J. Alleman. (1991). "Activities as Instructional Tools: A Framework for Analysis and Evaluation." *Educational Researcher* 20, 4: 9–23.

Bryk, A. S., and M. E. Driscoll. (1988). *The School as Community: Theoretical Foundations, Contextual Influences, and Consequences for Students and Teachers.* Madison, Wisconsin: National Center on Effective Secondary Schools.

Hom, A., and V. Battistich. (April 1995). "Students' Sense of School Community as a Factor in Reducing Drug Use and Delinquency." Presentation to the 1995 American Educational Research Association Annual Meeting.

Hopfenberg, W. (1993). *The Accelerated Schools.* San Francisco: Jossey-Bass.

Kohn, A. (1993). *Punished by Rewards: The Trouble with Gold Stars, Incentive Plans, A's, Praise, and Other Bribes.* Boston: Houghton Mifflin.

Lepper, M. R., and D. Greene. (1978). *The Hidden Costs of Reward: New Perspectives on the Psychology of Human Motivation.* Hillsdale, N.J.: Lawrence Erlbaum Associates.

Nicholls, J. (1989). *The Competitive Ethos and Democratic Education.* Cambridge, Mass.: Harvard University Press.

Palmer, P. J. (1983). *To Know as We Are Known: A Spirituality of Education.* San Francisco: HarperCollins.

Solomon, D., M. Watson, V. Battistich, E. Schaps, and K. Delucchi. (1992). "Creating a Caring Community: A School-Based Program to Promote Children's Prosocial Development." In *Effective and Responsible Teaching: The New Synthesis,* edited by E. Oser, J. L. Patty, and A. Dick. San Francisco: Jossey-Bass.

Catherine C. Lewis is the Formative Research Director, **Eric Schaps** is President, and **Marilyn S. Watson** is Program Director, of the Developmental Studies Center, 2000 Embarcadero, Suite 305, Oakland, CA 94606-5300.

Creating a Community of Learning for Homeless Children

The shocking truth is that the average age of a homeless person in the United States is 9 years. More than 750,000 homeless children are of school age. How are we educating these children?

Ralph da Costa Nunez and Kate Collignon

By 1997, more than 1 million American children were homeless, moving between shelters and overcrowded or inadequate housing. Of these, more than 750,000 were school-aged, and the overwhelming majority performed well below grade level (Education for Homeless Children 1994; Nunez 1996).

These children are at risk of far more than academic failure. Plagued by domestic violence, family substance abuse, parental uninvolvement, and the psychological devastation of homelessness, they need more than help with their homework: They need a safe haven where they will receive the educational and emotional support to keep them from falling farther into the cracks of society.

Many U.S. public schools provide academic assistance for homeless children, but only a handful of innovative model programs—whether functioning as shelters within schools or schools within shelters—provide comprehensive approaches to education. They have established "communities of learning" by incorporating referrals to adult education and family support services into *specialized*—rather than special—education for children. By broadening our vision beyond traditional children's education, we can learn from these models and effectively break the cycles of poverty and homelessness to ensure that the next generation will succeed.

Educational Pitfalls Facing Homeless Children

Homeless children face monumental obstacles in their pursuit of education. They lag far behind other children, both educationally and developmentally (Molnar et al., 1991; Rafferty 1991, 1995; Bassuk and Rubin 1987). Although all children in poverty fare similarly, homeless children face seemingly insurmountable logistical problems and emotional and psychological pressures.

The most visible hindrances to homeless children's education are the obstacles to enrollment and participation created by movement to and residence in a shelter. While allowed by law to continue at the school they attended before becoming homeless, many children end up in shelters so far from their previous home that they must choose between transferring schools or spending hours commuting. At new schools, the traumatized families face an obstacle course of residency, guardianship, and immunization requirements; inadequate record-keeping systems; and a lack of continuity of programs like special education and gifted education. For most homeless families, this happens two or three times during the school year (Rafferty 1991; Anderson et al. 1995).

Even after enrollment, homeless children struggle to reorient themselves to new schools, teachers, classmates, and curriculums; and teachers are forced to reassess their new students' skill levels and needs. Often teachers do not even know that their students are homeless. Even if they do, few teachers are trained in the special needs of homeless children. Homeless students are frequently left out of extended class projects and are three times more likely to be recommended for special education programs than their peers—and many never escape (Nunez 1996).

These impediments only hint at the devastation to a child's education caused by the psychological impact

From *Educational Leadership*, October 1997, pp. 56-60. © 1997 by the Association for Supervision and Curriculum Development.
All rights reserved. Reprinted by permission.

of homelessness. The loss of a home robs a child of the familiarity and sense of place that most people take for granted. At school, classmates are quick to ridicule homeless children, adding stigma to the displacement homeless children suffer.

What about the parents? The average homeless parent—a young single mother with one or two children—reads at or below the 6th grade level and left school by the 10th grade. Many parents feel alienated from school, and most are unable to reinforce school lessons. A constant crisis mode leaves parents no room for long-term goals such as education and stability. As a result, most homeless children fail to attend school regularly. One study found that homeless children in New York City had missed an average of three weeks of school even before entering the shelter system (Nunez 1996).

To help homeless children and their families move beyond the crises of homelessness, we must provide not just specialized tutoring but also a safe place, stability, and direct services. The Education of Homeless Children and Youth Program of the 1987 Stewart B. McKinney Homeless Assistance Act has taken significant steps toward ensuring equal access to public education for homeless children. But much remains to be done.

Communities of Learning

Schools must work to ameliorate the barriers to school attendance and participation, as well as the environmental conditions that fail to support—or at worst, sabotage—a child's education. Model programs have combined the educational expertise of schools with the experience and services of shelters into school- or shelter-based communities of learning.

Communities of learning immerse children in an environment of education, while enabling them to see their parents embracing learning as well, and to receive the basic care that schools usually assume children receive at home. A community of learning includes the following:

■ Specialized education for homeless children.

■ Contextualized education for parents.

■ Linkages to needed services.

The educational curriculums for children at these centers incorporate traditional techniques used for special education, but do not replace regular school attendance. The centers work to accommodate the frequent and unpredictable disruptions in participation common among homeless children, not to isolate homeless children from the educational mainstream.

> The Brownstone after-school program provides one-on-one tutoring, homework help, and creative educational activities that are organized around themes to provide continuity from one day to the next.

Again, what about the parents? Many homeless parents are embarrassed by their lack of literacy skills and feel humiliated by memories of academic failure. By addressing the educational needs of parents, we can encourage parental involvement and pave the way to much-needed stability. Here are some guidelines for an adult education curriculum:

■ Be basic enough to help those with even the lowest literacy skills.

■ Be flexible to accommodate the same unpredictable participation rates that plague homeless children.

■ Be relevant to a parent's day-to-day life.

■ Be provided in a one-on-one or workshop format—anything to avoid negative associations with previous classroom-based experiences.

Model Programs

The Brownstone School, operated by Homes for the Homeless at the Prospect Family Inn in the Bronx, is a shelter-based after-school program that takes an accelerated—rather than remedial—approach to helping homeless children address specific academic difficulties while keeping up with their peers. The Brownstone provides one-on-one tutoring, homework help, and creative educational activities that are organized around themes to provide continuity from one day to the next. The tutors modify these activities for multiple skill levels and offer them in brief cycles to accommodate new students who arrive at the shelter (Nunez 1994).

At the Prospect Family Inn, adult education begins with basic literacy workshops. In these, parents read, write, and talk about parenting, health and nutrition, stress management, budgeting, housing, and apartment maintenance. Many parents attend an alternative high school on site at the shelter that prepares them to receive their General Equivalency Diploma (GED). Parents then attend employment workshops and qualify for internships and placement. Parents' participation in these programs and children's participation in Brownstone and on-site day care supplement parenting and literacy training with the opportunity for parents and children to read and spend time together in a structured and safe place (Nunez 1994).

Yet homeless parents and children cannot be expected to make education their priority so long as they must continue to worry about where they will be sleeping the next night or when an abuser will resurface. Communities of learning must attend to these other issues.

Such attention begins by providing for basic needs. The Recovering the Gifted Child Academy, a public alternative middle school in Chicago founded by Corla "Momma Hawk" Hawkins to serve children who come from poverty (and many from homelessness), maintains a "survival kit" including clean underwear, socks, deodorant, toothpaste, and toothbrushes for any student who needs them. The Academy also offers three meals a day for its students—operating on the assumption that no assumptions can be made about what children are provided with outside of school (Pool and Hawk 1997). Once these basic needs are attended to, communities of learning still must attend to less visible needs, such as the effects of domestic violence and substance abuse. Teachers can listen when children want to talk, be prepared to discuss personal issues, and provide resources and referrals for specialized counseling and direct services.

Housing referrals and placement are critical needs. The Benjamin Franklin Day Elementary School—"B.F. Day"—a public school in Seattle with a high percentage of homeless students and a specialized program to meet their needs, acts as a liaison between landlords and families to ensure that buildings in undesirable neighborhoods do not fall into disrepair, but remain occupied and maintained by families (Quint 1994).

Community and School Partnerships

Communities of learning must establish lines of communication between schools and community-based organizations. This common thread of communication and collaboration unites the efforts of model programs to make them successful. Yet this critical step in providing a safe haven for homeless children is the piece most often missing from many programs.

Although schools are legally responsible for making sure that homeless children receive the special educational attention they need, lack of understanding of the needs of homeless children among school administrators and staff has left the few existing programs woefully inadequate. On the other hand, the few shelters and community-based organizations offering children's education programs have difficulty in implementing educational curriculums. Even when children's education, adult education, and family support are well

provided within one environment or the other, the lack of communication between schools and shelters impedes the education of homeless children. Schools often lose track of students making frequent moves, and shelter programs fail to reach children who are *almost* homeless—who are being shuttled between the apartments of family and friends.

Both schools *and* shelters hold a treasury of institutional expertise and resources necessary to provide effective programs for homeless children. To make the best use of all these resources, schools must work with community-based organizations and shelters to develop their own communities of learning. Here are three important steps to follow:

1. Identify community resources and their locations.

2. Develop an information-sharing relationship between schools and these organizations. At a minimum, this relationship should facilitate the education of school administrators and staff about the presence and specific needs of homeless children.

3. Update administrators of both schools and shelters on progress and developments within their programs to ensure that the programs are complementary, not conflicting.

Even such basic communication can make a significant difference in the life of a homeless child. In South Bend, Indiana, children residing at the Center for the Homeless shelter would get on the school bus at the stop in front of the shelter to taunts and jeers by their nonhomeless classmates. Open lines of communication between the shelter and the school district made it possible to alter the route of the bus to make the shelter the first stop in the morning and last in the afternoon so that no students would be identified as "shelter kids."

From this information-sharing relationship, collaboration develops. The B.F. Day School developed a relationship with the Mercer Island United Methodist Church, which provided volunteers to assist in moving families into permanent housing and to collect and distribute household items. Volun-

teers also assisted parents with household maintenance, budgeting, and cooking. Then, other partnerships emerged. For example, a clinic sent a physician's assistant to the school every Monday to examine children and provide immunizations and prescriptions (Quint 1994).

In other school/community collaborations, schools have provided services on site at shelters. The Alternative High Schools, a New York City public preparatory and vocational training program for teen parents and high school dropouts, agreed to establish a branch at the Prospect Family Inn so that homeless parents attend class among familiar faces, rather than traveling across town and getting involved in yet another bureaucracy (Nunez 1994).

The ultimate goal of this collaboration is seamless integration of children's education, adult education, and support services, making full use of school and shelter resources to establish effective communities of learning either in schools or in shelters. Thus homeless children already living in shelters can receive the educational assistance they need to avoid returning to the shelters as adults, and children on the verge of homelessness can be linked to the services their families need to keep from having to enter a shelter.

Perhaps the greatest example is set by the Homeless Children and Families Program in the Salem Keizer Public School system in Oregon. In addition to identifying homeless students and ensuring that these children have continuous access to schooling, the program has become involved in the activities of five local family shelters to engage the parents of homeless children in education and case management services. Program staff members serve as a bridge between the schools and shelters. They work with homeless children while they are in school and then go to local shelters to provide after-school and preschool enrichment programs for the children and case management, referrals, and life-skills classes for their parents.

An Opportunity for Action

The challenge that faces our schools is less a mandate to stretch underfunded services still further and more an opportunity to fulfill their potential as the spine of society. Schools have the greatest ongoing contact with all members of the community—children, parents, aunts, uncles, grandparents, neighbors—and the ability to steer the direction of lives through supportive measures. By addressing children's needs through collaboration with local service providers, schools have the power to make a difference not only for homeless children in shelters but also for families on the verge of homelessness. Indeed, it is ironic that out of the problems of homeless children, solutions have developed that meet the needs of many children at risk of educational neglect.

Though the goal of communities of learning is to educate children, the process must first focus on educating the educators. Every school administrator and teacher must understand that childhood homelessness is not something that flares up only during periods of media attention. We must recognize that the boy or girl who acted up in math class may be missing far more than the principles of long division. Only then will all children—homeless and otherwise—receive both the educational and developmental support they need from schools.

> Schools must work with community-based organizations and shelters to develop their own communities of learning.

Individual schools can make a difference in their district, and individual teachers can make a difference in their schools. By learning about the needs of homeless children and accepting the opportunity to take responsibility for more than a child's grades, individual educators can begin the collaborative approaches needed to develop a community of learning.

References

Anderson, L.M., M.I. Janger, and K.L.M. Panton. (1995). *An Evaluation of State and Local Efforts to Serve the Educational Needs of Homeless Children and Youth.* Washington, D.C.: U.S. Department of Education, Office of the Undersecretary.

Bassuk, E.L., and L. Rubin. (1987). "Homeless Children: A Neglected Population." *American Journal of Orthopsychiatry* 57, 2: 279-286.

Education for Homeless Children and Youth Program. (1994). *Report to Congress: Fiscal Year 1994.* Washington, D.C.: U.S. Department of Education.

Molnar, J., W.R. Rath, T.P. Klein, C. Lowe, and A.H. Hartmann. (1991). *Ill Fares the Land: The Consequences of Homelessness and Chronic Poverty for Children and Families in New York City.* New York: Bank Street College of Education.

Nunez, R. (1994). *Hopes, Dreams and Promise: The Future of Homeless Children in America.* New York: Homes for the Homeless.

Nunez, R. (1996). *The New Poverty: Homeless Families in America.* New York: Insight Books/Plenum Publishing.

Pool, C.R., and M. Hawk. (April 1997). Hope in Chicago." *Educational Leadership* 54, 7: 33-36.

Quint, S. (1994). *Schooling Homeless Children.* New York: Teachers College, Columbia University.

Rafferty, Y. (1991). *And Miles to Go . . . Barriers to Academic Achievement and Innovative Strategies for the Delivery of Educational Services to Homeless Children.* New York: Advocates for Children of New York.

Rafferty, Y. (Spring 1995). "The Legal Rights and Educational Problems of Homeless Children." *Perspectives: Journals of the Children's Institute of the Dyson College of Arts and Sciences* (Vol. 2). New York: Pace University.

Ralph da Costa Nunez is President and CEO of the Institute for Children and Poverty and a Professor at Columbia University's School of International and Public Affairs. **Kate Collignon** is Research and Training Associate with the Institute for Children and Poverty. Contact the authors at the Institute for Children and Poverty, 36 Cooper Square, 6th Floor, New York, NY 10003 (e-mail: hn4061@handsnet.org). World Wide Web: http://www.opendoor.com/hfh/

Curricular Issues

Education will be very different as we move into the twenty-first century. The amount of information children are required to learn has increased over the past generation, and more is available every day. Children cannot possibly be responsible for knowing all this new information, but they will be required to know how they can access it. Where would be the best place to look? What Web site should they check? What information have they gathered, and what conclusions can they draw? These are the types of questions our young children will be asking themselves in the not-too-distant future.

At the end of a busy day, most teachers would relish the thought of walking into a restaurant where they would not have to make any choices about what to eat or to do any of the shopping and cooking. All the food would be prepared by others and set before the hungry teachers to consume. Sounds wonderful! Maybe for two or even three nights the idea would be appealing, but come the fourth night, some teachers really would not like what was being served, or would cook it differently. In this restaurant, there are no opportunities for customer suggestions.

Does this sound like some classrooms? The adults choose the topic of study and spend weeks preparing the materials and activities. The teachers then lay everything out in front of the children and wait for them to eagerly lap up the information and activities prepared by the teacher. Unfortunately, this is how many classrooms operate.

Teachers in these classrooms do all the work, with no input from the children, their families, or their environment. Topics of study are often decided months in advance. A strict schedule is adhered to so that all the teacher-chosen topics can be covered in a particular time frame. Each year, themes are covered at the same time, and little, if any, deviation from the master calendar occurs. Unknowingly, teachers are making more work for themselves by ignoring the ideas and expertise that children and their families could contribute. The skills children acquire, such as investigating, predicting, and hypothesizing, can be more useful in future learning than knowing specific facts about a particular topic. Every teacher cannot teach the same information about every possible topic of study. What every teacher can do, however, is ensure that all children have equal opportunities to develop the learning skills they will need as they move through their formal education and into their chosen professions. It is not important if a particular preschool teacher does an in-depth investigation of boats and her friend who teaches in another part of the country does not. What is important is that the children in both classrooms have opportunities to develop and use skills, such as exploring, expression, and investigating, that extend their learning. These are the skills they will need in the future, more so than specific information on boats or any other topic of study.

" 'Hey, Where's the Toys?' Play and Literacy in 1st Grade" answers questions related to the play-based, exploratory curriculum. No child should have to mourn the loss of opportunities to investigate, solve problems, and come to conclusions. These are skills that will be needed throughout life and should play a major role in any quality educational experience. Why do the quality learning experiences so readily available in early childhood programs have to end as children get older? A fourth grader remarked one day, "My brain works better when my hands are working too." The saying "Hands on = Minds on" is so true.

In the first unit article, "Off with a Theme: Emergent Curriculum in Action," teachers are encouraged to listen to the children as they all work together to develop learning opportunities that meet the interests and abilities of the children.

The other articles address issues related to developing a child-centered, hands-on curriculum that is appropriate for the abilities of each child. Just as teachers want a say in what they eat and how it is prepared, so do children want a chance to investigate topics and gather some of the information that interests them. A child-centered curriculum offers possibilities for investigating, exploring, predicting, and collaborating, among other skills that are the benchmarks of a successful school experience.

Documenting children's learning has emerged as a key responsibility for teachers. Teachers who collect, analyze, make appropriate comments, and display the work of the children are adding greatly to their overall program quality. Parents, administrators, children, and community members all benefit from having opportunities to view evidence of the learning that has taken place.

A truly child-centered curriculum in a developmentally appropriate program is constantly changing, just like the children who attend that program. It is the job of the teachers and caregivers to keep pace with the children's needs and interests as they grow and learn.

Looking Ahead: Challenge Questions

What changes can teachers make to their theme-based planning to make the learning more meaningful to the children?

How can math, science, and technology be an integral part of classroom learning?

How are the processes of learning to read and write connected? What can facilitate these processes in the classroom?

What role do the diverse lifestyles of the children in a classroom play in the development of the curriculum?

Develop a list of ideas for supplementing play in the block area.

What should you take into consideration when choosing software for use with young children?

What should teachers or parents consider when choosing literature for children?

What are the benefits of designing curriculum based on the interests of the children?

Off with a Theme: Emergent Curriculum in Action

Marilyn A. Sheerer,[2] Ernest Dettore,[1] and Jennifer Cyphers[1]

Early childhood teachers can plan developmentally appropriate classrooms through a fusion of thematic and emergent curriculum approaches. Ernie, a preschool teacher/university professor working in a campus laboratory setting, designed and implemented a space theme which was relevant to young children, allowed them many opportunities to demonstrate their knowledge and skills and expand upon them in significant ways, and incorporated a variety of materials and resources. Overall, the use of this theme reflected the initial and emergent interests of both the teachers and children, as they interacted in the social environment.

KEY WORDS: thematic planning; emergent curriculum.

INTRODUCTION

Over the past decade, the early childhood curriculum literature has reflected an emphasis on particular philosophical perspectives and planning strategies. The terms "thematic" and "emergent" appear frequently in articles and discussions on developmentally appropriate practice. What, exactly, do these words mean within the context of curriculum for young children?

THEMATIC AND EMERGENT CURRICULUM

The thematic approach is defined as the organization of curriculum and learning experiences around a chosen topic, or central focus, which lends itself naturally to the integration of curriculum content areas. Planning early childhood curriculum from a thematic perspective is certainly not new. Early in the century, John Dewey (1902) advocated the organization of curriculum around projects or themes that would interest and involve children. Many contemporary early childhood professionals and organizations (Bredekamp, 1986; Jacobs, 1989; Jalongo, 1992; Katz & Chard, 1989;

NAEYC, 1991; Schwartz & Robison, 1982) also support a thematic approach in helping teachers design a developmentally appropriate curriculum. More recently, Bredekamp & Rosegrant (1992) articulated the following principle as one of twenty to be adhered to by teachers as they make curriculum decisions: "Curriculum allows for focus on a particular topic or content while allowing for integration across traditional subject-matter divisions by planning around themes and/or learning experiences that provide opportunities for rich conceptual development" (p. 111).

Another significant concept in early childhood education is the idea of emergent curriculum, defined herein as learning experiences and activities generated by the interests and needs of the children and teachers in a given context. In a joint position statement issued by the National Association for the Education of Young Children and the National Association of Early Childhood Specialists in State Departments of Education (1991), there is a definite emphasis on curriculum planning that emerges from the interests demonstrated by children:

> Curriculum content reflects and is generated by the needs and interests of individual children within the group. Curriculum incorporates a wide variety of learning experiences, materials and equipment, and instructional strategies, to accommodate a broad range of children's individual differences in prior experience, maturation rates, styles of learning, needs, and interests. (p. 30)

[1]Department of Elementary Education, Edinboro University of Pennsylvania, Edinboro, Pennsylvania.

[2]Correspondence should be directed to Marilyn Sheerer, Department Chair, Elementary and Middle Grades Education, Speight Building, East Carolina University, Greenville, North Carolina 27858-4353.

From *Early Childhood Education Journal*, Vol. 24, No. 2, 1996, pp. 99-102. © 1996 by Human Sciences Press, Inc. Reprinted by permission.

Jones and Nimmo (1994) provide a deeper insight into the concept and design of emergent curriculum by identifying multiple sources for input. They see children's interests as a high priority, but they also include teachers' interests, developmental tasks, things and people in the physical and social environment, curriculum resource materials, unexpected events, living dilemmas, and values of the school and broader culture. From the perspective of these writers, emergent curriculum is still the teacher's responsibility but must reflect all of these sources if it is to be a dynamic planning process.

Early childhood teachers who design and implement classrooms that are responsive to the developmental levels of children can view the thematic and emergent curriculum approaches as congruent. The thematic approach provides a framework around which appropriate experiences can be organized; and within this framework, children's particular interests, ideas, and special abilities can emerge and be extended. Flexible scheduling and large blocks of time allocated for project work provide further support for this approach.

Thus, a fusion of the constructs of thematic and emergent curriculum can address the ongoing debate between content and process. The organization of curriculum around a theme can help teachers plan meaningful, important content; and the application of the idea of emergent curriculum should generate active engagement on the part of children and teachers in the classroom context, as illustrated in Figure 1.

CHOOSING A THEME

Thematic organization alone does not guarantee a well-planned, thoughtful curriculum (Brewer, 1995). The theme must allow for the generation of worthwhile activities and more than a superficial study of a topic. Katz and Chard (1989) cite several important considerations in selecting a theme: relevance, the opportunity for application of skills, the availability of resources, student and teacher interest, and the time of year. Moreover, a theme cannot be carried out merely through surface touches that appear to keep everything integrated. For example, one preschool teacher who chose "bears" as her theme had

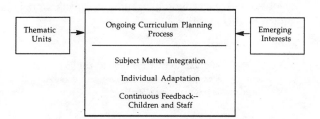

Fig. 1. Thematic and emergent curriculum constructs.

children color and cut out bears, construct a graph showing types of bears, use teddy bear counters, read stories about bears, eat gummy and graham cracker teddy bears, and talk about their own stuffed teddy bears during circle

time. This theme did not engage children in thought-provoking activities and experiences; nor did it promote exciting, long-term projects or investigations. Children left the thematic unit on bears with little knowledge beyond what they originally brought to their classroom experiences.

In another context, a teacher who focused on bears as part of a unit on animals had children build a mini library of books on different kinds of bears, make collages of bears and their habitats, build habitats for their small plastic or ceramic bears, dictate stories on bears, and visit a science museum with a display focusing on bears. A visit by Smokey the Bear to the classroom stimulated interest in forests and fire safety, which led to further projects related to this issue. In the first classroom the bears theme was exploited for its "cute" characteristics; in the second, children and teacher investigated "bears," through reading and writing experiences, field trips, in-depth play and thought-provoking discussions.

A SPACE THEME TAKES OFF

An analysis of a well-designed and implemented space theme in the preschool classroom of one of the writers, Ernie, provides clear examples of the fusing of thematic and emergent curriculum. His strong commitment to working in close conjunction with children is reflected in his remark that, "If you're aware and listening, the kids are creating the curriculum for you. If you believe they learn best through their interests, you want to hear their ideas and facilitate the expansion of those ideas."

Given these beliefs, where does the teacher begin in allowing ideas and approaches to play out in the classroom?

BUILDING ON CHILDREN'S PRIOR KNOWLEDGE AND EXPERIENCES

Ernie spends much of each day talking with and listening to children—one on one, in small groups, and with the whole group. In these discussions he finds out what children know about a particular topic or theme and what facets of the subject interest or excite them.

With respect to the space theme, which was an outgrowth of an all-school science theme, "Let the Forces be with You," Ernie began with a variety of pictures and books about space and engaged the children in dialogue around the materials. For example, after reading Eric Carle's (1986) *Papa Please Get the Moon for Me,* the children presented their own strategies for removing the moon from the sky. A favorite song (a parody of "I Know an Old Woman Who Swallowed a Fly") adapted to the space theme introduced new vocabulary and concepts:

> There was a space woman who swallowed a star;
> My, how bizarre, to swallow a star.

Words like "galaxy" and "asteroid" were explored as part of the singing at group time. During another whole group session, the children discussed a newspaper clipping showing astronauts testing new space gloves for cold weather. Since the gloves did not appear to keep the astronauts warm, the children were asked for ways to correct the problem. In yet another group discussion, Ernie introduced the sequence of the planets. The children learned the names of the planets, their different sizes, and some of their characteristics. This knowledge afforded one child the opportunity to explore a complex space mystery. The child stated, "There are good things and bad things about space. The bad things are that the aliens stole the craters from the moon and the rings from Saturn." Ernie videotaped this interview with the child, in which they explored together, both fictional and non-fictional information about space.

Extended conversations and videotapes generated the data for the teacher and assistant to begin designing activities and experiences that reflected children's true knowledge and interests relative to the topic. An important dimension of this process was a flexible time element which allowed the children to explore new and various aspects of an event or experience. After a trip to the campus planetarium, the children constructed their own classroom planetarium. This project necessitated changes in space utilization within the classroom; the reading area was moved to allow for the building of a space center. Old equipment (headsets, discarded computers, etc.) served as props for dramatic play in the center. When the area was lighted, the children interacted in the center by playing with control panels, headsets, a mini-projector showing space films from NASA, and a rocket ship in which they simulated flying to the moon. When the lights were turned off, the space center turned into a planetarium through the use of glow-in-the-dark paint and stickers. The children invited the campus planetarium director to view their meteors, galaxies, stars, moons, shooting stars, orbits, and planets.

As the project evolved, Ernie and his staff allowed his children to take it in other directions. One child's fascination with the air hose that fed oxygen into an astronaut's helmet led to an expanded investigation into breathing underwater and the need for humans to have oxygen. Concurrently, staff members continued to design additional learning experiences that built upon previous ones. Children explored the concept of weightlessness by physically demonstrating their abilities to "moon jump" (softly and thoughtfully) and to "earth jump" (loudly and demonstratively). Ernie facilitated the investigation of the crater concept by having the children make "moon eggs" (i.e. frying whites and yolks of eggs in a certain way to cause craters to form). In the gym, the teachers constructed orbits using jump ropes; and the children experienced the idea that the farther away they were from the sun, the longer it took to circle it.

INTERPRETIVE FRAMEWORK

Ernie articulates his perspective on his thematic/emergent approach by referring to Piaget's theories as follows:

> Knowledge of physical characteristics inherent in objects is acquired only by experience with those objects. The jump-rope activity, moon/earth jumping, and crater eggs are examples of putting this theory into practice.
>
> In our space communication center, children worked at launching and landing spacecraft and they experienced team work when collaborating on their play themes. The roles of rocket directors, air traffic controllers, and astronauts enabled children to express language and to problem-solve cooperatively while utilizing fantasy themes and expanding on them.

Ernie also expresses a strong belief in intrinsic motivation for learning. "When you make available materials and activities that really interest children, you don't have to worry about engaging them constructively in the classroom. Everything moves along in an exciting rhythm!"

The linking of space concepts could also be identified during transition periods. For example, covering the children with "invisible cloud spray" invited them to walk very quietly and pretend they were invisible. Other activities such as the moon walk and moon scream (silent scream) enhanced their concepts of conditions in space.

Ernie prepared the children for the dismantling of the space center; they pretended to blast off from the moon and return to earth and the study of the next theme, "Plants and Animals." (See Figure 2.) By the time the children returned following a school break, the space center had become a veterinary hospital. Then the children began a new investigation of concepts and possibilities around another exciting theme.

CONNECTION TO PARENTS

A monthly newsletter provided clear documentation of the teacher's belief that parents must be closely involved with everything happening in the classroom, as shown by this excerpt:

> Dear parents,
>
> We would like to take the time to tell you about some of the exciting activities we have been doing. Our space theme has really escalated!
>
> First we went to the campus planetarium at the end of January. From there we built our own planetarium. Our reading room has been moved out into the classroom to allow for a total space center.

Later, in a note to parents after an exciting morning, Ernie further invited them to carry over the children's interests and excitement into the home.

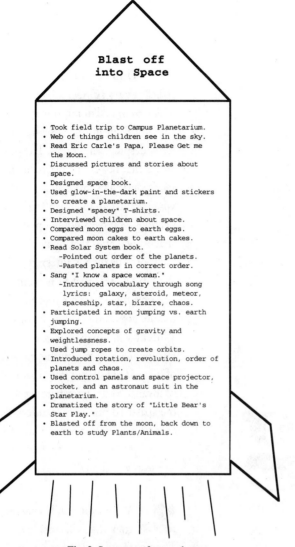

Fig. 2. Summary of space theme.

Within figure:

Blast off
into Space

- Took field trip to Campus Planetarium.
- Web of things children see in the sky.
- Read Eric Carle's Papa, Please Get me the Moon.
- Discussed pictures and stories about space.
- Designed space book.
- Used glow-in-the-dark paint and stickers to create a planetarium.
- Designed "spacey" T-shirts.
- Interviewed children about space.
- Compared moon eggs to earth eggs.
- Compared moon cakes to earth cakes.
- Read Solar System book.
    -Pointed out order of the planets.
    -Pasted planets in correct order.
- Sang "I know a space woman."
    -Introduced vocabulary through song lyrics: galaxy, asteroid, meteor, spaceship, star, bizarre, chaos.
- Participated in moon jumping vs. earth jumping.
- Explored concepts of gravity and weightlessness.
- Used jump ropes to create orbits.
- Introduced rotation, revolution, order of planets and chaos.
- Used control panels and space projector, rocket, and an astronaut suit in the planetarium.
- Dramatized the story of "Little Bear's Star Play."
- Blasted off from the moon, back down to earth to study Plants/Animals.

Dear Parents,

Ask your children about the "moon eggs" we had today to supplement our snack. The moon egg recipe is simple—five egg whites and one egg yolk. Drizzle the yolk through the white in a skillet; do not mix. Cook on low to medium heat. The yellow yolk becomes striated and the whites look like craters on the moon. The children really enjoyed our "moon eggs."

These examples of communicating with parents are not exceptions. Ernie believes that parents should always be informed of classroom activities and projects and invited to participate as often as possible.

CONCLUSION

An evaluation of the implementation of the space theme in Ernie's classroom strongly suggests that the criteria for selecting a theme were met. First, the topic was relevant to young children, who seem to be naturally fascinated by space if the concepts and experiences are developmentally appropriate. Second, the theme provided many opportunities for children to demonstrate their knowledge and skills and expand upon them in significant ways. Third, it allowed for the incorporation of a variety of materials and resources. And, finally, it reflected the initial and emergent interests of both the teachers and children, as they interacted in the social environment.

REFERENCES

Bredekamp, S., & Rosegrant, T. (1992). *Reaching potentials: Appropriate curriculum and assessment for young children*, (Vol. 1). Washington, D.C.: National Association for the Education of Young Children.

Bredekamp, S. (1986). *Developmentally appropriate practice in early childhood programs serving children from birth through age 8*. Washington, D.C.: National Association for the Education of Young Children.

Brewer, J. (1995). *Introduction to early childhood education: Preschool through primary grades*. Boston: Allyn and Bacon.

Carle, E. (1986). *Papa please get the moon for me*. USA: Picture Book Studio

Dewey, J. (1902). *The child and the curriculum*. Chicago: University of Chicago Press.

Jacobs, H., (Ed.). (1989). *Interdisciplinary curriculum: Design and implementation*. Washington, D.C.: Association for Supervision and Curriculum Development.

Jalongo, M. (1992). *Early childhood language arts*. Boston: Allyn and Bacon.

Jones, E., & Nimmo J. (1994). *Emergent curriculum*. Washington, D.C.: National Association for the Education of Young Children.

Katz, L., & Chard S. (1989). *Engaging children's minds: The project approach*. Norwood, NJ: Ablex.

NAEYC. (1991). Guidelines for appropriate curriculum content and assessment in programs serving children ages 3 through 8. *Young Children*, 21-38.

Schwartz, S., & Robison, H. (1982). *Designing curriculum for early childhood*. Boston: Allyn and Bacon.

10 *Ways to* Improve Your Theme Teaching

How to choose and manage terrific themes—while avoiding theme burnout and cutesiness

By Sean A. Walmsley

i taught my first theme with a class of seventh graders in a school in Somerset, England, in 1969. What was it? Graveyards. We explored a local cemetery and used it as a starting point for a theme on death, dying, and burial rites. It was gruesome—and the kids loved it. But they also gained substantive knowledge about local history and the whole business of dying, and I saw how worthwhile teaching with themes could be.

I've taught many themes since then. Along the way I've learned a lot about what makes themes work—and what makes them difficult to manage. Here are ten strategies that will improve your theme teaching, whether you're a veteran theme teacher or just starting out.

1. **Don't try to integrate every subject area into every theme.** I'm not sure who first started the all-in-one obsession, but it's widespread in schools. The problem is that not all themes naturally incorporate all subject areas, and when you try to force artificial connections, you risk ending up with shallow activities that dilute the focus of your theme. Integrate only the subject areas that fit naturally, and save the others for your next theme. For example, in a theme on Vincent Van Gogh, you *could* include math by measuring the area of his paintings—but does that really advance kids' understanding of the artist? I'd primarily focus on his art and his era. Just because you *can* fit a subject area into a theme doesn't mean you should!

2. **When you teach a theme, tuck the skills inside it.** Themes focus on content rather than skills, but the skills are nonetheless taught within the work that kids do while investigating the theme. For example, for a theme on pollution, your class might read Gail Gibbons's book *Recycle! A Handbook for Kids* (Little, Brown, 1992) to learn about the different ways that common items can be reused. While you're reading, you can teach comprehension, vocabulary, and word-recognition skills. You might teach math or science-process skills while students study recycling in their town. You can teach writing and research skills like note taking as children take notes from books and other material they're using to explore their topics.

From *Instructor*, August 1996, pp. 54-59. © 1996 by Scholastic, Inc. Reprinted by permission.

3. **Balance teacher-generated and student-created themes.** There's quite a debate among educators on this issue—some are adamant that all themes should be student-created. While I like the idea of students creating themes, I see nothing wrong with teacher-generated themes, provided that they are appropriate for kids. Many of my own interests were sparked by other people engaging me in topics I'm sure I wouldn't have selected for myself. So plan some themes yourself, create some collaboratively with students, and let some arise spontaneously.

4. **Avoid cutesy treatments of themes.** I'm sure children enjoy fun activities like coloring in dittos of bears, but the question is: What are they learning? The point of a theme is to explore a subject in some depth, and we defeat the whole purpose when we gloss over a concept with flimsy activities. Why not turn that cutesy theme on bears into something worthwhile? Explore all aspects of bears, including the concept of habitats, so children will develop a much better understanding of bears and their environments.

5. **Draw themes from a variety of arenas.** If you think of themes as digging deep into important ideas, then doesn't it make sense to draw themes from all sorts of realms? Here are six areas to consider.

● *Concepts* like survival or justice make excellent themes, although they work better if there's some tension built into them (e.g., surviving natural versus man-made disasters, and justice versus prejudice).

● *Content areas* such as science and social studies make good sources for themes, especially if you use themes to pursue a narrow rather than broad focus. For example, instead of swamping kids with a study of the entire Civil War, or even something as broad as conflict, focus on the concept of broken alliances, inviting students to study different examples of this. One group might research families that were divided over the slavery issue and fought brother against brother, while another might explore why the abolitionists and the suffragists broke their ties.

Stages of Teaching a Theme

Launching
● Connect the theme to children's prior experiences.
● Find out what children know or want to explore.
● Draw children in with a powerful read-aloud.

Exploring
● Reading aloud, guided/shared reading, and independent reading related to the theme
● Writing (such as journal entries related to the reading and theme-connected stories
● Speaking, listening, viewing (having children talk about their reading, watching a film on whales, listening to a speaker on birds of prey)
● Activities (such as making a class book about apples or measuring dinosaurs on the playground)
● Projects (such as having children explore a self-chosen or negotiated topic on their own or in small groups over several days or weeks)

Culminating
● Share what's been learned by making a display, putting on a readers' theater, or making a film strip or video.
● Take a field trip.
● Invite parents and friends into the classroom to learn about the theme.

Assessing
● If the theme's purpose is to enlarge children's understanding of an important concept, make sure your assessment focuses on this understanding.
● Use portfolios to have children show you what they've learned.
● Use checklists to see what skills have been mastered.
● Ask children and parents to give you feedback on the theme itself.

● *Current events* offers lots of high-interest themes. You might start with an event that's in the news and trace it backward, historically, politically, geographically, and so on. The 1996 Olympic Games in Atlanta are an obvious choice; the Iditarod is another (it can be explored in a number of ways, including the controversy over the treatment of animals).

● *People* make good themes. Explore the lives and contributions of people from different walks of life—authors and illustrators, composers, quilters, canoe builders, scientists, and so on.

● The *calendar* is a good source, too, especially in the early grades (for example, seasons, festivals, National Dairy Week).

● Finally, there are what I call *form* themes—themes that explore genres (mystery, humor, science fiction, and so on) and topics such as the alphabet or numbers. Form themes use the structure of a topic as their organizing framework. (For example, a mystery theme might examine the elements of a detective story.)

6. **Make sure your themes are the right size.** Have you ever become exhausted or bored with a theme that drags on forever? Are all your themes the same length? If you're nodding your head, maybe you should try adjusting the size of your themes. Think about three different sizes:

● A *mini-theme* might last less than a day in kindergarten (such as a focus on snails or magnets) or about a week in sixth grade (such as a current events theme devoted to a news item chosen by the students).

● A *regular theme* would last about a week in kindergarten (for example, bones and skeletons) and up to six weeks in the upper grades (for example, exploring the solar system).

● A *major theme* would last about two weeks in kindergarten (dinosaurs) and up to 12 weeks in the upper grades (ancient Greece).

Don't be afraid to cut short a regular or major theme that's dragging, or extend a theme that children have become absorbed in. But make sure that the major themes—those you'll be spending a lot of time preparing and carrying out—really are worthy of children's exploration.

7. **Approach yearlong and schoolwide themes with caution.** I have seen excellent schoolwide, yearlong themes. A science magnet school in Albany, New York, does a survival theme

---

YOUR Resources

The Basic School: A Community for Learning by Ernest Boyer (Carnegie Foundation for the Advancement of Teaching, 1994). Boyer lays out a broad set of themes for elementary school.

Bridging the Gap: Integrating Curriculum in Upper Elementary and Middle Schools by Cora Lee Five and Marie Dionisio (Heinemann, 1995). This profiles a "Discoveries" theme in a fifth-grade classroom and a "Trying on Someone Else's Skin" theme in middle school.

Learning and Loving It: Theme Studies in the Classroom by Ruth Gamberg, Winniefred Kwak, Meredith Hutchings, and Judy Altheim (Heinemann, 1988). Full of practical ideas, this is about a primary school in Nova Scotia that organizes much of its curriculum around themes.

The Author Studies Handbook: Helping Students Build Powerful Connections to Literature by Laura Kotch and Leslie Zackman (Scholastic Professional Books, 1995). This is an excellent, very practical look at how to prepare themes on authors and illustrators.

Theme Immersion: Inquiry-Based Curriculum in Elementary and Middle Schools by Gary Manning, Maryann Manning, and Roberta Long (Heinemann, 1994). This look at theme immersions is well written, easy to follow, and full of good ideas.

Using Literature in the Middle Grades: A Thematic Approach by Joy Moss (Christopher Gordon, 1994). Focusing on literature themes in middle school, Moss has great ideas on creating themes around books.

Theme Studies: A Practical Guide by Penny Strube (Scholastic Professional Books, 1994). Discussing both teacher-generated and student-generated themes, Strube provides a wealth of practical ideas.

Teaching Kindergarten: A Developmentally Appropriate Approach by Bonnie Brown Walmsley, Anne-Marie Camp, and Sean Walmsley (Heinemann, 1992). This describes the philosophy and practice of a kindergarten program based entirely on themes. It provides teaching plans for 37 themes. *Editor's Note: Each month in Instructor you'll find an integrated theme unit by Bonnie Walmsley and Anne-Marie Camp in the Primary Theme Club.*

Children Exploring Their World: Theme Teaching in Elementary School by Sean Walmsley (Heinemann, 1994). In the first half of this book, I lay out practical steps for creating and managing themes. In the second half of the book, teachers in grades K–6 share themes they have created (including insects, fish hatchery, architecture of a town, and Egyptian mummies).

that involves all grade levels. But I have some concerns. One is that if you're doing the same theme all yearlong, you're not doing other themes. And what about the child who's stuck in a yearlong theme he or she doesn't like? Another concern is that some yearlong themes are so abstract or all-encompassing (such as respect) that it's hard to create relevant activities for them. It's not unusual for these themes to run out of steam. Schoolwide themes are easier to create than yearlong themes, but you have to be sure that the theme is suitable for students across the grades.

8. **Bump up your own knowledge of the themes you're preparing.** If you prepare themes by simply gathering books and activities, you may be missing out on one the most important aspects of creating themes—learning about the topics yourself, what I call "bumping up" your knowl-edge. If you do a theme on dinosaurs, bring your own knowl-edge of dinosaurs up to date. You'll find your theme will be more sub-stantive, you'll have better sugges-tions for children as they pursue their projects, and you'll send a powerful message to children that you practice what you preach about learning. Bump up your knowledge through books, magazines and journals, talking to experts, explor-ing the Internet, and taking trips.

9. **Teach a theme at least twice and recoup your investment in it.** At a conference recently, a colleague told me that she never taught a theme twice because it would lose its interest and spon-taneity. I can see how this could be true for cutesy themes, but substan-tive themes usually go better the second or third time they are done.

I wouldn't repeat a theme if it really bombed or if I had become tired of it after several years because it wasn't growing or changing.

10. **Borrow theme ideas from others.** Some-times the best way to get started with themes is to use other people's, and then modify them with your own materials and activities. But I'd offer a couple of cautions. There are a lot of publishers out there who want you to buy their "theme" pack-ages, which are little more than sets of dittos loosely organized around a common label. Ask yourself: Will a child enlarge his or her knowledge of the world by using these materi-als, or are they just skills activi-ties? . . .

SEAN A. WALMSLEY is a profes-sor in the reading department at the State University of New York at Al-bany, where he teaches graduate courses in reading and writing, and works with schools to improve their literacy programs. He has taught in both elementary and secondary schools.

Documenting Children's Learning

Judy Harris Helm, Sallee Beneke and Kathy Steinheimer

Judy Harris Helm is an Early Childhood Specialist, Brimfield, Illinois.
Sallee Beneke is a Master Teacher, Oglesby, Illinois.
Kathy Steinheimer is a Preprimary Teacher, Peoria, Illinois.

doc·u·ment, -ment·ed, -ment·ing, -ments (dŏk´-ye-mènt´)
2. To support (an assertion or a claim, for example) with evidence or decisive information.
The American Heritage Dictionary of the English Language, Third Edition

Documenting children's learning may be one of the most valuable skills a teacher can learn. When teachers carefully collect, analyze, interpret and display evidence of learning, they are better able to understand how children learn and to help others recognize that learning. Regular and consistent documentation of children's work can benefit teachers in five ways.

1. Teachers who can document children's learning in a variety of ways are able to respond to demands for accountability.
An increased demand for accountability and program evaluation is a strong trend in education. Schools and other early childhood programs must prove their effectiveness to their constituencies. In an effort to meet these demands for accountability, some programs have turned to increased use of standardized tests. Such group administered tests, however, are especially inappropriate for assessing children younger than 3rd grade (Meisels, 1993). The Association for Childhood Education International's official position is that standardized testing should not occur earlier than Grade 3 (ACEI/Perrone, 1991). In contrast to achievement tests, comprehensive and quality documentation can:

- provide evidence of children's learning in all areas of their development: physical, emotional, social and cognitive
- provide insight into complex learning experiences when teachers use an integrated approach
- provide a framework for organizing teachers' observations and recording each child's special interests and developmental progress
- emphasize learning as an interactive process by documenting what children learn through active exploration and interaction with adults, other children and materials
- show the advantages of activities and materials that are concrete, real and relevant to young children, as opposed to abstract and artificial events such as group testing situations
- enable the teacher to assess childen's knowledge and abilities in order to increase activities' difficulty, complexity and challenge as children develop understanding and skills.

2. Teachers who document are more often able to teach children through direct, firsthand, interactive experiences that enhance brain development.
Documentation enables the teacher to provide evidence that children are learning as a result of firsthand experiences. Recent research on brain development (Sylwester, 1995) suggests that children learn better when they are active, engaged and involved. Learning

From *Childhood Education*, Summer 1997, pp. 200-205. © 1997 by the Association for Childhood Education International, 17904 Georgia Avenue, Suite 215, Olney, MD. Reprinted by permission.

is related to children's feelings and emotions; therefore, their dispositions towards learning are important (Katz, 1995). How a child feels about reading, and whether or not the child wants to learn to read, will affect that child's reading achievement over the long term. Traditional methods for monitoring children's progress, such as standardized tests, do not reveal such attitudes.

Brain research also shows that learning is interconnected and cannot be isolated or compartmentalized into subject areas (Howard, 1994). Subject matter tests and standardized achievement tests do not provide information about how children integrate their learning and apply content knowledge to real life challenges. A systematic collection of children's work documents how children integrate and apply what they learn. Teachers can then assess that integration and provide more meaningful experiences.

Sylwester also showed that the brain adapts and develops by exposure to continuously changing and challenging environments. Children learn from hands-on, thought-provoking experiences that challenge them to think and stimulate their brain's growth and development. Such experiences cannot be assessed easily by conventional methods.

As teachers strive to develop curricula that is brain enhancing, they must also be mindful of assessing students' growth, development and intellectual and social learning. The two circles in Figure 1 represent these simultaneous challenges.

3. Teachers are more effective when they document.

Perhaps the greatest value of comprehensive documentation is its power to inform teaching. Teachers who have good documentation skills will make more productive planning decisions, including how to set up the classroom, what to do next, what questions to ask, what resources to provide and how to stimulate each child's development. The more information a teacher can gather when making these decisions, the more effective a teacher is likely to be.

Lev Vygotsky's sociocultural theory explains the importance of teachers' decisions in maximizing learning. According to Vygotsky (1978), the teacher is most effective when teaching is directed towards a *zone of proximal development* for each child. Children learn best when learning experiences are within their

zone of development. The teacher needs to assess a child's development, probe the child's thinking on the topic and provide learning experiences that will build a bridge, or "scaffold," to higher level thought processes (Berk & Winsler, 1995). Data that reveal what the child partially understands, what the child is beginning to be able to do, or what the child is trying to integrate are often the most helpful pieces of information for teachers. Standardized tests primarily provide a limited sample of what the student has already mastered. By focusing only on what children already know, teachers cannot be as effective in helping them reach the next learning steps.

Documentation can also help the teacher decide if and when a child needs additional support systems. If the teacher collects a child's work over a period of time, the teacher can see if the child is progressing as expected or if mastery of a skill is just around the corner. When the teacher does not see mastery or emerging skills, she can seek additional help, such as early special assistance.

4. Teachers who can document children's work are better able to meet special needs.

Because of changing demographics early childhood teachers need even more skills than ever. Children with special needs are now part of many prekindergarten and primary classrooms. Some of these special needs include giftedness, physical disabilities, learning problems requiring individualized education plans, and challenges resulting from growing up in poverty. Teachers who know how to gather

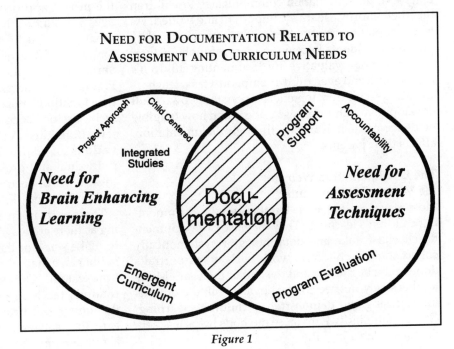

Figure 1

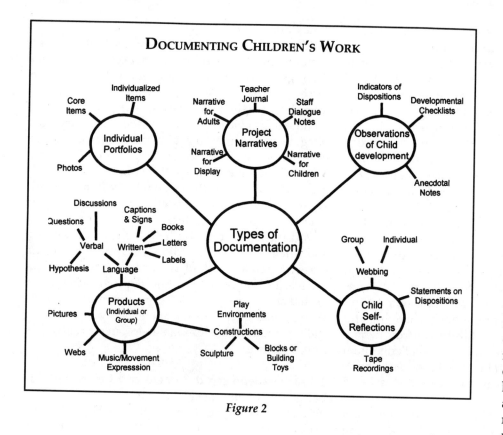

Figure 2

To be most effective, teachers should vary their documentation to match children's learning experiences and to meet the needs of the intended audience. A teacher who wants to discover what a child knows about a topic might collect the child's drawings and writings about that topic, but may not consider asking the child to help construct a beginning web about what he knows. The teacher may assemble a photographic display, but not think to have the child dictate an accompanying narrative. With a variety of ways to document at hand, the teacher will be able to obtain more accurate information about a particular child. A child who has not developed extensive language skills, for example, may not be able to dictate a narrative but may be able to draw a picture, or construct a block play environment, that shows his depth of understanding.

When teachers at the Valeska Hinton Early Childhood Education Center in Peoria, Illinois, introduced the project approach in their classrooms of children ages 3 through 6 they wanted to increase their documentation. The Professional Development Coordinator and Lead Teacher developed a web to illustrate the variety of ways that documentation could occur (see Figure 2). Teachers and other staff added to the web as they identified more ways to document. The resulting web classifies documentation methods into five clusters: Individual Portfolios, Project Narratives, Observations of Child Development, Products (both individual and group) and Self-reflections. Each of these types of documentation provides a way to view and understand children's work.

There are as many different ways to document learning as there are ways that active, engaged children try to make sense of their world. Therefore, the web is neither an exhaustive list nor an exclusive classification system. The documentation web informs and reminds teachers of the variety of ways they can document and provides a vocabulary and a structure for teachers to communicate with each other about documentation.

information and assess children's development are better able to identify the appropriate learning experiences for these children as well as for more typically developing children.

5. Children perceive learning to be important and worthwhile when teachers document their learning.

Extensive documentation communicates to children that their efforts to learn are important and valued. As teachers pay more attention to documentation, they find their students become more careful about their work and more evaluative. By documenting children's first, second and even third attempts at a task, teachers encourage children to reflect upon their own skill development. Children also understand how tangible evidence of their learning, through documentation, affects their parents.

The Documentation Web and the Valeska Hinton Center

Most teachers have some familiarity with documenting children's learning. They may use a developmental checklist, take anecdotal notes or systematically collect some of children's work, such as self-portraits done at the beginning and the end of the year. Many teachers may not recognize, however, all the options for assessing and demonstrating children's learning. Greater familiarity with these methods helps teachers document meaningfully.

Project Narratives

A narrative state-ment, which tells the story or history of a learning experience or project, is the most traditional method of documentation. Sto-ries are a powerful way of understand-

ing other people's events and experiences. Such narra-tives can take the form of stories for and by children, records of conversations with other teachers, teacher journals, narratives for adults in the form of books and letters, or visual displays. They are usually created over a period of time, marking change and growth in knowledge, skills and dispositions.

To take advantage of the interest that comes from an evolving project, teachers can write narratives that are continuously updated as the children's work proceeds. Kathy Steinheimer's pre-kindergarten class of 3- and 4-year-olds at the Valeska Hinton Center became engaged in constructing a mail system, for example. Kathy accompanied a photo display that illustrated the mailbag design process with the follow-ing narrative:

Karissa and Tim took on the job of creating a mailbag out of paper. This led to a lengthy interchange about the handle. Karissa drew a short handle using a picture on the cover of a book as her reference. Tim told her that it had to be bigger. Karissa drew a handle that was a little longer and wider. Tim told her that the handle was too fat. Karissa insisted that it would work and kept on cutting. Tim tried to convince Karissa that he needed the long strip on the edge of her paper. She did not agree and finished her cutting. Then, he showed her the picture on the book cover. Karissa kept on cutting. Next, she tried her handle on for size and discovered that it would not work. Therefore, she asked Tim to draw the handle. She cut out the long and narrow handle that he drew. It tore as she cut it out. However, they still thought that it would work after they cut it out. It did not. I gave them a yardstick and showed the pair how to draw a straight line with it. They made a long and wide handle for the bag, which they attached to the bag with tape. After a trial run with-out mail, they were satisfied with their accomplishment.

The problem-solving skills that the children developed through this experience would not be evi-dent to others without the teacher's narrative.

Observations of Child Development

Observing and re-cording development is a familiar practice for many teachers of young children. In general, child devel-opment observations

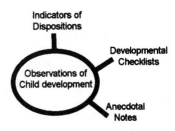

may be recorded as items on a developmental check-list, anecdotal notes or indicators of dispositions. These practices have been used primarily to report on mastery of discrete skills, to assess children's progress in school, or to indicate the frequency, duration and nature of a behavior at a particular point in time.

In recent years, observation systems such as the Work Sampling System have expanded the practical uses of checklists to document growth and skill de-velopment over time. Rather than focusing on whether a child has mastered a particular skill, some checklists, when systematically combined with an-ecdotal notes and children's work samples, enable a teacher to reliably identify skills, knowledge, behav-iors, dispositions and accomplishments as they emerge and become consistent. For example, Beth Crider-Olcott, a preprimary teacher at Valeska Hinton Center, recorded the following observation to document the growth in 4-year-old Thea's writing skills:

Our project has really encouraged Thea's writing devel-opment. She had been writing her name consistently, but with the drawing of the cages, Thea attempted to copy the word "cages." With her success, Thea began to copy any word put in front of her! She copied the words "shampoo" and "alcohol" to make labels for bottles in the clinic.

Crider-Olcott was able to record on the develop-mental checklist that Thea was able to complete the skill, "Copies or writes words needed for work or play" (Jablon, Marsden, Meisels & Dichtelmiller, 1994). (See Figure 3.)

Figure 3

Individual Portfolios

Collection of children's work is another familiar type of documentation. For years, teachers have saved children's work to share with parents and to use when evaluating a child's progress at the end of the year. Teachers often collect children's self-portraits or writing samples.

Teachers can observe and document growth by systematically collecting children's work over time. This documentation is more significant when it is linked to a "comprehensive and developmentally appropriate picture of what children can be expected to know and do across all domains of growth and learning" (Meisels et al., 1994, p. 8). Portfolio items are evidence of a child's progress, as measured on a checklist that is based on such a picture. Beth Crider-Olcott, for example, saved Thea's attempts to copy words, including a map that Thea labeled by copying names of vegetables (see Figure 4).

Child Self-reflections

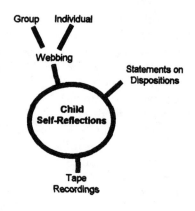

Self-reflections provide the most accurate assessment of a child's emotional involvement with a project's content area. The teacher can assess whether an experience is developmentally appropriate and the extent to which it will contribute to the child's disposition to learn. Observations of child self-reflections provide the most direct evidence of appropriate classroom experiences.

As part of a water project, some children in Pam Scranton's multi-age pre-kindergarten class at Valeska Hinton made foil boats. Scranton recorded 4-year-old Antonio's self-reflections:

Antonio has shown an increased disposition towards sticking with something. During the foil boat activity, he struggled

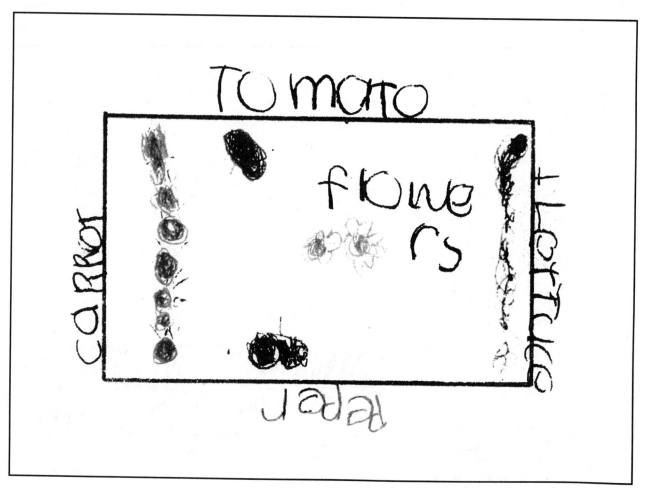

Figure 4

with his boat and how to connect the sides. He was beginning to become frustrated when he observed Rommel's boat and the way he pinched the sides closed. Antonio tried this and it worked. He exclaimed, "Look, Teacher, now my sides is gonna work good!" He manipulated both of his sides in this way and spent nearly 20 minutes perfecting the shape. Antonio's comments on his own progress and the length of his involvement with the boat indicate that Antonio was appropriately challenged and engaged.

Products

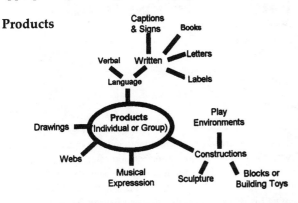

Products, the manifestations of children's learning, are the most obvious means of documenting learning. Adults probably consider writing samples to be the most visible signs of children's learning. Pictures, webs, musical expressions, constructions, and collections of data and oral language samples also produce significant documentation. These products can be produced either individually or by a group of children. Occasionally, the product speaks for itself; in general, however, this usefulness can be augmented by carefully selecting products for display and including an explanation of the product's significance. When displaying group work, a teacher may choose to select those products that are significant in telling the story of the project or in documenting an individual child's development through participation in the project. It is not usually necessary to display all of the children's pictures.

Group-constructed play environments are one of the most effective products to use when documenting children's knowledge and skills. What the children build reflects what they know, and the workmanship of the construction reflects their skills. Val Timmes' multiage kindergarten/1st-grade class constructed a grocery store in their classroom, for example, as an outgrowth of their investigation of fruits and vegetables.

The children visited the grocery story, made sketches of what they saw, and then drew and refined floor plans for their store. They made lists and diagrams. They measured, cut and created, forming teams to construct the store's various departments. The resulting play environment was rich with examples of the children's knowledge of the grocery store and their ability to measure, read, write, problem-solve, work with number concepts and create. By documenting

this play environment with written explanations of the various constructions, and by displaying photographs of the children in the process of constructing, Val Timmes was able to share the significance of these products with parents, children and other visitors.

Conclusion

Documentation is a powerful skill for the teacher. A letter from a parent at Valeska Hinton Center shows the effect that high quality documentation can have on parents' perceptions of a school. This parent was in the process of choosing a preschool program for her child and first encountered the project approach when she visited the center.

My first actual encounter with projects occurred in late spring at an open house for prospective parents . . . I was skeptical—the so-called traditional approaches had worked for me, so why wouldn't it also provide success for our child? . . . Walking around the school that night, I began to be impressed. I studied [the documentation on] a project on reflections. I marveled at the insights shared by the children. The critical thinking skills [that] their work exhibited was phenomenal. Direct quotations included sentences of greater length and complexity than I would have expected. Their vocabulary was very specific. I went home and attempted to describe what I had seen to my husband . . . After our discussion, we became convinced that this was the place for our daughter to learn.
—Nancy Higgins, parent

Ultimately, the teacher's skill and the time and effort spent in documentation benefited the children, the parents and the school.

◆

References

Association for Childhood Education International/Perrone, V. (1991). On standardized testing. A position paper. *Childhood Education, 67,* 132-142.

Berk, L., & Winsler, A. (1995). *Scaffolding children's learning: Vygotsky and early childhood education.* Washington, DC: National Association for the Education of Young Children.

Howard, P. (1994). *The owner's manual for the brain.* Austin, TX: Leornian Press.

Jablon, J. R., Marsden, D., Meisels, S., & Dichtelmiller, M. (1994). *Omnibus guidelines: Preschool through third grade* (3rd ed.) Ann Arbor, MI: Rebus Planning Associates.

Katz, L. (1995). *Talks with teachers of young children: A collection.* Norwood, NJ: Albex Publishing.

Meisels, S. (1993). Remaking classroom assessment with the work sampling system. *Young Children, 48,* 34-40.

Meisels, S., Jablon, J., Marsden, D., Dichtelmiller, M., Dorfman, A., & Steele, D. (1994). *An overview* (3rd ed.) Ann Arbor, MI: Rebus Planning Associates.

Sylwester, R. (1995). *A celebration of neurons: An educator's guide to the human brain.* Alexandria, VA: Association for Supervision and Curriculum Development.

Vygotsky, L. S., edited and translated by M. Cole, V. John-Steiner, S. Scribner, & E. Souberman. (1978). *Mind in society: The development of higher mental processes.* Cambridge, MA: Harvard University Press.

Fostering Creativity in the Early Childhood Classroom

Mary K. Smith, Ed.D.[1,2]

Most early childhood teachers would tell you that creativity is important; and that creativity should be considered an integral part of every early childhood classroom. Yet, too often, it is slighted in some areas or limited to being a part of art education. How can creativity can be nurtured and developed in all cognitive and social aspects of an early childhood classroom? The key to this fostering of creativity is for each teacher to examine his or her own filters that can help to foster, or hinder, as the case may be, creativity in that classroom setting. By examining adult attitudes, classroom atmosphere, and children's activities and materials, and adjusting, where necessary, to incorporate certain positive elements for creativity, early childhood educators are more likely to establish a trusting, flexible, and safe environment that allows and stimulates the creative process in an atmosphere of respect.

KEY WORDS: creativity; child autonomy; teacher attitudes; resourcefulness; classroom climate.

INTRODUCTION

Scott and Andy were playing in the housekeeping area. Suddenly Andy threw the fake fur piece on the floor and told Scott that there was a skunk and they should get out. The two boys proceeded to evacuate the area while pretending to call the fire department to come and help them. The teacher was working with another child close to this scene. She told the children that they had probably better move due to the skunk. More children got involved in the adventure. The original boys asked the teacher if the fire department was the right place to call. The teacher replied that she had never encountered the situation before, but if the fire department didn't respond, they might want to try the Humane Society.

This story is an entertaining example of the value of play in the early childhood classroom. But it is more than that. The story is also an example of children being creative; and it is an example of children being encouraged to be creative. Why is this important?

Most early childhood teachers realize the importance of educating the whole child. These teachers are

supported by the developmental guidelines published by the National Association for the Education of Young Children. These guidelines state that a curriculum of exploration and integration addresses the physical, emotional, social, and cognitive aspects of a child's education (Bredekamp, 1987; Haiman, 1991). Yet, the whole child in that early childhood classroom can never really be served unless the issue of developing creativity is also considered. Without considering creativity, a unique part of the individuality of each child is slighted. Thus, a key question for early childhood teachers to ask is "What is creativity for young children, and how can teachers in early childhood classrooms foster it?"

Creativity is the process of being original, spontaneous, and/or unique. The child, using previous knowledge, sees or acts upon selected appropriate new relationships (Edwards & Nabors, 1993; Meador, 1993; Isenberg & Jalongo, 1993; Whitson, 1994). The child uses all information available to arrive at this new way of thinking or acting. In fact, the child's awareness is heightened in general (Fowler, 1990). To illustrate, the child who turns the fur piece in the housekeeping area into a skunk and evacuates everyone is bring creative. He has taken his knowledge of skunks and extended that to the new setting of school where skunks would not likely be found. Likewise, a child, who draws a picture of the

[1]Teacher, Westgate Elementary, Westside Community Schools, Omaha, Nebraska, and Doctoral Student, Department of Educational Administration, University of Nebraska at Lincoln, Lincoln, Nebraska.

[2]Correspondence should be directed to Dr. Mary K. Smith, Westgate Elementary, 7802 Hascall, Omaha, Nebraska 68124.

 From *Early Childhood Education Journal*, Vol. 24, No. 2, 1996, pp. 77-82. © 1996 by Human Sciences Press, Inc. Reprinted by permission.

8-02-1980

Fig. 1. The painter.

painting contractor as a message for his mother to return the painter's call, is being creative (Figure 1). Combining knowledge of what the painter looks like and the knowledge of how to take a message, the child uses his crayons to make the picture of the painter as a unique way of communicating—without written words—the news of the painter's call to his mother.

From the example of the boys and the skunk, as well as from the example of the child noting the painter's call, cognition and skills are necessary because these serve as the base for creativity. However, the child does not actually cross over into creativity without taking some distinctive steps (Whitson, 1994; Tegano, Moran, & Sawyers, 1991). To take those extra steps, children must find themselves in an environment that not only supports this effort but, more importantly, encourages it in specific ways. Some teachers might be looking for a formula to make creativity happen. A formula like that cannot be given. What can be given are some ways of thinking, or facilitating strategies. Central to these ways of thinking or strategies will be the early childhood teacher who realizes and believes that creativity is not narrowly defined as a part of art education, but is, more broadly, able to be found and nurtured in every area of learning. Teachers cannot make children be creative. However, the teacher can provide a classroom that displays the appropriate attitude, the appropriate atmosphere, and the appropriate activities and materials for those children who wish to explore or demonstrate creative expression. These three ingredients—appropriate teacher attitude, appropriate classroom atmosphere, and appropriate activities and materials—which will be the focus of the rest of this article, can foster creativity. The absence of them can hinder creativity. The choice is really up to the teacher.

CREATIVITY CAN BE FOSTERED BY THE TEACHER'S ATTITUDE

An attitude of trust is paramount to developing creativity. Adults must trust that children will choose activ-

ities that will interest and engage them; and that children will self-regulate those choices without a lot of adult imposed regulations (Whitson, 1994). Most early childhood educators have been in a classroom where the teacher uses a planning board for the children to decide what area they will each work in for the next worktime period. This practice has the potential of limiting a child's thinking to just one area or aspect of the learning environment, particularly if every child is required to do the same task at that center. Further, many times children are asked to stay for a specified amount of time in order to "finish" that center before moving on to another choice. Surely, some of that practice is needed by teachers for accountability; but too much of it could hamper a child's potentially creative side. Now, think of a classroom without a daily planning board or without requirements for a certain number of centers to be visited or "completed" during worktime. This setting would allow each child to stay with a task for as long as he or she wished—or even continue the task when others have stopped working. The teacher is, in effect, telling the children that each of them is invited to go beyond the minimum amount of work or investment. "Getting done" is not the focus. The focus is on these children becoming competent decision makers, as well as on these young decision makers exploring fully and engaging in what interests them (Kamii & Devries, 1978). Engagement in a chosen activity fosters creative expression. Why? If a child knows that he was trusted to choose the activity in which he now finds himself engaged, he will also know that he will be trusted, if he wishes, to take a common or everyday activity and carry it to a new level (Whitson, 1994). An extension of this trust is demonstrated when the teacher elects to "teach to the moment" about something children find intriguing (Haiman, 1991). Trust, engagement, and extension are evident in this scene:

> Worktime was taking place after a group lesson on fire safety. Quite suddenly, half of the class met over in one corner of the room. The children had the scrap box with them. They were using the scrap paper to make fire badges for themselves; and they were splitting up into teams to check for fire hazards in the room. They were also making drawings of the play area and dividing that area up so that they could check the playground for safety when they went outside later.

These children absolutely went beyond the minimum expected, and their engagement led them into a creative way of expressing their combined knowledge. Consider the result if the teacher insisted that each child go back to the center area in which each had been working. Children, experiencing a situation similar to the one above, learn quickly that their interests are important; and that they are trusted to make decisions about what they choose in which to invest their time and inquiry.

Now, someone might suggest that in the real world, children must do certain work during certain times as well as stop work at certain times. Of course, sometimes that is true, but many times the subject matter or the stopping point is an arbitrary one chosen by the adult who has decided it is time to work on a particular idea or to move on simply because that was the original plan. When schedules cannot be changed to accommodate productive engagement, work can be saved and, therefore, respected until the child can resume the work.

There is, however, another important consideration regarding that sense of trust described in the scene of the children working on fire safety. That trust is not just immediately known by the children because trust is in the mind of the teacher. Communication of this sense of trust by the teacher to the students is critical. First, a teacher must be able to clearly state permission to try something new. Second, that teacher must state what it is that the children accomplished by the unique process or by the achievement of some form of novel work. Young children do not necessarily have the terms readily available to them to describe what is going on when they are thinking or working creatively; but children can be gradually helped and encouraged to learn to put these ideas into their own words. Third, that teacher must verbally give value to what is taking place (Segal & Segal, 1994). This does not mean a gushy display of enthusiasm, but rather a simple positive statement that can establish a climate of value. This climate is then made more meaningful when the communication interaction moves from teacher-to-student to student-to-student. This interaction is critical. Children should have access to each other and have permission to collaborate or discuss projects with which they are involved. Learning with and from peers should be seen as highly valuable. Children should be able to mingle freely, to display work that they wish to share, and to invite others to see and discuss the work. These concepts of interaction and collaboration among students can be seen in the following example:

> The children had just had a group lesson from the art teacher. Many of them were working on the activity which involved making flowers with small pieces of tissue paper wrapped around a pencil so that the pieces would stand up when glued onto the paper. Other children were working in the housekeeping area, the block area, or on other independent choice activities. The teacher noticed that Alex had crushed his tissue paper so that it had a flat appearance. When she asked him how he had discovered that technique, Alex launched into telling her about his "accident"—he lost his balance and crushed his work. He, quite dramatically, knocked his head with his palm and said that he was sure then that his work was ruined until he looked at it again. That second look made him decide that he liked it that way! When the teacher asked Alex if he would like to share the discovery of his technique with the other children, he used some of the teacher's descriptive words along with his own to describe his discovery and his feeling about it. Children stopped working and listened to him. Two other children joined in with comments about something that they had learned by experimenting with the tissue. Several children walked around to look at the various works in progress to get ideas.

Much of the above example would have been lost if the children had not had access to each other. Obviously, a ground work of trust had been developed and communicated to the students by the teacher long before this day. Such rich scenes do not just happen in a vacuum.

Someone might say that teachers do not have time for all this communication. That is true if they do not make time for it in their day. This does not mean adding it in like one more thing to do, but simply not crowding each day by "making sure that those kids are busy" every minute. A little flexibility with the day can go a long way.

CREATIVITY CAN BE FOSTERED BY THE ATMOSPHERE OF THE CLASSROOM

Children benefit creatively from an atmosphere that is relaxed and based on common sense and respect. That atmosphere tells children that they can test an idea as long as it falls within the confines of safety and appropriateness (Segal & Segal, 1994). The classroom climate communicates to students that it is all right to take a risk and make a mistake. No one can be permitted to "put down" another person for an unusual answer or approach. Everyone should have time to explain what it is that they are trying to say or do. Students should be able to brainstorm about the positive parts of any attempt. Lists can be made of what was learned from the attempt. Children learn from doing—and children learn to be creative from trying creative things.

According to Scott (1991), children need to develop their internal sense of worth before they will take risks. Therefore, the atmosphere needs, also, to be one of self-governance in regard to discipline. Earlier, trust was addressed in regard to work—now apply the same issue of trust to discipline or prosocial behavior. Children can be taught or given models of the ways of being prosocial. Then these tools of prosocial behavior can be used to allow children to "take care of themselves" without an adult watching their every move. Yes, children will make mistakes but they can correct these mistakes and modify the results of these mistakes without an atmosphere of consequences and retribution as you can see from this scene that took place after recess:

> The children had been outside with the paraprofessional. When they came in, the paraprofessional told the teacher that Andy had thrown a rock at Tommy. Luckily, it had missed. When the teacher sat down with the class to discuss the situation, Alex said that she didn't need to do that. He said that they just did what they would have done with her—the boys had talked about the problem. Their talking showed them that the running game they were playing was too hard for Andy; and he threw the rock when he got frustrated. The boys had then come up with a way to play that would keep the game fun for everyone, yet would make it easier for Andy; and, Andy, in return, had agreed not to throw rocks at his friends. The boys, with the paraprofessional's backing, told the teacher that they had all agreed and had successfully tried the new plan for the rest of recess. The teacher

declared the matter closed and outlined for the class
what the boys had achieved

These boys had learned that they could take care of
themselves and solve their own problems in an equitable
and agreeable manner. The internal motivation for self-
regulation that each student will have in such a setting
will help develop self-confidence and, therefore, the
comfort to take a risk regarding creativity not only in
problem solving but in all aspects of the classroom.

After reading the story of the boys and the rock
above, someone might strongly suggest that a rule was
broken; and that a consequence for breaking that rule
should be given. Of course, you need classroom rules but
some classrooms have too many, and place all the control
completely outside of the child. Further, sometimes consequences are imposed so often that they become mean-
ingless. The focus becomes one of remembering and
adhering to all the rules rather than on learning how to
get along, and on how to solve problems. Common sense
has to be the focus. Creativity will not be fostered in a
classroom that is a free-for-all place that is loud and out
of control. Who could think well enough to have a creative thought in a setting like that? But neither will creativity be fostered in a room where all the control lies
with the adult, and where conformity is the norm.

Because creative children may exhibit behaviors
that will be different from other children, the classroom
climate needs to reflect an atmosphere of respect for each
person and each person's individuality. All children may
be curious or sensitive, but a creative child may be those
and more. A creative child may be unusually quiet or
talkative, may have a strongly developed sense of humor,
may do things considered odd by others, may be outspo-
ken, or may be every bit a nonconformist (Meador, 1993;
Tegano et al., 1991). Even though a creative child might
be considered unusual, a pervasive atmosphere of respect
should help everyone (teacher included) to think of that
child as unique in some positive sense. An atmosphere of
acceptance must be in place so that children displaying
unusual tendencies along with their creativity do not
become ostracized or the recipient of negative behavior
and/or words. Consider this situation:

> Adam was a first grader in a multi-age classroom of first
> and second graders. He was a highly gifted child who
> was reading on the high school level as well as being a
> creative computer programmer in the class. Adam was
> also so highly disorganized that his messes often spilled
> over into areas belonging to classmates. One day, a
> small group of second graders approached Adam and
> said that they would be willing to help him organize his
> materials in order to help him, and the class in general.
> Adam gratefully accepted the offer; and worked right
> along with the organizing group.

The teacher had looked ahead to what might happen
and used a proactive approach by talking about and role
playing similar situations, thereby preparing all students
for both sides of such a situation; and by teaching and

modeling for them them tools of coping with such reactions (Segal & Segal, 1994). The teacher might have
given Adam a consequence for his disorganization or
chided the students for anger they might have directed at
Adam for the mess in their areas; but rather than using
rewards or punishments to handle such situations, the
teacher worked toward setting a tone that says everyone
respects each other, helps each other get through the difficult moments as quickly as possible, learns from those
moments, regroups, and goes on with life.

CREATIVITY CAN BE FOSTERED BY THE CLASSROOM ACTIVITIES AND MATERIALS

Activities based on the interests of the children are
conducive to fostering creativity. Young children are
capable of telling what they know about a topic of interest, what they want to know, and how they want to
explore the topic (Haiman, 1991; Scott, 1991). A toy or
nature sample brought to school by one of the children
may cause the other children to display a spontaneous
interest or curiosity. This is the time to explore that interest or curiosity; and let the interests drive the curriculum
rather than let the curriculum drive what children can do.

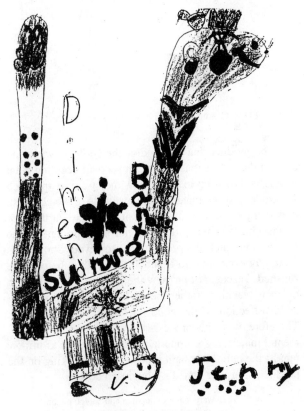

Fig. 2. Dimend Bartasorus.

Certainly, teachers often have curricular guidelines
to follow, however, almost any topic can be tied to some
element of the standard curriculum, and can offer the
promise of a new slant on the old. Both students and

teachers may experience creativity in such a setting. Teachers who value and act upon these ideas give children a sense of ownership in the work. Ownership leads to investment and engagement. Engagement leads to creative behavior. Examine this story about Jenny and her dinosaur:

> The children were asked to draw a favorite dinosaur and tell why it was their favorite. Jenny spent a great deal of time and used a great deal of detail in drawing a "princessasorus" complete with crown as well as scaly skin. She had a story to tell about this creature. When she was at home, she extended this by drawing a "Dimend Bartasorus" (Diamond Brontasaurus) for her teacher (Figure 2).

Jenny spent more time on this project because she had an investment with her imagination. She did follow the instructions, and she is still within the confines of the curriculum for "dinosaurs"—she just went further, combined some ideas, and ventured into something new.

Activities should also be open-ended. Rather than giving a strict model of what the product should be, dis-

Fig. 3. Columbus and his boat—the other two sank.

cuss the product that you and/or the students want and then let them have reasonable control over deciding what materials they want to use or how they want to approach the product. If the materials are available to the children, they can get the ones they want at any time. Further, for young children, the product is not as important as the process by which the product was achieved. Some children may even want to abandon the product before it is finished. Teachers often view the product as a reflection on their teaching, rather than what it really is—a concrete reflection of the child's work and work process. Therefore, in such a process-oriented classroom, supplemental materials are important, but maybe not as important as the child's thought process while working on the product. Consider David's thought processes:

> The children were making cut paper and crayon pictures of the voyage of the three boats of Columbus. David finished his work with one boat and a picture of an unidentified person. When the teacher asked him about his work, he told her that the person in the picture was Columbus; but there was only one boat because the other two had sunk (Figure 3). The teacher accepted his work readily.

No, David did not complete the project exactly, but the assignment was done to his satisfaction and his version of reality. He had done the basic task with, obviously, some extra thought processes if he could explain his work in the manner he did. His "supplemental" materials were not concrete. David's "extra" materials were in his mind, and consisted of the mental manipulation of ideas.

As for those optional concrete materials, teachers may feel stressed to "find" or provide them. However, one has to ask, how can children try the unusual if they never see or have the opportunity to work with anything unusual? Families can be a convenient and willing resource for donating or locating unusual materials. Parental involvement has another plus—this involvement gives parents more opportunity to notice and value creativity—especially if the child can convince them as to why certain "junk" would be considered outstanding material at school.

Classroom activities should be planned in such a way that an ample amount of uninterrupted worktime is given for investigation and discussion. Creativity will not develop in a vacuum. The main idea is to have children who have the time to see new concepts or extensions in the materials they have, rather than have children who need new materials to be stimulated. At first, the teacher can be the model by showing or telling about some extensions. Later, the children can take over this role, as Laura and Katie did:

> During worktime, Laura and Katie spent the better part of an hour sitting with the newly hatched chicks. They had an appropriate running conversation with each other during this time. They then approached the teacher with a song about chicks that they had created. The song was based on a familiar one that the children had learned about dinosaurs but it had been changed by the girls to incorporate what they knew or had learned about the chicks. The song was printed on the computer for the girls to use as they wished—for sharing, for a play, or for adding pictures for a story.

The girls were allowed to stay as long as they wished at the chicks, rather than being asked to leave after a certain amount of time or to leave in order to get another center done. This gave them the time and the permission to think of the chicks in a new way, and in combination with previous knowledge.

Finally, activities, processes, and products should be the intrinsic reward for learning. External rewards cause the shift of importance to go from the learning to "What do I get?" and cause creativity to drop off (Kohn, 1993). Why would a child want to invest time and interest in something after a reward was given for a minimal accomplishment? The focus should be on the description of what is taking place or has taken place—and what was learned. Again, the teacher takes the lead in establishing this, but the children will follow.

CONCLUSION

None of these classroom scenes are spectacular in any way. They are simply examples of what can happen to begin or continue to creative process. These samples are not ends in themselves but stepping stones to more creative ideas. If teachers can identify in themselves, and alter or eliminate, the filters that prevent or hinder children from trying something new, then creativity will have a greater chance to be fostered. Teachers may be more encouraged to modify or remove those filters if they keep in mind that "the creation of new ideas does not come from minds trained to follow doggedly what is already known. Creation comes from tinkering and playing around, from which new forms emerge" (Wassermann, 1991, p. 135).

REFERENCES

Bredekamp, S. (Ed.). (1987). *Developmentally appropriate practice in early childhood programs serving children from birth through age 8.* Washington, D.C.: NAEYC.

Edwards, L., & Nabors, M. (1993). The creative arts process. *Young Children, 48*(3), 77-81.

Fowler, C. (1990). Recognizing the role of artistic intelligences. *Music Educator's Journal, 77*(1), 24-27.

Haiman, P. (1991). Developing a sense of wonder in young children. There is more to early childhood education than cognitive development. *Young Children, 46*(6), 52-53.

Isenberg, J. P., & Jalongo, M. R. (1996). *Creative expression and play in early childhood* (2nd ed.). Englewood Cliffs, NJ: Merrill/Prentice Hall.

Kamii, C., & DeVries, R. (1978). *Physical knowledge in preschool education: Implications of Piaget's theory.* New York: Prentice Hall.

Kohn, A. (1993). *Punished by rewards.* Boston: Houghton Mifflin company.

Meador, K. (1993). Surviving a creative child's early years. *Gifted Child Today, 16*(2), 57-59.

Scott, M. (1991). Parental encouragement of gifted-talented-creative (GTC) development in young children by providing freedom to become independent. *The Creative Child and Adult Quarterly, 16*(1), 26-29.

Segal, J., & Segal, Z. (1994). Nurturing creativity in all your students. *LEARNING94, 23*(2), 26-27.

Tegano, D., Moran, J., & Sawyers, J. (1991). *Creativity in early childhood classrooms.* Washington, D.C.: National Education Association.

Wassermann, S. (1991). Serious play in the classroom: How messing around can win you the Nobel Prize. *Childhood Education, 68*(3), 133-139.

Whitson, S. (1994). The creative minority in our schools. *Childhood Education, 71*(1), 2-3.

Active Living: Physical Activities for Infants, Toddlers, and Preschoolers

Wayne Eastman[1,2]

Active Living is an approach that encourages people to be physically active every day. By targeting infants, toddlers, and preschoolers, early childhood educators will contribute to their lifestyles as Active Living Children. This article is designed as a framework for early childhood educators to support an active lifestyle among very young children. Various activities are described to promote active play for very young children and all of its associated benefits.

KEY WORDS: infants; toddlers; preschoolers; movement; physical activity; play.

INTRODUCTION

Why are movement experiences worthwhile and necessary? Physical activity is one of the most important mediums through which young children form impressions about themselves as well as about their surroundings. Physical activity exerts a positive relationship on good health, happiness, and vitality. In the context of the preceding statements, the concept of active living is a lifestyle in which physical activity is valued and integrated into daily life. More precisely, from an early childhood perspective, "when we think of very young children living actively, we see little girls and boys who are eager to explore their world and to move freely through it. Activity satisfies their curiosity and gives them real happiness" (Hanvey, 1992. p. 3).

Early childhood educators are in a unique position to support and encourage an active lifestyle among very young children. This article offers professionals in the field of early childhood a framework for examining the opportunities that they provide for young children to begin a life of active living.

[1]Department Coordinator, Early Childhood Education and Access Programs, Westviking College of Applied Arts and Technology, Corner Brook, Newfoundland, Canada.
[2]Correspondence should be directed to Wayne Eastman, Westviking College, P. O. Box 822, Corner Brook, Newfoundland A2H 6H6, Canada.

WHAT IS ACTIVE LIVING FOR YOUNG CHILDREN?

The mission for the promotion of active living infants, toddlers, and preschoolers can be best enunciated as follows: to support, to facilitate, and to promote the mobilization of adults to help young children participate in, enjoy, and value physical activity (Hanvey & Kinnon, 1993). Early childhood educators perform an essential role in providing active living opportunities for very young children. Therefore, it is crucial that they comprehend the values of active living. Listed below are some of the benefits to being an active child:

1. Movement is an important part of a child's physical, mental and emotional development.
2. Activity satisfies a child's curiosity of movement.
3. Good feelings are felt when early childhood educators, parents, and families are involved in physical activity and active play.
4. Activity can make young children feel good about themselves.
5. Games and activities allow for interacting with other children and develop social play.
6. Activity develops positive lifelong attitudes toward physical activity.
7. Young children solve problems and gain success through challenges and exploration (Newfoundland Department of Tourism, Culture, and Recreation, 1995).

Early childhood educators committed to active liv-

From *Early Childhood Education Journal,* Vol. 24, No. 3, 1997, pp. 161-164. © 1997 by Human Sciences Press, Inc. Reprinted by permission.

ing children need to be aware of the following nine principles:

1. Focus on the whole child, stressing the physical, emotional, social, and spiritual value of living actively. For young children, this builds on their natural love of physical activity and involves playing games and exercising with caring adults and friends.

2. Provide equal opportunities for physical activity, regardless of age, gender, language, ethnic background, and ability. Early childhood educators should use equipment which is not labeled by gender; for example, balls, hoops, bean bags and balance boards are used by all children and hence are gender neutral. By using simple and modifiable games, such as "Simon Says," early childhood educators can ensure that all children, including the disabled, have an opportunity to partake in active play.

3. Promote positive self-image, self-esteem, and personal control. This can be accomplished through activities such as parachute play where all children garner some measure of success.

4. Respect growth patterns and encourage physical activity at each stage. When infants commence crawling, they enjoy exploring. With this characteristic in mind, create a challenging setting that encourages crawling. Likewise, toddlers are often interested in throwing and catching, so centers should provide various size balls and bean bags to give this age group opportunities to practice there physical skills. Preschoolers begin to refine their abilities to kick and strike. These skills can be encouraged through modified games such as circle ball in small groups with an emphasis on cooperation.

5. Offer a variety of choices based on the needs, interests, and abilities of young children. For example, one activity for infants could be "crawl with me"; as the child learns to crawl, the early childhood educator could guide infants around objects and at the same time encourage the child to crawl under tables, around chairs, and to crawl forward and backward. An appropriate activity for toddlers is "Jack in the Box"; have the child squat and then yell "Jack in the Box" and jump up high. Preschoolers enjoy active play involving body parts; "my body" is a game where children are asked to touch various body parts while jumping, walking, etc. Because infants, toddlers, and preschoolers progress at their own rate, early childhood educators should not require children to perform, but merely assist in the motor development.

6. Keep activities enjoyable and nonthreatening. This can be accomplished by encouraging physical activity as a choice of play each day. Furthermore, to be effective, active play need not be structured. Early childhood educators need to provide young children with opportunities for active living throughout the day; for example, encourage walking, use the playground for throwing and kicking, or provide music which in turn stimulates young children to move.

7. Encourage a "for children by children" approach. Movement experiences must be designed so that each child can experience success, thus, the setting and the activities must be presented in an informal manner. Physical activities for young children should be diverse in nature with the caregiver creating a supportive setting in which children can achieve a broad range of motor experiences.

8. Aim programs at the appropriate developmental levels. Motor development, like the other areas of child development, is somewhat predictable. For example, infants explore their surroundings through movement and manipulation; they enjoy activities where they are required to attempt fundamental movements of walking, jumping, kicking, catching and throwing. Toddlers and preschoolers prefer active play which emphasizes swinging, sliding, balancing, riding, and pulling wheeled toys, water play and climbing, as well as loosely organized games like "Wheels The Bus" and "hide and seek."

9. Use contemporary, honest, and positive approaches that encourage a sense of belonging. Through the child-center approach, staff can ensure that movement activities are fun. A positive attitude toward physical activities can be enhanced through ample praise and encouragement, and where young children receive positive feedback (Active Alliance for Children and Youth, 1991; Eastman, 1994; Ontario Health and Physical Education Association, 1992; Department of Tourism, Culture, and Recreation, 1995).

SAMPLE ACTIVITIES FOR THE VARIOUS AGE GROUPS

For infants, toddlers, and preschoolers, there is a wide range in the level of physical abilities, so activities

Category	Typical Motor Development Stages	Movement Activities		
		You and Me Exercises	Games	Other Motor Activities
Infants (0 - 6 Months)	- reaching & grasping - rolling over - sitting - crawling - standing	- leg stretches - hand squeezes - supportive curl -ups - toothbrush tickle; light movements performed on particular areas of the child automatically make the foot move - tummy squeeze; with your whole hand, grasp the stomach gently and feel the baby pulling his/her tummy - head raises	* Focus on Simple games - peek-boo - bubble breaking; encourage the baby to reach and burst the bubbles - singing action games; for example, 'pat-a-cake' and 'This Little Piggy'	* Motor Development Activities: - Kick a bag; let the baby kick at a pillow - Baby rattle; encourage the baby to shake a rattle
Infants (6 - 12 months)	- reaching and grasping - sitting - crawling - standing - walking	- curl up; assist the child move from his/her back to a sitting position - stand-up; adult assist in raising the baby to a standing position. - rowing; the baby sits between the adult's leg, and both grasp a broom handle and reach forward and backward in a rowing motion.	- pull and tug; early childhood educators can use a variety of objects like towels - action singing rhymes - mirror game; a floor mirror encourages visual motor activities - climb about; with rolled up pillows, etc. have the child crawl over objects placed on the floor - pillow mountain; build a mountain have the children climb it.	- walk with me - crawl with me; lead the child in a crawling adventure - climb with me; crawl up a stairs with the child

Category	Typical Motor Development Stages	Movement Activities		
		You and Me Exercises	Games	Other Motor Activities
Infants (12 - 18 months)	- reaching - grasping - releasing and manipulating - sitting - crawling - climbing - walking	- pedalling; the child lies on his/her back and pedals with the legs - arm circles - helicopter; the child lies on his/her stomach and moves the hands & feet in a kicking motion. - watch me; have the child imitate the adult's actions - obstacle courses; have the child explore the concepts of over, under, etc. - reach for a toy held over head	* Focus on Simple Games - Jack in the Box; the child curls up in an imaginary box and then springs up - follow the leader - singing rhymes; for ex. 'Head & Shoulders' & 'Hokey Pokey' - in and out; the child crawls in and out of a variety of household items, for ex. chairs - drop and pick up; have the child drop an object like a ball and then pick it up.	* Motor Development Activities: -walk a block; practice walking with the child - Hand manipulation; have the child do activities with both hands - kicking; have the child kick at a large beach ball
Toddlers	- reaching - grasping - releasing and manipulating - climbing - walking - running - jumping	- wet dog shake; shake arms and legs like a wet dog - flower growing; each child pretends they are growing a flower - helicopter - tight rope; place a piece of masking tape on the floor and have the child walk along the tape	* Active Games - follow the leader - singing rhymes; for ex. 'Wheels on the Bus' - musical chairs - cookie monster tag; the adult(cookie monster) chases the child(cookie), then hugs him/her - target games - hide-and-seek	* Motor Development Activities: -Pathways; create an obstacle course with various objects - Zoo loo; imitate various animals - stop and go; practice stopping and starting

Category	Typical Motor Development Stages	Movement Activities		
		You and Me Exercises	Games	Other Motor Activities
Preschoolers	- reaching - grasping - releasing and manipulation - climbing - walking and running - jumping and landing	- windmills; have children rotate their arms in circles. - rocking rolls; while sitting on the floor with their hands under their knees, the children gently rock back and forth	* Active games - "Simon Says" - Parachute games, for example popcorn and waves. - jump the brook; make two stripes on the floor and have the children jump over them.	* Three specific movement designs: - Theme approach; based on a theme, for example transportation, the early childhood education would develop a lesson plan premised on the theme, related skill development and activities focusing on large muscle pursuits. - skill theme travel maps; children progress from the simple to learn activities to the more advanced. An example of this design is a locomotor travel map with the sequence as follows: walking - marching - galloping - hopping - running - skipping. aerobic play; aerobic exercising can follow the same sequence as for adults - warm up (action songs), workout (large muscle activities) and cool down (transition from active play to tranquil activities)

Fig. 1. Activity chart: Physical activities for infants, toddlers, and preschoolers (Sources: Canadian Institute of Child Health, 1991; Fitness Canada, 1991; Eastman, 1994; Department of Tourism, Culture and Recreation, 1995; Ontario Health and Physical Education Association, 1992).

and exercises should be specific for each child. Early childhood educators should concentrate on each child's actions rather then the outcome. Rather than telling a child what to do or doing the activity for him/her, allow the preschooler to utilize his/her imagination to conceive simple games and activities (Newfoundland Department of Tourism, Culture, and Recreation, 1995). Figure 1 summarizes appropriate physical activities for infants, toddlers, and preschoolers.

CONCLUSIONS

Young children often devise their own ideas of how and what they want to play. Furthermore, young children become bored with routine games/rules and enjoy creating their own activities. Identifying ways to utilize a child's imagination to create activities is a foundation to the active living approach. Below is a list of ideas to enhance the preceding goal:

1. Do not always follow rules of games.
2. Allow time for free play. Make equipment and materials available and allow children to explore.
3. Urge children to think of how to modify a game.
4. Cooperative games will lead to a much greater use of imagination. Ensure that there are no single winners. All children should feel successful as an outcome of the game.
5. Allow children's choices to become a reality. This will reinforce the use of the imagination (Newfoundland Department of Tourism, Culture, and Recreation, 1995).

There are a myriad of benefits to being an active child. Active play contributes to the mental, social, and emotional development of young children. Not only does movement enable children to feel good about themselves, but inactivity can contribute to health risks. More specifically, the research evidence confirms that physical activity can help young children become fit and healthy, develop social skills, improve self confidence, cope with stress and anxiety, and express ideas and feelings (Ontario Health and Physical Education Association, 1992).

REFERENCES

Active Alliance For Children and Youth (1991). *Changing times: Times to changes*. Ottawa: Active Alliance for Children and Youth.

Canadian Institute of Child Health (1991). *Moving and growing exercises and activities for two's, three's, and four's*. Ottawa: Government of Canada.

Department of Tourism, Culture, and Recreation (1995). *Active living for infants, toddlers, and preschoolers*. St. John's: Government of Newfoundland

Eastman, W. (1992). The values and purposes of human movement. *Day Care and Early Education, 19*(4), 21-24.

Eastman, W. (1994). Aerobics for young children. *Canadian Association for Health, Physical Education, Recreation and Dance Journal, 60*(1), 17-20.

Eastman, W. (1995). Developing skilled movers: Designing skill theme travel maps for young children. *Canadian Association for Health, Physical Education, Recreation, and Dance Journal, 61*(1), 9-12.

Fish, H. T. (1989). *Starting out well*. Champaign, IL: Leisure Press.

Fitness Canada (1991). *Moving and growing: Exercises and activities for the first two years*. Ottawa: Government of Canada.

Hanvey, L. (1992). *Young children living actively: A background paper*.

Hanvey, L., and Kennon, D. (1993). Because They're Very Young: Active Living for Infants, Toddlers, and Preschoolers. Working Document.

Ontario Health and Physical Education Association (1992). *Moveability*. Toronto: Ontario Health and Physical Education Association

Sanders, S. (1992). *Designing preschool movement designs*. Windsor: Human Kinetics Publishers.

World Book (1987). *Getting ready for school*. Chicago: Author.

"Hey! Where's the Toys?"

Play and Literacy in 1st Grade

**Mary Martin Patton
and Jennifer Mercer**

*Mary Martin Patton is Assistant Professor, School of Education, Texas Christian University, Fort Worth.
Jennifer Mercer is Director and K/1st Teacher, Sandia Heights Academy, Albuquerque, New Mexico.*

My son Austin galloped into his 1st-grade classroom exhibiting the same robust enthusiasm for school with which he had greeted kindergarten. He stopped abruptly. Looking around in astonishment he turned to me and asked, "Where's the toys?" I could see the confusion on his face; surely we must be in the wrong classroom! Ms. Chandler, his teacher, quickly assured him that the closet held games for rainy days. Austin was not reassured, however, as we were living in the desert where the average yearly rainfall is eight inches! I felt an immediate pang of regret and sorrow for my child, who would be experiencing the painful rite of passage from "playing" in kindergarten to doing "real work" in 1st grade.

The generally acknowledged difference between kindergarten and 1st grade becomes obvious when you walk into a "traditional" 1st-grade classroom. Opportunities for child-initiated learning barely exist. Most notably, such classrooms lack centers for construction, sand and water play, sociodramatic/housekeeping play and woodworking. The centers that are present tend to be skills-based and ditto-driven.

"Playing" in child-initiated learning centers is considered the domain of preschool and kindergarten, while 1st grade marks the transition into a "work" environment. It is as if educators believe that during the short span between kindergarten's end and 1st grade's beginning, children magically transform into abstract learners who no longer need to interact with their environment in active, playful ways. Early childhood experts generally agree, however, that learning occurs "primarily through projects, learning centers, and playful activities that reflect current interests of children" (Bredekamp, 1987; Katz & Chard, 1989). This discrepancy in theory and practice might be explained by the fact that 1st grade historically was not considered a part of early childhood education. Today, however, the National Association for the Education of Young Children defines early childhood as birth through age 8, and many school districts are beginning to include 1st, 2nd and sometimes 3rd grade in their early childhood curricula.

Developmental continuity describes the natural progression of children's developmentally appropriate education experiences as they move from preschool through the primary grades (Barbour & Seefeldt, 1993). The transition from kindergarten to 1st grade is the most abrupt transition for young children, as evidenced by frequent comments such as, "He'll never make it in 1st grade—he's just not ready!" We think these ideas will help make 1st-grade classrooms ready for all children.

The 1st-Grade Teacher's Dilemma

First-grade teachers must often contend with administrators', 2nd-grade teachers' and parents' expectations that all students will be reading by the time they leave 1st grade. Teachers often cite this pressure as the

From *Childhood Education*, Fall 1996, pp. 10-16. © 1996 by the Association for Childhood Education International, 17904 Georgia Avenue, Suite 215, Olney, MD. Reprinted by permission.

reason their curriculum is so worksheet-driven. We believe, however, that child-initiated learning centers are not incompatible with literacy development. Child-initiated learning centers support literacy acquisition by encouraging children to construct their own learning in an environment that promotes exploration and engagement. In this setting, critical 1st-grade skills of reading and writing are integrated throughout the day's activities. All learning centers foster literacy with carefully chosen materials and props that promote literacy behaviors (Strickland & Morrow, 1989). This article will describe a "How To" approach for creating a 1st-grade learning environment that is simultaneously developmentally appropriate and supportive of 1st-graders' literacy development.

Playing To Learn

Play can be defined as an activity that is pleasurable, voluntary, spontaneous, devoid of imposed tasks or regulations, intrinsically motivated, undertaken for the process rather than an expected outcome and that requires active participation (Frost, 1992). "Quality play is not a luxury but a necessity in the lives of young children. . . . Play contributes to learning and cognitive maturity as children consolidate what they know with what they are learning as they play" (Zeece & Graul, 1990, p. 15). Child-initiated learning centers promote learning through play by motivating students to engage in active learning experiences. Child-initiated learning centers are active-learning areas where students choose to engage in learning opportunities for large blocks of time (45 minutes or more). We will describe ten learning centers that we believe should be a part of every 1st-grade classroom: sociodramatic, block building, puppetry, library, construction/woodworking, sand and water, creative arts, science/math, writing and cooking. Lists of appropriate children's literature and props/materials for each center are included throughout this article. The centers should be both individually appropriate and age appropriate (i.e., materials and experiential activities should accommodate and engage all learning styles and span a diverse range of skills, interests and abilities). The aim can be accomplished if the centers support:

- social development through opportunities to practice cooperation and self-regulation
- cognitive development through incorporation of reading and writing materials in all centers
- creative growth through music, movement, creative arts, puppetry and dramatic play opportunities

The *Puppetry Center*

should occupy an area of the room where children can put on performances for an audience. Make available a variety of store-bought and child-made puppets. Discarded soft dolls and stuffed animals can be made into wonderful puppets by opening up the seams and removing some of the stuffing.

CHILDREN'S LITERATURE:
Piggies, A. & D. Wood
The Napping House, A. Wood
Women at Their Work, B. English
The Gingerbread Boy,
P. Galdone
People, P. Spier

MATERIALS/PROPS:
hand puppets, finger puppets, masks, costumes, rubber noses, stick puppets, paper, pens, flannel board and figures, puppet theater (use a cardboard television box) and materials for making puppets (egg cartons, cardboard tubes, doll clothes, fur and fabric scraps, pompons, toothpicks, pipe cleaners, Ping-Pong™ balls, yarn, wigs, beads, shells, felt, sequins, glue, paint, markers, jewelry, paper bags, drinking straws and buttons).

The *Sociodramatic Center* can reflect different themes by changing its books, props and materials. It can be the ocean floor, doctor's office, zoo, etc. Boxes from refrigerators and big-screen televisions can easily become stores, spaceships, zoos, cars, houses and barns.

CHILDREN'S LITERATURE:
My House, Mi Casa: A Book in Two Languages, R. Emberley
William's Doll, C. Zolotow
Evan's Corner, E. S. Hill
The Quilt Story, T. Johnston & T. dePaola
Hats, Hats, Hats, A. Morris
My Mother's House, My Father's House, C. B. Christiansen

MATERIALS/PROPS:
hats, clothes, food replicas, empty food containers, broken toaster, brooms, alarm clock, pillows, blankets, ethnically diverse dolls, mirror, newspapers, magazines, telephone, message pads, phone books, bed or cradle, play iron, silverware, dishes, hand towels, pots and pans, aprons, napkins, baskets, food coupons, grocery store flyers, cookbooks, recipe cards, blank recipe cards, message board, play money, calendars, kimonos, fans, serapes, African masks, moccasins, turbans and sashes.

Design Consideration and Material Selection

DIMENSION	PROVISIONS
Soft/Hard Classrooms have many hard surfaces for writing activities; soft places are needed for reading, listening to story tapes and playing.	Soften the learning environment by adding pillows, carpet, stuffed animals and comfortable furniture in the library, sociodramatic and writing centers.
Open-Ended Materials Materials that can be used in many ways encourage creativity and experimentation.	Provide lots of "beautiful junk" for the creative arts, puppetry and construction centers.
Intrusion/Seclusion and Noise Level Boundaries created by the placement of furniture and centers in the classroom determine how children move about and interact. A carefully planned environment supports individual, small group and large group interactions. While a busy hum is appropriate in any active learning environment, less noise is desirable in some centers.	Invite solitude and individual endeavors with private, quiet spaces (reading nook made from a large box, listening carrel with tape and head set) near the writing, science/math, library and creative arts centers. Invite cooperation and collaboration by providing flexibility (children can change the room arrangement) and by adjoining centers that complement each other and promote socialization: sociodramatic next to construction/block building, puppetry next to the library, and sand and water next to creative arts.
Organization and Storage of Materials Support decision making, responsibility and organizational skills by encouraging children to self-select and return materials to designated positions.	Materials are organized on low, open shelves to provide easy access and clean-up.

Figure 1

■ physical development through active manipulation of materials and props.

You can assure yourself, parents and your school's administration that you are meeting your district's objectives by posting the center's purpose and how it teaches students certain concepts and skills. As you begin to include child-initiated learning centers in the curriculum, you will be able to say with confidence, "Yes, I have a developmentally appropriate 1st-grade curriculum."

The Literate Environment

All the learning centers we will be describing include literacy materials, allowing children to playfully practice reading and writing in a purposeful setting, without pressure or expectations. Morrow and Rand (1991) propose that classrooms with an abundant supply of reading, writing and oral language materials provide an optimum literacy environment. The centers promote literacy at developmentally appropriate levels, whether a child is reenacting a story with puppets, making a book in the writing center or recording an observation in the science center.

Literacy materials that reflect life outside the classroom help children see the purpose and necessity of reading and writing. In addition to children's literature, teachers will want to include science reference books, magazines, maps, medical forms, business cards, grocery lists, newspapers and advertising flyers, as well as a variety of writing implements and paper. Storytelling and dramatization, using props such as puppets, flannel boards, hats, masks and costumes, can further extend literacy. Center time enables students to self-initiate a myriad of literacy activities when the teacher is occupied with an individual or small group.

Designing and Provisioning Learning Centers

Learning centers' success greatly depends upon design considerations and material selection. The classroom's physical arrangement influences how children interact in and react to the environment. Careful planning will ensure productive, conflict-free center time (Isenberg & Jalongo, 1993; Jones & Prescott, 1984) (see Figure 1).

Learning center materials should be open-ended and inexpensive. Open-ended materials offer unlimited possibilities for use. These include the traditional

The *Creative Arts Center* includes open-ended art materials, as well as music and movement activities. Materials for creating the right atmosphere for this center include multicultural instruments and masks, and song charts and tapes of favorite music, such as Raffi's *Down by the Bay*. *Kids in Motion* tapes are a favorite choice for movement activities, because they easily integrate instruments. The children can make instruments, masks or puppets, and choose their favorite music.

CHILDREN'S LITERATURE:
The Art Lesson, T. dePaola
Kites Sail High: A Book About Verbs, R. Heller
The Very Busy Spider, E. Carle
When the Sun Rose, B. H. Berger
Little Rabbit's Loose Tooth, L. Bate
Ben's Trumpet, R. Isadora
Thump, Thump Rat-a-Tat-Tat, G. Baer
The Usborne Story of Music, S. Mundy
The Diane Goode Book of American Folk Tales and Songs, A. Durell
One Light, One Sun, Raffi
Down by the Bay, Raffi

MATERIALS/PROPS:
easels, drying racks, loom, clothespins, aprons/old shirts, clay, play dough, paint, paintbrushes, finger-paints, pens, crayons, chalk, paper in all sizes and colors (drawing, newsprint, tag board, construction, tissue, foil, wax, wallpaper), fabric scraps, cotton balls, pipe cleaners, straws, sponges, yarn, glue, stapler, scissors, attractive found objects, song charts, song books, tape recorder with microphone, record player, records, kazoos, tambourine, shakers, assorted bells, drums, tone blocks, rhythm sticks, gongs, maracas, cymbals, piano, pictures of instruments, handmade instruments and cassettes/records of music from a variety of cultures.

manipulatives as well as "beautiful junk" (i.e., all those collected and donated materials that become important construction materials for the classroom). We suggest sending a letter home asking for "beautiful junk" to help begin your classroom collection of props and materials. The classroom library should include books for research, storybooks and books that reflect ethnic diversity and feature non-stereotypical characters.

Getting Started
Making the transition from a teacher-directed environment to a child-initiated one is a gradual process. You should explore what works best for you. As teachers who have been through this process, we recommend the following steps:

- Start with a few basic centers and add others as time and energy permit.
- Build upon your students' natural enthusiasm by involving them in the centers' development. A sense of ownership will encourage them to gather materials, organize the space and dictate the rules. We are always delighted at our students' innovations!
- Investigate community resources and thrift shops and encourage parents to contribute discarded materials.
- Include books, writing materials, signs, catalogs and environmental print in all centers.
- Incorporate multicultural materials in all learning centers through thoughtful selection of books, props and other materials.
- Encourage fluidity of materials and groupings by allowing students to move materials to different locations and by not limiting the number of students

The *Cooking Center* can be as simple as a hot plate with measuring and cooking utensils for making simple snacks. If space is available, it may include a stove, microwave and a sink. Individual portion recipe books create sheer delight for those independent, budding chefs.

CHILDREN'S LITERATURE:
Bread, Bread, Bread, A. Morris
Stone Soup, M. Brown
Daddy Makes the Best Spaghetti, A. G. Hines
Johnny Appleseed, S. Kellogg
Eating the Alphabet, L. Ehlert
The Very Hungry Caterpillar, E. Carle
Strega Nona, T. dePaola
Pancakes, Pancakes!, E. Carle

MATERIALS/PROPS:
aprons, utensils, bowls, ingredients, chef hats, dish towels, recipe cards and books, cooking magazines, grocery lists, food charts, measuring charts, grocery store ads, food poems, food posters and familiar restaurant and grocery store signs

The *Sand and Water Center* is often the most used. The material in the "water table" should be changed frequently to reflect both the students' interests and your theme. You can use water, sand, beans, macaroni and birdfeed (especially for outdoors in the spring and fall). Mixing sand and water together will create a whole new experience!

CHILDREN'S LITERATURE:
Swimmy, L. Lionni
Our Home Is the Sea, R. Levinson
Hermit the Crab, E. Carle
A First Look at Sea Shells, Selman & Hunt
Life in the Oceans: A Planet Earth Book, N. Wu
The Sand Horse, A. Turnball
A Water Snakes Year, D. Gove
Whales, G. Gibbons

MATERIALS/PROPS:
water wheel, shovels, scoops, plastic containers, sponges, cookie cutters, pans, straws, tubing, funnels, squeeze bottles, strainers, sinking and floating objects, corks, sifters, pans, PVC pipe and fittings, spades, spoons, pitchers, tin cans with holes, water pump, toys (trucks, boats, cars, people, animals and trees), seashells, muffin tins, cake and Jello™ molds, and food coloring.

The *Science/ Math Center* should include literature that supports specimens students bring in, as well as the current theme. Every student should have a journal for recording observations and discoveries. You will want to provide objects for measuring (Popsicle™ sticks, string, tape measure, ruler); objects to sort, weigh, classify, count and order; a variety of pets (hamster, guinea pig, rabbit, bird, snake) and other living things to observe and care for (plants, fish, crayfish, pillbugs, ants, etc.)

who work or play together at any center. If the space cannot accommodate the number of children who want to use it, make more space, rather than limit the possibilities.

Whether you begin with one basic child-initiated learning center or ten, introducing the center and establishing rules are crucial to success. We recommend introducing only one or two centers at a time. All the centers are "closed" at the beginning of the year. We wrap them up like packages and open one or two each day over the first two weeks of school. The anticipation and excitement delight the children. Students generate rules for using the centers and review them when necessary. Any problems arising in a center can be resolved in class meetings.

Finally, child-initiated learning centers should not be saved for use only when children have completed their seatwork or for the last 15 minutes of the day. Centers must be

CHILDREN'S LITERATURE:
Chickens Aren't the Only Ones, R. Heller
The Brambleberry's Animal Book of Big and Small Shapes, M. Mayer & G. McDermott
Cactus Hotel, B. Guiberson
Brother Eagle, Sister Sky: A Message from Chief Seattle, S. Jeffers
Planting a Rainbow, L. Ehlert
Anno's Counting Book, M. Anno
Anno's Math Games, M. Anno
Over in the Meadow, J. Langstaff
The Magic School Bus series, J. Cole
Rain Forest Secrets, A. Dorros
Fish Eyes: A Book You Can Count On, L. Ehlert
The Seasons of Arnold's Apple Tree, G. Gibbons
Wilfrid Gordon McDonald Partridge, M. Fox
Charlie's House, R. Schermbrucker
Ranger Rick magazine
Discovery magazine

MATERIALS/PROPS:
puzzles, pattern blocks, geoboards, shape sorters, nesting toys, Erector Sets™, Cuisenaire™ rods, foreign coins, materials to string patterns (beads, macaroni, seeds), pegboards, Tinker Toys™, dominoes, bulbs, batteries, magnets, microscopes, magnifying glasses, prisms, compasses, scales, timers and natural materials (seed pods, pine cones, feathers, raw cotton and birds' nests).

The *Writing Center* will house an author's table, mailbox, computer for desktop publishing and a tape recorder for story dictation. Environmental print, favorite books, word boxes, poem charts and sentence strips make writing accessible to both emergent and accomplished writers. Here, journal writing becomes published work, the Big Bad Wolf may get a letter of warning and children can create individual "thank-you" letters for the firefighters they met on a field trip.

CHILDREN'S LITERATURE:
The Secret Birthday Message, E. Carle
A Letter to Santa Claus, R. Impey & S. Porter
The Jolly Postman or Other People's Letters, J. & A. Ahlberg
Rain Makes Applesauce, J. Scheer
How a Book Is Made, Aliki

MATERIALS/PROPS:
markers, pens, paper, chalk and chalkboard, a whiteboard, variety of paper and stationery, index cards, typewriter, word processor, alphabet stamps, picture stamps, hole punches, staplers, blank books, picture file, old calendars, posters, magazines, newspapers, catalogs, stencils and stickers.

viewed as an important part of the curriculum, and students must have large blocks of time in which to engage in the learning center activities on a daily basis.

Summary

While 1st-grade teachers must be mindful of state and district curriculum guidelines, strict adherence to using only textbooks and workbooks is not necessary. Curriculum objectives *can* be met in a literacy-rich, developmentally appropriate environment. Take a few moments to set up a list of objectives for your centers. You will be amazed at the number of skills that these centers can reinforce across all content areas. After choosing your initial centers, heighten parents' interest in the environment by asking them to help you gather materials and literature. If you are still skeptical, try one center for a few weeks and simply observe. You will be astounded by the children's literacy behaviors, language, learning and enthusiasm! You will be well on your way to creating an interesting, motivating and developmentally appropriate learning environment. In turn, your students will perceive their playful journey into literacy as exciting, positive and meaningful.

◆

References

Barbour, N. H., & Seefeldt, C. (1993). *Developmental continuity across preschool and primary grades.* Wheaton, MD: Association for Childhood Education International.

Bredekamp, S. (1987). *Developmentally appropriate practice in early childhood programs serving children from birth through age 8.* Washington, DC: National Association for the Education of Young Children.

Frost, J. (1992). *Play and playscapes.* Albany, NY: Delmar.

Isenberg, J. P., & Jalongo, M. R. (1993). *Creative expression and play in the early childhood curriculum.* New York: Macmillan.

Jones, E., & Prescott, E. (1984). *Dimensions of teaching-learning environments: A handbook for teachers in elementary schools and day care centers.* Pasadena, CA: Pacific Oaks College.

Katz, L., & Chard, S. (1989). *Engaging children's minds: The project approach.* Norwood, NJ: Ablex Publishing Company.

Morrow, L., & Rand, M. (1991). Promoting literacy during play by designing early childhood classroom environments. *The Reading Teacher, 44*(6), 396-402.

Strickland, D., & Morrow, L. (1989). *Emerging literacy: Young children learn to read and write.* Newark, DE: International Reading Association.

Zeece, P. D., & Graul, S. K. (1990). Learning to play: Playing to learn. *Day Care and Early Education, 18*(1), 11-15.

The *Block Building / Manipulatives Center* works well when situated next to the sociodramatic center, because play will often spill over from one center to the other. This center's area must be large enough to support structures. Children will be delighted by displays of Polaroid pictures and written stories or descriptions of their creations. Pictures of local businesses and of your students' homes will help make connections to "real life."

CHILDREN'S LITERATURE:
A House Is a House for Me, M. A. Hoberman
Anno's USA, M. Anno
City Seen from A to Z, R. Isadora
Grandmother's Adobe Dollhouse, M. M. Smith
Animals and the New Zoos, P. Curtis
What It Feels Like To Be a Building, F. Wilson
This Is My House, A. Dorros
Up Goes the Skyscraper!, G. Gibbons
Castle, D. Macaulay

MATERIALS/PROPS:
solid wood blocks, hollow blocks, interlocking blocks (large and small), cardboard blocks, milk carton blocks, adobe blocks boxes, cardboard tubes, construction toys, hard hats, pictures of construction projects, Lincoln Logs™, road signs, manipulatives, toys of farm/zoo/wild animals, miniature people, toy dinosaurs, vehicles, blueprints, writing materials for making traffic signs and billboards, sheets and fabric for constructing tents.

The *Library Center* will house anything you can scrounge from your libraries, donations, book clubs, etc. Books on tape at the listening center give non-readers the opportunity to "read" along. Books written and illustrated by your students are always popular!

CHILDREN'S LITERATURE:
The Wednesday Surprise, E. Bunting
Chicka Chicka Boom Boom, B. Martin, Jr. & J. Archambault
Jambo Means Hello: Swahili Alphabet Book, M. Feelings
A Jewish Holiday ABC, M. Drucker & R. Pocock
Animalia, G. Base
Fables, A. Lobel
Handmade ABC, L. Bourke
Knots on a Counting Rope, B. Martin Jr. & J. Archambault

MATERIALS/PROPS:
shelves, rug, pillows, bulletin board, felt board and felt figures, stuffed animals, rocking chair, alphabet chart, tactile letters (plastic, magnetic, wooden, felt, etc.), bookmarks, checkout sheet, ABC index cards, posters of children's books, headphones/tape player, book/tape sets, magazines, catalogs, newspapers and big books.

The *Construction/Woodworking Center* works well beside the block center. Promote safety with goggles and hard hats as children enthusiastically plan and build everything from bird houses to original sculptures. This center often lures even the most introverted children into action! Close supervision is necessary.

CHILDREN'S LITERATURE:
How a House Is Built, G. Gibbons
Houses and Homes, A. Morris
My Screwdriver, My Hammer, My Saw, My Drill, and *My Wrench*, Warner Juvenile Book Series
Need a House, Call Ms. Mouse, G. Mendoza
Animal Architecture, J. O. Dewey
Architects Make Zigzags: Looking at Architecture from A to Z, D. Maddex
Round Buildings, Square Buildings, & Buildings That Wiggle Like a Fish, P. M. Isaacson
Unbuilding, D. Macaulay

MATERIALS/PROPS:
safety goggles, workbench, wood scraps, nails, screws, nuts and bolts, rulers, sandpaper, paint, glue, hammer, screwdriver, wrench, saw, pliers, vise, compass, clamps, scrap materials (e.g., Popsicle™ sticks, tile samples, latches, hinges, packing "popcorn," bottle caps), shoe boxes, home design magazines, house designs, paper and drawing instruments.

TEACHER RESOURCE BOOKS

Many resource books are available to teachers; we found these to be particularly helpful.

Blackwell, F., & Hohmann, C. (1991). *High/Scope K-3 curriculum series-science.* Ypsilanti, MI: The High/Scope Press.

Hill, D. M. (1993). *Mud, sand, and water.* Washington, DC: National Association for the Education of Young Children.

Hirsch, E. S. (Ed.). (1993). *The block book.* Washington, DC: National Association for the Education of Young Children.

Hohmann, C. (1991). *High/Scope K-3 curriculum series-mathematics.* Ypsilanti, MI: The High/Scope Press.

Lorton, M. B. (1995). *Mathematics their way.* Reading, MA: Addison Wesley.

McNeill, E., Allen, J., & Schmidt, V. (1981). *Cultural awareness for young children.* Mt. Rainier, MD: Gryphon House.

Renfro, N., & Hunt, T. (1982). *Puppetry in early childhood education.* Austin, TX: N. Renfro Studies.

Routman, R. (1988). *Transitions: From literature to literacy.* Portsmouth, NH: Heinemann.

Routman, R. (1991). *Invitations: Changing as teachers and learners K-12.* Portsmouth, NH: Heinemann.

Skeen, P., Garner, A. P., & Cartwright S. (1993). *Woodworking for young children.* Washington, DC: National Association for the Education for Young Children.

Veitch, B., & Harms, T. (1981). *Cook and learn: Nutritious foods from various cultures* (Pictorial single portion recipes). Reading, MA: Addison Wesley.

Sharing Books with Infants and Toddlers: Facing the Challenges

Barbara N. Kupetz and Elise Jepson Green

Read to the children in an infant or toddler group? You must be kidding! All they want to do is chew and grab at the book or just walk away. Trying to read to this age is a very frustrating experience for everyone.

Hearing early childhood educators and child care providers respond in this way about reading to the young children in their care is not uncommon. Although the literature on the importance of reading to the very young is extensive (Kontos 1986; Lamme & Packer 1986; Dinsmore 1988; Trelease 1989; Hasson 1991) and most early childhood professionals realize the value of introducing books early, it is the frustration they feel in actually implementing book sharing that stands in the way of frequent and early book experiences.

Barbara N. Kupetz, *Ed.D., was an early childhood educator for many years before becoming an associate professor in the Department of Professional Studies at Indiana University of Pennsylvania. Currently she teaches courses in early childhood education and children's literature.*

Elise Jepson Green, *M.Ed., has diverse and extensive teaching experience in the field of early childhood education. She currently is a teaching associate and a doctoral student in the Department of Professional Studies at Indiana University of Pennsylvania.*

It is never too early to begin reading to children! As one works with the very youngest audiences, it is easy to see the beauty, imagination, and magic the world of books can bring to children. The reading of Dorothy Butler's (1980) *Babies Need Books* as well as some of the more recent writings by Fields (1987); Glazer (1986); Goodman (1986); Jalongo (1990); Larrick (1980); Oppenheim, Brenner, and Boegehold (1986); Silvern (1985); Smith (1989); Snow and Ninio (1986); and Taylor (1983) clearly identify the many benefits derived from reading to infants and toddlers. Barclay, Benelli, and Curtis (1995) believe that infant and toddler child care settings are capable of developing and promoting children's literacy skills when the environment is structured to support interactions similar to those found in homes of early readers.

The benefits of early book experiences include helping the infants' eyes to focus and their recognition of objects, development of language, and enhancement of listening skills; in addition to building sensory awareness, reinforcing basic concepts, stimulating the imagination, extending experiences, providing a good reading model, and establishing physical closeness so critical to the young child's emotional and social development.

The sharing of a book is also just one of many ways a child may form social bonds and necessary attachments. In this intertwining of the social and emotional dimension of behavior, very young children begin to find ways to communicate with adults and become involved in the social process. The infant who has interest in sights and sounds can begin to show interest in the people around her. Greenspan and Greenspan (1985) call this "falling in love." During this "courtship," infants will look eagerly into faces and share emotions that are most expressive when the attachment figure is involved (Dworetzky 1990). Reading a book to an infant gives opportunities to interact in this social way.

Reading books to young children is a powerful way of introducing them to a lifelong relationship with quality literature. It has also been one of the early experiences identified as making a significant difference in later reading success (Anderson et al. 1985). Friedberg (1989) believes that teachers and caregivers can enrich the lives of children by providing an abundance of good books, offering a routine that includes daily storytimes, and finding time for spontaneous book sharing. Who can forget the dramatic statement resulting from the findings of the Commission on Reading: "The single most important activity for building the knowledge required for eventual success in reading is reading aloud to children" (Anderson et al. 1985, 23)?

Who can forget the dramatic statement resulting from the findings of the Commission on Reading: "The single most important activity for building the knowledge required for eventual success in reading is reading aloud to children"?

What are the parameters and the challenges?

In spite of all the support for introducing books early and often, why then do we hear early childhood educators saying, "But it's so hard to do"? Why do we see a reading center in early childhood centers but find it primarily used by the three- and four-year-olds? Reading to the youngest of audiences can be problematic unless early childhood centers and the professionals working in them recognize the parameters, face the challenges, and work together to transcend the difficulties.

When reading to young audiences, it is not necessary or appropriate to have a structured reading time. Caregivers who require a group of toddlers to sit and listen to a story together are asking for trouble. The following scenario pictures the potentially disastrous situation that can occur when structure is enforced. David, an experienced caregiver, describes the experience:

David is reading to a group of 12 toddlers, ranging in age from 14 to 30 months, and two caregivers who are seated on the floor in front of him. One child stands up and begins walking away but is corralled and reseated by a vigilant caregiver. Two children begin quarreling over the caregiver's lap that they co-occupy, each attempting to dethrone the other. The youngest toddler escapes the watchful eye of a caregiver and starts to play on a nearby climbing structure. A caregiver plucks the toddler from the climber and returns

her to the story area, kicking and screaming to be released from the caregiver's hold. David has been reading less than three minutes, but the scene has already become a chaotic battleground of restless toddlers and determined caregivers.

Knowing appropriate strategies for sharing books with infants and toddlers could mean the difference between having a pleasant experience, for both the adult and child, or one that you might prefer to quickly forget. The following is a scenario that

© Barbara N. Kupetz

Reading to infants and toddlers is certainly not a large-group activity. It can effectively occur only in very small groups or in a one-to-one pairing.

illustrates a positive approach to reading books with infants and toddlers.

Maggie, a young toddler, has been clutching a book as she wanders around the classroom, being careful not to put it down. She glances across the room and notices another toddler leaving the lap of a caregiver. She seizes the opportunity and quickly plops down in the recently vacated caregiver's lap.

Maggie then takes the caregiver's hands and guides them around her waist to form a secure embrace while opening the book. She looks back at the caregiver as if to say, "I'm ready for you to begin reading." Since Maggie has control of the book, the "reading" begins from the back of the book, with the pages turned at Maggie's discretion.

The caregiver begins describing the illustrations and comments on the things found on each of the pages, taking cues from Maggie's deliberate pointing and questioning. Maggie is intensely focused throughout this interactive process as she turns the pages back and forth.

With each passage through the same book, Maggie develops an ever-increasing command of her language. She communicates her understanding of these concepts by pointing and naming objects and symbols throughout the book. Maggie is later seen testing a newly acquired concept as she declares a rectangle to be a "trunk" like the one the pirates had in the book she read.

In examining early childhood programs, it is clear that most often it is an issue of organization or a lack of information that makes book sharing difficult. Reading to infants and toddlers is certainly not a large-group activity. It can effectively occur only in very small groups or in a one-to-one pairing. With infants, this shared experience must be intimate and familiar. These requirements mean that child caregivers hoping to provide book experiences must reduce their facility's child-adult ratio to offer optimum interactions. The NAEYC recommendations for toddler programs suggest a 4:1 child-adult ratio and a one-to-one pairing for infants (Bredekamp 1987). Therefore, a center may need to hire additional staff, make changes in staffing patterns, or often schedule parent and other volunteer assistants to facilitate the practice of "reading" informally and on an impromptu basis to toddlers.

What books are best?

Even the youngest children can be connoisseurs of books. They do enjoy a wide variety of literature. It is the sound of the reader's voice that gets the young child's attention even before he can focus on the pictures. The warmth and security of being held and the melodic, soothing sound of the reader's voice make for a very pleasurable combination.

Even when a children's book is not available, using one's voice effectively to read any printed material is a soothing experience and an opportunity for dialoguing or "dancing" with the child. The simple conversations you have with children while dressing or rocking provide opportunities for them to respond to the sound of the human voice and enjoy the rhythm of language.

Toddlers love the repetitive language of such predictable books as Bill Martin Jr.'s *Brown Bear, Brown Bear, What Do You See?* (1967) as well as many of the familiar retold classics, including Paul Galdone's version of *The Gingerbread Boy* (1975). These books offer repetitive language patterns and phrases that invite children to actually participate in the story.

Rhythmical-language books

Books with rhythmical language may be the first books children encounter. Very young children focusing on the comforting voice of the reader enjoy "Mother Goose" rhymes and lullabies, which allow even the youngest child to explore the rhythm and music of language. Consider the alliteration of "Diddle, diddle, dumpling" and "Peter, Peter pumpkin eater." They call out to be said again and again. Some other good choices with enjoyable rhythmical qualities include *The Three Little Kittens* (Cauley 1982) and *Chicka Chicka Boom Boom* (Martin & Archambault 1989).

Point-and-say books

As the name implies, these books are best used with children as they begin to focus on pictures. This happens around the ages of four to six months and continues into toddlerhood. These books should have simple, uncluttered illustrations that allow the reader to point to the familiar pictures, such as animals, toys, family members, or trucks, and clearly name them. "See the kitty? Where's the kitty in the picture? That looks like Grandma's kitty doesn't it?"

After a time of adult pointing and naming, the child will begin to point to pictures that the reader refers to. Some good point-and-say books with familiar objects include Tana Hoban's *What Is It?* (1984) or any of Helen Oxenbury's books, such as *Family, Friends,* or *Playing* (1981), which are especially appropriate for very young children. Raines and Isbell (1988) recommend following the story's main character throughout the scenes, focusing on the individual's actions to assist the child with story progression.

Touch-and-smell books

These books give young children the opportunity to use their senses and invite them to participate in the reading experience as they learn about their world. A classic, such as *Pat the Bunny* (Kundhardt 1962), provides a variety of textures and manipulative activities as children *feel* Daddy's rough beard and *smell* the bouquet of flowers. Other participatory books include *Where's My Fuzzy Blanket?* (Carter 1991), which continues to give children enjoyment over and over again as they open cupboard doors and toy boxes in search of the soft blue blanket.

Board books

This type of book is designed to take the abuse of the youngest reader and last through teething, when everything is put into a child's mouth, as well as the exploration and testing of new-found skills of grabbing, tearing, and throwing. The thick, laminated cardboard of the board book endures more child handling than does the traditional paper book. Because of this, adults can allow children to look at the book independently, even if their hands are going from mouth to book as they often are. As a child reaches eight to ten months, adults should begin to encourage proper handling of books and to identify a special place for storing books. This is a time when children, if given the opportunity, are eager to participate in turning pages and holding the book. They love to

be actively "reading"! Some excellent choices in a board book would be *Goodnight Moon* (Brown 1947) or any of the books in the series by Jan Omerod (1985), Helen Oxenbury (1981), or Rosemary Wells (1985). Other child-tested choices include *1,2,3* (Hoban 1985) and *Bye Bye Daddy* (Ziefert & Ernst 1988).

© Ron Juliette

Early picture storybooks

As children approach their first birthday, many become interested in looking at pictures and listening to short, simple stories. These selections should have few words per page and simple illustrations. At this stage a child's interests center around self and the familiar. They need books that can be shared a few pages at a time or in a brief sitting. Many short storytimes are better than one long one.

By this age, children will begin to respond to books in several ways. Very young listeners may demonstrate verbal behaviors as they giggle and coo, or they also may turn toward the reader to watch the action of reading rather than what is being read. As children move toward toddlerhood, they begin to follow the adults pointing cues. They are able to know

a picture by its name and point to the appropriate picture as an adult reads. They may be curious about what will happen next and show increased interest in the story itself.

Some good choices for the young child who is ready to hear an early picture storybook would include *Ten, Nine, Eight* (Bang 1983), *The Runaway Bunny* (Brown 1972), *The Very Hungry Caterpillar* (Carle 1969), *Peekaboo Bunny* (Capucilli 1994), *Are You My Mother?* (Eastman 1960), *The Snowy Day* (Keats 1962), *Our Home Is the Sea* (Levinson 1988), and *Edward in Deep Water* (Wells 1995).

Young children need materials and real experiences that support concepts they are learning. The child who has planted a tomato seed, watered it, watched it grow, and ultimately picked and ate it will have a much better idea of what the word *tomato* or the illustration represents when seeing it in a book. Pictures and words are symbols that stand for real things in a child's life. Caregivers need to provide opportunities for infants and toddlers to have meaningful experiences. It is from these concrete experiences that young children make connections between the abstract knowledge they are constructing and their environment. Children make inferences from books and compare what happens in stories with what they know about the world (Miller 1990).

Today, more than ever before, the diversity of participants in our programs will include individuals whose home language is not English. Bilingualism is valuable and should be nurtured when possible. You may be fortunate to have bilingual caregivers, parents, or community volunteers working with you in your program. Young children learn to use language in natural settings while

Don't Say No!

Anne Sibley O'Brien

> **Books with rhythmical language may be the first books children encounter. Very young children focus on the comforting voice of the reader.**

playing with people and things in their environment. The sharing of books is a great way of supporting a child's home language or for introducing a second one.

Guidelines for book selection

The books identified here are a very small sample of the many quality books available for children. Rather than specifically citing additional books, identifying some general guidelines for book selection will be more valuable for those who want to become more involved in individual or small-group reading with infants and toddlers. By keeping these tips for choosing books in mind, you can make good selections in any children's library or bookstore (see box at right).

Guidelines for reading

"But," you say, "even with the best of books, reading to a very young child is a struggle. What am I doing wrong?" It may not be that you are doing something wrong, but just expecting too much. A well-chosen book isn't everything. There are many other things that make sharing books with young children easy and fun, too! Here are some guidelines to help early childhood professionals experience successful infant and toddler book reading sessions.

• **Read to a young child when you are in the mood to do so.** If you are having a bad day or have disturbing things on your mind, your reading will be affected.

• **Choose a book that is not only appropriate for the youngster but also that is one you like.** Enjoying the book you choose makes the experience more pleasurable, and you'll probably do a better job!

• **Timing is really important.** Don't expect a book to quiet a fussy baby or rambunctious toddler. The child must be ready to hear a story. The time must be

Mother's Helper

Helen Oxenbury

Tips for Infant and Toddler Book Selection

• Does the book appeal to you, the reader?
• Is the book well constructed and durable?
• Is the book safe? Does it have any pointed, sharp corners or small removable parts?
• Are the pictures simple and clear on an uncluttered background?
• Does the book use bright colors that contrast each other for easier focusing by the young child?
• Is the book accurate in content (puppies should not be purple and bunnies should not be green)?
• Are the pictures predominantly familiar objects in the child's environment, mixed with a few unfamiliar objects to stimulate the young child's curiosity?
• Does the book invite the child to participate and interact?
• Is the book short for an active child with a short attention span?

---

one when the child seems alert, curious, and interested.

• **Have a special reading routine established.** Although books can be read at any time, having a special reading time helps children know when to expect a story. Routines are important in the lives of young children. Establish a reading routine in your early childhood program, but do not expect or even urge any child to participate.

• **Position the child so that pictures can be easily seen.** For the newborn, your voice is more important than the pictures. However, as very young children reach the point at which holding up their heads is possible, pictures do become interesting. Also keep in mind the curiosity of the toddler. They want to see the puppy in the story and seeing encourages dialogue with the adult.

• **Allow the child to assist you in the reading experience.** Particularly with board books, very young children can help turn pages if you keep all of the pages in your right hand, except the next one to be turned. In this way, only one of the sturdy cardboard pages will turn at a time.

• **Point to and identify things in the pictures as you read.** As children get older, you can encourage their pointing to the pictures as you name objects and read about them.

• **React positively to all of the child's attempts in nam-**

ing objects, turning pages, or attempting any form of verbalization. Remember, even the smallest attempt is a step in the right direction, and positive reinforcement does make a difference—even with babies.

• **Use your voice as a tool, which makes reading exciting and interesting.** In general, using a quiet, soft voice is best, but there are times when your voice can show excitement, surprise, or any number of other emotions. The best way to read to young children is to sound like you're having a good time, too!

• **Tune into the developmental stages of children.** If you know that from about five to nine months of age a baby usually will attempt to handle a book as he or she does most things by mouthing, hitting, tugging, twisting, and pulling, you will not be surprised when this happens. Have something else ready for the baby to chew, pull, or tug on while you maintain possession of the book.

• **Be responsive to your audience.** This should be an enjoyable time for adult and child alike! If, for whatever reason, both child and adult cannot enjoy the experience—*stop*. Watch for the visual cues children present that tell you they have had enough. These may include crying, pushing to get off your lap, arching their backs in an attempt to push away, or simply walking away from the reader. You know the children in your care. You'll know when it's time to put the book down.

Conclusions

As early childhood professionals, we must not fail to introduce infants and toddlers to books simply because such experiences present challenges. We cannot put book experiences off until later, merely assuming children will encounter books as they move through childhood. If early childhood educators wait until children are four or five to share with them the wonder and excitement books have to offer, we have waited too long.

Babies and toddlers are enriched by books. Equally important, the relationship between the child and the adult is enriched. So, the next time you are considering sharing a book with an infant or toddler, think no more. Do it! Both reader and listener will be glad you did!

References

Anderson, R.C., E. Hiebert, J.A. Scott, & I.A.G. Wilkinson. 1985. *Becoming a nation of readers: The report of the Commission on Reading.* Washington, DC: National Academy of Education.

Barclay, K., C. Benelli, & A. Curtis. 1995. Literacy begins at birth: What caregivers can learn from parents of children who read early. *Young Children* 50 (4): 24–28.

Bredekamp, S., ed. 1987. *Developmentally appropriate practice in early childhood programs serving children from birth through age 8.* Exp. ed. Washington, DC: NAEYC.

Butler, D. 1980. *Babies need books.* New York: Atheneum.

Dinsmore, K.E. 1988. Baby's first books. *Childhood Education* 64 (4): 215–19.

Dworetzky, J.P. 1990. *Introduction to child development.* St. Paul, MN: West Publishing.

Fields, M. 1987. *Let's begin reading right: A developmental approach to literacy.* Columbus, OH: Merrill.

Friedberg, J. 1989. Food for thought. Helping today's toddlers become tomorrow's readers: A pilot parent participation project offered through a Pittsburgh health agency. *Young Children* 44 (2): 13–16.

Glazer, J. 1986. *Literature for young children.* Columbus, OH: Merrill.

Goodman, Y. 1986. Children coming to know literacy. In *Emergent literacy: Writing and reading,* eds. W. Teale & E. Sulzby, 1–14. Norwood, NJ: Ablex.

Greenspan, S., & N.T. Greenspan. 1985. *First feelings: Milestones in the emotional development of your baby and child.* New York: Viking.

Hasson, E.A. 1991. Reading with infants and toddlers. *Day Care and Early Education* 19 (1): 35–37.

Jalongo, M.R. 1990. *Early childhood language arts.* Boston: Allyn & Bacon.

Kontos, S. 1986. What preschool children know about reading and how they learn it. *Young Children* 42 (1): 58–66.

Lamme, L.L., & A.B. Packer. 1986. Bookreading behavior of infants. *The Reading Teacher* 39 (6): 504–08.

Larrick, N. 1980. *Children's reading begins at home.* Winston-Salem, NC: Starstream Products.

Miller, J. 1990. Three-year-olds in their reading corner. *Young Children* 46 (1): 51–54.

Oppenheim, J., B. Brenner, & B.O. Boegehold. 1986. *Choosing books for kids.* New York: Ballantine.

Raines, S.C., & R. Isbell. 1988. Tuck talking about wordless books into your classroom. *Young Children* 43 (6): 24–25.

Silvern, S. 1985. Parent involvement and reading achievement: Research and implications for practice. *Childhood Education* 62 (1): 44–51.

Smith, C.B. 1989. Reading aloud: An experience for sharing. *The Reading Teacher* 42 (4): 320.

Snow, C., & A. Ninio. 1986. The contracts of literacy: What children learn from learning to read books. In *Emergent literacy: Writing and reading,* eds. W. Teale & E. Sulzby, 116–38. Norwood, NJ: Ablex.

Taylor, D. 1983. *Family literacy: Young children learning to read and write.* Portsmouth, NH: Heinemann.

Trelease, J. 1989. *The new read aloud handbook.* New York: Penguin.

Children's books

Bang, 1983. *Ten, nine, eight.* New York: Greenwillow.

Brown, M.W. 1947. *Goodnight moon.* New York: Harper & Row.

Brown, M.W. 1972. *The runaway bunny.* New York: Harper & Row.

Capucilli, A. 1994. *Peekaboo bunny.* New York: Scholastic.

Carle, E. 1969. *The very hungry caterpillar.* Cleveland, OH: Collins-World.

Carter, N. 1991. *Where's my fuzzy blanket.* New York: Scholastic.

Cauley, L.B. 1982. *The three little kittens.* New York: Putnam.

Eastman, P.D. 1960. *Are you my mother?* New York: Random House.

Galdone, P. 1975. *The gingerbread boy.* New York: Clarion.

Hoban, T. 1984. *What is it?* New York: Greenwillow.

Hoban, T. 1985. *1, 2, 3.* New York: Greenwillow.

Keats, E.J. 1962. *The snowy day.* New York: Viking.

Kundhardt, D. [1940] 1962. *Pat the bunny.* New York: Golden Books.

Levinson, R. 1988. *Our home is the sea.* New York: Dutton.

Martin Jr., B. 1967. *Brown bear, brown bear, what do you see?* New York: Holt, Rinehart & Winston.

Martin, B., & J. Archambault. 1989. *Chicka chicka boom boom.* New York: Simon & Schuster.

Omerod, J. 1985. *Dad's back. Messy baby. Reading. Sleeping.* Baby Books series. New York: Lothrop.

Oxenbury, H. 1981. *Family. Friends. Playing.* The Baby Board Books series. Boston: Simon & Schuster.

Wells, R. 1985. *Max's bath. Max's bedtime. Max's birthday. Max's breakfast.* Baby's First Books series. New York: Dial.

Wells, R. 1995. *Edward in deep water.* New York: Dial.

Ziefert, J., & L. Ernst. 1988. *Bye bye daddy.* New York: Viking.

Regie Routman

Back to the Basics of Whole Language

Assuring parents that students are learning both basic and higher-order language arts skills goes a long way in promoting your program's success—and student achievement.

© Susie Fitzhugh

The ongoing debate about the best way to teach reading and writing has heated up to a rolling boil that shows no signs of simmering down. Across the United States, politicians, policymakers, and the media are having a field day bashing public schools.

In particular, the controversy rages over whole language and phonics, especially at the primary grade levels. Good news—such as the successes of whole language programs in schools in states like New Jersey, Virginia, and Ohio—tends to get lost.

Low test scores in reading on the 1994 National Assessment of Educational Progress (NAEP) further fueled the controversy debate. According to these scores, most U.S. students can decode and comprehend literally; they can read at basic levels. However, they have difficulty thinking about and constructing knowledge from the information they have read. Ironically, media reports continue to emphasize that we are not teaching decoding skills and the basics and that students are failing to learn how to read. Much of the backlash against whole language is based on incomplete reporting. For example, the most recent Gallup Poll reports:

> The public has been negatively affected by distorted, biased, or inadequate media coverage. The public believes, for example, that American student achievement does not compare favorably with that of students in other developed countries, even though recent studies show American students near

the top in reading and no worse than average in math (Elam, Rose, and Gallup 1996).

Whole Language Versus Phonics in California and Elsewhere

In part because California is our most populous and diverse state, language arts instruction there has greatly influenced the rest of the country. In 1987 the California Department of Education adopted its "English-Language Arts Framework," which moved away from a skills model of teaching reading. Educators from more than 30 states either adopted or adapted the model of quality literature as the heart of the reading program. Erroneously, what was never more than a "literature-based" reading program became equated with whole language.

When California's students had dismally low scores on the 1994 NAEP, the media made whole language the scapegoat. Critics rarely mentioned other problems in the state: the highest class sizes in the nation, low education funding, inadequate school and public libraries, great numbers of students whose primary language is not English, and insufficient staff development for teachers.

After California's poor test results—even among white students and children of college graduates—a state task force studied the problem. After reviewing extensive research and hearing testimony from many reading and curriculum experts, the task force recom-

From *Educational Leadership,* February 1997, pp. 70-74. © 1997 by the Association for Supervision and Curriculum Development. All rights reserved. Reprinted by permission.

mended that teachers use a "systematic skills instruction program."

Admirably, the task force called for a "balanced and comprehensive" approach that continues to incorporate rich literature. In actuality, however, the state's recent advisory on how to teach reading emphasizes instruction in phonemic awareness (the ability to hear and manipulate the discrete sound chunks of words), letter names and shapes, and systematic, explicit phonics (letter/sound correspondence) (California Department of Education 1996).

These new recommendations are having ramifications across the United States—both in textbook adoptions and in state and district mandates. As responsible educators, however, we must remember that if we just teach kids how to decode words and not how to read and write for meaning and think critically, we will continue to be disappointed with reading achievement and continue to have students who are unable to use reading and writing for problem solving in the world.

Examining the Controversy Over Whole Language

Critics of whole language proclaim that teachers are not teaching phonics and basic language arts skills. Phonics-first advocates believe that phonics teaching must be systematic and intense and that phonics knowledge must precede reading. Whole language advocates place phonics and skills in the context of reading whole and predictable texts and view phonics as one of the cueing systems—along with the meaning and structure of the text—that readers use.

Much of the change (to whole language) has been cosmetic, with lots of innovation, but little actual, deep change. Many school districts simply exchanged basal reading texts and accompanying workbooks for children's literature and free-choice writing. But teachers received only spotty professional development and were allowed scant time for collaboration and reflection. Success came to **teachers who were experienced and knowledgeable—who took the time to put research and theory into prac-**

tice, collaborate with colleagues, and constantly monitor how they taught and how their students were doing.

Unfortunately, this has not happened in many places. As Stan Pogrow (1996) states, "Large-scale reform requires highly specific, systematic, and structural methodologies with supporting materials of tremendously high quality" (p. 52). Successful reform means that student achievement is high. Favorable results require "meaningful teamwork; clear, measurable goals; and the regular collection and analysis of performance data" (Schmoker 1996, p. 2). In reality, there have been only pockets of successful change, and the public has become impatient.

> **If we just teach kids how to decode words and not how to read and write for meaning and think critically, we will continue to be disappointed with reading achievement.**

Looking Closely at Whole Language

Though whole language is taking the brunt of what's gone wrong in reading and writing, there is no simple solution. Where whole language plays a role, it has been the misinterpretation, poor application, and inadequate articulation of whole language, rather than its sound principles and practices, that are to blame. Though many critics see

whole language as a passing fad, its principles are based on more than 20 years of research on language learning from around the world.

Perhaps one of the problems has been that many whole language principles are based on what children who come to school already reading and writing have done in the home. These are the children who have listened to stories for up to thousands of hours and had many opportunities for role playing, reading, meaningful discussion, writing, and language play. They enter school ready for phonics to make sense. But for other children who have not had such opportunities, how do teachers make up those hours? Increasingly, the number of these children appears to be growing—and they often struggle with learning phonics and making sense of texts.

Recently I was working with a 3rd grader new to our school district. In doing an informal reading assessment, I asked him to bring me the book he was reading. The simple picture book began, as many tales do, "Once upon a time. . ." He could not decode "upon," reading it as two separate words, "up" and "on." When I asked him to think about how lots of stories begin, he was at a loss. Without the experience of the familiar language of stories, he was reduced to "sounding out." Though he will benefit from phonics, even more so, he needs a volunteer to read to him so he becomes familiar with, understands, and enjoys the cadence and rhythms and words of storybook language.

Another major difficulty has been that whole language is difficult to define. In a whole language classroom, learners are continually supported to purposefully use language (in many subject areas and contexts) to inquire and to construct and evaluate their own understanding of texts and real-world issues. Whole language classrooms are student-centered, problem-solving, democratic communities where students experience a wide range of literature and literary experiences. Expectations for quality work are high and rigorous. Students are decision makers and independent thinkers.

The emphasis on students as decision makers upsets some people. Phonics is systematic and not open to interpretation and discussion. The belief that a piece of literature can have many valid interpretations can make a poorly informed public uneasy. Yet the public is even less comfortable with accepting students' well-thought-out approximations, such as the invented spellings of emerging writers. People often view these approximations as an indication of neglect and poor teaching. They don't realize that students' approximations inform teachers of the student's stage of development, how much practice is needed, and what needs to be taught and demonstrated next.

Perhaps most important, whole language classrooms rely on highly knowledgeable teachers—not prescriptive manuals of how and what to teach. Teachers must know how to use fiction and nonfiction by award-winning authors and illustrators to meaningfully teach reading and writing across the curriculum. In extreme cases, teachers have had to write their own curriculum in every subject area. It is no wonder that some teachers have floundered.

Without adequate professional development, many educators misinterpreted whole language to mean that all you need to do is immerse kids in books and they will learn to read as easily as they learn to speak. Also, some educators saw the teaching of phonics and skills as anti-whole language, and that has never been true. Phonics has always been part of whole language. And when some educators imply that spelling and grammar don't matter, they contribute to

Excerpt from a Newsletter to Parents

Dear Families,
I wanted to take this time to talk a little more about our spelling program. Attached you will find the 3rd grade spelling list I told you about at Open House. It would be great if you encouraged your child to put this on his or her desk or homework area and use it when writing letters, doing homework, or writing in the writer's notebook.

This list of words was compiled by the 3rd grade teachers. The students will be tested on these words weekly (about five a week). I group the words according to the spelling rule or pattern we are focusing on that week. If students get all the words correct, they look for words in their writer's notebook, math log, reading log, or science or social studies notebooks. Each child should have five to eight words each week.

I thought it might be helpful to give you a list of the rules and patterns I stress in the 3rd grade (see attached). I will try to keep you informed of the spelling focus each week so you can reinforce it at home.

—*From Your Child's Teacher*

destroying the credibility and rigor of successful whole language teaching.

Enabling Effective Change

When educators and communities have given adequate time, training, and resources to whole language instruction and learning, the results have been overwhelmingly positive.

One such example is Union City, New Jersey, a small urban center, which began to move to whole language in the late 1980s after standardized test scores were "discouragingly low, and the state was demanding a plan to turn the district around." In 1996, 1st graders' districtwide test scores on the reading section of the California Achievement Test averaged at the 78th percentile, as

compared to the 34th percentile in 1989 (Flanagan 1996). Other examples include the Shaker Heights, Ohio, City School District, and the Fairfax County, Virginia, School District. The following are some common actions incorporated by districts that have successfully implemented whole language.

■ *Plan for change.* Union City teachers and administrators spent a year planning for change—reading recent research; writing a schoolwide philosophy; and setting aside a daily, almost two-hour, uninterrupted block of time for language arts in kindergarten through grade 3.

■ *Involve parents in the planning process.* In successful districts, educators share current research findings about language learning, and they are clear and articulate about their beliefs and practices. Parents feel confident that the new practice is right for their kids, not just a new fad or experiment. Unless the community understands curricular changes, questions will eventually arise that may sabotage the change process.

■ *Go slowly and build in ongoing professional development.* In successful programs, funds are allocated for releasing teachers from the classroom for daytime professional development, and teachers are paid for ses-

Many children need volunteers to read to them so they become familiar with, understand, and enjoy the cadence and rhythms and words of storybook language.

sions outside of school hours. Continuing professional development in the teaching of phonics, spelling, and reading skills is critical to the success of any language arts program.

Without informed practice, collaboration, and feedback, the program will fail. In some elementary schools in the Shaker Heights district, principals hire substitutes for teachers planning student-led conferences and portfolio assessment. Teachers meet together, develop procedures and conference guidelines, write letters to parents, and even hold one-to-one conferences with students.

For the past decade, teachers in K–4 buildings in Shaker Heights have been voluntarily meeting each week before school. They discuss current articles from educational journals and books, share practices that work, hold dialogues about all areas of the curriculum, and study authentic assessment procedures.

■ *Provide adequate resources.* In addition to the school library and a knowledgeable librarian, teachers and students have classroom libraries that include hundreds of books—fiction, informational books, and multiple resources and references. Some schools also have a professional library for teachers and, often, one for parents.

■ *Reassure parents that the basic skills are being taught.* Even when parents are supportive of whole language teaching, they still want to know that the basics are included. Parents are comfortable with spelling tests, phonics, and "skill and drill" because it's the way many of them were taught. They do not see the value of invented spelling for young writers or understand the developmental spelling stages all students go through unless teachers can clearly articulate the research and explain the process. As one parent said at back-to-school night, "I don't want to hear anything about that invented spelling. I get enough of that from my secretary."

Newsletters to parents—explaining the traditional disciplines that are being taught, such as phonics, spelling, and handwriting—as well as written work

that is sent home, contribute to parents' confidence in their child's growing competency. Figure 1 on the previous page shows an excerpt from a newsletter to parents.

■ *Communicate clearly to parents and avoid jargon.* Use clear definitions of terms to help parents and community members understand what's going on. When educators have carefully communicated what they are doing in the classroom and can demonstrate positive results, most parents and community members are supportive.

In Fairfax County, Virginia, teachers have written booklets to explain current approaches to language learning and teaching. Other districts invite teachers and students to show what portfolio assessment looks like at a board of education meeting. There is nothing so convincing as students who can talk clearly about the purposes of education, what they are learning and why, and what goals they have set.

■ *Value parents as experts.* In successful programs, parent feedback is welcomed, and parents feel welcome in the school. Such a climate is rare in many schools, despite all the rhetoric about parents as partners. In the Shaker Heights district, parent volunteers are integral to the success of our program: they run the 1st grade publishing program, organize building literature collections, and build bridges between the schools and the community.

In an effort to determine how parents were responding to K–4 changes in the conferencing and reporting system, one principal set up a before-school meeting that was attended by most of the staff and about 50 parents. Educators listened to parents' concerns, took them seriously, and made adjustments in the reporting process.

■ *Put standardized testing in perspective for parents.* In Shaker Heights, only a small portion of conference time with parents is spent discussing standardized test results. Overattention to standardized testing gives the message that these tests alone show achievement. In conferences, talk is about students' work, setting goals, and celebrating learning, with students

often playing an integral role. Because parents have seen ongoing examples of their child's work, they come to see the standardized test for what it is—one isolated indicator on a given day that provides little information for improving instruction and learning.

■ *Report the good news about our public schools.* Where whole language has been accepted, local reporters have been invited into schools, and local newspapers have carried "good news" stories. Sometimes, these articles have been written and submitted by educators who want to make sure that the public receives accurate information about our schools so that the naysayers don't continue to dominate the news.

As knowledgeable educators, we must speak loudly and eloquently so that our rational voices join the literacy conversations. We must do everything in our power to ensure that the media fairly and accurately represent what is going on in education.

References

California Department of Education. (June 1996). *Teaching Reading: A Balanced, Comprehensive Approach to Teaching Reading in Prekindergarten Through Grade 3.* Sacramento, Calif.: Author.

Elam, S.M., L.C. Rose, and A.M. Gallup. (September 1996). "The 28th Phi Delta Kappa/Gallup Poll of the Public's Attitudes Toward the Public Schools." *Phi Delta Kappan* 78, 1: 42.

Flanagan, A. (1996). "Whole Language Philosophy Guides Instruction in New Jersey District." *The Council Chronicle* 6, 1: 4–5.

Pogrow, S. (September 25, 1996). "Commentary: On Scripting the Classroom." *Education Week*, p. 52.

Schmoker, M. (1996). *Results: The Key to Continuous School Improvement.* Alexandria, Va.: ASCD.

Regie Routman is a language arts resource teacher in the Shaker Heights, Ohio, City School District. Her latest book is *Literacy at the Crossroads: Crucial Talk About Reading, Writing, and Other Teaching Dilemmas* (Portsmouth, N.H.: Heinemann, 1996). She can be reached at Mercer Elementary School, 23325 Wimbledon Rd., Shaker Heights, OH 44122 (phone: 216-295-4066).

Kathryn Button
Margaret J. Johnson
Paige Furgerson

Interactive writing in a primary classroom

Interactive writing provides a means for teachers to engage in effective literacy instruction, not through isolated skills lessons, but within the framework of constructing texts filled with personal and collective meaning.

"We're going to finish up our list for our story map," Paige Furgerson explains to her kindergarten students. "Let's read what we have so far."

As Ali points to the words written on the paper attached to the easel, her classmates read along with her: "Trees, 3 bowls, 3 spoons, 3 chairs, house, 3 beds, 3 bears."

"I know that there are some other things that we need. Can you think about the story of 'Goldilocks and the Three Bears'? What else do we need to write on our list?" Miss Furgerson asks.

Brody suggests, "A window."

Joey requests, "Three bathrooms. One for each bear."

Katelin volunteers, "Goldilocks."

"Oh, you know what?" Furgerson says. "I think we really do need her. Did you hear what Katelin said, that we needed Goldilocks?"

"Goldilocks," the children repeat in unison.

"Goldilocks," Furgerson replies. "We need a Goldilocks. We're almost out of room

right here." Furgerson points to the bottom of the list of items needed for the class story map. "So where should we write *Goldilocks*?" After the children decide that a new column needs to be started, they help Furgerson hear the sounds in the word *Goldilocks* and proceed to write the word.

"Let's say the word together, slowly," Furgerson reminds the children.

"Goldilocks. *O*, I hear an *o*," Adam states.

"I hear a *d*," Quang suggests.

"A *g*, a *g*," repeats Katelin.

After observing her children and listening to them encode *Goldilocks*, Furgerson explains. "There is an *o* and a *d* and a *g*. The *g* is at the beginning, Katelin. You come up and write the *g*, and then we'll let Adam write the *o* that he heard. Do you know what? This is a person's name, *Goldilocks*. Do you know what kind of a *g* we have to use?

Rosa replies, "A capital."

"A capital *g* because it's somebody's name." Furgerson then leads the class forward in their task. "That's a good capital *g*. Now, Adam, you come up and write the *o*. Class, let's say the word again to see if we hear any other sounds. Help me."

This scene took place in a kindergarten classroom at Ramirez Elementary School in Lubbock, Texas, USA. Of the 17 students in the class, 2 were Asian, 8 Hispanic, 6 non-Hispanic White, and one African American. Fifteen of the children received free or reduced-price lunch, and 6 had attended a prekindergarten program. The teacher, Paige Furgerson, and the children spent their days engaged in a variety of literacy activities, including interactive writing lessons like the one described above.

Roots of interactive writing

Interactive writing has its roots in the language experience approach developed by Ashton-Warner (1963) in which children dictated a text and the teacher acted as scribe. The text was then used as reading material for the youngsters. McKenzie (1985), working with British teachers, developed a process she called "shared writing" in which the teacher and children collaborated on a text to be written. The focus of the writing could come from a children's literature selection, an event experienced by the children in the class, or a topic under study in social studies or science. In McKenzie's model, the teacher served as scribe and usually used chart paper to create a text that then served as the students' reading text. As the charts accumulated, they were displayed around the room, surrounding the children with meaningful print.

Interactive writing, a form of shared writing, is part of the early literacy lesson framework (see Figure 1) developed by educators at The Ohio State University (Pinnell & McCarrier, 1994) to provide rich, educative experiences for young children, particularly those considered to be educationally at risk. The framework draws on the concept of emergent literacy, a term coined by Clay (1966), and is explicated by other early childhood educators (see Strickland & Morrow, 1989; Teale & Sulzby, 1986).

In the early literacy framework, the use of quality literature (Huck & Kerstetter, 1987) scaffolds the development and integration of all literacy processes (reading, writing, speaking, listening, thinking). Three to five trade books, which represent various genres, are read aloud to children each day. Prior to the construction of the students' list for their story map of "Goldilocks and the Three Bears," Miss Furgerson had read aloud Galdone's (1972) version several times. The repeated readings helped students reconstruct the story line and recall characters and story sequence, the information necessary to generate their lists and construct the actual map. Often the focus of the daily interactive writing lesson was an extension of a book read aloud to the class.

Clay (1991) explained that children are active constructors of their own language and literacy. Their competence grows as they gain inner control over constructing meaning from print. This growth does not take place without environmental support. Rather, with supportive instruction, children develop in language and literacy competence (Vygotsky, 1962). The early literacy framework is a balanced program of instruction and independent exploration. Interactive writing provides opportunities for teachers to engage in instruction precisely at the point of student need.

Interactive writing provides opportunities for teachers to engage in instruction precisely at the point of student need.

Interactive writing differs from shared writing in two important ways. First, children take an active role in the writing process by actually holding the pen and doing the writing. Second, the teacher's role changes as she scaffolds and explicates the children's emerging knowledge about print (Button, 1992). Through questioning and direct instruction, the teacher focuses the children's attention on the conventions of print such as spaces between words, left-to-right and top-to-bottom directionality, capital letters, and punctuation. Clay (1979) reminds teachers to utilize the child's strengths and not to do for the child "anything that she can teach him to do for himself" (p. 4).

Interactive writing in practice

To guide the interactive writing process and make children's knowledge about print explicit, the teacher might ask questions such as these:

"How many words are there in our sentence?"

"Where do we begin writing?"

**Figure 1
The Ohio State University Early Literacy Learning Initiative
A framework for early literacy lessons**

Element	Values
1. Reading aloud to children (rereading favorite selections)	Motivates children to read (shows purpose). Provides an adult demonstration. Develops sense of story. Develops knowledge of written language syntax and of how texts are structured. Increases vocabulary and linguistic repertoire. Supports intertextual ties through enjoyment and shared knowledge; creates community of readers.
2. Shared reading Rereading big books Rereading retellings Rereading alternative texts Rereading the products of interactive writing	Demonstrates early strategies. Builds sense of story and ability to predict. Demonstrates process of reading. Provides social support from the group. Provides opportunity to participate, behave like a reader.
3. Guided reading	Provides opportunity to problem solve while reading for meaning. Provides opportunity to use strategies on extended text. Challenges the reader and creates context for successful processing on novel texts. Provides opportunity for teacher guidance, demonstration, and explanation.
4. Independent reading	Children read on their own or with partners from a wide range of materials.
5. Shared writing	Children compose messages and stories; teacher supports process as scribe. Demonstrates how writing works.
6. Interactive writing	Demonstrates concepts of print, early strategies, and how words work. Provides opportunities to hear sounds in words and connect with letters. Helps children understand "building up" and "breaking down" processes in reading and writing. Provides opportunities to plan and construct texts.
7. Guided writing and writers' workshop Teacher guides the process and provides instruction	Demonstrates the process of writing. Provides opportunity for explicit teaching of various aspects of writing. Gives students the guidance they need to learn writing processes and produce high-quality products.
8. Independent writing Individual retellings Labeling "Speech balloons" Books and other pieces	Provides opportunity for independence. Provides chance to write for different purposes. Increases writers' ability to use different forms. Builds ability to write words and use punctuation. Fosters creativity and the ability to compose.
9. Letters, words, and how they work	Helps children learn to use visual aspects of print.

Extensions and themes: Drama, murals, story maps, innovations on text, surveys, science experiments, and others.
• Provides opportunities to interpret texts in different ways.
• Provides a way of revisiting a story.
• Fosters collaboration and enjoyment.
• Creates a community of readers.
• Provides efficient instruction through integration of content areas.

(continued)

Figure 1
The Ohio State University Early Literacy Learning Initiative (cont'd.)

Documentation of progress
- Provides information to guide daily teaching.
- Provides a way to track the progress of individual children.
- Provides a basis for reporting to parents.
- Helps a school staff assess the effectiveness of the instructional program.

Home and community involvement
- Brings reading and writing materials and new learning into children's homes.
- Gives children more opportunities to show their families what they are learning.
- Increases reading and writing opportunities for children.
- Demonstrates value and respect for children's homes.

Oral language is the foundation for all elements of the framework.

The Ohio State University, July 1995. Copyright 1995, OSU Early Literacy Learning Initiative. Used with permission.

"After writing one word, what do we have to remember to do? Why?"

"What word are we writing next?"

"Say the word slowly. What sounds do you hear?"

"Can you write the letter that stands for that sound?"

"Can you find the letter on our alphabet chart that we need to write?"

"What comes at the end of the sentence?"

"Would that make sense?"

"Does that look right?"

"Would you point and read what we have written so far?"

These questions and the instruction they represent vary according to the knowledge and needs of the children (see Figure 2). For children beginning the process, the teacher may need to attend more to letter formation. At times the teacher may show a child a model or assist the child with the formation of the needed letter. As children gain competence, attention may shift to punctuation, capitalization, prefixes, suffixes, and phonetic structures such as digraphs, consonant blends, and vowel patterns.

An interactive writing lesson need not be lengthy. On the first day of kindergarten, Furgerson and her students engaged in interactive writing for 15 minutes. As the year progressed, lessons lasted from 20 to 30 minutes. The power of the lesson lies not in the length of the text constructed but in the quality of the interaction. Typically the children are seated on a carpet facing an easel holding unlined chart paper, a marking pen, correction tape,

and a pointer. The teacher usually sits within easy reach of the easel, facing the children. Teachers have found interactive writing to be successful with classes that range in size from 15 to 32 children.

The environment the teacher creates during this process should support risk taking. Children are encouraged to take an active role in negotiating the text. The teacher assumes that the children are in the process of learning about print and that some of their responses will be approximations. The teacher explains to the children that because they and other people will be reading the story, it is important that the words be conventionally constructed. The teacher uses correction tape to mask preconventional attempts (the child's approximations) and helps the child to write the word, letter, or punctuation mark conventionally. Teacher sensitivity is needed to value the knowledge reflected in the attempt yet also to teach the standard conventions of print used in books such as the ones the children read.

For example, during the construction of a class big book about the incubation of eggs, a classroom experience that occurred late in the school year, the children decided to write the sentence: "When the chicks get bigger, we will send the chicks to the farm." After everyone repeated the sentence aloud, Furgerson asked the class what word needed to be written first. They agreed that the first word should be *when.* Rosa stepped up to the easel and wrote *wen.* Furgerson said, "It does sound like *w-e-n,* but we need an *h* before the *e.*" She then cov-

Figure 2
Interactive writing expectations and guidelines in primary classrooms over a school year

Beginning of the year ──────────➤ Later in the year ──────────➤

Establish routine
Negotiate simple text (a label)
Construction of text may be completed in one
    day (news)
Repeat orally word or line to be written

The teacher will
Model hearing sounds in words
Model sound/symbol relationships
Support letter recognition (using alphabet chart
    or chart listing class members' names)
Model and question for Concepts About Print
    (CAP): spacing, left-to-right directionality,
    top-to-bottom directionality, word-by-word
    matching during shared reading
Link words to be written with names of children
    in the class

The teacher may
Write more of the text
Write challenging parts of word/text
Assist with letter formation

Routine established
Negotiate a more complex text
Construction of text continues over several days
Count the words to be written before starting to
    write

Students will
Hear dominant sounds in words
Represent sounds with symbols (letters)
Write letters without copy
Have control of core words
Begin linking known words to unknown words
Leave spaces between words
Use familiar chunks (-*ed*; -*ing*)
Control word-by-word matching during shared
    reading
Punctuate sentences on the run
Write text with little support
Make generalizations about print

ered the letters *en* with a piece of correction tape and asked Rosa to write an *h* and then the *en* that she initially had written. During the writing of the word *the* Simon wrote *teh*. For some of the children *the* was a known word, but Simon could not yet spell it conventionally. Xuchen responded, "You have the right letters but in *the* the *h* comes before the *e*." One of the children tore off a piece of correction tape and handed it to Simon to place over the letters *eh*. He then wrote *he*. Jane asked Furgerson, "What did it say?" After the teacher pronounced *teh*, Jane commented that it didn't make sense. The children agreed that *the* looked right and that *teh* neither made sense nor looked like a word they knew. This information confirmed for Furgerson that some of her students knew that what they wrote needed to make sense (semantics).

Texts for interactive writing represent many forms of writing. Children might want to create a list of characters from a story as part of the process of forming a story map. Survey questions might be used as a basis for interactive writing. For example, after reading the books written by their visiting author, Rafe

Martin, the children created a survey chart to display their favorite book title. Children might retell a story they have read or write an alternative text. After students read *The Farm Concert* (Cowley, 1990), they wrote their own variant entitled "The Classroom Concert." Children might compose an invitation to a class party or write a letter to pen pals in another city. Recipes, a review of a trip, class news, and many other forms of communication can also serve as topics for interactive writing.

What interactive writing looks like in one classroom

At the beginning of the school year, Furgerson used informal assessments, including Clay's Observation Survey (Clay, 1993a), to determine the strengths and knowledge of her students. She found about half her children could write their names. Only two of the children could name all the letters of the alphabet. All of the children could identify the front of a book, distinguish between illustrations and print, and indicate where they would begin to read. They all knew print carried a message.

On the first day of kindergarten, Furgerson began with an interactive writing experience based on the focus book of their first thematic unit. After reading Galdone's (1975) *The Gingerbread Boy*, the class took a walking tour of the school to find gingerbread boys hidden in certain spots throughout the building. When they returned to the classroom, they created a list of the spots where the gingerbread boys were found. After explaining the purpose of the writing, Furgerson asked the students what word they wanted to write first on their list.

They decided to begin with the word *lab*. She asked the children where they should start writing. One child stepped forward to point to the upper left-hand corner of the chart paper. Furgerson asked the students to say the word aloud—*lab*—listening for the sounds they heard. Some of the students heard a *b* and some an *l*. At this initial point in the process, Furgerson took the responsibility of seriating the sounds. "Yes," she told the children, "we do hear a *b* and an *l*. When we write the word *lab*, the *l* comes first."

Furgerson knew Larry could write his name. "Larry," she said, "you come and write the *l*. You have an *l* in your name." After Larry wrote the letter *l*, the children said the word again, listening for additional sounds. Brody heard the sound represented by the letter *b*. While Brody came up to write the *b*, Furgerson explained to the class that Brody's name began with a *b*. Before he wrote the *b*, however, she explained that the letter *a* came before the *b* although it was hard to hear. Brody wrote the *a* and then the *b*.

Furgerson then called another child to come up to the chart and, using the pointer, point under the word they had just written for the class to read. She then asked where else they found gingerbread boys. They followed a similar process with other items on their list. Furgerson chose to write three words at this sitting and to add to the list on subsequent days. Interactive writing was a daily event in her classroom.

Furgerson built on the knowledge students had about the sounds represented by letters in their names. She used everything the children appeared to know at the time of the lesson and then, through demonstration and explanation, extended their knowledge by providing the letters representing unfamiliar sounds. Clay (1993b) states, "At the beginning of the school year what the child can write is a good indicator of what the child knows in detail about written language" (p. 11). As the children finished writing a word, a list, or a sentence, they read it. One child pointed under each word to help the others to track the print while reading. This process demonstrates in a powerful and immediate way the reciprocal nature of reading and writing.

Later in the year, the children were thoroughly familiar with the routine of interactive writing and much more sophisticated in their knowledge about the conventions of print. They were able to analyze the phonological features of the message to be written (hear sounds in words), sequence the sounds heard, represent the sounds they heard with letters, and discern many different patterns. The children were also aware that their purpose for writing dictated the type of writing they would undertake. When the class decided to reply to their Ohio pen pals, they knew their letter would begin with the line, "Dear Miss Patacca's Class," and what followed would be written from left to right across the page.

On the first day of kindergarten, Furgerson began with an interactive writing experience based on the focus book of their first thematic unit.

In the spring the children decided to retell the story of Michael Rosen's (1989) *We're Going on a Bear Hunt*. They had spent several days listening to repeated readings of the book. Using interactive writing, they had made lists of the characters and the different settings from the story, which then served as references for an elaborate story map. To accompany the map, the children spent several days writing a retelling of the story.

Furgerson and the children negotiated the first line of the retelling. Borrowing in part from the text of the story, they decided to write: "The children walked through the forest, stumble trip, stumble trip." They repeated the sentence several times to fix the message clearly in their minds and to give them something against which to monitor their writing. Furgerson then asked the children to count the words as they said the sentence. She asked them what word they would write first. At this point in the school year, *the* was a known word for all the children in the room. Miss Furgerson asked the children what they needed to remember. Most knew that they start writing in the upper left-hand corner of the page, begin the first word of the sentence with a capital letter, and leave a "hand space" between the words.

Although the focus of Furgerson's curriculum was not to teach her children to read, but to immerse them in meaningful print rich activities, most of them were reading by spring of their kindergarten year.

After writing and reading *the*, the children told Furgerson that the next word they needed to work on was *children*. This was not a known word for most of them. Following a routine well established at this point, the students said the word together slowly, yet naturally, thinking about the order of the sounds in the spoken word. One child commented that the word had two parts—*chil* and *dren*. Furgerson turned the child's observation into a teaching moment, explaining that, indeed, *children* had two syllables and showing the class how to clap as they said the word, one clap for each syllable. Capitalizing further on the observation, she told the students they would be listening for the sounds in the first syllable. They heard the first sound easily and all knew the digraph *ch*. Furgerson asked Chaz to come up to the easel and write the first two letters while the class said the first syllable again, listening for additional sounds.

Rosa said she heard an *i* like in *him*. At this point, most of the children were beginning to connect known words and new words. Rosa came up, took the marker from Chaz, and wrote the *i*. As Rosa repeated the word aloud while writing, she said she also could hear an *l*. Furgerson said, "You are right. You may write the *l*." She then asked the children to say the word again, listening for the sounds in the last syllable. Quang said he heard a *tr*. Furgerson said, "Yes. It does sound like a *tr*, but in this word it is a *dr*. TR and *dr* do sound almost alike." Quang came up to the easel and wrote the *dr*. After saying the word one more time, Joshua said he heard an *n*. Furgerson said, "Yes, you are right, there is an *n*. But before the *n*, there is an *e* which is harder to hear. Would you like to come up and write *en* for us?"

Throughout the school year the children also had 20 to 30 minutes every day to write independently either in their journals or at the writing center. This gave students time to use the knowledge gained from interactive writing instruction and time to take further risks as writers. They made independent choices about what to write about and how to organize their texts. They were encouraged to use invented spelling, copy from environmental print, and make use of their growing core of known words. Furgerson's observations of what the students wrote and how they wrote independently informed her teaching for future interactive writing sessions.

Literacy assessment

Assessment in the early literacy framework is ongoing as the teacher documents the children's growth over time. Furgerson used a checklist she developed to monitor the growth children exhibited through their journal writing. Although the children varied in their control of the conventions of print, they all thought of themselves as readers and writers. Although the focus of Furgerson's curriculum was not to teach her children to read but to immerse them in meaningful print-rich activities, most of them were reading by spring of their kindergarten year.

To document the growth her students made during the year and to provide information for next year's first-grade teacher, Furgerson and a class of trained undergraduate language/literacy students administered the Observation Survey (Clay, 1993a) in May to all of the children. She analyzed the children's scores on each of the six tasks assessed and then compared the May scores with the September scores.

The children exhibited growth in all areas measured by the Observation Survey. In the spring of the year, 13 of 17 children were able to read with 90% or better accuracy books like *The Chick and the Duckling* (Ginsburg, 1972) and *Mary Wore Her Red Dress and Henry Wore His Green Sneakers* (Peek, 1985). These books have illustrations that provide moderate support for the reader and stories that tell about familiar objects. The stories contain varied, often repetitive, simple sentence patterns that include action such as, "'I am taking a walk,' said the Duckling." (See Peterson, 1991, for characteristics of texts to support beginning readers.)

The children improved the most in their ability to hear sounds in words as measured by the Dictation Task. In this task, children are asked to record a dictated sentence containing a possible 37 phonemes. Each child's attempt is scored by counting the number of letters (graphemes) written by the child that represent the sounds (phonemes) analyzed by the child. In the fall the children had a mean dictation score of 9.8 (maximum score = 37). The children represented primarily initial consonants. In the spring, the children's mean dictation score was 29 (almost three times higher than in the fall). The children's ability to hear sounds in words, practiced daily during interactive writing, enabled them to represent initial and final sounds heard in each word. In addition, they could accurately spell high-frequency words like *the, is,* and *it.* This growth in the Dictation Task is particularly significant given the importance of phonemic awareness as a predictor of success in learning to read (see Adams, 1990).

On the Writing Vocabulary Task of the Observation Survey children were asked to write as many words as they could in a 10-minute period. In the fall, the children's scores ranged from 0 to 20 with a mean score of 4.8. Many children were able to write their first name and names of family members like *mom* and *dad.* In the spring, the Writing Vocabulary scores ranged from 1 to 56 words written in a 10-minute period with a mean score of 23.9. In addition to writing names of family members and friends, the children wrote high-frequency words like *on, the, in, go,* and *to* and favorite words like *pizza* and *dog.*

Meeting individual students' needs

Furgerson used information from the Observation Survey, anecdotal notes, and writing checklists to help her meet the needs of each of her students. Valerie's fall Observation Survey summary indicated that she could recognize 14 of 54 letters, no high-frequency words, and 7 out of 24 concepts about print; could represent no phonemes on the Dictation Task; and could write no words during the Writing Vocabulary Task. During the interactive writing lesson, Furgerson built on Valerie's strengths, asking her to write the *l* and *a* when they were needed in words the class was writing, as these were 2 of the 14 letters Valerie knew. Valerie delighted everyone one day when she announced that the particular sentence the class was writing needed a question mark at the end. She quickly became in charge of question marks. As the year progressed, Furgerson also worked individually with Valerie at the teacher table during center time and guided her during journal writing. At the end of kindergarten Valerie recognized 46 of the 54 letters, no high-frequency words, and 14 of the 24 concepts about print; she could represent 3 phonemes on the Dictation Task, and on the Writing Vocabulary Task she could write her name. Furgerson stated that Valerie's spring scores exhibited growth even though the growth was atypical for children her age. Valerie also showed marked growth in other areas such as art and oral language. Even with the most supportive literacy framework, some children require more intensive instruction. Valerie would be a prime candidate for Reading Recovery (see Pinnell, Fried, & Estice, 1990).

Concluding remarks

Interactive writing provides an authentic means for instruction in phonics and other linguistic patterns within the context of meaningful text. Children learn the conventions of spelling, syntax, and semantics as they engage in the construction of letters, lists, and stories. Interactive writing is a tool that puts reading and learning about conventions into a dynamic relationship. As children attend to meaningful text, they develop their knowledge of the conventions embedded in that text. As they gain more knowledge of conventions, they are able to construct and interpret more sophisticated messages.

Interactive writing is an important part of the early literacy lesson framework (see Figure 1) because it provides so many opportunities to teach directly about language conventions, sense of story, types of writing, and concepts about print. These teaching moments do not follow a specified sequence but evolve from the teacher's understanding of the students' needs. The early literacy lesson framework blends independent problem solving, shared literacy experiences, and teacher instruction within a literacy-rich classroom.

Too often teachers feel they must choose between using holistic literacy experiences and teaching basic skills. In interactive writing sessions, teachers do both at the same time. Interactive writing provides a means for teachers to engage in effective literacy instruction, not through isolated skills lessons, but within the framework of constructing texts filled with personal and collective meaning.

Button teaches early literacy courses and Johnson teaches language and literacy courses at Texas Tech University. Furgerson teaches kindergarten in the Lubbock Independent School District. Button may be contacted at Texas Tech University, Box 41071, Lubbock, TX 79409-1071, USA.

References

Adams, M.J. (1990). *Beginning to read: Thinking and learning about print.* Cambridge, MA: MIT Press.

Ashton-Warner, S. (1963). *Teacher.* New York: Simon & Schuster.

Button, K.A. (1992). *A longitudinal case study examination of the theoretical and practical changes made by three urban kindergarten teachers during participation in early literacy training.* Unpublished doctoral dissertation, The Ohio State University, Columbus.

Clay, M.M. (1966). *Emergent reading behavior.* Unpublished doctoral dissertation, University of Aukland, New Zealand.

Clay, M.M. (1979). *The early detection of reading difficulties: A diagnostic survey with recovery procedures.* Portsmouth, NH: Heinemann.

Clay, M.M. (1991). *Becoming literate: The construction of inner control.* Portsmouth, NH: Heinemann.

Clay, M.M. (1993a). *An observation survey of early literacy achievement.* Portsmouth, NH: Heinemann.

Clay, M.M. (1993b). *Reading Recovery: A guidebook for teachers in training.* Portsmouth, NH: Heinemann.

Huck, C.S., & Kerstetter, K.J. (1987). Developing readers. In B. Cullinan (Ed.), *Children's literature in the reading program* (pp. 30-40). Newark, DE: International Reading Association.

McKenzie, M.G., (1985). Shared writing: Apprenticeship in writing. *Language Matters, 1-2,* 1-5.

Peterson, B. (1991). Selecting books for beginning readers. In D.E. DeFord, C.A. Lyons, & G.S. Pinnell (Eds.), *Bridges to literacy: Learning from Reading Recovery* (pp. 119-147). Portsmouth, NH: Heinemann.

Pinnell, G.S., Fried, M.D., & Estice, R.M. (1990). Reading Recovery: Learning how to make a difference. *The Reading Teacher, 43,* 282-295.

Pinnell, G.S., & McCarrier, A. (1994). Interactive writing: A transition tool for assisting children in learning to read and write. In E. Hiebert & B. Taylor (Eds.), *Getting reading right from the start: Effective early literacy interventions* (pp. 149-170). Needham, MA: Allyn & Bacon.

Strickland, D.S., & Morrow, L.M. (1989). *Emerging literacy: Young children learn to read and write.* Newark, DE: International Reading Association.

Teale, W.H., & Sulzby, E. (Eds.). (1986). *Emergent literacy: Writing and reading.* Norwood, NJ: Ablex.

Vygotsky, L. (1962). *Thought and language.* Cambridge, MA: MIT Press.

Children's books cited

Cowley, J. (1990). *The farm concert.* Bothell, WA: The Wright Group.

Galdone, P. (1972). *The three bears.* New York: Clarion.

Galdone, P. (1975). *The gingerbread boy.* New York: Clarion.

Ginsburg, M. (1972). *The chick and the duckling.* New York: Macmillan.

Peek, M. (1985). *Mary wore her red dress and Henry wore his green sneakers.* New York: Clarion.

Rosen, M. (1989). *We're going on a bear hunt.* New York: McElderry.

Computers and Young Children

Outstanding Developmental Software

Susan Haugland, Department Editor

INTRODUCTION

The past year has been packed with new early childhood computer software releases. Selecting the best software to facilitate young children's development among the array of choices is indeed a challenge.

Software publishers were invited to submit entries for the Developmental Software Awards in seven categories: creativity, language, math, multicultural, multipurpose, problem solving, and thematic focus. Software was evaluated using the Haugland/Shade Developmental Scale, Revised Edition (Figure 1). The Revised Edition includes three changes.

First, and most importantly, the nonviolence criteria was added. The nonviolence criteria includes two characteristics: first, software is free of violent characters and actions, and second, software models positive social values. To receive credit for nonviolence, software must not contain any objects which could ultimately be used for aggressive acts including guns, knives, swords, etc., even if their use is not modeled in the software. If the software contains any of these objects, it is unrealistic to expect that at some point children will not use these for violent actions. The addition of the nonviolence criteria is a significant change to the software evaluation scale. This is especially true in light of the increasing prevalence of violence in software as well as the level of violence in our society (NAEYC, 1990; NAEYC, 1993; Levin, 1995). Violence in software is of particular concern because children are the initiators and control the violence. When violence occurs in other media such as television, videos, and books, children observe the violence rather than control or initiate it. Thus, the inclusion of the nonviolence criteria is an important improvement to the Developmental Scale.

The second revision is closely connected. To maintain the ten criteria, trial and error was omitted as a separate criteria and included as a characteristic under child control. Providing children opportunities for trial and error is one aspect of the amount of control children have over their computer experiences.

Third, technical features are expanded to reflect the vast improvements that have occurred in the hardware and software industry. Additional characteristics added include: installs easily, prints, and saves children's work. Anyone who has struggled with installing software with complicated procedures and then left the software in total frustration can appreciate the importance of simple installation. Time is valuable and not all teachers and parents are computer experts. Directions for loading the software need to be concise, specific, and easy to follow. Graphics and/or verbal instructions are included on the screen as needed to make each step clear. A manual highlights software installation, allowing users to preview installation if desired. A troubleshooting guide is included for solving common difficulties that emerge during installation and while operating the program. Printing is an important technical quality, as well, for several reasons. First, it is a tangible record of children's computer experiences. This is valuable for parents as an avenue for talking with children, particularly young children who have limited verbal and recall skills, about their computer experiences. Second, it is an important resource for teachers who can use children's printed work for portfolio development. Third, it is a useful learning resource for children. Printing gives children more opportunities to integrate their computer experiences with concrete activities. Fourth, printing provides children an important tangible record of their computer experiences. It also provides children valuable opportunities to reflect upon their computer experiences and even ponder over problem situations. Fifth, children need to be able to save within the program their progress and/or computer activities. They should be able to exit software and then re-enter wherever they have stopped. Children may be interrupted during their computer experiences for a variety of reasons: it's time for lunch or they have to go home, etc. It is important that children know they can stop and revisit the software right where they left it, if they so desire. Saving also gives children the opportunity to reflect over time on an activity and make changes, thereby enhancing the learning experience.

From *Early Childhood Education Journal*, Vol. 24, No. 3, 1997, pp. 179-184. © 1997 by Human Sciences Press, Inc. Reprinted by permission.

HAUGLAND/SHADE DEVELOPMENTAL SCALE
REVISED EDITION

Title [   ] Ages [   ]
Publisher [   ] Cost [   ]
Date Evaluated [   ] Hardware Eval. On [   ] Updated [   ]
Evaluated by [   ] Multiple Platforms [   ] Copyright [   ]

Description

[   ]

Comments   PICTURE

[   ]

Age Appropriate [   ]   ☐ Realistic Concepts
                              ☐ Appropriate Methods   Subscore [   ]
Child in Control [   ]   ☐ Actors not Reactors   Anti-Bias [   ]
                              ☐ Can Escape   TOTAL [   ]
                              ☐ Children Set Pace
                              ☐ Trial & Error

Clear Instructions [   ] ☐ Picture Choices
                              ☐ Simple, Precise Directions
                              ☐ Verbal Instructions

Expanding Complexity [   ] ☐ Low Entry, High Ceiling
                                ☐ Learning Sequence is Clear
                                ☐ Teaches Powerful Ideas

Independence [   ]   ☐ Adult Supervision Not Needed After Initial Exposure

Non-Violence [   ]   ☐ Software is free of violent characters and actions
                              ☐ Software models positive social values

Process Orientation [   ] ☐ Discovery Learning, Not Skill Drilling
                               ☐ Intrinsic Motivation
                               ☐ Process Engages, Product Secondary

Real World Model [   ]   ☐ Concrete Representations
                              ☐ Objects Function
                              ☐ Simple, Reliable Model

Technical Features [   ] ☐ Animation
                              ☐ Colorful
                              ☐ Installs Easily
                              ☐ Operates Consistently
                              ☐ Prints
                              ☐ Realistic Corresponding Sound Effects or Music
                              ☐ Runs Quickly
                              ☐ Saves Children's Work
                              ☐ Uncluttered Realistic Graphics

Transformations [   ]   ☐ Objects and Situations Change
                              ☐ Process Highlighter

Multiple Languages   ☐ Multiple Languages
Universal Focus   ☐ Universal Focus

Mixed Gender and Role Equity ☐ Mixed Gender and Role Equity
                             ☐ Exempt

People of Diverse Cultures   ☐ People of Diverse Cultures
                             ☐ Exempt

Differing Ages and Abilities ☐ Differing Ages and Abilities
                             ☐ Exempt

Diverse Family Styles   ☐ Diverse Family Styles
                             ☐ Exempt

©1996 Revised by Susan W. Haugland

Fig. 1

THE OUTSTANDING DEVELOPMENTAL SOFTWARE

The following brief reviews highlight the best developmental software in the seven categories. Software is divided into two age categories: 3–8 and 7–12. Publisher's sources for obtaining the software are located in Table I, following the software reviews. These programs provide a sound basis for beginning a software library or can enrich and update the resources already available to young children.

Ages 3–8

Creativity

Software: Blocks in Motion
Publisher: Don Johnston, Inc.
Developmental Rating: 8.5
Cost: $99.00
Description:
An awesome shape builder program full of drawing, building, and movement options. Numerous background templates available such as arctic trek, middle ages, rain forest, space, etc. Children can type text related to their creations.
Outstanding Features:
- Extensive, diverse program options with varying levels of difficulty.
- Children can program speed of movement, discover gravity, create their own machines, and/or construct graphs.
- Detailed manual includes supplemental activities.

Language

Software: Stanley's Sticker Stories
Publisher: Edmark Corporation
Developmental Rating: 8.5
Cost: $40.00
Description:
Children animate stories, write letters, and/or create alphabet and counting books. They select from 300 stickers to compose their stories, record sounds, and/or write words and sentences. Stickers are animated with the click of a key.
Outstanding Features:
- Child friendly picture menu.
- Builds reading, writing, and problem-solving skills as well as creativity.
- Numerous backgrounds including scenes from Millie's Math House, Bailey's Book House, Sammy's Science House, and Trudy's Tune and Place.

Math and Science

Software: Math Keys: Unlocking Probability
Publisher: MECC
Developmental Rating: 9.0
Cost: $99.00
Description:
An excellent classroom learning experience focusing on the laws of probability. Children explore coins, spinners, cubes, marbles, and/or play three games: Crazy Creatures, Chance Crossing, and Cloud Hop. After finishing a problem, children write about their solution.
Outstanding Features:
- Provides "hands on" experiences, teaching the nature of probability through discovery.
- Integrates language and math skills.
- Extensive teacher resources including learning objectives, activities, guidelines for teachers, and student handouts.

Multicultural

Software: Zurk's Alaskan Trek
Publisher: Soleil Software, Inc.
Developmental Rating: 8.0
Cost: $32.00
Description:
Children access two cabins and 11 cultural and environmental videos. They explore these activities: Animal Theater, create a scene and watch animals move and plants react; Moviemaker, create a movie by selecting a background, animals and text; Balancing Act, explore relative weight of animals or use a scale to answer 560 questions.
Outstanding Features:
- Children explore animals, plants, habitats and weight as well as the Alaskan culture.
- A portfolio option encourages children to make observations and record discoveries.
- A field guide provides information about 36 animals and 18 plants.

Multipurpose

Software: Paint, Write, and Play
Publisher: The Learning Company
Developmental Rating: 9.0
Cost: $60.00
Description:

Children draw, write stories, utilize Rebus pictures, and/or explore ten microworlds. Text to speech enables children to hear stories read. Pick and click word lists allow children to add words without typing. Drawing includes eight tools, 48 colors, cut, and paste.

Outstanding Features:
- Easy for young children to operate.
- Rebus pictures and spoken text help nonreaders and beginning readers build literacy skills.
- Includes ten diverse microworlds from Africa to the North Pole.

Problem Solving

Software: Mixed-Up Mother Goose Deluxe
Publisher: Sierra On-Line
Developmental Rating: 8.5
Cost: $39.95
Description:

Mother Goose has hidden objects from the characters in nursery rhymes. Children are asked to find the objects and return them to their owner. Builds mapping and directional skills; enhances planning skills, memory, and critical thinking.

Outstanding Features:
- Verbal instructions make this program now accessible to young children.
- Captures children's attention for extended periods of time.
- Children select program leader from diverse options varying in age, racial background, and gender.

Thematic Focus

Software: Let's Explore the Airport with Buzzy
Publisher: Humongous Entertainment
Developmental Rating: 8.0
Cost: $29.95
Description:

Children explore 40 locations at the airport. They investigate the ticket counter, the cockpit, the parking garage, the baggage processing area, the rental car area, etc.

Outstanding Features:
- Children access an extensive glossary by clicking objects on the screen.
- Verbal instructions and spoken information enable even nonreaders to learn in-depth information.
- A functioning microworld which gives children control of their computer experience.

Ages 7–12

Creativity

Software: Widget Workshop
Publisher: Maxis, Inc.
Developmental Rating: 8.5
Cost: $44.95
Description:

Widget Workshop is an elaborate, electronic, science/construction set. Children design their own widgets and/or solve puzzles. Widgets can be experiments, strange inventions, machines, or even puzzles themselves. Millions of different widgets are possible with diverse parts available.

Outstanding Features:
- Children learn about the weather, the human body, sound, light, distance, speed, time, gravity, and numbers.
- An activity book includes over 30 experiments to challenge children's thinking.
- Children stretch their minds becoming totally absorbed and, in the process, learn scientific and mathematical concepts and problem-solving skills.

Language

Software: Opening Night
Publisher: MECC
Developmental Rating: 8.5
Cost: $79.00
Description:

Children create and direct their own plays in a multimedia theater. Software includes 110 scenery backgrounds, 110 set props, and 40 costumed actors. Children write dialogue, hear it spoken, direct the movement of actors, select sound effects, and program their emotions.

Outstanding Features:
- Includes a Behind-the-Scenes CD from Children's Theater Company, Minneapolis, Minnesota.
- Extensive manual includes classroom activities and handouts.
- Motivates children to build language skills in a meaningful context which challenges their problem solving and creativity.

Math and Science

Software: Fun With Electronics
Publisher: Phillips Interactive

Developmental Rating: 8.5

Cost: $44.99

Description:

Children manipulate a "hands-on" electronic workbench to construct intercoms, engine sounds, radio, burglar alarm, etc. Children can also meet a cast of components that explain their functions, visit behind the scenes to hear how telephones, light bulbs, electric guitars, etc., use electricity.

Outstanding Features:

- Children are highly motivated as they explore these "hands-on" activities.
- A question-and-answer segment reviews children's understanding of electricity.
- Twenty-five experiments are available for children to conduct on the workbench.

Multicultural

Software: Africa Trail

Publisher: MECC

Developmental Score: 8.5

Cost: $79.00

Description:

Children plan and execute a 12,000 mile bike trek from Tunisia to the tip of South Africa. Includes 1,000 photos and video clips from an actual bike trek, maps, a guide book, and entries from the leader's journal.

Outstanding Features:

- Provides children a realistic view of Africa and its people.
- Children choose team members, supplies, equipment, buy visas, determine routes, drive bikes, handle emergencies, repair bikes, etc.
- Children are challenged to do their best as they face this amazing journey.

Multipurpose

Software: Windows Draw 4.0

Publisher: Micrografx, Inc.

Developmental Score: 7.5

Cost: $49.00

Description:

A graphics program with 15,000 clip art and photo images, 250 type faces, 40 special effects, and 150 templates. ABC Media Manager, enables children to integrate graphics from any Windows '95 application.

Outstanding Features:

- Very sophisticated graphics, publication, and presentation software.
- Includes desktop publishing and presentation applications, allowing children to position text anywhere on the page and create interactive computer slide shows.
- Enables classrooms or families to implement any desktop publishing or multimedia presentation they can imagine!

Problem Solving

Software: Top Secret Decoder

Publisher: Houghton Mifflin Interactive

Developmental Rating: 8.0

Cost: $49.95

Description:

Children code and decode messages. There are 22 codes to select, including sign language. Three codes have a decode button, and the computer can decode these messages.

Outstanding Features:

- Extensive variety of codes.
- A challenge panel gives messages to decode.
- Children enjoy sending and receiving secret messages from friends.

Thematic

Software: Imagination Express: Ocean

Publisher: Edmark Corporation

Developmental Rating: 8.0

Cost $35.00

Description:

As in the previous imagination programs, children begin by selecting a background and then adding people, animals, plants, and objects. Text, sound, music, and narrative can be added to each page. Ocean provides the additional features of "smart stickers" which animate as they are dragged.

Outstanding Features:

- Move Tools record and playback the path of the sticker.
- The zoom option enables children to closely examine ocean creatures.
- A Fact Book and Story Ideas stimulate children's thinking and enhance learning.

Table I.
Software Publishers

Don Johnston, Inc.
1000 North Rand Road Bldg. 115
Wauconda, IL 60084
(800) 999-4600

Edmark Corporation
6727 185th Avenue, N.E.
Redmond, WA 98052
(800) 426-0856

Humongous Entertainment
16932 Woodinville-Redmond Road
Suite 204
Woodinville, WA 98073
(800) 499-8386

Houghton Mifflin Interactive
222 Berkeley Street
Boston, MA 02116
(800) 225-3362

Learning Company, The
6493 Kaiser Drive
Fremont, CA 94555
(800) 852-2255

Maxis
2121 North California Blvd.
Suite 600
Walnut Creek, CA 94596-3572
(800) 52-MAXIS

MECC
6160 Summit Drive
North Minneapolis, MN 55430
(800) 215-0368

Micrografx
1301 Arapaho
Richardson, TX 75081
(800) 417-8312

Phillips Interactive
10960 Wilshire Blvd. 7th Floor
Los Angeles, CA 90024
(310) 444-6500

Sierra On-Line
3380 146th Suite 300
Bellevue, WA 98
(800) 757-7707

Soleil Software, Inc.
3853 Grove Court
Palo Alto, CA 94303
(415) 494-0114

Reflections

As a profession, early childhood education is relatively new. Teachers are still experiencing the growing pains always associated with the emergence of new institutions. We are creating our own traditions as a profession and, in the process, we are discovering "authentic practice." Lyn Fasoli and Janet Gonzalez-Mena ask us to consider how authentic we are in teaching young children. Their article, "Let's Be Real!" is packed with interesting vignettes of teachers engaging in authentic practice. They invite us to create first-hand experiences for children and be honest in all our dealings with children and colleagues. This is the way we, as early childhood educators, can be our real selves. Even more significantly, it is the way the profession will match beliefs and actions.

The American family of the 1830s is not so different from families of today. Diversity and ethnicity have always characterized families. So says Stephanie Coontz in "Where Are the Good Old Days?" For people who long to return to the good old days when fathers went to work and mothers cared for young children in the home, this is a wake-up call. Families have continually been affected by extremes of war and peace, poverty and wealth. Care for children outside the home is not a new trend but an old tradition in America.

An important addition to this unit is not an article, but a list of addresses. "Child Advocacy Directory" is a comprehensive listing of national organizations that advocate for young children. A concise mission statement is included for each of the 24 organizations. A valuable learning project might be to contact these organizations for more information on their early childhood involvement.

Today, early childhood educators are being called on to make extensive changes in instruction. This revolution in teaching flows from the latest research on how young children learn. Constructivist teaching practice is the new (but old) way of teaching. By emphasizing active learning, work in context, and ongoing assessment, teachers can more effectively match the ways children learn. Mary Heuwinkel describes these latest innovations in teaching in her article "New Ways of Learning = New Ways of Teaching."

The United States has a rich heritage of early care and kindergartens. It has produced many wonderful early childhood educators and leaders. We close with the words of one of them— Dorothy Hewes—about the importance of our field: "As we prepare to enter the twenty-first century, it is time to move beyond charity, sentimentality, and sisterhood with evidence that child care is a worthwhile public investment."

Looking Ahead: Challenge Questions

How close to "life on the outside" is "life on the inside" of child care?

What was the status of children in colonial families, in post–Civil War era families, and in 1950s families?

Name three national organizations that advocate for young children. Where are they located?

What are some of the newest teaching practices in early childhood education today?

What are the components of constructivist practice?

UNIT 6

Let's Be Real!

Authenticity in Child Care

by Lyn Fasoli and Janet Gonzalez-Mena

D*o you ever catch yourself speaking pleasantly when you don't feel pleasant at all? Do you sometimes feel that you are acting a part, and that the real you is left at home? Are you being your version of a professional, but you don't feel professional? Perhaps you are having an authenticity crisis.*

Jim Greenman (1992) talks about how children spend their childhoods in child care. It's a sobering thought, a childhood in child care.

What kinds of childhoods are we professionals creating for children? How authentic are they? How honest are the emotional exchanges children see and experience? How rich and authentic are the conversations? How close to "life on the outside" is "life on the inside" of child care? How often do real events, real objects, real people from the outside world have a real impact on the child-centered world in which children spend up to five years of their lives?

Lyn Fasoli teaches early childhood education at Northern Territory University in Darwin, Australia.

Janet Gonzalez-Mena divides her time between teaching, writing, and family life. She is on the faculty at Napa Valley College in California.

How influenced are we by the kinds of packaged environments, curricula, materials, and toys available on the market? Do we understand what happens if a child never has a chance to wander, rummage around in a shed, barn, attic, basement, or other clutter-gathering space? When we protect children from the real world, do we inadvertently discourage the very qualities we say we value in children: curiosity, inquisitiveness, initiative, risk taking, and persistence?

What about opportunities to investigate and explore what exists in the home? Old things such as broken radios, sewing machines, screwdrivers, strips of material to make into dress up, real kitchen bowls, spoons, and stuff for concoctions. Do we rely too much on pretend tool kits, toy construction kits, store-bought play dough? Toys are not the same as real things that adults use. Children deserve the chance to learn firsthand about their culture through playing with real things that come from their culture.

The child care center is a relatively new institution still in the process of formation. We are at the precedent setting stage in developing places where childhoods do indeed happen. Unlike schools, child care centers are not encumbered by centuries of tradition. In our short history, we have acquired few impediments to creating a new institution. What kinds of tradition will we create? Can we dream a healthy vision of what can be or will we today produce baggage that those who follow us will have to carry?

We are making strides. We, as a profession, have established codes of ethics and developmentally appropriate practices to guide us in examining the experience we provide for young children in care. Ever since the groundbreaking document by the NAEYC in 1987 (Bredekamp, 1987) defined nationally agreed upon guidelines for practice (known as developmentally appropriate practices, or DAP), we have focused our attention increasingly on the issue of what is appropriate.

From *Child Care Information Exchange*, March 1997, pp. 35-40. © 1997 by Exchange Press, Inc. Reprinted by permission of *Child Care Information Exchange*, P.O. Box 2890, Redmond, WA 98073. (800) 221-2864.

We continue to make strides. DAP is not a static concept. It has been expanded in the brand new edition to include more cultural sensitivity. We would like to suggest that appropriate practice must also be examined in terms of authenticity. We ask the question — is it truly appropriate if it isn't also authentic?

Authenticity is a dimension sometimes neglected in discussions of practices with young children. Thinking in terms of authenticity of experience may help identify the feelings of discontent reflected in the questions we asked in the first paragraph.

Here are some examples of teachers engaging in small samples of what we consider authentic practice.

❖ ❖ ❖

Three toddlers and two four year olds are sitting in front of the TV at 5:40 PM. They are the last to go and there is still 20 minutes to wait. Jean, their caregiver, looks at them and asks, "Do you want to count money?" Without hesitation, they shout, "Yes!" They know and love "counting money." Jean takes them out to the front office and asks the director if she has any money that needs counting. The director tips out the change drawer, spilling hundreds of coins onto the carpeted floor. The children settle down happily to count the money, which means making piles of coins that go together. The 20 minutes fly by.

❖ ❖ ❖

A seven year old is allowed to spend several hours combining parts of several old ball-point pens into a new creation of his own that is short and stubby, doesn't look like a pen, but writes like one. He shows more pride in this creation than any of the craft projects presented him in his after-school care program.

❖ ❖ ❖

A teacher looking for a way to lock the new trike shed discovers an abandoned box full of locks and keys, but doesn't have time to pick through and find one that works. A four year old who has a notably short attention span happens along and shows interest in the jumble in the box. He spends the rest of the morning matching keys to padlocks, and proudly presents the box of keys in locks to the teacher right before lunch.

❖ ❖ ❖

A tired, filthy three year old remarks while showing off a hole out in the back corner of the play yard, "That's the best thing I ever did in nursery school." His teachers tell his mother when she comes to pick him up and confirm that he worked hours digging the hole with a small adult shovel. It was his own idea. Nobody suggested it to him. The next day he filled the hole back in without being asked.

❖ ❖ ❖

Tom, a caregiver of three year olds, decides he will bring his motorbike to work to fix it. Why not? He used to help his dad when he was a little fellow. Soon he is surrounded by small bits of motorcycle, tools, and rags. Off to the right there is a line of small mechanics also tinkering with their tricycles.

❖ ❖ ❖

What is authentic to one person, place, or situation will not necessarily hold for another. However, we all seem to recognize an authentic experience when we have one. It feels right. It sounds right. When we only consider appropriateness, is there a danger that we leave out this personal check point of authenticity?

Authenticity is a useful word. Authenticity wears its association with personal value judgments on its sleeve. Appropriateness, on the other hand, depends on what some group somewhere considers to be acceptable in some general sense. Appropriateness is arrived at by consensus decision making. When we try to decide what is appropriate, invariably we refer to higher, broader, and more remote authorities than ourselves and our immediate community. We often forget to consult our own beliefs and gut feelings and consider the requirements of the contexts we work in. It is when we trust ourselves and what we, as the local "expert," know that we access authenticity.

Here are some examples of familiar practices that cause many of us to feel that something inauthentic is happening.

❖ ❖ ❖

Sam: It's a box I got from my Nan and my brother got one, too, but his is already broken when my dog got it.

Sarah: So, what shape would you call that box, Sam?

Sam: A box.

Sarah: But what shape is it?

Sam: A box shape?

Sarah: It's a square shape, isn't it?

Sam: Uh huh.

Sarah: Actually there are lots of square shapes on your box, aren't there? Can you show the children a square on your box?

Sam: (Holds the box aloft for the children to see.)

How authentic is it to talk about shapes when the dog ate your brother's box?

❖ ❖ ❖

Marie is asked by another caregiver to take over in the sleep room. Marie groans inwardly. She absolutely hates patting children to sleep. It is boring. She always falls asleep herself and, besides, she's no good at it. They never go to sleep when she does it because she just doesn't believe in it. It's no good for children to be patted to sleep. It just makes them dependent on adults to get them to sleep. They should learn to do it themselves. There's no point in thinking such thoughts, though. The policy at this center is to pat, so pat she will.

Is authentic to do something you don't like, don't feel is effective, and don't want to do?

❖ ❖ ❖

Wendy is an assistant teacher in the toddler room. She is also the mother of four. She has been assigned to supervise finger painting with chocolate pudding. She watches several children hold back, and is told to encourage them because it is important for young children to have sensory experiences. She is repulsed by the activity and wonders how this practice might conflict with what the children are being taught at home about touching food (or feces). She wonders if, at this age, they can distinguish between a sensory activity and a "no, no."

How authentic is it to carry out a practice that disgusts you — one you don't believe in?

❖ ❖ ❖

These next examples push the issue of authenticity a bit further.

❖ ❖ ❖

Dawn uses the saying "You capture more flies with honey than with

vinegar" to guide her interactions with children and co-workers. She has a 100% positive approach to everything and can twist children around her finger with sweet talk. She manages to waylay most behavior problems by distracting offenders with new activities or promises of "surprises." Her techniques work. Are her manipulations appropriate? Are they authentic? How would you know?

❖ ❖ ❖

On the contrary, Lilly, is gruff and stern with children. She confronts behavior head on. Nobody gets away with anything around her and she uses no sweet talk. She's always got an eye out for misbehavior and issues regular warnings when she sees something coming. As stern as she is in the face of misbehavior, that's how warm and loving she is at other times. She handles the children a lot. Some are in awe of her sternness, but melt in her warmth.

Is Lilly appropriate? Is she authentic? How would you know?

❖ ❖ ❖

Samantha has been working with Jim for a week now. He is great with the kids, but he does get them stirred up. For instance, this morning he was horsing about with them pretending to be a lion and one of the children actually started crying. He cuddled her and got her screaming with laughter again soon after but Samantha doesn't really think this is appropriate behavior for a teacher.

Is Jim's behavior authentic? Is it appropriate? Does it have to be both?

❖ ❖ ❖

Research in early childhood education has begun to recognize that personal as well as formal knowl-

edge has a place in teachers' and caregivers' decision making. In studies of teachers' and caregivers' thinking about their practice, researchers highlight stories of practice that "ring true" or sound authentic (Jalongo and Isenberg, 1995). These studies emphasize the knowledge that teachers and caregivers themselves generate. Authentic, personal, and contextualized knowledge can be found in stories that teachers tell about their own practice. More formal knowledge sources tend to eliminate this kind of knowledge as being too specific and context bound.

It is the formal, principled knowledge that we find in curriculum guides, textbooks, directives from higher authorities, and indeed the NAEYC *Developmentally Appropriate Practice* document. Principled knowledge is what it sounds like — knowledge that is expressed in terms of principles or generalities and, as such, it is perceived to be context free (Mclean, 1993).

As early childhood educators, we are trained, in-serviced, and pressured by others to value principled knowledge more than the personal, practical, context-specific knowledge we generate ourselves, know on an intuitive level, and accumulate through our everyday experiences with young children. The stories of practice we tell each other and the practical knowledge embodied within them connect with what we know to be true, with what we believe.

This is not an argument to discard or denigrate principled knowledge. Both kinds of knowledge are important. But one always needs to be examined in light of the other. Some who work in child care only operate out of personal knowledge and experience and miss the broader view of principled knowledge that comes from research and formal study. They are one sided. On the other hand, some neglect to examine their principled knowledge in the light of personal feelings and experience. They fail to go beyond what they've been taught. They lack trust in their own ability to determine what is authentic for the circumstances and setting (Stonehouse, 1993).

Those who operate as professionals but fail to balance principled knowledge with personal knowledge and authenticity may have some of the feelings alluded to in the opening paragraph.

Some professionals who are also parents may operate authentically at home and feel guilty that they don't act more "professional" with their own children. How many of us yell in anger and frustration at our own children, but would never raise our voices or show anger around the children with whom we work? How many of us feel guilty at the inconsistency? (Gonzalez-Mena, 1995)

We suggest that perhaps child care teachers should balance principled knowledge with gut knowledge and aim for increased authenticity. This kind of balance may change both their teacher roles and their parent roles to some extent. That is not to say that we propose teachers and parents should act alike. Teachers, after all, must be more thoughtful, plan more for learning, not become overly attached, and be concerned about fairness to all children.

Parents, on the other hand, should accept the fact that parenting is a passionate job. Parents are, and should be, more attached, more spontaneous, more emotional, and a champion for their own child. It's not that they shouldn't be thoughtful about what they are doing, but too much analysis creates "analysis paralysis" and gets in the way of healthy parenting (Katz, 1977). Both teachers and parents should operate out of principled knowledge and

personal, practical knowledge. Both parents and teachers should be authentic.

How do we know and recognize authentic experiences, objects, interactions, conversations? Where does what is developmentally appropriate fit with what is authentic? Like everything else in life, there are many diverse ideas about what constitutes authenticity in child care. If authentic is that which reflects reality, one common definition, then the question is "whose reality?" Do we know what constitutes an authentic experience for the children we work with — for their families as well? How do we find out? There are likely to be many authentic ways to work with children and they won't all look the same.

Like "quality," authenticity is a complex and elusive characteristic and best understood as occurring along a continuum. Most experience can probably be located somewhere between entirely authentic and entirely unauthentic rather than at either end of the spectrum. Perhaps thinking along these continua will help in evaluating the authenticity of an experience.

An authentic experience is one that:

• is closer to being true than false in nature;

• is the real thing more often than a replica;

• is characterized more by honesty than deception;

• is richer, wider, deeper than its synthetic counterpart;

• feels more right than wrong;

• is more evocative than evoking no feeling at all.

The key is to avoid dichotomies of right and wrong, appropriate and

inappropriate, but consider that almost every situation is potentially both. We must tap into our personal knowledge base and that of others with whom we work and live to discover the knowledge held in the variety of beliefs and views. That knowledge must work in conjunction with principled knowledge in determining what is appropriate and authentic. We can't use books or sets of guidelines alone, but must use our gut reactions as well.

We must bring our "real selves" to work with us. Consider the caregiver who is angry and frustrated about a child who continually hits other children. For the tenth time, she hustles over to intervene when Matthew and Tommy are struggling over the red-handled shovel. She arrives just in time to stop Matthew from whapping Tommy in the head with a blue-handled shovel. She squats down next to Matthew and says in a calm, even tone, "Matthew, use your words. Tell Tommy what you want." She's well trained. She hides her true feelings about the situation.

How authentic is it to speak as if you were ordering a cappuccino when, in fact, you are completely fed up? Shouldn't children perhaps know when an adult is feeling something deeply?

How bad would it be for children to see adults being natural in a child care setting? Consider this scene. The director glances up and sees the new caregiver, Miriam, talking and laughing once again with another caregiver while they're both sitting on the edge of the sand pit. Miriam is almost weeping with the hilarity of some incident. So is the other caregiver. A few children approach them and stand watching them laugh. Soon there is a circle of children all standing around the two women laughing. They have big smiles on their faces. They start giggling. In no time, the whole group is laughing.

Why shouldn't children see adults enjoying themselves, having a good laugh? At home, children are likely to see adults expressing all sorts of feelings. If they are to have a childhood in child care, shouldn't they see adults being more authentic than they are when acting in an unemotional "professional" manner?

We must not miss the opportunity we have today to expand our definitions of good quality care and education to include not only what we, as a profession, believe is appropriate, but what we, as professional individuals, know is authentic. This is not going to be an easy process. It will require much discussion, argument, and compromise as groups of early childhood professionals and parents determine what they mean by "authentic" for the children who spend their childhoods in child care. In doing this, we won't be generating new sets of guidelines for others to follow. Accommodating the principle of personal authenticity will always remain within the domain of the personal and local. Nevertheless, determining a process for distinguishing what is authentic from what is not provides a growth point for the profession.

References

Bredekamp, S. (editor). *Developmentally Appropriate Practice in Early Childhood Programs Serving Children From Birth through Age 8.* Washington, DC: National Association for the Education of Young Children, 1987.

Gonzalez-Mena, J. *Dragon Mom: Confessions of a Child Development Expert.* Napa, CA: Rattle OK Publications, 1995.

Greenman, J. "Living in the Real World." *Child Care Information Exchange,* July 1992, pp. 21–23.

Jalongo, M. R. and J. P. Isenberg. *Teachers' Stories: From Personal Narrative to Professional Insight.* San Francisco: Jossey-Bass, 1995.

Katz, L. G. *Talks with Teachers.* Washington, DC: National Association for the Education of Young Children, 1977.

Mclean, V. "Learning from Teachers' Stories." *Childhood Education.* Annual Theme Issue, 1993, pp. 265–268.

Stonehouse, A. "Is Appropriate Practice the Same Whatever the Setting?" Symposium address given at the Creche and Kindergarten Association of Queensland National Early Childhood Conference, Brisbane, June 1993.

In Search of the American Family

WHERE ARE THE GOOD OLD DAYS?

Raising a family is hard enough without having to live up to myths. In fact, the American family is as strong—and as fragile—as it ever was.

Stephanie Coontz

Family historian Stephanie Coontz is the author of The Way We Never Were: American Families and the Nostalgia Trap *(Basic Books, 1992) and* The Way We Really Are: Coming to Terms with America's Changing Families (Basic Books, 1997). *A recipient of the Dale Richmond award from the American Academy of Pediatrics, Coontz teaches history and family studies at The Evergreen State College, Olympia, WA.*

T HE AMERICAN FAMILY IS UNDER SIEGE. To listen to the rhetoric of recent months, we have all fallen down on the job. We're selfish; too preoccupied with our own gratification to raise our children properly. We are ungrateful; we want a handout, not a hand.

If only we'd buckle down, stay on the straight and narrow, keep our feet on the ground, our shoulder to the wheel, our eye on the ball, our nose to the grindstone. Then everything would be all right, just as it was in the family-friendly '50s, when we could settle down in front of the television after an honest day's work and see our lives reflected in shows like *Ozzie and Harriet* and *Father Knows Best.*

But American families have been under siege more often than not during the past 300 years. Moreover, they have always been diverse, both in structure and ethnicity. No family type has been able to protect its members from the roller-coaster rides of economic setbacks or social change. Changes that improved the lives and fortunes of one family type or individual often resulted in losses for another.

A man employed in the auto industry, for example, would have been better off financially in the

EARLY DAYS

In 1745 in Massachusetts, any child age 6 who did not know the alphabet was removed from the home and placed with another family.

During the Civil War, the number of orphans in almshouses increased by 300 percent. In 1825, there were two orphanages in New York State; by 1866, there were 60, but still not enough to meet the need. Homeless children swarmed in the cities' streets and "menaced the gentry."

1950s than now, but his retired parents would be better off today. If he had a strong taste for power, he might prefer Colonial times, when a man was the undisputed monarch of the household and any disobedience by wife, child, or servant was punishable by whipping. But woe betide that man if he wasn't born to property. In those days, men without estates could be told what to wear, where to live, and whom to associate with.

His wife, on the other hand, might have been happier in the 1850s, when she might have afforded two or three servants. We can be pretty sure, though, that the black or Irish servants of that day would not have found the times so agreeable. And today's children, even those scarred by divorce, might well want to stay put rather than live in the late 19th century, when nearly half of them died before they reached their late teens.

From *Modern Maturity,* May/June 1996, pp. 36–43. © 1996 by Stephanie Coontz. Reprinted by permission.

THE AMERICAN FAMILY HAS ALWAYS BEEN VULNERABLE TO SOCIAL AND ECONOMIC CHANGE

A History of Tradeoffs

These kinds of tradeoffs have characterized American family life from the beginning. Several distinctly different types of families already coexisted in Colonial times: On the East Coast, the Iroquois lived in longhouses with large extended families. Small families were more common among the nomadic Indian groups, where marital separation, though frequent, caused no social stigma or loss of access to group resources. African-American slaves, whose nuclear families had been torn apart, built extended family networks through ritual co-parenting, the adoption of orphans, and complex naming patterns designed to preserve links among families across space and time.

White Colonial families were also diverse: High death rates meant that a majority spent some time in a stepfamily. Even in intact families, membership ebbed and flowed; many children left their parents' home well before puberty to work as servants or apprentices to other households. Colonial family values didn't sentimentalize childhood. Mothers were far less involved in caring for their children than modern working women, typically delegating the task to servants or older siblings. Children living away from home usually wrote to their fathers, sometimes adding a postscript asking him to "give my regards to my mother, your wife."

A Revolution of Sorts

Patriarchal authority started to collapse at the beginning of the Revolutionary War: The rate of premarital conception soared and children began to marry out of birth order. Small family farms and shops flourished and, as in Colonial days, a wife's work was valued as highly as her husband's. The revolutionary ferment also produced the first stirrings of feminism and civil rights. A popular 1773 Massachusetts almanac declared: "Then equal Laws let custom find, and neither Sex oppress: More Freedom give to Womankind or to Mankind give less." New Jersey women had the right to vote after the Revolution. In several states slaves won their freedom when they sued, citing the Declaration of Independence.

But commercial progress undermined these movements. The spread of international trade networks

---

SOME DO WELL . . .

In the 1840s and '50s, a respectable woman was expected to be passionless and to show "becoming abhorrence" to sexual advances.

In his classic book, Democracy in America, *French social philosopher Alexis de Tocqueville commented admiringly on the American family of the 1830s:* "Democracy stretches social bonds but tightens natural ones. It brings relatives together even as it pulls citizens apart."

---

and the invention of the cotton gin in 1793 increased slavery's profits. Ironically, when revolutionary commitment to basic human equality went head-to-head with economic dependence on slavery, the result was an increase in racism: Apologists now justified slavery on the grounds that blacks were *less* than human. This attitude spilled over to free blacks, who gradually lost both their foothold in the artisan trades and the legal rights they'd enjoyed in early Colonial times. The subsequent deterioration in their status worked to the advantage of Irish immigrants, previously considered nonwhite and an immoral underclass.

Feminist ideals also faded as industrialization and wage labor took work away from the small family farms and businesses, excluding middle-class wives from their former economic partnerships. For the first time, men became known as breadwinners. By the post-Civil War era of 1870–90, the participation of married women in the labor force was at an all-time low; social commentators labeled those wives who took part in political or economic life sexual degenerates or "semi-hermaphrodites."

Women Lose; Children Lose More

As women left the workforce children entered it by the thousands, often laboring in abysmal conditions up to ten hours a day. In the North, they worked in factories or tenement workshops. As late as 1900, 120,000 children worked in Pennsylvania's mines and factories. In the South, states passed "apprentice" laws binding black children out as unpaid laborers, often under the pretext that

---

. . . OTHERS DO NOT

Between 1890 and 1915, 18 million immigrants entered the country; then tenement homes often doubled as sweatshops for child labor.

By 1900, the U.S. had the highest divorce rate in the world. Birthrates among the educated had plummeted to an alarming degree, prompting Teddy Roosevelt to call it "race suicide" in 1903. Some state legislatures passed laws prohibiting abortions in order to boost the nation's birthrate.

---

their parents neglected them. Plantation owners (whose wives and daughters encased themselves in corsets and grew their fingernails long) accused their former female slaves of "loaferism" when they resisted field labor in order to stay closer to home with their children.

So for every 19th-century middle-class family that was able to nurture its women and children comfortably inside the family circle, there was an Irish or German girl scrubbing floors, a Welsh boy mining coal, a black girl doing laundry, a black mother and child picking cotton, and a Jewish or Italian daughter making dresses, cigars, or artificial flowers in a sweatshop.

Meanwhile, self-styled "child-saver" charity workers, whose definition of an unfit parent had more to do with religion, ethnicity, or poverty than behavior, removed other children from their families. They sent these "orphans" to live with Western farmers who needed extra hands—or merely dumped them in a farm town with a dollar and an earnest lecture about escaping the evils of city life.

The Outer Family Circle

Even in the comfortable middle-class households of the late 19th century, norms and values were far different from those we ascribe to "traditional" families. Many households took in boarders, lodgers, or unmarried relatives. The nuclear family wasn't the primary focus of emotional life. The Victorian insistence on separate spheres for men and women made male-female relations extremely stilted, so women commonly turned to other women for their most intimate relationships. A woman's diary would rhapsodize for pages about a female friend, explaining how they carved their initials on a tree, and then remark, "Accepted the

marriage proposal of Mr. R. last night" without further comment. Romantic friendships were also common among young middle-class men, who often recorded that they missed sleeping with a college roommate and laying an arm across his bosom. No one considered such relationships a sign of homosexuality; indeed, the term wasn't even invented until the late 19th century.

Not that 19th-century Americans were asexual: By midcentury New York City had one prostitute for every 64 men; the mayor of Savannah estimated his city had one for every 39. Perhaps prostitution's spread was inevitable at a time when the middle class referred to the "white meat" and "dark meat" of chicken to spare ladies the embarrassment of hearing the terms "breast" or "thigh."

The Advent of the Couple

The early 20th century brought more changes. Now the emotional focus shifted to the husband and wife. World War I combined with a resurgence of feminism to hasten the collapse of Victorian values, but we can't underestimate the role the emergence of a mass consumer market played: Advertisers quickly found that romance and sexual titillation worked wonders for the bottom line.

Marriage experts and the clergy, concerned that longer lifespans would put a strain on marriages, denounced same-sex friendships as competitors to love; people were expected to direct all their emotional, altruistic and sensual impulses into marriage. While this brought new intimacy and sexual satisfaction to married life, it also introduced two trends that disturbed observers. One was an increased dissatisfaction with what used to be considered adequate relationships. Great expectations, social historian Elaine Tyler May points out in her book of the same name, could generate great disappointments. It's no surprise that the U.S. has had both the highest consumption of romance novels and the highest divorce rates in the world since the early part of the 20th century.

The second consequence of this new cult of married bliss was the emergence of an independent and increasingly sexualized youth culture. In the late 19th century, middle-class courtship revolved around the institution of "calling." A boy was invited to call by the girl or her parents. It was as inappropriate then for a boy to hint he'd like to be asked over as it was in the 1950s for a girl to hint she'd like to be asked out. By the mid-1920s, calling had been almost totally replaced by dating, which took young people away from parental control but made a girl far more dependent on the

EVEN IN THE LATE 1800s FAMILY VALUES VARIED A GREAT DEAL FROM THOSE OF THE 1950s

boy's initiative. Parents especially worried about the moral dangers the automobile posed—and with reason: A middle-class boy was increasingly likely to have his first sexual encounter with a girlfriend rather than a prostitute.

The early part of the century brought a different set of changes to America's working class. In the 1920s, for the first time, a majority of children were born to male-breadwinner, female-homemaker families. Child labor laws and the spread of mass education allowed more parents to keep their children out of the workforce. Numerous immigrant families, however, continued to pull their offspring out of school so they could help support the family, often arousing intense generational conflicts. African-American families kept their children in school longer than other families in those groups, but their wives were much more likely to work outside the home.

There Goes the Family

In all sectors of society, these changes created a sense of foreboding. *Is Marriage on the Skids?* asked one magazine article of the times; *What Is the Family Still Good For?* fretted another. Popular commentators harkened back to the "good old days," bemoaning the sexual revolution, the fragility of nuclear-family ties, the cult of youthful romance, and the threat of the "emancipated woman."

The stock market crash, the Great Depression, and the advent of World War II moved such fears to the back burner. During the '30s and '40s, family trends fluctuated from one extreme to another. Depression hardship—contrary to its television portrayal on *The Waltons*—usually failed to make family and community life stronger. Divorce rates fell, but desertion and domestic violence rose sharply; economic stress often translated into punitive parenting that left children with emotional scars still apparent to social researchers decades later. Murder rates in the '30s were as high as in the 1980s; rates of marriages and births plummeted.

WWII started a marriage boom, but by 1946 the number of divorces was double that in 1941. This time the social commentators blamed working women, interfering in-laws and, above all, inadequate mothers. In 1946, psychiatrist Edward Strecker published *Their Mothers' Sons: The Psychiatrist Examines an American Problem*, which argued that women who were old-fashioned "moms"

THE DAWN BEFORE . . .

The clock has struck "sex o'clock" shrieked a tabloid headline in 1913. The 1920s brought flappers, short skirts, and "necking parties."

In the '20s, the average annual income was about $1,000; only middle-class families earning $3,000 or more could afford domestic help. By 1927, 60 percent of homes had electricity and some of the new-fangled labor-saving appliances were showing up (the electric iron was a big hit).

---

instead of modern "mothers" were emasculating American boys.

Moms, he said disapprovingly, were immature and unstable and sought emotional recompense for the disappointments of their own lives. They took care of aging parents and tried to exert too much control over their children. Mothers, on the other hand, put their parents in nursing homes and derived all their satisfaction from the nuclear family while cheerfully urging independence on their children. Without motherhood, said the experts, a woman's life meant nothing. Too much mothering, though, would destroy her own marriage and her son's life. These new values put women in an emotional double-bind, and it's hardly surprising that tranquilizers, which came on the scene in the '50s, were marketed and prescribed almost exclusively to housewives.

The '50s: Paradise Lost?

Such were the economic and cultural ups and downs that created the 1950s. If that single decade had actually represented the "tradition" it would be reasonable to argue that the family has indeed collapsed. By the mid 1950s, the age of marriage and parenthood had dropped dramatically, divorce rates bottomed out and the birthrate, one sociologist has recently noted, "approached that of India." The proportion of children in Ozzie-and-Harriet type families reached an all-time high of 60 percent.

Today, in contrast, a majority of mothers, including those with preschool children, work outside the home. Fifty percent of children live with both bio-

. . . THE DARK YEARS

During the Depression, divorce rates dropped; desertion soared. Half of all births were in families on relief or making under $1,000 a year.

World War II years: The GNP soared: from $90 billion in 1939 to $213 billion in 1945. So did divorces: from 264,000 in 1940 to 610,000 in 1946. Women and teenager built aircraft, ships, tanks, weapons. Fewer than half the teenagers who entered high school graduated.

It's All Relative

Why then, do many people remember the 1950s as so much easier than today? One reason is that after the hardships of the Depression and WWII, things *were* improving on many fronts. Though poverty rates were higher than today, they were falling. Economic inequality was also decreasing. The teenage birthrate was almost twice as high in 1957 as today, but most young men could afford to marry. Violence against African-Americans was appallingly widespread, yet many blacks got jobs in the expanding manufacturing industries and for the first time found an alternative to Southern agriculture's peonage.

What we forget when politicians tell us we should revive the 1950s family is that the social stability of that period was due less to its distinctive family forms than to its unique socioeconomic and political climate. High rates of unionization, heavy corporate investment in manufacturing, and generous government assistance in the form of public-works projects, veterans' benefits, student loans and housing subsidies gave young families a tremendous jump start, created predictable paths out of poverty, and led to unprecedented increases in real wages. By the time the "traditional male breadwinner" reached age 30, in both the 1950s and '60s, he could pay the principal and interest on a median-priced home on only 15–18 percent of his income. Social Security promised a much-needed safety net for the elderly, formerly the poorest segment of the population. These economic carrots combined with the sticks of McCarthyism and segregation to keep social dissent on the back burner.

logical parents, almost one quarter live with single parents and more than 21 percent are in stepfamilies. Three quarters of today's 18–24-year-olds have never been married, while almost 50 percent of all first marriages—and 60 percent of remarriages—will end in divorce. Married couples wait longer to bear children and have fewer of them. For the first time there are more married couples without children than with them. Less than one quarter of contemporary marriages are supported by one wage earner.

Taking the 1950s as the traditional norm, however, overstates both the novelty of modern family life and the continuity of tradition. The 1950s was the most atypical decade in the entire history of American marriage and family life. In some ways, today's families are closer to older patterns than were '50s families. The median age at first marriage today is about the same as it was at the beginning of the century, while the proportion of never-married people is actually lower. The number of women who are coproviders and the proportion of children living in stepfamilies are both closer to that of Colonial days than the 1950s. Even the ethnic diversity among modern families is closer to the patterns of the early part of this century than to the demographics of the 1950s. And the time a modern working mother devotes to childcare is higher than in Colonial or Revolutionary days.

The 1950s family, in other words, was not at all traditional; nor was it always idyllic. Though many people found satisfactions in family life during that period, we now know the experiences of many groups and individuals were denied. Problems such as alcoholism, battering, and incest were swept under the rug. So was discrimination against ethnic groups, political dissidents, women, elders, gays, lesbians, religious minorities and the handicapped. Rates of divorce and unwed motherhood were low, but that did not prevent 30 percent of American children from living in poverty, a higher figure than at present.

The New Trends

Because the '60s were a time of social protest, many people forget that families still made economic gains throughout the decade. Older workers and homeowners continued to build security for their retirement years. The postwar boom and government subsidies cut child poverty in half from 1949 to 1959. It was halved again, to its lowest levels ever, from 1959 to 1969. The high point of health and nutrition for poor children came in 1970, a period that coincided with the peak years of the Great Society, not the high point of the '50s family.

Since 1973, however, a new phase has emerged. Some things have continued to improve: High school graduation rates are at an all-time high; minority test scores rose steadily from 1970 to 1990; poverty rates among the elderly have continued to fall while life expectancy has risen.

GENEROUS FEDERAL PROGRAMS GAVE YOUNG 1950s FAMILIES A TREMENDOUS JUMP START

Other trends show mixed results: The easy availability of divorce has freed individuals from oppressive or even abusive marriages, but many divorces have caused emotional and economic suffering for both children and adults. Women have found new satisfaction at work, and there's considerable evidence that children can benefit from having a working mother, but the failure of businesses—and some husbands—to adjust to working mothers' needs has caused much family stress and discord.

In still other areas, the news is quite bleak. Children have now replaced seniors as the poorest segment of the population; the depth and concentration of child poverty has increased over the past 20 years so it's now at 1965 levels. Many of the gains ethnic groups made in the 1960s and '70s have been eroded.

History suggests that most of these setbacks originate in social and economic forces rather than in the collapse of some largely mythical traditional family. Perhaps the most powerful of these sources is the breakdown of America's implicit postwar wage bargain with the working class, where corporations ensured labor stability by increasing employment, rewarding increased productivity with higher wages, and investing in jobs and community infrastructure. At the same time, the federal government subsidized home ownership and higher education.

Since 1973, however, real wages have fallen for most families. It increasingly requires the work of two earners to achieve the modest upward mobility one could provide in the 1950s and '60s. Unemployment rates have risen steadily as corporations have abandoned the communities that grew up around them, seeking cheap labor overseas or in nonunionized sectors of the South. Involuntary part-time work has soared. As *Time* magazine noted in 1993, the predictable job ladders of the '50s and '60s have been sawed off: "Companies are portable, workers are throwaway." A different article in the same issue found, "Long-term commitments . . . are anathema to the modern corporation."

During the 1980s the gap between the rich and middle-class widened in 46 states, and each year since 1986 has set a new postwar record for the gap between rich and poor. In 1980 a CEO earned 30 to 40 times as much as the average worker; by 1994 he earned 187 times as much. Meanwhile, the real wages of a young male high school graduate are lower today than those earned by his 1963 counterpart.

A MIXED BAG

The 1950s: Father knew best; mother stayed home; wages grew; divorces dropped; teen pregnancies peaked (so did teen marriages).

Many black families moved north, leaving the agricultural South to share in the postwar industrial boom. But racism was rampant. In 1957, Life magazine noted that of the 10,000 blacks working at the Ford Motor Company's Dearborn plant, not one was allowed to live in Dearborn.

These economic changes are not driven by the rise in divorce and unwed motherhood. Decaying wage and job structures—not changing family structures—have caused the overwhelming bulk of income redistribution. And contrary to what has been called a new bipartisan consensus, marriage is not the solution to poverty. According to sociologist Donald J. Hernandez, Ph.D., formerly with the U.S. Census Bureau, even if every child in America were reunited with both biological parents, two thirds of those who are poor today would still be poor.

Our Uncertain Future

History's lessons are both positive and negative. We can take comfort from the fact that American families have always been in flux and that a wide variety of family forms and values have worked well for different groups at different times. There's no reason to assume that recent changes are entirely destructive. Families have always been vulnerable to rapid economic change and have always needed economic and emotional support from beyond their own small boundaries. Our challenge is to grapple with the sweeping transformations we're currently undergoing. History demonstrates it's not as simple as returning to one or another family form from the past. Though there are many precedents for successfully reorganizing family life, there are no clear answers to the issues facing us as we enter the 21st century.

Child Advocacy Directory

The following national organizations engage in advocacy in the early childhood arena. The person listed as CEO is in most cases the organization's executive director. When a separate person is listed after ECE, this person leads the organization's early childhood division.

Alliance of Work/Life Professionals
465 Carlisle Drive
Herndon, VA 22070
(800) 874-9393
CEO: Brad Googins, Mary Ellen Gornick

Mission: The Alliance of Work/Life Professionals is a membership organization with the vision of promoting work/family and personal life balance. Through sharing cutting edge thinking, promising practices, and helpful resources, the Alliance strives both to improve the professionalism of those working in the work/life arena and to influence the better integration of work and family life.

American Academy of Pediatrics
141 Northwest Point Boulevard
Elk Grove Village, IL 60007
(800) 433-9016
Fax: (847) 228-1281
CEO: Joe M. Sanders, Jr., MD
ECE: Kathleen Sanabria

Mission: The American Academy of Pediatrics is committed to the attainment of optimal physical, mental, and social health for all infants, children, adolescents, and young adults.

Association for Childhood Education International
11501 Georgia Avenue, Suite 315
Wheaton, MD 20902
(301) 942-2443/(800) 423-3563
Fax: (301) 942-3012
CEO: Gerald C. Odland

Mission: ACEI's mission is to promote the inherent rights, education, and well-being of all children to bring into active cooperation all individuals and groups concerned with children; to raise the standard of preparation for those actively involved with the care and development of children; and to focus the public's attention on the rights and needs of children.

Board on Children, Youth, and Families
(of the National Research Council and the Institute of Medicine)
2101 Constitution Avenue NW, HA 156
Washington, DC 20418
(202) 334-2998
Fax: (202) 334-3829
CEO: Deborah Phillips
ECE: Anne Bridgman

Mission: The Board on Children, Youth, and Families was created in 1993 to provide a national focal point for authoritative, nonpartisan analysis of child, youth, and family issues relevant to policy decisions. It does so primarily by establishing committees to synthesize and evaluate research from scientific disciplines that are relevant to critical national issues, including child care.

Center on Effective Services for Children
PO Box 27412
Washington, DC 20038-7412
(202) 785-9524
Fax: (202) 833-4454
CEO: Jule M. Sugarman

Mission: The Center on Effective Services for Children is dedicated to improving the efficiency and effectiveness of child and family services. Its current focus has been preparing states and localities to take advantage of impending federal changes to improve services and offering guidance on how multiple programs and funding sources can be combined.

Child Care Action Campaign
330 7th Avenue, 17th Floor
New York, NY 10001-5010
(212) 239-0138
Fax: (212) 268-6515
CEO: Barbara Reisman

Mission: The Child Care Action Campaign (CCAC) is a national non-profit coalition of individuals and organizations whose goal is to improve the lives of children and their families by expanding the supply of good quality, affordable child care. CCAC uses its information resources and strategic skills to engage parents, policymakers, business leaders, and child care providers in improving child care and early education.

Child Welfare League of America
440 First Street NW, Suite 310
Washington, DC 20001
(202) 638-2952
Fax: (202) 638-4004
CEO: David Liederman
ECE: Bruce Hershfield

Mission: CWLA believes that every child is entitled to live in a loving, stable, and protective family, free from abuse and neglect. CWLA is the nation's oldest and largest organization devoted entirely to the well-being of America's vulnerable children. CWLA's almost 1,000 members provide a wide range of services to strengthen and support families for children.

Children's Defense Fund
25 E Street NW
Washington, DC 20001
(202) 628-8787
Fax: (202) 662-3560
CEO: Marian Wright Edelman
ECE: Helen Blank

Mission: CDF exists to provide a voice for all American children. Our staff includes

From *Child Care Information Exchange*, September/October 1996, pp. 25, 27-28. © 1996 by Exchange Press, Inc. Reprinted by permission of *Child Care Information Exchange*, P.O. Box 2890, Redmond, WA 98073. (800) 221-2864.

specialists in children's issues, including child care. CDF gathers data and disseminates information on key children's issues involving child care and Head Start. We monitor the development and implementation of federal and state policies.

Children's Foundation
725 15th Street NW, #505
Washington, DC 20005
Voice/Fax: (202) 347-3300
CEO: Kay Hollestelle
ECE: Sandra Gellert

Mission: The Children's Foundation is a national educational non-profit organization striving to improve the lives of children and those who care for them. Our mission is to provide a voice for caregivers, children, and their families on issues of critical concern. We conduct research and provide information and training.

National Association for the Education of Young Children
1509 16th Street NW
Washington, DC 20036-1426
(202) 232-8777/(800) 424-2460
Fax: (202) 328-1846
CEO: Marilyn M. Smith
ECE: Barbara Willer, M. Therese Gnezda

Mission: NAEYC exists for achieving healthy development and high quality education for all young children. To accomplish its mission, NAEYC promotes improvements in professional practice and working conditions in all family child care homes, early childhood programs, and centers. Building and maintaining a strong, diverse, and inclusive organization enables NAEYC to achieve these goals.

National Association for Family Child Care
206 6th Avenue, Suite 900
Des Moines, IA 50309
(515) 282-8192
Fax: (515) 282-9117
CEO: Deborah E. Eaton

Mission: NAFCC is the national membership organization dedicated to strengthening and expanding the more than 400 local and state family child care provider associations. NAFCC facilitates the professional development of the field in identifying and developing existing and emerging leaders; administering a provider accreditation program; and producing and disseminating informational materials.

National Association of Child Care Resource and Referral Agencies
1319 F Street NW
Washington, DC 20004
(202) 393-5501
Fax: (202) 393-1109
CEO: Yasmina S. Vinci
ECE: Rachel Bly

Mission: NACCRRA's mission is to promote the growth and development of quality child care resource and referral services and to exercise national policy leadership to build a diverse, quality child care system with parental choice and equal access for all families.

National Black Child Development Institute
1023 15th Street NW, #600
Washington, DC 20005
(202) 387-1281
Fax: (202) 234-1738
CEO: Evelyn Moore

Mission: NBCDI is dedicated to improving the quality of life for Black children and families through services and advocacy. As a national, membership organization, NBCDI keeps its members informed about critical issues in child care, education, child welfare, and health that face Black children and families. NBCDI's affiliate network is composed of dedicated volunteers who help to educate their communities about national, state, and local issues facing Black children and families.

National Center for Children in Poverty
154 Haven Avenue
New York, NY 10032
(212) 927-8793
Fax: (212) 927-9162
CEO: J. Lawrence Aber
ECE: Ann Collins

Mission: The National Center for Children in Poverty (NCCP) uses demographic research and program and policy analyses to identify and communicate strategies that reduce the incidence of young child poverty and improve the lives of poor young children.

National Center for the Early Childhood Work Force
733 15th Street NW
Washington, DC 20005
(202) 737-7700
Fax: (202) 737-0370
CEO: Claudia E. Wayne

Mission: NCECW is a policy, research, and advocacy organization dedicated to enhancing the compensation, working conditions, and training of child care staff and providers. It coordinates the Worthy Wage Campaign, a grassroots initiative empowering the work force itself to press for staffing solutions, and the Early Childhood Mentoring Alliance, a network for mentors and mentoring programs nationwide.

National Child Care Association, Inc.
1029 Railroad Street
Conyers, GA 30207
(800) 543-7161
Fax: (770) 388-7772

CEO: Lynn White
ECE: Nancy Granese

Mission: The purpose of NCCA is to promote the growth of quality child care focusing on licensed, proprietary, tax-paying providers with emphasis on efforts to (1) provide the public with information concerning the benefits of licensed, center-based child care services; (2) assist legislative, regulatory, standard-setting bodies in the development of policies affecting child care services; and (3) expand the availability of professionally managed, licensed, proprietary child care centers.

National Coalition for Campus Child Care
PO Box 258
Cascade, WI 53011
(414) 528-7080/(800) 813-8207
Fax: (414) 528-8753
CEO: Michael Kalinowski
ECE: Todd Boressoff

Mission: NCCCC is a non-profit educational membership organization. NCCCC supports research and activities affecting college and university early childhood education and service settings, family and work issues, and the field of early childhood education in general. NCCCC expresses this mission through its newsletters, publications, conferences, and grants.

National Head Start Association
1651 Prince Street
Alexandria, VA 22314
(703) 739-0875
Fax: (703) 739-0878
CEO: Sarah M. Greene
ECE: James A. Delaney

Mission: The National Head Start Association (NHSA) strives to (1) define and implement strategies for funding the Head Start program; (2) be a direct provider of training and professional development services; (3) advocate for the provision of quality services to the Head Start community; (4) advocate for measures that support the development of children; (5) advocate for measures that assist parents to meet the needs of their children and families; (6) advocate for professional development for Head Start staff; and (7) develop and disseminate research, information, and resources.

National Women's Law Center
11 Dupont Circle NW, #800
Washington, DC 20036
(202) 588-5180
Fax: (202) 588-5185
CEO: Nancy Duff Campbell
ECE: Elisabeth Donahue

Mission: The National Women's Law Center is a national organization that has been working since 1972 to advance and protect women's legal rights. The center focuses on major policy issues of importance to women and their families, including employment, education, family support, income security, and reproductive rights and health.

Southern Early Childhood Association
7107 West 12th, Suite 102
Little Rock, AR 72215
(800) 305-7322
Fax: (501) 663-2114
CEO: Dr. Clarissa Leister-Willis

Mission: For almost 50 years, the Southern Early Childhood Association (SECA) has provided teachers and caregivers of young children with practitioner-oriented publications, opportunities for professional growth and development, and has become a regional organization dedicated to providing for all children.

USA Child Care
2104 East 18th Street
Kansas City, MO 64127
(816) 474-3751, ext. 603
Fax: (816) 474-1818
CEO: Shirley Stubbs Gillette
ECE: Cliff Marcussen

Mission: The mission of USA Child Care is to provide a national voice for direct service providers to ensure quality, comprehensive childhood care, and education that is affordable and accessible for all families. The primary focus of the organization is the provision of quality childhood care and education for low- and moderate-income families.

YMCA of the USA
101 North Wacker Drive
Chicago, IL 60606
(312) 977-0031
Fax: (312) 977-9063
CEO: David Mercer
ECE: John Brooks

Mission: The YMCA, one of the nation's largest providers of child care, is a not-for-profit agency which puts Christian principles into practice through programs that build healthy spirit, mind, and body for all. YMCA child care centers are family centered with an emphasis on building self-esteem and character.

YWCA of the USA
624 9th Street NW, 3rd Floor
Washington, DC 20001
(202) 628-3636
Fax: (202) 783-7123

CEO: Dr. Prema Mathai-Davis
ECE: Rhea Staff

Mission: The YWCA is a women's membership movement to empower women and girls and eliminate racism.

Zero to Three/National Center for Infants, Toddlers, and Families
734 15th Street NW, Suite 1000
Washington, DC 20005
(202) 638-1144
Fax: (202) 638-0875
CEO: Matthew Melmed, JD
ECE: Beverly Roberson Jackson, Ed.D.

Mission: Zero to Three's urgent mission is to advance the healthy development of America's young children, by: (1) increasing public awareness of the critical importance of the first three years of life; (2) fostering professional excellence through training and related activities; (3) inspiring tomorrow's leaders by identifying and engaging promising young professionals; (4) promoting the discovery and application of new knowledge; (5) stimulating effective service approaches and responsive policies; and (6) educating parents and other caregivers.

New Ways of Learning = New Ways of Teaching

Mary K. Heuwinkel

Mary K. Heuwinkel is a doctoral student in Elementary Education, University of Northern Colorado, Greeley.

Since the late 1970s, educators have been researching such concepts and practices as mastery learning, programmed learning, behavioral objectives, ability grouping, Bloom's Taxonomy, word attack skills and classroom management. Teachers have been taught that specific teaching behaviors result in higher standardized test scores for their students (Brandt, 1988/89; Elmore, 1992; Resnick & Klopfer, 1989).

More recently, journal articles, in-service training programs and education courses are emphasizing such ideas as whole language, reader's and writer's workshops, NCTM (National Council of Teachers of Mathematics) Standards, discourse, Grand Conversations, literacy, self-directed learners and learning communities. Now, teachers are being taught that student learning is a process that requires students to be actively, purposefully engaged.

Clearly, education reformers are calling for far-reaching changes in instructional practices. Teachers implementing these new practices experience a dramatic shift in their role. Others considering implementation are wondering how best to start. Some teachers, parents, legislators and members of business and industry question the efficacy of such different strategies, often sparking acrimonious public debates. School board members are voted in or out according to their views on these methods. All who are aware of the changes are making decisions about their merit and effective use. Yet seemingly few of these teachers, decision-makers and other stakeholders understand the philosophical roots of these innovations, their assumptions and intents, or the connections among them (Battista, 1994; Peterson & Knapp, 1993; Watson, 1994).

What is this "revolution" in teaching? How did it come about? What are the fundamental differences from traditional practices? Can the new practices mesh with more established ones? Are these innovations more effective than traditional strategies? Are these ideas just the latest fad or are they solid, research-based alternatives?

These questions and others will be answered only by studying the principles of learning and teaching that underlie the innovations. With such an understanding, parents, legislators and educators can make sound and reasoned decisions regarding implementation. When teachers understand the foundations as well as the surface features of new instructional practices, they will be able to use them more effectively (Battista, 1994; Peterson & Knapp, 1993; Watson, 1994).

Current Innovations in Reading and Language Arts

A visitor to Mr. R's 3rd-grade class hears a low hum of activity and sees children scattered around the room, some working alone and some in groups. Seven children are clustered around Mr. R, who is giving a mini-lesson on using commas. The students are focused on a big book and discussing the patterns they see in comma placement. Mr. R directs the children's attention to individual trade books they have chosen and asks them to find more examples of commas. Later, he will ask them to choose a piece of writing from their writing folders and work in pairs to place commas correctly.

In another part of the room, four students are discussing their reactions to the book *Freckle Juice* by Judy

From *Childhood Education*, Fall 1996, pp. 27-31. © 1996 by the Association for Childhood Education International, 17904 Georgia Avenue, Suite 215, Olney, MD. Reprinted by permission.

Blume (1971). One student seems to be posing questions, while all are eager to voice their ideas.

A student teacher listens to a child explain how he decoded an unfamiliar word from his trade book. Occasionally, the student teacher asks a question or restates what she has heard; mostly she listens and jots brief notes on her clipboard.

Current practice in language arts and reading emphasizes developing the learner's ability to use language through reading real, whole texts and through composing purposeful text. Language literacy skills and strategies are developed in meaningful contexts and as they are needed, rather than as separate skills to be applied later. Mr. R's students, for example, are learning to place commas by examining their practical

Students learn by working independently, as well as with others, and by actively making sense of mathematical situations.

use in literature and then using them in their own writing. The teacher perceived a need for a lesson on commas by examining the students' writing. In contrast, a teacher using a more traditional approach would have first taught the rules for comma use and then asked students to insert commas in a series of sentences. Such an instructional approach has little connection to the students' writing or the need for commas.

Teachers adhering to the whole language philosophy attempt to integrate all of the language areas. Students combine writing, reading, spelling and handwriting to communicate real messages to real audiences, such as writing a letter to an author. Literacy learning is a developmental process that the teacher facilitates by providing modeling, authentic experiences, mini-lessons on specific topics and frequent opportunities for students to consult with and learn from each other. Students learn as they create their own meaning and actively take charge of their own learning.

Current Innovations in Mathematics

A math lesson has just begun in Ms. C's 4th-grade class. Ms. C is explaining, "Yesterday when we were measuring distances in social studies, Malik and Alisha said that 1/4 and 4/16 are really the same thing, and we spent a little time discussing their theory. Some of you gave reasons why you think it would always work and some of you talked about why it wouldn't. Today, I want you to work alone or in groups to prove or disprove their idea. Malik and Alisha, let's have you go

over your discovery again to refresh us."

As Alisha and Malik use the overhead projector, a rule and some Cuisenaire rods to explain the concept of equivalent fractions, other students listen and ask questions or make comments to clarify their understanding. A few students point out inconsistencies and pose other situations where the theory does not seem to work. As more students become involved, Ms. C directs the other students to demonstrate equivalent fractions themselves, using whatever manipulative they wish. Students choose fraction circles or bars, rods, geoboards or counters to set up their fraction problems. Ms. C circulates around the room, asking students what they are doing and thinking and requesting them to explain their rationale. Often, she presents additional or even contrary evidence, asking students to explain it in light of their ideas. Later, she will bring the whole class together again to discuss new theories, ideas and processes.

Innovative mathematics instruction today is guided by the National Council of Teachers of Mathematics' (NCTM) *Curriculum and Evaluation Standards for School Mathematics* (1989) and *Professional Standards for Teaching Mathematics* (1991). These standards call for students to independently discover mathematical concepts and skills through active exploration and reflection. They emphasize building students' mathematical reasoning and problem-solving abilities so that every student develops mathematical insights, rather than simply memorizing formulas. Mathematics is kept "whole" by connecting traditional areas (e.g., fractions and subtraction) to each other and to practical applications. The teacher facilitates active student learning by providing motivating mathematical situations, engaging students in thoughtful discourse and stimulating mathematical thinking. Students learn by working independently, as well as with others, and by actively making sense of mathematical situations.

Changing Views of Learning and of Teaching

The innovations described above, as well as others in science and social studies, reflect interrelated paradigm shifts in views regarding the purpose of learning, the content or knowledge to be learned and how learning occurs.

Purpose. Dewey, Brownell and the Progressive Movement initially proposed in the early part of the 20th century an emphasis on *meaningful* learning.

In their lives and work and thought, people do not need simply to be able to recall facts or preset procedures in response to specific stimuli. They need to be able to plan courses of action, weigh alternatives, think about problems and issues in new ways, converse with others about what they know and why, and transform and create new knowledge for themselves; they need, in short, to be able "to make sense" and "to learn." (Peterson & Knapp, 1993, p. 136)

This approach subsequently was deemphasized in favor of more measurable rote learning. Rote learning will not suffice in education today; rather, education requires meaningful learning that allows one to manipulate and reflect on knowledge in order to solve unforeseen problems. This view underscores the need for teaching methods that promote *understanding*, not memorization, and is the impetus behind many new practices.

Content. Educators traditionally treated mathematics as a set of rules and procedures developed by highly trained mathematicians that must be memorized and applied. In a more recent view of mathematics, Lauren Resnick calls it " . . . an organized system of thought that [students] are capable of figuring out" (Brandt, 1988/89, p. 14). Thus, students make sense of patterns and invent understanding, which they use in solving problems. Similarly, today's language literacy is not a set of phonics, punctuation and spelling rules to be absorbed and applied. Rather, it is a process that allows one to create text to communicate ideas to a specific audience and to make sense of someone else's writing. Neither math nor language learning is a linear sequence of specific skills; both areas emphasize conceptual learning over procedural learning (Keene, 1994; NCTM, 1989).

Student attitudes are important considerations in both areas. Students are encouraged to see themselves as authors, readers and mathematicians at all ages and stages of development. The NCTM *Standards* (1989) assert that students should value mathematics and feel confident of their mathematical abilities.

Process. Traditional methods of teaching are based on associationist and behaviorist views of learning proposed by Thorndike in the 1920s and B. F. Skinner in the 1940s (Peterson & Knapp, 1993; Silverman, 1985). These views assume that students learn in a stimulus-response manner; thus, students do drill-and-practice exercises and are rewarded for correct answers (Brandt, 1988/89; Elmore, 1992; Peterson & Knapp, 1993; Resnick & Klopfer, 1989). Constance Weaver (1990) calls this a *transmission* model of teaching, wherein the teacher possesses the knowledge and directly imparts it to the students. No proof exists, however, that this model is effective in advancing *meaningful* learning. Research in cognitive and developmental psychology and related fields (Brandt, 1988/89; Resnick & Klopfer, 1989; Weaver, 1990) point instead to what Weaver (1990) calls the *transactional* model of teaching, in which the student learns through active *engagement* in authentic tasks designed to create personal meaning. In this model, the teacher is a facilitator who stimulates and guides learning. This process capitalizes on children's natural learning patterns that are present before formal schooling; that is, language acquisition becomes a model for learning to read and write (Weaver, 1990) and a preschooler's informal math knowledge and intuitive processes provide the basis for formal mathematical education (Peterson & Knapp, 1993).

This emerging paradigm of learning and teaching, now known as constructivism, is not entirely new. As mentioned previously, it is derived from the ideas of Dewey, Piaget and Brownell and has influenced such reforms as the "New Math" of the 1950s and 1960s (Peterson & Knapp, 1993; Silverman, 1985). Neither is the clash between constructivist and traditional ideas new; at several junctures in this century educators have argued for one paradigm or the other. Today, dissatisfaction with public schools and subsequent calls for reforms are prompting educators and researchers to move away from Thorndike's and Skinner's traditional views and look more closely at constructivist ideas.

Constructivist Principles
Proponents of constructivism believe that knowledge should be constructed by the learner rather than transferred from the teacher to the student. For example, students might learn about the commutative property for multiplication (3x4=4x3) by counting objects in equal groups and observing that four groups of three is the same as three groups of four. After conducting further testing to prove that this property holds true for all numbers, the student explains the discovery to the teacher. In contrast, behaviorist teaching typically requires the teacher to define the commutative property for the students, explain it with examples and then ask the students to practice using it with a set of exercises. Behaviorists view knowledge as being an accumulation of facts; constructivists see it as understandings that are continually developed and modified by the learner.

One of constructivism's basic tenets is that knowledge is subjective; that is, everyone creates his own meaning of any particular experience, including what he hears or reads. Thus, any two people reading the same material will interpret it differently. One of Mr. R's students reading *Freckle Juice* may consider the main character to be foolish, while another student may view him as inventive. Regardless of how tightly the curriculum is sequenced and delivered, students will construct their own unique meanings.

Another basic tenet holds that children learn through integrating new ideas into their existing knowledge structures. Piaget described this integration as the processes of assimilation and accommodation (Bodner, 1986; Fosnot, 1989). Assimilation occurs when new information can be interpreted in light of what the child already knows; thus, it simply extends existing knowledge. Accommodation occurs when the new experience contrasts with preexisting schema, which then must be modified so that the new information "fits." It is important to recognize that these processes are within the child; new information cannot be manipulated by the teacher either to "fit" with existing schema or to change it in some predetermined way. The teacher's role is to create disequilibrium; that is, to provide stimuli that cause children to examine, expand and/or modify their existing knowledge. Thus, Ms. C may ask Malik and Alisha how many twelfths (which are not on the ruler) would equal 1/4 and 4/16. Through this investigation, Alisha and Malik would examine their rationale for 1/4=4/16 and either confirm it or modify it in order to apply to other situations.

Constructivist Teaching Practices

Constructivist teaching practices share several major characteristics:

■ *Active Learning.* In order for students to create their own meanings and build their own knowledge, they must be mentally and physically *engaged* in their work.

Students in innovative classrooms do most of the thinking and talking and the teacher provides guidance.

The students in Mr. R's and Ms. C's classrooms read books of their own choice and respond to them by writing in journals or discussing them with peers and/or the teacher. They learn how to write, punctuate and spell by examining how authors do it. They learn math concepts by exploring with manipulatives, looking for patterns and solving problems. In all subjects, students learn by making discoveries, *reflecting* on them and discussing them rather than blindly imitating the teacher or completing exercises to absorb what the teacher tells them.

■ *Work in Context.* Meaningful learning that is conceptual rather than procedural occurs in authentic situations, not from memorizing facts and skills to be transferred and applied later. Students in constructivist classrooms read children's literature and compose stories and letters that have a real purpose. They solve math problems that they create from their studies and their lives outside school. They use strategies that adult readers, writers and mathematicians use. Consequently, less separation exists between in-school and out-of-school learning. Keeping in mind the axiom "The whole is greater than the sum of its parts," the whole is what students experience.

■ *Student Autonomy.* Students cannot create their own learning in tightly controlled situations. Thus, teachers should allow students to take more control of their learning by choosing their own books to read and topics to write about, selecting the materials from which they want to learn and setting up their own investigations. Students in innovative classrooms do most of the thinking and talking, and the teacher provides guidance.

■ *Social Learning.* The construction of knowledge is greatly enhanced through discourse, in which ideas are discussed and "proven" (Fielding & Pearson, 1994; NCTM, 1991; Peterson & Knapp, 1993). Students work collaboratively on projects, challenging and confirming each other's discoveries. Students in "learning communities" have grand conversations (Peterson & Eeds, 1990) about their reading and writing, as in Mr. R's room, and "argue" about their mathematical ideas, as in Ms. C's class. The teacher asks questions not to elicit the "right" answers, but rather to provoke students to examine and expand upon their thoughts. Hence, the teacher needs to foster a safe environment for such risk-taking.

■ *Teacher As Facilitator.* In such learner-centered classrooms, the teacher moves away from dispensing information and toward guiding students' efforts to make sense of their work. The teacher designs situations that allow the students to learn by doing and that actively promote the students' thinking and investigating. The teacher listens, watches and questions students to bring forth their prior knowledge, thus revealing misconceptions and miscues. The teacher can then help students learn from these events by providing further learning experiences, pointing out discrepancies and asking students to resolve them, and occasionally supplying additional information.

■ *Ongoing Assessment.* Individually constructed meanings cannot be measured within the constraints of standardized tests. Innovative classrooms permit learning to be continuously assessed as students work, not through contrived questions at artificial checkpoints. Math and language portfolios (containing work in progress as well as finished products), individual conferences where students discuss their strategies, and written and verbal explanations of student reasoning demonstrate progress. Alternative assessment practices such as these are consonant with a constructivist view of learning.

Alignment of Beliefs and Practice

Constructivist classrooms are not diametrically opposed to those based upon behaviorist views of learning and teaching. Teachers will continue to use some direct instruction in mini-lessons and demonstrations, the teacher still decides which critical concepts and skills must be learned and students will require a great deal of structure if they are to be productive with their choices. The fundamental differences lie in contrasting beliefs and assumptions about learning and teaching. Those involved in making decisions about education practices, including teachers, administrators, parents, policymakers and legislators, must examine their own beliefs to determine what should receive the greatest emphasis in classrooms:

- children learning through putting together separate skills, or through immersion in authentic situations
- children learning basic information, or building their own understanding of subject matter
- teachers who *tell* children what they must know, or who trust children to learn through experience and reflection with teacher guidance
- teachers who are the only ones with the answers, or who engineer learning situations whereby students make their own discoveries.

Effective implementation of current instructional innovations requires an open mind toward (if not agreement with) a constructivist philosophy of learning. Struggling with the above questions may help policymakers and practitioners alike determine their willingness to embrace this philosophy, which may be an indication of their potential for success.

◆

References and Resources

Angeletti, S. (1993). Group writing and publishing: Building community in a second-grade classroom. *Language Arts, 70,* 494-499.

Ball, D. (1991). What's all this talk about "discourse"? *Arithmetic Teacher, 39,* 44-48.

Battista, M. (1994). Teacher beliefs and the reform movement in mathematics education. *Phi Delta Kappan, 75,* 462-470.

Blume, J. (1971). *Freckle juice.* New York: Four Winds Press.

Bodner, G. (1986). Constructivism: A theory of knowledge. *Journal of Chemical Education, 63,* 873-878.

Brandt, R. (1988/89). On learning research: A conversation with Lauren Resnick. *Educational Leadership, 46*(4), 12-16.

Brandt, R. (1994). On making sense: A conversation with Magdalene Lampert. *Educational Leadership, 51*(5), 26-30.

Brooks, J. G. (1990). Teachers and students: Constructivists forging new connections. *Educational Leadership, 47*(5), 68-71.

Brooks, J. G., & Brooks, M. (1993). *In search of understanding: The case for constructivist classrooms.* Alexandria, VA: Association for Supervision and Curriculum Development.

Brophy, J. (1992). Proving the subtleties of subject matter teaching. *Educational Leadership, 49*(7), 4-8.

Burns, M. (1994). Arithmetic: The last holdout. *Phi Delta Kappan, 75,* 471-476.

Davis, R., Maher, C., & Noddings, N. (Eds.). (1990).

Constructivist views on the teaching and learning of mathematics. *Journal for Research in Mathematics Education.*

Elmore, R. (1992). Why restructuring alone won't improve teaching. *Educational Leadership, 49*(7), 44-48.

Fielding, L., & Pearson, P. D. (1994). Reading comprehension: What works. *Educational Leadership, 51*(5), 62-68.

Fosnot, C. T. (1989). *Enquiring teachers, enquiring learners: A constructivist approach for teaching.* New York: Teachers College Press.

Kamii, C., & Lewis, B. (1990). Constructivist learning and teaching. *Arithmetic Teacher, 38,* 34-35.

Keene, E. (1994). A new paradigm for reading instruction. *Colorado Reading Council Journal, 5,* 39-41.

Leinhardt, G. (1992). What research on learning tells us about teaching. *Educational Leadership, 49*(7), 20-25.

Loucks-Horsley, S., Kapitan, R., Carlson, M., Kuerbis, P., Clark, R., Melle, G. M., Sachse, T., & Walton, E. (Eds.). (1990). *Elementary school science for the '90s.* Alexandria, VA: Association for Supervision and Curriculum Development.

National Council of Teachers of Mathematics. (1989). *Curriculum and evaluation standards for school mathematics.* Reston, VA: Author.

National Council of Teachers of Mathematics. (1991). *Professional standards for teaching mathematics.* Reston, VA: Author.

Palincsar, A., & Brown, A. (1989). Instruction for self-regulated reading. In L. Resnick & L. Klopfer (Eds.), *Toward the thinking curriculum: Current cognitive research* (pp. 19-39). Alexandria, VA: Association for Supervision and Curriculum Development.

Peterson, R., & Eeds, M. (1990). *Grand conversations: Literature groups in action.* New York: Scholastic.

Peterson, P., & Knapp, N. (1993). Inventing and reinventing ideas: Constructivist teaching and learning in mathematics. In G. Cawelti (Ed.), *Challenges and achievements of American education* (pp. 134-157). Alexandria, VA: Association for Supervision and Curriculum Development.

Resnick, L., & Klopfer, L. (1989). Toward the thinking curriculum: An overview. In L. Resnick & L. Klopfer (Eds.), *Toward the thinking curriculum: Current cognitive research* (pp. 1-18). Alexandria, VA: Association for Supervision and Curriculum Development.

Romberg, T. (1993). NCTM's standards: A rallying flag for mathematics teachers. *Educational Leadership, 50*(5), 36-41.

Russell, S., & Corwin, R. (1993). Talking mathematics: "Going slow" and "letting go." *Phi Delta Kappan, 74,* 555-558.

Silverman, F. L. (1985). Mathematics curriculum and its roots from the 40's forward. *Focus on Learning, 11,* 67-74.

Siu-Runyan, Y. (1993). Whole math: A research base. *Teachers Networking: The Whole Language Newsletter, 12*(3), 1, 12-15.

Smith, S., Smith, M., & Romberg, T. (1993). What the NCTM standards look like in one classroom. *Educational Leadership, 50*(8), 4-7.

Watson, D. (1994). Whole language: Why bother? *The Reading Teacher, 47,* 600-607.

Weaver, C. (1990). *Understanding whole language: From principles to practice.* Portsmouth, NH: Heinemann.

Wiske, M., & Levinson, C. (1993). How teachers are implementing the NCTM standards. *Educational Leadership, 50*(8), 8-12.

Yackel, E., Cobb, P., Wood, T., & Merkel, G. (1990). Experience, problem solving, and discourse as central aspects of constructivism. *Arithmetic Teacher, 38,* 34-35.

Credits/Acknowledgments

Cover design by Charles Vitelli

1. Perspectives
Facing overview—© 1998 by Cleo Freelance Photography.

2. Child Development and Families
Facing overview—Photo courtesy of Gina Mulqueen.

3. Care and Educational Practices
Facing overview—© 1998 by Cleo Freelance Photography.
71—Illustration by Brenda Grannan.

4. Supporting Young Children and their Families
Facing overview—© 1998 by Cleo Freelance Photography.

5. Curricular Issues
Facing overview—Apple Computer, Inc., photo by Jeff Haeger.

6. Reflections
Facing overview—© 1998 by Cleo Freelance Photography.

ANNUAL EDITIONS ARTICLE REVIEW FORM

■ NAME: _____ DATE: _____

■ TITLE AND NUMBER OF ARTICLE: _____

■ BRIEFLY STATE THE MAIN IDEA OF THIS ARTICLE: _____

_____

■ LIST THREE IMPORTANT FACTS THAT THE AUTHOR USES TO SUPPORT THE MAIN IDEA:

_____

_____

_____

_____

■ WHAT INFORMATION OR IDEAS DISCUSSED IN THIS ARTICLE ARE ALSO DISCUSSED IN YOUR TEXTBOOK OR OTHER READINGS THAT YOU HAVE DONE? LIST THE TEXTBOOK CHAPTERS AND PAGE NUMBERS:

_____

_____

_____

_____

_____

■ LIST ANY EXAMPLES OF BIAS OR FAULTY REASONING THAT YOU FOUND IN THE ARTICLE:

_____

_____

_____

_____

■ LIST ANY NEW TERMS/CONCEPTS THAT WERE DISCUSSED IN THE ARTICLE, AND WRITE A SHORT DEFINITION:

_____

_____

_____

_____

_____

*Your instructor may require you to use this ANNUAL EDITIONS Article Review Form in any number of ways: for articles that are assigned, for extra credit, as a tool to assist in developing assigned papers, or simply for your own reference. Even if it is not required, we encourage you to photocopy and use this page; you will find that reflecting on the articles will greatly enhance the information from your text.

We Want Your Advice

ANNUAL EDITIONS revisions depend on two major opinion sources: one is our Advisory Board, listed in the front of this volume, which works with us in scanning the thousands of articles published in the public press each year; the other is you—the person actually using the book. Please help us and the users of the next edition by completing the prepaid article rating form on this page and returning it to us. Thank you for your help!

ANNUAL EDITIONS: EARLY CHILDHOOD EDUCATION 98/99
Article Rating Form

Here is an opportunity for you to have direct input into the next revision of this volume. We would like you to rate each of the 40 articles listed below, using the following scale:

1. **Excellent: should definitely be retained**
2. **Above average: should probably be retained**
3. **Below average: should probably be deleted**
4. **Poor: should definitely be deleted**

Your ratings will play a vital part in the next revision. So please mail this prepaid form to us just as soon as you complete it.
Thanks for your help!

Rating	Article	Rating	Article
	1. How to Build a Baby's Brain		21. Together Is Better: Specific Tips on How to Include Children with Various Types of Disabilities
	2. New Brain Development Research—A Wonderful Window of Opportunity to Build Public Support for Early Childhood Education		22. Challenges to Family Involvement
	3. Highlights of the Quality 2000 Initiative: Not by Chance		23. Beyond Discipline to Guidance
	4. The National Television Violence Study: Key Findings and Recommendations		24. Getting Along: How Teachers Can Support Children's Peer Relationships
	5. Child Care		25. The Caring Classroom's Academic Edge
	6. A Bundle of Emotions		26. Creating a Community of Learning for Homeless Children
	7. Prenatal Drug Exposure: Meeting the Challenge		27. Off with a Theme: Emergent Curriculum in Action
	8. Families and Schools: Building Multicultural Values Together		28. 10 Ways to Improve Your Theme Teaching
	9. The Education of Hispanics in Early Childhood: Of Roots and Wings		29. Documenting Children's Learning
	10. Integrating Learning Styles and Multiple Intelligences		30. Fostering Creativity in the Early Childhood Classroom
	11. It May Cause Anxiety, But Day Care Can Benefit Kids		31. Active Living: Physical Activities for Infants, Toddlers, and Preschoolers
	12. Meeting Basic Needs: Health and Safety Practices in Feeding and Diapering Infants		32. "Hey! Where's the Toys?" Play and Literacy in 1st Grade
	13. Who Cares for the Children? Denmark's Unique Public Child-Care Model		33. Sharing Books with Infants and Toddlers: Facing the Challenges
	14. Nurturing Kids: Seven Ways of Being Smart		34. Back to the Basics of Whole Language
	15. The New Preschool		35. Interactive Writing in a Primary Classroom
	16. Understanding through Play		36. Outstanding Developmental Software
	17. Your Learning Environment: A Look Back at Your Year		37. Let's Be Real!
	18. Labeled for Life?		38. Where Are the Good Old Days?
	19. "SMART" Planning for Inclusion		39. Child Advocacy Directory
	20. "Can I Play Too?" Adapting Common Classroom Activities for Young Children with Limited Motor Abilities		40. New Ways of Learning = New Ways of Teaching

(Continued on next page)

ABOUT YOU

Name _____ Date _____

Are you a teacher? ☐ Or a student? ☐

Your school name _____

Department _____

Address _____

City _____ State _____ Zip _____

School telephone # _____

YOUR COMMENTS ARE IMPORTANT TO US!

Please fill in the following information:

For which course did you use this book? _____

Did you use a text with this *ANNUAL EDITION*? ☐ yes ☐ no

What was the title of the text? _____

What are your general reactions to the *Annual Editions* concept?

Have you read any particular articles recently that you think should be included in the next edition?

Are there any articles you feel should be replaced in the next edition? Why?

Are there any World Wide Web sites you feel should be included in the next edition? Please annotate.

May we contact you for editorial input?

May we quote your comments?

ANNUAL EDITIONS: EARLY CHILDHOOD EDUCATION 98/99

BUSINESS REPLY MAIL		
First Class	Permit No. 84	Guilford, CT

Postage will be paid by addressee

**Dushkin/McGraw·Hill
Sluice Dock
Guilford, CT 06437**

No Postage
Necessary
if Mailed
in the
United States